About Island Press

Island Press is the only nonprofit organization in the United States whose principal purpose is the publication of books on environmental issues and natural resource management. We provide solutions-oriented information to professionals, public officials, business and community leaders, and concerned citizens who are shaping responses to environmental problems.

In 2006, Island Press celebrates its twenty-first anniversary as the leading provider of timely and practical books that take a multidisciplinary approach to critical environmental concerns. Our growing list of titles reflects our commitment to bringing the best of an expanding body of literature to the environmental community throughout North America and the world.

Support for Island Press is provided by the Agua Fund, The Geraldine R. Dodge Foundation, Doris Duke Charitable Foundation, The William and Flora Hewlett Foundation, Kendeda Sustainability Fund of the Tides Foundation, Forrest C. Lattner Foundation, The Henry Luce Foundation, The John D. and Catherine T. MacArthur Foundation, The Marisla Foundation, The Andrew W. Mellon Foundation, Gordon and Betty Moore Foundation, The Curtis and Edith Munson Foundation, Oak Foundation, The Overbrook Foundation, The David and Lucile Packard Foundation, The Winslow Foundation, and other generous donors.

The opinions expressed in this book are those of the author(s) and do not necessarily reflect the views of these foundations.

Defending the Environment

Defending the Environment:
Civil Society Strategies to Enforce International Environmental Law

Linda A. Malone
& Scott Pasternack

 Island Press
Washington · Covelo · London

(c) 2006 Linda A. Malone and Scott Pasternack

Previously published in hardcover by Transnational Publishers, Inc. in 2004

All rights reserved under International and Pan-American Copyright Conventions. No part of this book may be reproduced in any form or by any means without permission in writing from the publisher: Island Press, 1718 Connecticut Ave., N.W., Washington, DC 20009

ISLAND PRESS is a trademark of The Center for Resource Economics.

Library of Congress Cataloging-in-Publication Data

Malone, Linda A.
Defending the environment : civil society strategies to enforce international environmental law / Linda A. Malone, Scott Pasternack.
   p. cm.
Includes bibliographical references and index.
ISBN 1-59726-066-5 (pbk. : alk. paper)
1. Environmental law, international. 2. Environmental justice.
3. Civil society. I. Pasternack, Scott. II. Title.
K3585.M35   2006
344.04'6   dc22

2006001438

Printed on recycled, acid-free paper ♻

Manufactured in the United States of America
10 9 8 7 6 5 4 3 2 1

For Erin and Corey always, for their children, and in memory of Joan Fitzpatrick.

For Deb, who tolerated all those just-fifteen-more-minute hours.

CONTENTS

Foreword by Philippe Sands xvii
Preface by Alexandre Kiss xix
About the Authors xxi
Acknowledgments xxiii

Introduction 1
I.   Layout of the Book 2
II.   Layout of Each Chapter 3
III. Strategy Tools 4
    A. Petition 4
    B. Letter Petition or Letter Request 5
    C. Written Statement (Includes Issue Papers) 5
    D. Oral Statement 5
    E. Critique of National Report 5
    F. *Amicus Curiae* Brief 6
IV. Summary of Sources of International Law 6

Chapter 1: Exercising Environmental Human Rights and Remedies in the United Nations and Regional Systems 9
I.   Introduction 9
II.   Determining Valid Environmental Human Rights Claims 9
III. Determining Where to File the Environmental Human Rights Claim 14
IV. Submitting the Environmental Human Rights Claim to the Selected Forum 17
    A. United Nations System 17
        1. Human Rights Committee 18
        2. Committee on Economic, Social, and Cultural Rights 24
        3. Committee for the Elimination of Racial Discrimination 26
        4. Committee for the Elimination of Discrimination Against Women 28
        5. Committee on the Rights of the Child 31
        6. Commission on Human Rights and UN Special Rapporteurs 32

		7. Subcommission on Promotion and Protection of Human Rights 34
		8. Commission on the Status of Women 36
		9. The 1235 and 1503 Procedures for Dealing with Gross Human Rights Violations 36
		10. UNESCO 40
		11. International Labor Organization 41
	B.	African System 45
	C.	American System 48
		1. Inter-American Commission on Human Rights 50
		a. Scope of Authority 51
		i. Party to the American Convention 51
		ii. Non-Party to the American Convention 52
		b. Prerequisites 53
		c. Procedure 54
		2. Inter-American Court of Human Rights 57
		a. Eligibility to File Cases 58
		b. Contentious Jurisdiction 58
		c. Advisory Jurisdiction 60
		3. Additional Strategies 62
		a. *Amicus Curiae* 63
		b. Lobbying OAS Members to Pursue Inter-State Mechanisms 63
	D.	European System 64
		1. European Commission 64
		2. European Court 66
		3. Dispute Resolution Under the European Social Charter 68
		4. European Parliament and the Charter 69
V.	Newly Emerging Rights and Fundamental Rights Recognized as Customary International Law 69
VI.	Seeking Enforcement if a Claim Prevails and a Nation-State Fails to Comply 71
	A.	United Nations System 71
		1. Notify the UN High Commissioner for Human Rights 71
		2. Encourage the HCHR to Notify the UN Secretary General 72
		3. Encourage the UN Security Council to Take Enforcement Action 72
	B.	African System 73
	C.	American System 74
	D.	European System 74

Table of Contents • xi

		1.	Council of Europe 74
		2.	European Parliament 75
VII.	Conclusion. 76
VIII.	Tables. 77
	A.	Sources of International Law Applicable to Environmental Human Rights 77
	B.	Jurisdiction of Human Rights Body Over the Claim 107
	C.	Private Rights of Action Available 124

Chapter 2: Advocating for International Finance and Trade Institutions to Adhere to Environmental and Public Health Standards. 131

I. Introduction. 131
II. World Bank Inspection Panel 132
    A. Overview. 132
    B. Eligibility to Submit a Request 133
    C. Submitting the Request 134
    D. Decision Making 135
    E. Locating Requests for Inspection, Inspection Panel Reports, and Management Responses. 135
III. The International Finance Corporation—Compliance Advisor Ombudsman 137
    A. Overview. 138
    B. Eligibility to Submit a Complaint 138
    C. Submitting the Complaint 139
    D. Response 140
    E. Results. 140
    F. CAO and the Panel. 141
IV. Inter-American Development Bank—Independent Investigation Mechanism 143
    A. Overview. 143
    B. Preliminaries 144
    C. Eligibility to Submit a Request 144
    D. Submitting the Request 144
    E. Deciding Whether to Authorize an Investigation. 145
        1. Eligibility Determination 145
        2. Frivolity Determination 145
        3. Management Response 145
        4. Investigation Authorization 146
        5. Exception 146
    F. Investigation and Reports. 146
        1. Panel Investigation Report. 146
        2. Management Reply 146
        3. Board's Report and Response. 147

xii • Defending the Environment

V.	Asian Development Bank—Accountability Mechanism	147
	A. Overview	147
	B. Consultation Phase	148
	C. Compliance Review	149
	1. Filing Compliance Review Requests	149
	2. Compliance Review Process	152
	3. Remedial Actions	154
	4. Requester and Third Party Participation	154
VI.	European Bank for Reconstruction and Development—Independent Recourse Mechanism	155
VII.	European Parliament—Committee on Petitions	156
VIII.	African Development Bank Group—Independent Review Mechanism	157
IX.	North American Commission on Environmental Cooperation	159
	A. Overview	159
	B. Eligibility	160
	C. Making a Submission	160
	D. Decision Making	161
X.	Canada-Chile Commission on Environmental Cooperation	163
	A. Overview	163
	B. Eligibility	163
	C. Making a Submission	163
	D. Decision Making	165
XI.	Conclusion	166

Chapter 3: Preventing New International Trade and Investment Dispute Resolution Mechanisms from Undermining Current Environmental and Public Health Regulations ... 167

I.	Introduction	167
	A. The Impact of Increased Globalization on Environmental and Public Health Regulations	167
	B. Strategically Targeting Globalization Processes	170
	C. Why New Strategies?	170
II.	Strategy No. 1: *Amicus Curiae* Submissions to Trade and Investment Bodies	172
	A. Strategy Summary	172
	B. Bodies to Whom Such Submission May Be Made	172
	1. World Trade Organization	172
	2. NAFTA	174
	a. NAFTA Chapter 11	174
	b. NAFTA Chapter 20	177

		3. Canada-Chile Free Trade Agreement 179
		4. Court of Justice of the Andean Community 180
		5. EU Court of Justice and Court of First Instance 180
		6. Common Market for Eastern and Southern Africa (COMESA) 181
		7. East African Community Court of Justice (EAC) 181
		8. Economic Community of Western African States (ECOWAS) 181
		9. Others (APEC, OECS, Mercosur, BITs) 182
	C.	Preparing and Filing Your *Amicus Curiae* Brief 183
III.	Strategy No. 2: Persuading a Domestic Government to File a Trade or Investment Dispute to Prevent the Weakening of Environmental or Public Health Laws 184
IV.	Strategy No. 3: Submitting Public Comments to Environmental Reviews of Trade and Investment Agreements. 185
V.	Strategy No. 4: Demanding Transparency and Public Participation from Domestic Governments on Trade and Investment Issues Adversely Affecting the Environment and Public Health 186
VI.	Conclusion 188

Chapter 4: Encouraging Secretariats of Multilateral Environmental and Public Health Agreements to Enforce Current International Environmental Standards 189

I.	Introduction 189
II.	Strategy No. 1: Making Submissions Pursuant to Specific MEA Processes Open to Non-Party Participation 191
III.	Strategy No. 2: Petitioning MEA Secretariats 194
	A. Strategy Summary 194
	B. Creating the Petition 195
	1. Select a Treaty Secretariat. 195
	2. Prepare an Argument on the MEA Secretariat's Authority 195
	3. Present Your Case 195
IV.	Strategy No. 3: Lobbying State Parties to Initiate Dispute Resolution Proceedings 196
V.	Strategy No. 4: Participating at MEA Conferences of the Parties or in Appropriate Bodies of Charter-Based Institutions 197
	A. United Nations 199
	B. United Nations Environmental Program ("UNEP") 199
	C. United Nations Division for Sustainable Development 201

        D. United Nations Food and Agriculture ("FAO")........... 201
        E. United Nations Educational, Scientific, and Cultural
           Organization ("UNESCO") 201
        F. Organization of American States ("OAS") 202
VI. Conclusion.. 202
VII. Table–Sample MEAs 205

Chapter 5: Enforcing International Environmental Law in
              Tribunals of General Jurisdiction................. 221
I.   Introduction.. 221
II. International Court of Justice 221
III. The Law of the Sea Treaty Regime 225
IV. The International Criminal Court 233
V.   Regional Tribunals of General Jurisdiction 241
     A. European Union Court of Justice 241
     B. African Union Court of Justice 243
VI. International Arbitral Bodies.............................. 243
     A. Permanent Court of Arbitration 243
     B. International Court of Environmental Arbitration and
        Conciliation... 245
VII. Conclusion... 248

Chapter 6: Enforcing International Environmental Law Through
              Domestic Law Mechanisms 249
I.   Introduction.. 249
II. Non-Litigation Strategies.................................. 250
     A. Corporate Citizenship 250
     B. Participating on Advisory Committees 251
     C. Demanding Transparency from Domestic
        Governments on Matters Adversely Affecting the
        Environment Abroad 252
     D. Calling for U.S. Federal Agency Compliance with
        Executive Order 12114 253
     E. Lobbying Congress to Impose Environmental Standards
        on Appropriations 254
     F. Pelly Amendment 255
III. Litigation Strategies 257
     A. The Alien Tort Claims Act 258
     B. Extraterritorial Application of United States
        Environmental Laws to U.S. Government Activity
        Abroad.. 267
        1. Common Law Tort Actions Against a Domestic
           Government 268

   2. Administrative Procedures Act 268
    a. Claims of a Violation of the National Environmental Policy Act 270
    b. Claims that an Agency Action, Finding or Conclusion Made Pursuant to Any Other U.S. Federal Environmental Law *Except NEPA* Was Arbitrary, Capricious and/or an Abuse of Agency Discretion 271
   3. Citizen Suit Provisions 274
  C. Court Action to Demand Transparency on Domestic Actions Affecting the Environment Abroad 276
  D. Court Action to Assure Environmental Representation on Federal Advisory Committee Act 277
  E. General Obstacles 278
IV. Newly Independent States 283
V. Conclusion 285

Conclusion 289

Appendix: List of Practitioner Experts 297

Bibliography 313

Index 341

FOREWORD

I am pleased to introduce this impressive exposition of legal strategies and resources that civil society can use internationally in its efforts to protect the environment and health. International environmental initiatives undertaken by governments will remain marginal unless they are addressed in an integrated manner with those international economic endeavors that continue to retain a primary role in international law-making and institutional arrangements. The involvement of civil society has helped to balance long term environmental goals and shorter term economic priorities. This book contributes greatly to the continued involvement of civil society in strengthening these international environmental obligations by providing civil society with useful legal tools for use in both the international and domestic arenas. The focus on enforcement, particularly by civil society, is now central to the evolution of an effective international environmental law.

Malone and Pasternack identify options for enhancing accountability for environment and health obligations at international and domestic levels. Problem resolution strategies are offered in numerous arenas—human rights commissions, international financial institutions, trade regimes, treaty dispute resolution processes, and international and domestic courts and tribunals—all with the aim of promoting access to environmental information. The emphasis is strongly on the practical application of environmental claims. This is apparent from the book's emphasis on the pursuance of an environmental claim through multilateral environmental and public health agreements. Chapter 5, for example, assesses the selection of an international court or tribunal, such as the International Court of Justice, the International Tribunal for the Law of the Sea, the International Criminal Court and the Permanent Court of Arbitration, as well as the International Court of Environmental Arbitration and Conciliation.

In providing a framework Malone and Pasternack identify and assess three approaches to the protection of non-human species and habitats through environmental human rights. The examination provides a practical outline for using international human rights law and institutions, such as UNESCO, the UN Rapporteur on Health and the UN Human Rights Committee. They also propose that international financial institutions such as the World Bank should be encouraged to adhere to applicable environmental and health standards. The book then examines formal dispute resolution processes for enforcement of environmental protection standards.

In addition to this most useful discussion of international strategies, the concluding chapter identifies domestic tools for implementing an integrated strategy. The discussion of the usage of domestic mechanisms ranges from public information campaigns and the Code of Corporate Citizenship to the Alien Tort Claims Act. Again, the book addresses the proper choice of forum and the complexities of U.S. federal courts for the enforcement of environmental claims that have international affects. They encourage the use of the Administrative Procedures Act and the National Environmental Policy Act as a basis for these claims and also promote use of the Freedom of Information Act as a tool for access to environmental information.

This is a comprehensive and accessible work that will be of considerable utility to practitioners and others who are interested in the enforcement of environmental and health standards. Identifying the mechanisms for bringing to an end international environmental violations, as well as identifying the substantive elements of what may constitute a violation, are two vital steps to environmental improvement, sustainable development, and the promotion of health. This book guides the reader to the critical third stage—meaningful and committed enforcement. The book promises to make a serious, useful and sustained contribution to the development of international environmental law.

Philippe Sands QC
Professor of Laws, University College London
Barrister, Matrix Chambers

PREFACE

The objective of this volume is to aid those who seek to defend the environment. It succeeds very well in this purpose, describing the different procedures in international and American fora that may be used by environmental activists. The exhaustive review of the possibilities which can be used by all elements of civil society and of the rules which may be invoked presents at the same time an overall picture of international environmental law, a relatively new field of law. In addition to its practical usefulness, this work thus also contributes to a better understanding of that legal system, whose age can be estimated at little more than thirty years.

The importance of the legal protection of the environment is generally recognized and based on an understanding that care for the survival of our biosphere is a fundamental part of the common concern of humanity. Still, such recognition has not resulted so far in the establishment of proper international institutions or tribunals to ensure compliance with the norms of the new branch of international law. This enhances the importance of the possibility to utilize compliance mechanisms outside environmental institutions, in favor of those where the development of international law is more advanced, like the international protection of human rights. Even where mechanisms are more recent, such as those concerning international trade, the availability of quasi-judicial proceedings allows environmental claims to be heard.

The description of such mechanisms and the opportunities they offer for environmental protection also leads to some thinking on the nature of present international law as a whole. The indirect means for defending the interests of the environment, which can be used, may recall the reaction of a living organism which lacked a proper organ necessary to serve a vital function and which then developed another organ to ensure its continued health and well-being. Such reaction is proof of the importance of the given function, but also of the vitality and the capacity of adaptation of the whole system. In other words, outside its practical value, the research by the authors of the present book shows both the fundamental importance of environmental protection by international means, and the strength of present international society. It demonstrates that despite certain negative manifestations, international law is able to defend fundamental interests of the whole of mankind.

Thus, while some derive a negative impression from the lack of proper international legal mechanisms to ensure compliance with international environmental law, a positive conclusion can be reached. This book also shows the emergence and the vitality of international civil society and can greatly contribute to enhancing its possibilities of action. One may think of the image of a poet who described the state of a society by the following comparison: although the sailors think they govern their ship, the real master of their destiny is the sea itself.

Professor Alexandre Kiss
President of the European Council on Environmental Law
Member of the Permanent Court of Arbitration

ABOUT THE AUTHORS

LINDA A. MALONE is the Marshall-Wythe Foundation Professor of Law at The College of William and Mary School of Law. She has been a Visiting Professor at the University of Virginia Law School, Washington and Lee Law School, Duke University, the University of Arizona, and University of Denver law schools and has taught at the University of Illinois Law School and University of Arkansas Law School in Fayetteville. She is the author of numerous publications, including several books on international law, human rights, and environmental law. She was also the Associate Editor of the Yearbook of International Environmental Law and has served on the Advisory Council to the National Enforcement Training Institute of the U.S. Environmental Protection Agency, Board of Visitors of Duke Law School, and the Board of Directors of the American Agricultural Law Association and as chair of the agricultural law section of the American Association of Law Schools. She was a delegate to the United Nations Conference on the Environment and Development in Rio in 1992, co-counsel to Bosnia-Herzegovina in its genocide case against Serbia and Montenegro before the World Court, and co-counsel to Paraguay in it challenge to the death penalty in Paraguay v. Virginia. In 1998 she received the Fulbright/OSCE Regional Research Award to conduct research on women's and children's rights in Eastern Europe. Professor Malone received her B.A. from Vassar, her J.D. from Duke, where she was Research and Managing Editor of the Duke Law Journal, and her LL.M. from the University of Illinois. Prior to joining the William and Mary faculty in 1988, she served as a law clerk for the Honorable Wilbur F. Pell, United States Court of Appeals for the Seventh Circuit, and practiced law in Chicago and Atlanta. She is presently serving on the ABA's Special Subcommittee on the Rights of the Child, which is working on passage of the Convention on the Elimination of Discrimination Against Women and the Convention on the Rights of the Child, on two committees of the National Academy of Sciences, and is the author of the water quality chapter of the forthcoming report of the Congressionally created U.S. Ocean Commission. In 2000 she received the first Millenium Award of the Virginia Women's Bar Association, given to a professor, a judge, and a practitioner for their contribution to the role of women and women's rights in the law.

SCOTT PASTERNACK is Senior Counsel in the Environmental Division of the New York City Law Department. Prior to joining the Law Department, Mr. Pasternack was the Klipstein Fellow in the International Program at

Earthjustice, a U.S. non-profit environmental law organization, where he represented NGOs and community groups before international and domestic courts and tribunals on matters concerning environmental human rights, international environmental law and policy, and the affects of international trade and investment on the environment. Prior to Earthjustice, Mr. Pasternack clerked for the Honorable Jacob Mishler, United States District Court for the Eastern District of New York and practiced law in New York and San Francisco. He received his A.B. from the College of William and Mary where he was a Phi Beta Kappa and his J.D. from New York University School of Law where he was a Ford Foundation Fellow with the Center for International Studies directed by Professor Thomas M. Franck and where he served as Articles Editor of the New York University Journal of International Law & Politics. Although Mr. Pasternack has published several scholarly articles, *Defending the Environment* is his first book.

ACKNOWLEDGMENTS

Professor Malone gratefully acknowledges the support of grants provided by the Fulbright Association, the International Research and Exchange Board with funds provided by the United States Department of State through the Title VIII Program and the National Endowment for the Humanities, and the Reves Center for International Studies and the Marshall-Wythe Law School at the College of William and Mary. None of these organizations is responsible for the views expressed.

Both authors also gratefully acknowledge the extraordinary support provided by the library and support staff of the law school, particularly Felicia Burton and Della Harris. In addition, the book benefited from the research assistance of Maggie Collins, Amanda Owens, and Ryan Igbanol.

Finally, we want to express our appreciation to the World Conservation Union (IUCN), which dedicated a session of its 2004 meeting in Bangkok to discussion of an earlier iteration of the book. We thank the session participants for their comments and suggestions, and specifically wish to acknowledge Professor Nicholas Robinson for his support of this project.

INTRODUCTION

The past few decades in international law have seen tremendous development of legal protections for the environment and public health. Many nations have drafted, signed, and/or ratified numerous multilateral environmental agreements ("MEAs") to protect the air, water, land, and biodiversity. Despite these efforts to confront environmental and public health problems, the public's concern over sufficient clean water resources, climate change, desertification, endangered species protection, the AIDS epidemic, ocean oil spills, ozone depletion, and other similar matters seems to have increased rather than decreased. A key reason for this result is the failure of many countries and their leaders to implement adequately and effectively and/or enforce the standards in these new MEAs to overcome the mounting problems that the MEAs were designed to combat. Such inadequacy and ineffectiveness includes the simultaneous development of international legal protections for trade and investment that often run afoul of these new MEA standards.

Faced with an ever widening gap between environmental rights and environmental remedies, the public now more than ever needs tools to encourage, if not compel, their leaders to act. *Defending the Environment: Civil Society Strategies to Enforce International Environmental Law* provides the public with these tools. This book promotes use and awareness of several different international, regional, and domestic strategies designed to safeguard the environment and public health.

Defending the Environment emphasizes practice as well as theory. Unlike works devoted exclusively to theoretical aspects of international environmental law and policy or generally to international courts and tribunals, this book provides the what, how, when, where, and why for resolving environmental and public health problems in front of international courts, tribunals, commissions, committees, secretariats, and, at times, their domestic counterparts. In many countries where environmental and public health harms occur, the inadequacies of the judiciary—whether corruption or a lack of sufficient authority to review legislative and/or executive actions—make citizen access to international courts and tribunals essential for obtaining sufficient relief.

Furthermore, an appendix at the end of the book lists individuals and organizations that can assist the reader with these various strategies. The authors cannot emphasize enough how essential notifying and seeking assistance from either the authors or these individuals and organizations is to the continued development of the strategies discussed in this book. These individuals and organizations specialize in these kinds of strategies and have direct experience with how the international courts and tribunals operate and what claims will or will not prevail. More importantly, any strategy that a reader of this text decides to pursue may affect strategies that these individuals and groups are themselves pursuing or plan to pursue.

The strategies in the book serve different purposes for different audiences. For non-governmental organizations ("NGOs") and community groups focused on environmental and public health concerns, the book provides suggestions for and guidance about several different legal and political approaches that may help such organizations achieve some of their goals. For law and policy students, the book informs them about supra-national institutions and processes available to address environmental and public health issues and encourages such students to work with their faculty through law and policy clinics to assist needy individuals and groups with these approaches. For academics, the book reveals the growing number of supra-national processes designed to handle environmental and public health matters and allows such scholars to assess the effectiveness of existing mechanisms and propose new ones. For government attorneys and policymakers, the book suggests new ways in which such officials permit the public to participate in environmental and public health decision making and problem solving and invites such elected and appointed representatives not only to strengthen these processes but to take the initiative of safeguarding the environment and public health by creating even more effective regimes. For the general public, the book raises awareness about supra-national dispute resolution and current global environmental and public health problems and calls upon citizens to demand that government take action to enhance these mechanisms and better protect the environment and public health.

I. LAYOUT OF THE BOOK

In assessing the potential legal and political strategies available, the authors found that grouping them into six thematic categories was the best organizational method for presenting them. Each chapter discusses a different set of strategies as follows:

Chapter 1: Exercising Environmental Human Rights and Remedies in the United Nations and Regional Systems.

Chapter 2: Advocating for International Finance and Trade Institutions to Adhere to Environmental and Public Health Standards.

Chapter 3: Preventing New International Trade and Investment Dispute Resolution Mechanisms from Undermining Current Environmental and Public Health Regulations.

Chapter 4: Encouraging Secretariats of Multilateral Environmental and Public Health Agreements to Enforce Current International Environmental Standards.
Chapter 5: Enforcing International Environmental Law in International Tribunals.
Chapter 6: Enforcing International Environmental Law Through Domestic Law Mechanisms.

One significant set of institutions and processes that this book does not address separately are United Nations Specialized Agencies, (*e.g.*, International Maritime Organization) and United Nations Related Organizations (*e.g.*, International Atomic Energy Organization). Some of these entities are included where dispute resolution at that entity relates to the theme of a chapter (*e.g.*, the World Trade Organization in Chapter 3). However, one should consult http://www.un.org/aboutun/chart.html for more information and web links to these institutions as they may sometimes offer an alternative forum to remedy the environmental degradation at issue.

II. LAYOUT OF EACH CHAPTER

Each chapter addresses three core aspects of a given set of strategies. Those aspects are:

Aspect No. 1: A description of the institutional mechanisms that can potentially receive, review, and remedy the alleged violation of environmental or public health standards.

Aspect No. 2: A set of guidelines that explain how the reader can access and employ a particular strategy.

Aspect No. 3: An example that indicates the effectiveness of a given strategy.

Thus, for example, Chapter 1 presents various strategies involving the presentation of a human rights claim to an appropriate human rights body that if resolved would protect the environment or public health. First, the chapter outlines the components of an environmental or public health human rights claim and explains how to determine which human rights fora can consider such a claim. Second, the chapter discusses the types of submissions one can make to each human rights forum, when to use each type of submission, what information to include in each type of submission, how to locate rules and procedures regarding submissions to each forum, and where to make each type of submission. Third, the chapter provides an example of an environmental human rights claim presented to a human rights body that led to some degree of protection of the environment and public health.

To keep the information discussed in a given chapter of *Defending the Environment* as current as possible, the text refers the reader to forum websites often in lieu of summarizing such material in the chapter itself. This approach allows the chapter to serve as a coordinator of information from varying places, sewn together with analysis, commentary, and precedent not available in the same place on the Internet.

III. STRATEGY TOOLS

The cornerstone of *Defending the Environment* is arguably the second aspect of each chapter—the guidelines for accessing and using particular strategies. Many of these strategies center on various written and oral submissions that individuals and groups can make to the different international, regional and domestic courts, tribunals, commissions, and committees. Therefore, the guidelines for these strategies focus on how to prepare these submissions. The submissions usually share a similar format whether presented to a human rights tribunal, financial institution, treaty secretariat, court, or other international or domestic body.

To prepare the reader for the chapters that follow, below is an overview of these types of submissions. Each chapter will then detail prerequisites, pieces of information to include, and logistics (*e.g.*, length, mailing address, etc.) for a given submission.

A. Petition

A petition is a formal written document that sets forth facts and law related to a particular claim for relief, including environmental and public health claims for relief. In addition, "petition" is sometimes used loosely among international legal practitioners to refer to any writing permitted by a supra-national instrument that one submits to a supra-national forum.

Once submitted, a petition often is reviewed by lawyers and judges who will scrutinize greatly the proof cited to support the facts and the authority cited to support the law. These reviewers usually issue a decision that directly responds to the claim presented, as compared with the more general decisions provided in response to written statements.

In a petition, the facts must be specific and the law must be precise. A petition should include, where permitted, documentary and/or testamentary evidence to support particular facts. Moreover, it should include complete and accurate citations to legal and policy sources or should attach copies whenever such sources seem difficult to locate. Finally, the petition not only needs to state the facts and the law but also has to apply the law to the facts to demonstrate that the particular violation that has occurred or is occurring qualifies the individual or group to the relief requested.

B. Letter Petition or Letter Request

Similar to a petition, a letter petition or request takes the form of a letter addressed to a particular decision maker. It still must include specific facts and accurate law with as much support as possible.

C. Written Statement (Includes Issue Papers)

A written statement is usually submitted to a political body that issues resolutions or decisions aimed at solving a more general problem of which the subject matter of the written statement is just one example. While facts should still be specific and law and policy should be accurate, such written statements will not be scrutinized as heavily as petitions and not necessarily by lawyers or judges.

D. Oral Statement

An oral statement is usually presented to a political body that issues resolutions or decisions or to a judicial or quasi-judicial body that issues opinions. Again, facts should be specific, and law and policy should be accurate. The political body likely demands from the oral statement an explanation of how the particular problem presented in the statement relates to a larger issue that the political body can handle. By contrast, the judicial or quasi-judicial body likely demands from the oral statement greater precision in the statement to guide that body in understanding the dispute before it and what that judicial or quasi-judicial body ought to write in its opinion. Moreover, please note that oral statements may serve as the entry point for an impromptu question-and-answer session between the submitter and the decision making body.

E. Critique of National Report

Most treaties and a few other international instruments pertaining to the environment and public health require nations that obligate themselves to that instrument to submit continual reports, usually annually, to a secretariat or office responsible for administering the treaty or other instrument. In the case of environmental and public health instruments, the secretariats and offices receiving these national reports usually will not forbid the receipt from non-state actors of critiques of these reports. However, for such a critique to encourage a response from the secretariat, office, or nation itself, the critique needs to respond justly and fairly to the national report submitted and not serve as a vehicle for promoting other issues. Should an individual or group find that their critique primarily promotes other issues rather than commenting on the national report, the individual or group should consider using a different device for making the submission.

F. *Amicus Curiae* Brief

Amicus curiae is Latin for "friend of the court" and is the name given to a brief submitted in a dispute to which the submitter is not a party but has expertise, information, and/or concern about the dispute or the larger issue to which the dispute relates. Such submissions are made to courts and dispute resolution bodies authorized to hear particular disputes between two or more parties. *Amicus curiae* briefs usually emphasize legal analysis over, or at the exclusion of, fact development. They are designed to explain to the decision maker about the larger consequences of the decision and persuade the decision maker to consider certain legal arguments or factual information not necessarily explained well or properly emphasized in the party submissions.

Amicus curiae briefs are a more recent development among international courts and dispute resolution bodies entertaining environmental and related disputes. Consequently, some of these fora have not yet drafted procedural rules permitting or denying such briefs. Nevertheless, experience has shown that when one submits an *amicus curiae* brief in the absence of a particular rule permitting or denying such a brief, the decision making body considers it at least informally.

Similar to petitions (and even moreso), *amicus curiae* briefs will be reviewed by lawyers and judges with expertise in international law, particularly procedural matters. Therefore, precise law and specific facts are imperative. The brief should provide complete and accurate citations to legal and policy sources or should attach copies whenever such sources seem difficult to locate. Moreover, the brief should provide, where permitted, documentary and/or testamentary evidence to support particular facts included. Finally, where significant factual discussion takes place in the brief, an application of the law to those facts should follow along with a related analysis.

In general, *amicus curiae* briefs must be well written and convincing. One should seek counsel from the appropriate individuals and organizations on the List of Practitioner Experts in the appendix to this book.

These five oral and written submissions discussed above comprise most of the strategies in the book. However, other strategies mentioned in the text include attending treaty party conferences as an observer; lobbying international, regional, and domestic legislatures and/or executives; litigating international and foreign environmental law and policy matters in domestic courts; and participating on domestic government advisory committees that address international environmental law and policy issues. Consequently, additional strategy tools may exist or emerge.

IV. SUMMARY OF SOURCES OF INTERNATIONAL LAW

Employing the strategies in this book often will require researching international law. Such research can be more complicated than domestic law research, largely because of the difficulty in determining whether the documents encountered constitute a legitimate source of international law upon which one can rely as legal authority in presenting a legal or even quasi-legal argument. Generally speaking, the sources of international law are set forth in Article 38(1) of the Statute of the International Court of Justice:

- a. international conventions, whether general or particular, establishing rules expressly recognized by the contesting states;
- b. international custom, as evidence of a general practice accepted as law;
- c. the general principles of law recognized by civilized nations;
- d. subject to the provisions of Article 59, judicial decisions and the teachings of the most highly qualified publicists of the various nations, as subsidiary means for the determination of rules of law.[1]

Often, documents which themselves do not clearly qualify for one of these categories either may qualify or have evidentiary value in demonstrating one of these sources of law. For example, international conventions are understood to include conventions, agreements, treaties, and protocols. Declarations, resolutions, decisions and reports from multilateral organizations among other documents, even if otherwise nonbinding, are of evidential value in demonstrating international custom or general principles of international law. Third, a sufficient number of domestic constitutions recognizing the same right may be used to establish general principle of law recognized by civilized nations.

In sum, this book encourages non-state actors to compel governments to implement and enforce existing international environmental and public health obligations, remedy existing environmental and public health harms, and seek new ways to guard against future environmental and public health problems. The book also looks to academia to support such undertakings and governments to resolve them. Pursuing some of these strategies will be fruitful and open doors to some degree of relief; pursuing others will be wasteful and close doors tighter than they were before. However, to prevent the weakening of the viable strategies and to altogether strengthen the weak ones requires constant third party enforcement against member states. Ultimately, that is what *Defending the Environment: Civil Society Strategies to Enforce International Environmental Law* hopes to achieve.

---

[1] *See* 59 Stat. 1031, 1060, T.S. No. 993, *available at* http://www.icj-cij.org/icjwww/ibasicdocuments/Basetext/istatute.htm.

CHAPTER 1

EXERCISING ENVIRONMENTAL HUMAN RIGHTS AND REMEDIES IN THE UNITED NATIONS AND REGIONAL SYSTEMS

I. INTRODUCTION

Whenever environmental degradation results in a human harm that violates accepted human rights norms, an international, regional, or domestic human rights committee, commission, and/or court may provide a remedy that can contribute effectively to rectifying the underlying environmental degradation as well as the human rights violation. This chapter chronicles in the United Nations ("UN") system and regional systems of Africa, the Americas, and Europe,[1] the array of environmental human rights claims, how to determine and establish jurisdiction in the proper forum, the functions of varying fora where such claims may be filed, and newly emerging rights that have been recognized and legitimized in international law through this process.

II. DETERMINING VALID ENVIRONMENTAL HUMAN RIGHTS CLAIMS

When undertaking a human rights approach to resolving environmental degradation problems, the first step is to determine whether a valid claim exists. Essential to the understanding of what validates a human rights claim in an international forum is the concept that environmental human rights refer to the link between human rights and the environment. This link involves the deprivation of human rights as a result of environmental degradation. More specifically, an environmental human rights claim alleges that an act or omission of a nation-state has proximately caused environmental degradation that deprives individuals or groups within the jurisdiction of that nation-state of certain rights that the nation-state is obligated to safeguard for those individuals or groups. In more limited circumstances

---

[1] Human rights systems in the Middle East, Asia, and Oceania either do not exist or are still in the preliminary stages of formulation.

a claim may be brought against a corporation or individual for such degradation, or violations of human rights in furtherance of the degradation.

In general, an environmental human rights claim will not persevere unless it satisfies three conditions: (1) existence of environmental degradation; (2) a nation-state action or omission that results in or contributes to that environmental degradation; and (3) a deprivation of human rights that results from the environmental degradation.

Establishing that environmental degradation has occurred is the preliminary condition to satisfy in this process. Environmental degradation involves harm to the atmosphere, lithosphere, hydrosphere, and/or biosphere. Such degradation includes, but is hardly limited to, emission of hazardous pollutants into the air (for example, from oil refineries and chemical plants); discharge of hazardous materials into internal waters, coastal waters, the ocean, and the soil (for example, from mining, petroleum exploration, and other extraction projects); and destruction of ecosystems, including forests (for example, to build roads in connection with dam projects, to construct a pipeline in connection with a natural gas project, to obtain timber products, or to eradicate illicit agricultural crops).

Usually, a valid environmental human rights claim will also require a specific act or omission from a nation-state, commonly referred to as "state action." Examples of state action that result in or contribute to environmental degradation include, but once again are hardly limited to, the granting of permits to emit air pollutants and discharge hazardous waste, the allowance of or failure to prevent ecosystem destruction, especially from development and extraction projects that often result in air, water, or soil pollution and/or ecosystem destruction, the forbiddance of or affirmative efforts to combat protests against environmental degradation, and the provision of military or other support to safeguard an activity giving rise to environmental harm.[2]

Once one establishes that environmental degradation has occurred and, in most circumstances, that state action exists, the final condition underlying an actionable human rights claim is proof that an actual human right was violated. Such an assessment involves considering how an environmental degradation harmed individuals and/or groups and whether such harm translates into the violation of any accepted human rights norms. For some human rights remedies, it is important to ensure that claims are made only on behalf of actual victims.[3]

---

[2] One distinct exception to the state action requirement is the possibility of a complaint in United States federal court pursuant to the Alien Tort Claims Act ("ATCA"), 28 U.S.C. § 1350, to hold non-state actors accountable for human rights violations. Chapter 6 on the expansion of the scope of domestic mechanisms discusses this aspect of the ATCA, among others, in greater detail.

[3] *See, e.g.*, Optional Protocol to the International Covenant on Civil and Political Rights, Dec. 16, 1966, art. 1, 999 U.N.T.S. 302, *available at* http://www.unhchr.ch/html/menu3/b/a_opt.htm ("Optional Protocol to ICCPR").

Generally speaking, environmental degradation adversely impacts human existence. Among other things, the types of environmental degradation described above can make air unhealthy for humans to breathe, water unhealthy for humans to consume or clean with, and soil unhealthy for humans to grow on or inhabit. Air, water, and ground pollution can invade the privacy of one's home, adversely affect one's food, or disturb the balance of the ecosystem necessary for continued human existence. The question is whether any of these elements of human existence rise to the level of a legal right.

The debate over environmental human rights seems to demarcate three categories for such rights. There are existing human rights that are mobilized to combat environmental degradation, existing human rights that are reinterpreted to apply to environmental degradation, and new human rights that safeguard against environmental degradation.[4]

Mobilized existing human rights are those human rights found repeatedly in human rights treaties, many of which have crystallized into customary international law, that either enable or motivate individuals and/or groups to take civil action in response to existing or potential environmental degradation. Examples include the:

a. Right to information,[5]
b. Right to public participation,[6]
c. Right to freedom of expression,[7]

---

[4] See Alan Boyle, *Human Rights Approaches to Environmental Protection: An Overview*, in HUMAN RIGHTS APPROACHES TO ENVIRONMENTAL PROTECTION 2–10 (Alan Boyle & Michael Anderson eds., 1996); *see also* "Human Rights and the Environment," Chapter 15 of A. Kiss and D. Shelton, INTERNATIONAL ENVIRONMENTAL LAW (3d ed. 2004).

[5] *See, e.g., Report on the Situation of Human Rights in Ecuador*, Inter-Am. C.H.R., OEA/ser. L./V./II.96, doc. 10 rev. 1 (Apr. 24, 1997), *available at* http://www.cidh.oas.org/countryrep/ecuador-eng/index%20-%20ecuador.htm ("Ecuador Report"). *See also* Aarhus Convention on Access to Information, Public Participation in Decision-making and Access to Justice in Environmental Matters, *available at* http://www.unece.org/env/pp/documents/cep43e.pdf, arts. 4–5; Protocol on Strategic Environmental Assessment to the Convention on Environmental Impact Assessment in a Transboundary Context, *available at* http://www.unece.org/ env/eia/documents/protocolenglish.pdf, art. 8; Protocol on Pollutant Release and Transfer Registers to the Aarhus Convention, *available at* http://www.unece.org/env/pp/prtr/docs/ PRTR%20Protocol%20English.pdf, art. 11.

[6] *Id. See also* Aarhus Convention on Access to Information, Public Participation in Decision-making and Access to Justice in Environmental Matters, *available at* http://www.unece.org/env/pp/ documents/cep43e.pdf, arts. 6–8; Protocol on Strategic Environmental Assessment to the Convention on Environmental Impact Assessment in a Transboundary Context, *available at* http://www.unece.org/env/eia/documents/protocolenglish.pdf, art. 8; Protocol on Pollutant Release and Transfer Registers to the Aarhus Convention, *available at* http://www.unece.org/env/pp/prtr/ docs/PRTR%20Protocol%20English.pdf, art. 13.

[7] International Covenant on Civil and Political Rights, Dec. 16, 1966, art. 19, 999 U.N.T.S. 171 ("ICCPR").

d. Right to freedom of association,[8] and
e. Right to vote.[9]

Reinterpreted, existing human rights are those human rights found repeatedly in human rights treaties, some of which have crystallized into customary international law, that apply to environmental degradation when reinterpreted with sufficient breadth. Examples include the:

a. Right to life,[10]
b. Right to health,[11]
c. Right to residence,[12]
d. Right to privacy and/or inviolability of the home and family,[13]
e. Right to food,[14]
f. Right to sustenance,[15]
g. Right to property,[16]
h. Right of liberty or security of person,[17]

---

[8] In *Wiwa v. Royal Dutch Shell Petroleum Co.*, No. 96 Civ. 8386, 2002 U.S. Dist. LEXIS 3293 (S.D.N.Y. Feb. 22, 2002), four Nigerians, including three United States residents, sued Royal Dutch Petroleum of the Netherlands and Shell Transport and Trading Company of the United Kingdom. *Id*. at *3. Allegedly Shell Nigeria recruited the Nigerian police and military to attack villages and suppress opposition to its oil development activities in the Ogoni region. *Id*. at *5. In addition, the complaint states that Shell encouraged Nigerian government officials to imprison, torture, and kill plaintiffs and their families, and forcibly took land without adequate compensation while causing pollution of the air and water. *Id*. at *4, *41. Shell allegedly gave the Nigerian military money, weapons, vehicles, ammunition, and other logistical support in the village raids. *Id*. at *42. On February 22, 2002, the district court rejected almost all of the grounds for dismissal, allowing the case to move to discovery. *Id*. at *101. The human rights violations from environmental harm include crimes against humanity against Doe and Owens Wiwa, torture of Doe, cruel, inhuman, and degrading treatment of Doe and Wiwa, violation of the right to peaceful assembly and association for Doe and Wiwa, as well as the rights to life, liberty, and security of person for Doe.

[9] *Id*. art. 25, 999 U.N.T.S. at 179.

[10] E.g., *Ecuador Report*, *supra* note 5; K.H.W. v. F.R.G., 40 I.L.M. 773 *passim* (2001).

[11] E.g., *The Yanomami Case*, Res. 12/85, Case 7615, Inter-Am. C.H.R., OEA/ser. L./V./II.66, doc. 10 rev. 1 (Mar. 5, 1985), *reprinted in* 1985 INTER-AM. Y.B. ON HUM. RTS. (Inter-Am. C.H.R.) 264, 272-76.

[12] ICCPR, *supra* note 7, art. 12, 999 U.N.T.S. at 176.

[13] E.g., *Lopez Ostra v. Spain*, App. No. 16798/90, 20 Eur. H.R. Rep. 277 (Dec. 4, 1994); *Hatton & Others v. U.K.*, Application No. 36022/97 (Feb. 10, 2001).

[14] International Covenant on Economic, Social, and Cultural Rights ("ICESR"), Dec. 16, 1966, art. 11(1)-(2), 993 U.N.T.S. at 7.

[15] *See e.g.*, Sierra Club Politics, Environmental Justice Principles, art. 1(E), *available at* http://www.sierraclub.org/policy/conservation/justice.asp.

[16] E.g., *The Mayagna (Sumo) Awas Tingni Community Case*, Case No. 11.557, Inter-Am. C.H.R. 79 (Aug. 31, 2001), *available at* http://www1.umn.edu/humanrts/iachr/AwasTingnicase.html; *see generally*, S. James Anaya, *The Awas Tingni Petition to the Inter-American Commission on Human Rights: Indigenous Lands, Loggers, and Government Neglect in Nicaragua*, 9 ST. THOMAS L. REV. 157 (1996).

[17] ICCPR, *supra* note 7, art. 9(b), 999 U.N.T.S. at 175.

Exercising Environmental Human Rights and Remedies • 13

i. Right to freedom from inhumane treatment,[18]
j. Right to equal protection,[19] and
k. Right to culture.[20]

Lastly, new human rights are those rights not yet codified or well-codified in treaties but strongly evident in sources of customary international law that protect against environmental degradation. Examples include the:

a. Right to a clean and healthy environment,
b. Right to clean and healthy air,
c. Right to clean and healthy water,[21]
d. Right to clean and healthy soil,
e. Right to environmental protection, and
f. Right to biodiversity.

The above three groups of human rights enable one to validly claim that the environmental degradation resulting from the act or omission of a nation-state proximately caused a harm that violated the human rights of the individuals and/or groups within the jurisdiction of that nation-state.

Additional sources of international law to which a petitioner can cite to support many of the aforementioned rights can be found in Table A in Part VIII of this Chapter. With every treaty provision listed in Table A, one must determine whether the nation-state against which the environmental human rights claims are alleged either has ratified, acceded, accepted, or at least signed the convention in which the provision appears. In contrast, declarations or resolutions that determine if the nation-state in question voted in favor of that document are helpful but not essential. One can easily find the above information on the Internet site where the human right instrument is located or in the official records for that instrument cited in Table A.[22]

To the degree that claims presented in human rights petitions rely primarily on sources of customary international law rather than on treaties, general principles of law, international court and tribunal decisions, or scholarly writings (as is frequently necessary), the articulation of the environmental human rights through custom is more complex. Consequently,

---

[18] *Id.* art. 10(1), 999 U.N.T.S. at 176.

[19] *E.g., Lubicon Lake Band v. Canada*, U.N. Hum. Rts. Comm. (HRC), Comm. No. 167/1984, Supp. No. 40, U.N. Doc. A/45/40 (1990).

[20] *E.g., id.; Universal Declaration of Human Rights*, G.A. Res. 217 A (III), U.N. GAOR, 3rd Sess., Supp. No. 2, art. 15, U.N. Doc. A/810 (1948), *available at* http://www1.umn.edu/humanrts/instree/b1udhr.htm ("UDHR").

[21] *See General Comment No. 15 (2002), The Right to Water (arts. 11 and 12 of the International Covenant on Economic, Social and Cultural Rights)*, U.N. Comm. on Econ., Soc., & Cultural Rts., U.N. Doc. E/C.12/2002/11 (2002), *available at* http://www.unhchr.ch/html/menu2/6/gc15.doc.

[22] *See id.* and Table A, Part VIII, *infra*.

this Article devotes Part IV to the topic and encourages the reader to consider that material as well.

Finally, if environmental degradation has occurred but either no state action is present or no accepted human rights standards were violated, thus precluding a valid environmental human rights claim, other colorable judicial avenues most likely exist by which to remedy the harm. Such avenues may include tort actions, nuisance actions, administrative proceedings, and/or citizen enforcement proceedings brought by individuals or a class of individuals against a nation-state and/or a non-state actor. Chapter 6 on domestic mechanisms comments briefly on aspects of these actions whenever they involve the extraterritorial application of a domestic law. However, most of the subject is beyond the scope of this book.

III. DETERMINING WHERE TO FILE THE ENVIRONMENTAL HUMAN RIGHTS CLAIM

After the determination has been made that a valid environmental human rights claim exists, the second step is selecting the most effective forum in which to present the claim. This determination depends on whether the forum has jurisdiction over the subject of the claim, the defendant, and the petitioner (*i.e.*, whether a private right of action exists for the petitioner). Table B is designed to assist the reader in this process.

The UN and regional human rights systems of Africa, the Americas, and Europe provide fora for resolving various human rights environmental claims.[23] The UN human rights system includes charter-based and treaty-based bodies within or linked to the UN Economic and Social Council, as well as UN specialized agencies such as the UN Educational, Scientific and Cultural Organization ("UNESCO") and the International Labor Organization ("ILO"). The regional human rights systems of Africa, the Americas, and Europe usually involve a two-part, treaty-based process before a commission and a court. It is important to note, however, that individuals and groups can seek the assistance of some of these human rights bodies only

---

[23] *See, e.g.*, Optional Protocol to the ICCPR; African Charter on Human and Peoples' Rights, June 27, 1981, *available at* http://www.achpr.org/africancharter.doc, at arts. 55–56 ("African Charter"); American Convention on Human Rights, Nov. 22, 1969, *available at* http://wwwcidh.oas.org/Basicos/ basic3.htm ("American Convention"), at art. 44; [European] Convention for the Protection of Human Rights and Fundamental Freedoms, Nov. 4, 1950, 312 U.N.T.S. 221, *available at* http://conventions.coe.int/Treaty/EN/CadreListeTraites.htm, ("European Convention"), at art. 34.

In addition to supra-national dispute resolution fora, domestic courts may be able to exercise jurisdiction over such matters. Chapter 6 on the expansion of domestic mechanisms addresses this issue in the context of the U.S. Alien Tort Claims Act, 28 U.S.C. § 1350. In addition, *see generally* Richard L. Herz, *Litigating Environmental Abuses Under the Alien Torts Claim Act: A Practical Assessment*, 40 VA. J. INT'L L. 545 (2000).

after exhausting or simultaneously resorting to domestic remedies.[24] In addition, individuals and groups often can seek the assistance of UN human rights bodies only at the exclusion of seeking assistance from other supranational bodies.[25]

The first step in determining which of these various UN human rights fora to approach requires assessing the subject matter jurisdiction of each body—that is, what rights the forum is authorized to consider. For treaty-based human rights fora (*e.g.*, the UN Human Rights Committee, Inter-American Committee on Human Rights), relevant rights are primarily those listed in the treaty creating that forum.[26] For charter-based human rights fora (*e.g.*, UN Commission on Human Rights), rights come from the charter provisions creating that forum, and are often elaborated in a related declaration or resolution.[27] Table B summarizes the relevant human rights instrument for each body and the list of rights to which the jurisdiction of that forum is usually limited.[28]

Despite the limitations of an individual forum's jurisdiction as reflected in Table B, limitations are only relevant to determine the correct forum to which one makes a submission. Once a specific forum is selected, the human rights body will usually consider arguments in a given submission that depend on sources of international law outside the specific treaty or charter creating that institution.[29] For example, in submitting an environ-

---

[24] *See, e.g.*, Optional Protocol to the ICCPR, art. 5(2)(b); African Charter, at art. 56(5); American Convention, at art. 46(1)(a); European Convention, at art. 35(1).
See also, e.g., M.A. v. Canada, Committee Against Torture (CAT) Comm. No. 22/1995, CAT/C/14/D/22/1995 (Jurisprudence), 14th Sess., Annex (May 5, 1995) (denying evaluation by the Committee Against Torture because the claimant had not exhausted all available domestic remedies as required by the Convention Against Torture and did not fit within the exception), *available at* http://193.194.138.190/tbs/doc.nsf/c12563e7005d936d4125611 e00445ea9/dc94422b8e0f1a86802567a6004f36f7?OpenDocument; *Velásquez Rodríguez Case*, Preliminary Objections, Judgment of June 26, 1989, Inter-Am.Ct.H.R. (Ser. C) No. 1 (1994).

[25] *See, e.g.*, Optional Protocol to the ICCPR, at art. 5(2)(a); African Charter, at art. 56(7); American Convention, at art. 46(1)(c); European Convention, at art. 35(2)(b).
See also, e.g., Cameroon v. Nigeria, 1998 I.C.J. 275, 359 (June 11) (noting the "final and binding force" of the Court's decisions), *available at* 1998 WL 1148893; *Concerning Application of Convention on Prevention and Punishment of the Crime of Genocide*, 1996 I.C.J. 595, 619 (July 11) (noting same), *available at* 1996 WL 943410.

[26] *See, e.g.*, Introduction to the U.N. Human Rights Committee, *available at* http://193.194.138.190/html/menu2/6/a/introhrc.htm. The site explains that the U.N. Human Rights Committee was created to monitor the implementation of the ICCPR.

[27] *See infra* Table B in Part VIII of this Chapter.

[28] *Id.*

[29] *See, e.g., Concerning the Arrest Warrant of 11 April 2000*, 2000 I.C.J. 182, 206–07, 233 n.9 (Dec. 8), *available at* 2000 WL 33942512; *Concerning the Aerial Incident of 10 August 1999*, 2000 I.C.J. 12, 45 (Jun. 21) (Koroma, J., separate opinion), *available at* 2000 WL 33942493; *Concerning Kasiki/Sedudu Island*, 1999 I.C.J. 1045, 1045 (Dec. 13), *available at* 1999 WL 1693057. *See generally* American Convention, *supra* note 23, at art. 29.

mental human rights claim based on the right to life acknowledged by the UN Human Rights Committee ("HRC"), the petition can cite not only the appropriate provision of the ICCPR and prior HRC decisions, but also (1) any similar right to life provisions in other treaties, whether international or regional, as well as evidence of customary international law on the right to life such as declarations, resolutions, and reports; (2) evidence of general principles among civilized nations, documented in national constitutions and statutes, judicial and quasi-judicial decisions; and (3) opinions of scholars, so long as they are all relevant to the right to life.[30]

The second criteria in considering whether a human rights forum has jurisdiction over the alleged nation-state is whether the nation-state has accepted the jurisdiction of the human rights forum or whether the nation-state is a party to any international instruments which automatically subject that nation-state to the jurisdiction of that human rights forum. The last column in Table B summarizes this information.

The last step in determining an appropriate human rights forum is to strategize on which of the competent human rights fora is preferred. Factors to consider are: whether the forum has handed down favorable decisions on the factual claims and/or legal issues at stake; whether exhaustion of domestic or regional remedies is required before filing a claim with that forum; whether submission to that forum is to the exclusion of all other forums; whether the forum entertains requests for provisional measures; where the forum meets so as to determine travel expenses to the forum for any oral hearings; and how quickly the forum disposes of matters on its docket, determined in part by how often the forum meets and how well-funded the forum is; and whether the forum's decisions are enforceable. Information about various human rights fora discussed in the next part highlights advantages and disadvantages of each one that can help with selecting a preferred forum.

Regarding what private rights of actions are available to the petitioner, not every avenue available to address international human rights problems is open to non-state actors and not every human right is redressable before those bodies where private rights of action do exist. Consequently, one must consider what kind of submissions can be made through each available human rights body and/or process. Table C summarizes these possibilities.[31]

With respect to the enforceability of a forum's decisions, one should note that generally speaking, such decisions can only *persuade* the nation-state in question to take steps to curtail the human rights violations resulting from the environmental degradation. In other words, only a public shaming occurs. However, additional procedures discussed separately in Part V may be available to obtain enforcement of these decisions.[32] In addi-

---

[30] See *infra* Table B in Part VIII of this Chapter.
[31] See *infra* Table C in Part VIII of this Chapter.
[32] See *infra* Part V of this Chapter.

tion to the information provided in this part, the discussion in the next part about how to file a claim in each forum may serve to highlight additional advantages and disadvantages that can help with selecting a preferred forum.

IV. SUBMITTING THE ENVIRONMENTAL HUMAN RIGHTS CLAIM TO THE SELECTED FORUM

With a valid environmental human rights claim in one hand and a selected human rights forum in the other, the next major step is the actual filing of the claim. The information below introduces each UN and regional human rights forum and explains briefly how to bring an environmental human rights claim to various human rights fora. Tables B and C in Part VIII provide guidance on use of these fora, including which states are parties to what processes.

Before turning to each specific forum, it is extremely important to note that before non-governmental organizations ("NGOs") can make written and/or oral submissions to most of these fora, such NGOs often must have consultative status of some kind with the UN or must identify an NGO with such status and ask that NGO to make the submission. The authorization for NGO consultative status with the UN is found in Article 71 of the UN Charter,[33] and the procedure for obtaining such status is set forth in Economic and Social Council ("ECOSOC") Resolution 1996/31.[34] These instruments have led to the creation of the Committee on Non-Governmental Organizations and the NGO Section of ECOSOC.

NGOs seeking consultative status should contact the NGO Section of ECOSOC. Such contact information as well as a consultative status application and answers to many questions can be found at http://www.un.org/esa/coordination/ngo. Again, consultative status is often required for an NGO to make use of the strategies discussed herein. Consequently, one can either obtain such consultative status or ask another NGO with such status to assist.

A. United Nations System

Readers should be sure to consult appropriate individuals on the List of Practitioner Experts, in the appendix to this book, when proceeding with these strategies.

---

[33] "The Economic and Social Council may make suitable arrangements for consultation with non-governmental organizations which are concerned with matters within its competence. Such arrangements may be made with international organizations and, where appropriate, with national organizations after consultation with the Member of the United Nations concerned." U.N. CHARTER art. 71, *available at* http://www.un.org/aboutun/charter.

[34] *See* E.S.C. Res. 1996/31, U.N. ESCOR, 51st Sess., 49th plen. mtg., U.N. Doc. E./1996/96 (1996), *available at* http://www.un.org/documents/ecosoc/res/1996/eres1996-31.htm.

1. Human Rights Committee[35]

One potential forum for voicing human rights grievances is the HRC established by the ICCPR.[36] The HRC consists of 18 members who are nominated by the states and serve in their individual capacities, not as government representatives.[37]

The HRC has various functions, all designed to ensure a state's compliance with the ICCPR.[38] The HRC has adjudicative functions under the Optional Protocol to the ICCPR, which establishes a right to individual petition.[39] Individuals and groups can present environmental human rights claims to the HRC in four different ways: filing an individual petition under the Optional Protocol;[40] making an *amicus* submission to any Article 41 and 42 dispute; encouraging a state to initiate an inter-state dispute;[41] or submitting a critique of Article 40 reports.[42]

The first method for presenting environmental human rights claims is the filing of an individual petition under the Optional Protocol.[43] The Protocol enables private parties to file individual communications and complaints with the HRC.[44] Since 1976, the HRC has dealt with an increasing number of individual communications. Many of these are ruled inadmissible, usually because the complaint is already being examined under another procedure of international investigation or there has been no exhaustion of domestic remedies.[45] The HRC has developed a body of case law interpreting and applying the Covenant and Protocol.[46] Individual complaints may only be filed against state parties to the Covenant that have also ratified the Optional Protocol.[47]

---

[35] The official website for the Human Rights Committee may be found at http://www.unhchr.ch/html/menu2/6/hrc.htm.

[36] See ICCPR, *supra* note 7, art. 28, 999 U.N.T.S. at 179.

[37] *Id.*

[38] *Id.*

[39] Optional Protocol to the ICCPR, *supra* note 3, art. 5, 999 U.N.T.S. at 303.

[40] *Id.* art. 2, 999 U.N.T.S. at 303.

[41] ICCPR, *supra* note 7, arts. 41-42, 999 U.N.T.S. at 182-84.

[42] *Id.* art. 40, 999 U.N.T.S. at 181-82.

[43] See Optional Protocol to the ICCPR, *supra* note 3, art. 2, 999 U.N.T.S. at 302.

[44] It is important to distinguish in all UN processes between "individual" complaints with respect to who may petition and with respect to what claims can be brought. For example, under the 1235 and 1503 procedures, individuals may file petitions but they must allege widespread or systematic violations. See E.S.C. Res. 1235, U.N. ESCOR, 42d Sess., Supp. No. 1A, at 17, U.N. Doc. E/4393 (1967), *available at* http://www.oup.co.uk/pdf/bt/cassese/cases/part3/ch16/1602.pdf ("E.S.C. Res. 1235").

[45] See *id.*

[46] For a list of case law decisions, see the HRC website, *Documents on Jurisprudence, available at* http://193.194.138.190/tbs/doc.nsf/FramePage/TypeJurisprudence?OpenDocument&Start= 1&Count=15&Expand=3.

[47] Optional Protocol to the ICCPR, *supra* note 3, art. 1, 999 U.N.T.S. at 302.

The review process for the Optional Protocol has two stages. In the first stage, the HRC must decide on the admissibility of the communication under Articles 2, 3, and 5 of the Protocol. Article 2 requires that the complaining party must have exhausted all available domestic remedies and must submit a written communication.[48] Article 3 requires that a communication is deemed inadmissible if it is anonymous, if the committee considers it to be an abuse of the right of submission, or if the committee considers it to be incompatible with the provisions of the covenant.[49] Article 5(a) states that the Committee consider each communication in light of all the written information made available to it by the individual and the state involved.[50] The complaining party must also prove that they have exhausted all available domestic remedies per Article 5(b), which provides that the Committee will not consider a communication unless it has ascertained that the same matter is not being examined under another procedure of international investigation or settlement, and that the individual has exhausted domestic remedies.[51] Furthermore, meetings are closed while the committee examines each communication, and the Committee must forward its views to both the state and the individual.[52]

Once the Committee has decided that a communication is admissible, it informs the state of the matter and the state has six months to respond to the charges.[53] The Committee reviews written communications of the state and the individual and communicates its findings to the parties.[54] The Committee also provides the UN General Assembly with a summary of the findings in its annual report.[55] As a result of the increasing number of parties that have ratified the Optional Protocol, the Committee now issues its annual report in two volumes, using the second volume to report on practice under the Protocol.[56]

The HRC has strengthened the effectiveness of the human rights mechanism established by the Optional Protocol. The HRC now has the power to propose interim measures to avoid irreparable damage to the victim of a violation.[57] The HRC also now requires state parties to indicate in their reports what measures they have taken to give effect to the HRC's recommendations in cases in which the HRC has found the state

---

[48] *Id.* art. 2, 999 U.N.T.S. at 302.
[49] *Id.* art. 3, 999 U.N.T.S. at 302-03.
[50] *Id.* art. 5(a), 999 U.N.T.S. at 303.
[51] *Id.* art. 5(b), 999 U.N.T.S. at 303.
[52] *Id.* art. 5(c), 5(d), 999 U.N.T.S. at 303.
[53] *Id.*, art. 4, 999 U.N.T.S. at 303.
[54] *Id.* art. 5(4), 999 U.N.T.S. at 303.
[55] ICCPR, *supra* note 8, art. 45, 999 U.N.T.S. at 184.
[56] *Report of the Human Rights Committee*, U.N. GOAR, Hum. Rts. Comm., 54th Sess., Supp. No. 40, U.N. Doc. A/54/40, Vol. II (1999), *available at* http://www.unhchr.ch/tbs/doc.nsf/(Symbol)/64f3eba65d74c527c12569b900554f3d?Opendocument.
[57] *See* Optional Protocol to the ICCPR, *supra* note 3, art. 4(1), 999 U.N.T.S. at 303.

to be in violation of the Optional Protocol, particularly stressing the remedy that has been given to the victim.[58]

A second method for bringing a complaint within the HRC is achieved with an *amicus* submission to the Article 41 and 42 dispute process for interstate complaints.[59] When an environmental rights claim is presented to the Human Rights Committee, individuals and groups who do not directly suffer from the harm alleged but are nonetheless aware of and concerned about the outcome of such claim—both in terms of the relief for the petitioner and the impact on human rights jurisprudence—are usually unable to file their own petition. However, they may be able to play a formal role in the process by filing an *amicus curiae* or "friends of the court" brief in support of the petitioner's claim.[60] Nothing in the text of the ICCPR or the HRC's rules of procedure appears to prevent a non-party from filing such an *amicus* brief.

Generally speaking, *amicus* submissions should: (1) explain how the case relates to the work of the NGO or community group filing it; (2) elaborate on legal arguments not adequately addressed in the petition; and (3) provide additional, supportive factual information not presented in the petition.[61]

1.1 Llaka Honhat

In *Association of Lhaka Honhat Aboriginal Communities (Nuestra Tierra/Our Land) v. the State of Argentina, Precautionary Measures Request*,[62] filed with the Inter-American Commission on Human Rights, two NGOs—the Center for Human Rights and the Environment in Cordoba, Argentina[63] and the Center for International Environmental Law in Washington, D.C.[64]—jointly filed an *amicus curiae* brief[65] to support the petitioner's claim that Argentina's plan to cut through the center of the protected land of the indigenous Wichi,

---

[58] *Id.* art. 4(2), 999 U.N.T.S. at 303.
[59] *See* ICCPR, *supra* note 7, arts. 41–42, 999 U.N.T.S. at 182–84.
[60] *See id.*
[61] *See, e.g.*, Brief of Amici Curiae American Civil Liberties Union AIDS Project, Cahill v. Rosa, 674 N.E.2d 274 (N.Y. 1996) (Nos. 180, 181).
[62] Brief of Amici Curiae Center for Human Rights and the Environment and Center for International Environmental Law, *Ass'n of Lhaka Honhat Aboriginal Communities (Nuestra Tierra/Our Land) v. Argentina*, Precautionary Measures Request, Inter-Am. C.H.R. (2000) (No. P12.094), *available at* http://www.ciel.org/Publications/WichiAmiciCuriae2.pdf.
[63] The Center for Human Rights and the Environment ("CEDHA") is a non-profit organization promoting sustainable development through the promotion of the symbiotic relationship existing between the environment and people, and striving to build awareness of the importance of addressing human rights and environmental protection in all development processes. *See* CEDHA, About CEDHA, *available at* http://www.cedha.org.ar/cedha.htm.
[64] The Center for International Environmental Law ("CIEL") is a public interest, not-for-profit environmental law firm founded in 1989 to strengthen international and comparative environmental law and policy around the world. *See* CIEL, CIEL's Goals, *available at* http://www.ciel.org/reciel.html.
[65] Brief of Amici Curiae CEDHA and CIEL, *Supra,* note 62.

1.1 Llaka Honhat *(continued)*

Chorote, Chulupi, Toba, and Tapiete peoples to build a transnational road through Argentina linking Brazil to Chile would violate their right to life and their right to a clean and healthy environment.[66]

In October 2000, the Inter-American Human Rights Commission ordered the Argentine government to come to a meaningful agreement with the Wichi and other indigenous people. The Commission gave the Argentine government 30 days to demonstrate that it was taking significant steps to resolve the conflict over the road construction. This was one of the first cases in which an international tribunal recognized a connection between indigenous people and their land and more importantly, a link between environmental abuses and human rights violations.[67] Presumably, submission of the *amicus* papers helped persuade the Commission to order that a serious meet-and-confer process occur.

A third, indirect method found under Articles 41 and 42 of the ICCPR is through the inter-state complaint machinery, which enables one state party to charge another with a violation of the treaty.[68] Although the machinery is optional and can be used only by and against parties that have recognized HRC's jurisdiction to receive these complaints,[69] NGOs can encourage a state party to make use of the machinery so that the complaint might bring attention to human rights issues occurring in another country. In practice, the system establishes little more than a formal conciliation machinery. If a state believes another state is in violation of the ICCPR, it can make a formal statement to the other state, addressing the alleged violation.[70] If the two states do not resolve their differences within six months, each has the right to submit their case to the HRC.[71] Each side is invited to present its case and submit evidence.[72] If a friendly solution is reached within 12 months, it is reported by the HRC.[73] Otherwise, the HRC must prepare a report on the situation, including a brief statement of the facts, and the written and oral statements of the parties.[74] The role of the HRC ends there, unless the states consent to the appointment of an *ad hoc* Conciliation Committee,[75] consisting of five members approved by the states.[76]

---

[66] See id.
[67] Press Release, Human Rights Commission Halts Argentine Plan That Would Lead to Genocide of Indigenous Communities (Oct. 12, 2000), *available at* http://www.ciel.org/Announce/wichipressrelease2.html (last visited June 21, 2005).
[68] See ICCPR, *supra* note 7, arts. 41–42, 999 U.N.T.S. at 182-84.
[69] Id. art. 41(1), 999 U.N.T.S. at 182.
[70] Id. art. 41(1)(a), 999 U.N.T.S. at 182.
[71] Id. art. 41(1)(b), 999 U.N.T.S. at 182.
[72] Id. art. 41(1)(f), 999 U.N.T.S. at 182.
[73] Id. art. 41(1)(h)(i), 999 U.N.T.S. at 183.
[74] Id. art. 41(1)(h)(ii), 999 U.N.T.S. at 183.
[75] Id. art. 42(1)(a), 999 U.N.T.S. at 183.
[76] Id. art. 42(1)(b), 999 U.N.T.S. at 183.

After examining the case, the Commission attempts to negotiate a friendly settlement and then can make its own findings of the relevant facts and suggest a resolution.[77] The parties are not required to accept the suggested resolution,[78] but the Commission can call a failure to do so to the attention of the General Assembly in the HRC's annual report.[79]

A fourth method for bringing a complaint within the HRC is under Article 40(1) of the ICCPR.[80] Because all state parties must submit reports on the measures they have adopted in compliance with the Covenant,[81] NGOs can bring attention to environmental human rights concerns occurring within or committed by state parties that submits reports. Such NGOs can prepare and submit to the HRC a critique that focuses on material omissions and/or misrepresentations in the state report regarding environmental human rights.[82] The HRC is responsible for examining these reports and any NGO critiques, and has developed a set of reporting guidelines and procedures for dealing with the reports to ensure state compliance with their obligations, and to assist states in overcoming any difficulties.[83] Although the ICCPR does not vest the HRC with the power to verify state reports or conduct investigations, it can seek permission to do so from the states concerned.[84] In addition, each state's representatives must be present when the HRC reviews its reports.[85] This requirement allows the HRC to ask for supplemental information and to pinpoint serious compliance problems.[86] The HRC can then call any problems to the attention of the UN General Assembly in an annual report.[87] In the past few years, the report-

---

[77] *Id.* art. 42(7), 999 U.N.T.S. at 184.
[78] *Id.* art. 42(7)(d), 999 U.N.T.S. at 184.
[79] *Id.* art. 45, 999 U.N.T.S. at 184.
[80] *Id.* art. 40(1), 999 U.N.T.S. at 181.
[81] *See id.*
[82] *See, e.g., Concluding Observations of the Human Rights Committee (Hong Kong): China 12/11/99*, U.N. GOAR, HRC, 67th Sess., U.N. Doc. CCPR/C/79/Add.117(1999) (noting NGO's participation in report filed by the Hong Kong Special Administrative Region), *available at* http://www.unhchr.ch/tbs/doc.nsf/(Symbol)/CCPR.C.79.Add.117.En?Opendocument; George E. Edwards & Mark Zuckerman, *Rights Monitoring Under Threat?: Hong Kong at the United Nations*, CHINA RTS. F.: J. OF HUM. RTS. IN CHINA (1996), *available at* http://iso.hrichina.org/iso/article.adp?article_id=339& subcategory_id=26.
[83] ICCPR, *supra* note 7, art. 40(4), 999 U.N.T.S. at 182.
[84] *Id.* art. 40(5), 999 U.N.T.S. at 182.
[85] *Rules of Procedure of the Human Rights Committee*, U.N.GAOR, Hum. Rts. Comm. (HRC), 56th Sess., Supp. No. 40, 1924th mtg., at rule 68, U.N. Doc CCPR/C/3/Rev. 6 (2001), *available at* http://www.unhchr.ch/tbs/doc.nsf/(Symbol)/CCPR.C.3.Rev.6.En?Opendocument ("*HRC Rules*"). *See also Reporting Obligations of State Parties under Article 40 of the Covenant: General Comment No. 30*, U.N. GAOR, HRC, 57th Sess., Supp. No. 40, 2025th mtg., U.N. Doc. CCPR/C/21/Rev.2/Add.12 (2002), *available at* http://www.unhchr.ch/tbs/doc.nsf/(Symbol)/452ffba066e323b8c1256c480036f5ca?opendocument (explaining that in an effort to remedy noncompliance with delegation obligations, the HRC may proceed to review a report in the absence of a delegation from a state party).
[86] *HRC Rules, supra* note 84, at 68.
[87] ICCPR, *supra* note 7, art. 45, 999 U.N.T.S. at 184.

ing system has evolved into an increasingly more effective instrument for ensuring compliance with the ICCPR. Among the activities increasing the reporting system's effectiveness is the HRC's decision to bring information concerning any grave violations of human rights revealed in the reporting system to the UN Secretary General.[88] In addition, the HRC has adopted a number of General Comments that spell out the meaning of provisions of the ICCPR and are similar to advisory opinions that interpret the ICCPR.[89]

It is important to remember to consult appropriate individuals on the List of Practitioner Experts, in the appendix to this book, as one proceeds with these strategies.

1.2 Finland

In December 1990, four Finnish reindeer breeders wrote a communication to the United Nations Human Rights Committee alleging that the Finnish Wilderness Act would allow logging to interfere with their reindeer's breeding area.[90] The authors of the communication specifically complained that the Central Forestry Board would control large portions of wilderness area and the Board would have the power to carry out full-scale logging with the approval of the Ministry for the Environment.[91] The authors claimed that the Act not only threatened the general and economic future of reindeer herding, but that the Act was an interference with the authors' rights to enjoy their own culture under Article 27 of the Covenant.[92] The authors requested that they be afforded interim protection measures while the Act was being investigated.

The State argued that the authors could not be considered "victims" because fear of logging and road construction in the future did not translate to an actual violation of their rights.[93] An executive decision or action would have to be taken under the Wilderness Act before the authors could actually claim a violation of Covenant rights.

In July 1991, the Human Rights Committee found the authors' communication admissible and requested that the State "adopt such measures as

(continued)

---

[88] *See* PHILIP ALSTON & HENRY J. STEINER, INTERNATIONAL HUMAN RIGHTS IN CONTEXT: LAW, POLITICS, MORALS 619-21 (2d ed. 2000).

[89] A list of all General Comments from the HRC under ICCPR are available at the UN website at http://www.unhchr.ch/tbs/doc.nsf.

[90] United Nations, Decisions of the Human Rights Committee declaring communications inadmissible under the Optional Protocol to the International Covenant on Civil and Political Rights, Communication No. 431/1990 (Dec. 18, 1990), *available at* http://www.unhchr.ch/tbs/doc.nsf/(SymbolSearch)/d9b7883d6531d3ea8025672a0041705e?Opendocument (last visited June 22, 2005).

[91] *Id.* at ¶ 2.4.

[92] ICCPR, *supra* note 7.

[93] United Nations Human Rights Committee, *supra* note 90, at ¶ 4.5.

1.2 Finland *(continued)*

appropriate to prevent irreparable damage to the authors."[94] The State requested a review of admissibility and restated their argument that current road construction and logging activities were not causing damage to reindeer breeding. In response, the authors cited a world trend of interference with indigenous peoples' possibility to enjoy their culture and carry out traditional economic activities.[95] The authors also stated that road construction was causing noise and traffic that disturbed the reindeer, changing the pattern of reindeer movement, and that any roads or logging in the area would further disturb the reindeer.

In March 1994, the Human Rights Committee, upon reexamination of admissibility considerations, decided that the authors needed to exhaust domestic remedies under Article 27 because Finland had adopted the Covenant into domestic law. While the authors filed a domestic suit, the Committee ordered the Central Forestry Board to take no further action in the wilderness area under examination.[96]

2. Committee on Economic, Social, and Cultural Rights[97]

The Committee on Economic, Social and Cultural Rights ("ESC") carries out duties under the International Covenant on Economic, Social and Cultural Rights ("ICESCR").[98] Designed to address human rights violations within the UN, the ICESCR itself does not establish a formal complaint system. It only requires that state parties submit reports on steps that they have taken and progress that has been made toward the observance of the rights the ICESCR recognizes.[99] Furthermore, it was not until the establishment of the ESC that there existed a permanent committee dedicated to the review of these reports.[100]

The ESC consists of 18 members who serve in their individual capacities.[101] Prior to the ESC's first meeting in March 1987, the Sessional Working

---

[94] *Id.* at ¶ 5.6.
[95] *Id.* at ¶ 7.3.
[96] *Id.* at ¶ 8.4.
[97] The official website for the Committee on Economic, Social and Cultural Rights may be found at http://www.unhchr.ch/html/menu2/6/cescr.htm.
[98] E.S.C. Res. 1985/17, U.N. ESCOR, 2d Sess., 22d mtg., U.N. Doc. S/RES/1985/17 (1985) *available at* http://www.un.org/esa/coordination/ecosoc/archives.htm. (establishing the ESC).
[99] International Covenant on Economic, Social and Cultural Rights, Dec. 16, 1966, art. 16(1), 993 U.N.T.S. 3, 9 ("ICESCR").
[100] UNITED NATIONS, FACT SHEET NO. 16 (REV. 1), Comm. on Econ., Soc. & Cultural Rts. (2002), *available at* http://www.unhchr.ch/html/menu6/2/fs16.htm ("FACT SHEET NO. 16").
[101] *Id.*

Group on the Implementation of the International Covenant on Economic, Social and Cultural Rights was responsible for the review of the reports.[102] The working group's members were drawn from the ECOSOC and its findings were reported back to ECOSOC, the UN Commission on Human Rights, and to the specialized agencies of the UN concerned with economic, social and cultural rights.[103] With the establishment of the permanent committee, efforts to promote the implementation of the ICESCR became more effective.[104] The ESC has used general comments and analyses to clarify ambiguities in the language of the Convention.[105] In particular, it was the Committee's analysis of Article 2(1) of the ICESCR in General Comment No. 3 (1990) that solidified the immediate, although progressive, nature of the state parties' obligations.[106]

Unlike the ICCPR, the ICESCR allows for progressive implementation.[107] Article 2(1) of the ICESCR requires that the state parties "take steps ... with a view to achieving progressively the full realization of the rights recognized in the present Covenant by all appropriate means, including particularly the adoption of legislative measures,"[108] and Article 2(2) requires that state parties "undertake to guarantee" that these rights will be exercised without discrimination.[109] In its General Comment No. 3, the ESC made clear its opinion that this language does impose obligations of immediate effect.[110] With regard to the undertaking of non-discrimination, the Committee notes that "the enjoyment of the rights recognized, without discrimination, will often be appropriately promoted, in part, through the provision of judicial or other effective remedies."[111]

---

[102] International Covenant on Human Rights, G.A. Res. 40/115, U.N. GAOR, 40th Sess., Supp. No. 24, at 231, U.N. Doc. A/Res/40/115 (1985).

[103] U.N. ESCOR, E.S.C. DEC. 1978/10, 2d Sess., 12th mtg., U.N. Sales No. #.80.I.1 (1978), *reprinted in* 1978 U.N.Y.B. 727-28 (establishing the Working Group).

[104] *See* Philip Alston, *Out of the Abyss: The Challenges Confronting the New U.N. Committee on Economic, Social and Cultural Rights*, 9 HUM. RTS. Q. 332, 340-342 (1987) (detailing the shortcomings of the Working Group). *But see* PHILIP ALSTON & JAMES CRAWFORD, THE FUTURE OF UN HUMAN RIGHTS TREATY MONITORING 139-44 (2000) (cataloguing improvements in the effectiveness of the Committee).

[105] *Implementation of the International Covenant on Economic, Social and Cultural Rights*, U.N. ESCOR, 21st Sess., Supp. No. 2, U.N. Doc. E/2000/22-E/C.12/1999/11+Corr.1 (1999).

[106] *The Nature of State Parties' Obligations (art. 2, par. 1), General Comment 3*, U.N. ESCOR, 5th Sess., Supp. No. 3, U.N. Doc. E/1991/23-E/C.12/1990/8+Corr.1 (1991) ("*Nature of State Parties' Obligations, Gen. Comment 3*").

[107] *Compare* ICESCR, *supra* note 91, art. 2(1), 993 U.N.T.S. at 5 *with* ICCPR, *supra* note 8, art. 2(1), 999 U.N.T.S. at 173.

[108] ICESCR, *supra* note 91, art. 2(1), 993 U.N.T.S. at 5.

[109] *Id*. art. 2(2), 993 U.N.T.S. at 5.

[110] *Nature of State Parties' Obligations, Gen. Comment 3*, *supra* note 98.

[111] *Id.*

Further, the ESC recognizes that legislation is necessary to combat discrimination effectively.[112] Concerning the progressive nature of the implementation requirements, the Committee states that "while the full realization of the relevant rights may be achieved progressively, steps toward that goal must be taken within a reasonably short time after the ICESCR's entry into force for the states concerned."[113] In addition, while the rights enumerated in the ICESCR in many cases cannot be ensured without significant technical, economic, or educational resources, it is incumbent upon state parties to maximize their available resources.[114] In other words, a state party is obligated to meet at least a minimum essential level of each right, and if it ascribes its failure to do so to a lack of resources, "it must demonstrate that every effort has been made to use all resources that are at its disposition in an effort to satisfy, as a matter of priority, those minimum obligations."[115]

As with the HRC, NGOs can similarly submit written comments to the ESC.[116] Such comments either can focus on particular environmental degradation adversely impacting economic, social and cultural rights, or can critique a state report submitted to the ESC that materially omits or misrepresents an environmental human rights issue.[117]

3. Committee for the Elimination of Racial Discrimination[118]

The Committee for the Elimination of Racial Discrimination ("CERD") was created pursuant to the International Convention on the Elimination of All Forms of Racial Discrimination ("CERD Convention").[119] The CERD Convention prohibits racial discrimination, which it defines as

---

[112] *Id.* at 3.

[113] *Id.* at 2.

[114] ICESCR, *supra* note 91, at art. 2(1), 993 U.N.T.S. at 5.

[115] *Nature of State Parties Obligations, Gen. Comment 3, supra* note 98.

[116] *See NGO Participation in Activities of the Committee on Economic, Social and Cultural Rights*, U.N. ESCOR, 8th Sess., ¶ 354, U.N. Doc. E/1994/23 (1993), *reprinted in* FACT SHEET NO. 16, *supra* note 92 (accepting written comments or allowing your client to make oral comments to the Committee itself on the first day it meets or to its Working Group in advance of the Committee meeting). *See also Rules of Procedure of the Committee on Economic, Social, and Cultural Rights*, U.N. ESC, 3d Sess., at rule 69, U.N. Doc. E/C.12/1990/4/Rev.1 (1989).

[117] *See Concluding Observations of the Committee on Economic, Social and Cultural Rights: Honduras*, U.N. ESCOR, 25th mtg., UN Doc. E/C.12/1/Add.57 (2001), *available at* http:// www.unhchr.ch/tbs/doc.nsf/(Symbol)/E.C.12.1.Add.57.En?Opendocument. *See, e.g.*, Ctr. for Econ. & Soc. Rts., *The Price of Gold: Gold Mining & Human Rights Violations in Honduras*, Report to the U.N. ESC (2001), *available at* http://www.cesr.org/PROGRAMS/honduras/ Honduras%20Report%20Revised.pdf. The ESC considered this report for its May 2001 concluding observations for Honduras.

[118] The official website for the Committee for the Elimination of Racial Discrimination may be found at http://www.unhchr.ch/html/menu2/6/cerd.htm.

[119] International Convention on the Elimination of All Forms of Racial Discrimination, Mar. 7, 1966, 660 U.N.T.S. 195, 216 ("ICERD").

any distinction, exclusion, restriction or preference based on race, colour, descent, national or ethnic origin which has the purpose or effect of nullifying or impairing the recognition, enjoyment or exercise, on an equal footing, of human rights and fundamental freedoms in the political, economic, social, cultural or any other field of public life.[120]

The basic human rights and fundamental freedoms it protects include the rights enumerated in the Universal Declaration of Human Rights, the ICCPR, and the ICESCR.[121] Not only is it incumbent upon state parties to eliminate governmental discrimination, they must also "prohibit and bring to an end, by all appropriate means, including legislation as required by circumstances, racial discrimination by any persons, group or organization."[122]

The CERD Convention does allow that "special measures" may be required for the protection or adequate advancement of the enjoyment of fundamental rights and freedoms for certain racial or ethnic groups, and that such action "shall not be deemed racial discrimination" as long as such measures do not "lead to the maintenance of separate rights for different racial groups and that they shall not be continued after the objectives for which they were undertaken have been achieved."[123] States are also obligated to prevent, prohibit and eradicate the practice of apartheid in their territories.[124]

As an enforcement mechanism, the CERD Covention establishes the CERD[125] not only to review the periodic reports that the states parties are obligated to submit,[126] but also to handle the inter-state and individual complaints systems.[127] Submission to the inter-state complaint system is not optional for the state parties under the CERD Convention as it is under the ICCPR.[128]

The inter-state complaint system as laid out by Article 11 of the CERD Convention is a two-stage process.[129] The CERD first rules on the admissibility of the complaint.[130] All state parties concerned are obligated to supply any

---

[120] *Id.* art. 1(1), 660 U.N.T.S. at 216.
[121] *Compare* ICERD, *supra* note 111, art 5, 660 U.N.T.S. at 220-21 *with* UDHR, *supra* note 20, at 135 *and* ICCPR, *supra* note 8, pt. III, 999 U.N.T.S. at 174-79, *and* ICESCR, *supra* note 91, pt. III, 993 U.N.T.S. at 6-9.
[122] ICERD, *supra* note 111, art. 2(1)(d), 660 U.N.T.S. at 218.
[123] *Id.* art 1(4), 660 U.N.T.S. at 216.
[124] *Id.* art 3, 660 U.N.T.S. at 218.
[125] *Id.* art. 8(1), 660 U.N.T.S. at 224.
[126] *Id.* art. 9(1), 660 U.N.T.S. at 224.
[127] *Id.* art. 11(1), 660 U.N.T.S. at 226.
[128] *Compare* ICERD, *supra* note 111, art. 11(1), 660 U.N.T.S. at 226 *with* ICCPR, *supra* note 7, art. 41(1), 999 U.N.T.S. at 182-83.
[129] ICERD, *supra* note 111, art. 11, 660 U.N.T.S. at 226.
[130] *Id.* art. 11 (1-3), 660 U.N.T.S. at 226.

information that CERD deems relevant.[131] After the fact-finding process is complete, CERD establishes an *ad hoc* Conciliation Commission,[132] which will complete a report on the dispute[133] and issue recommendations to the state parties concerned.[134] No inter-state complaint has ever been filed.[135]

The individual complaint system, on the other hand, is optional and therefore requires that the state parties separately declare that they recognize the jurisdiction of CERD to hear the complaint.[136] CERD does not use an *ad hoc* Commission to deal with individual complaints.[137] CERD reviews information from the state concerned and the petitioner,[138] summarizes its findings and makes recommendations.[139] These recommendations are published in its annual report to the General Assembly.[140] The International Court of Justice ("ICJ") may also address disputes regarding interpretation and application if the respondent state has agreed to its jurisdiction.[141] In addition, non-parties with a legitimate interest in the outcome of a petition may be able to file an *amicus* brief. Nothing in the CERD appears to prevent that possibility.

4. Committee for the Elimination of Discrimination Against Women

The first international document to recognize equal rights without regard to sex was the UN Charter.[142] The Convention on the Elimination of All Forms of Discrimination against Women ("CEDAW Convention"), which was adopted by the General Assembly on December 18, 1979, and entered into force on September 3, 1981,[143] focuses on the status of women and provides an extensive bill of rights for women including the right to equal education, health care, and equality before the law.[144] State parties to the CEDAW Convention have an obligation to condemn discrimination against women and to implement measures to advance the enjoyment of equal rights by women from all walks of life.[145]

---

[131] *Id.* art. 11(4), 660 U.N.T.S. at 226, art. 12(8), 660 U.N.T.S. at 228.
[132] *Id.* art. 12(1)(a), 660 U.N.T.S. at 228.
[133] *Id.* art. 13(1), 660 U.N.T.S. at 230.
[134] *Id.*
[135] *See* Alston & Steiner, *supra* note 87, at 776.
[136] ICERD, *supra* note 111, art. 14(1), 660 U.N.T.S. at 230.
[137] *Id.* art. 14(2), 660 U.N.T.S. at 230.
[138] *Id.* art. 14(7)(a), 660 U.N.T.S. at 232.
[139] *Id.* art. 14(7)(b), 660 U.N.T.S. at 232.
[140] *Id.* art. 14 (8), 660 U.N.T.S. at 232.
[141] *Id.* art. 16, 660 U.N.T.S. at 234.
[142] U.N. CHARTER, art. 7.
[143] Covenant on the Elimination of All Forms of Discrimination against Women, Dec. 18, 1979, 1249 U.N.T.S. 13, 14 n.1 ("CEDAW").
[144] *Id.* art. 1-16, 1249 U.N.T.S. at 16-20.
[145] *Id.* art. 2, 1249 U.N.T.S. at 16.

"Discrimination against women" is defined as:

> any distinction, exclusion or restriction made on the basis of sex which has the effect or purpose of impairing or nullifying the recognition, enjoyment or exercise by women, irrespective of their marital status, on a basis of equality of men and women, of human rights and fundamental freedoms in the political, economic, social, cultural, civil or any other field.[146]

Under Article 3 of the CEDAW Convention:

> [S]tate parties shall take in all fields, in particular in the political, social, economic and cultural fields, all appropriate measures, including legislation, to ensure the full development and advancement of women, for the purpose of guaranteeing them the exercise and enjoyment of human rights and fundamental freedoms on a basis of equality with men.[147]

Special measures designed to achieve equality between men and women shall not be considered discrimination, but shall be discontinued when the objective of equality has been achieved.[148] The CEDAW Convention also requires that state parties must take all "appropriate measures"

> (a) To modify the social and cultural patterns of conduct of men and women, with a view to achieving the elimination of prejudices and customs and all other practices which are based on the idea of the inferiority or the superiority of either of the sexes or on stereotyped roles for men and women.
>
> (b) To ensure that family education includes a proper understanding of maternity as a social function and the recognition of the common responsibility of men and women in the upbringing and development of their children.[149]

In ratifying the CEDAW Convention, many states made reservations in order to preserve national or religious institutions that are in conflict with the CEDAW Convention.[150] These reservations have undermined the

---

[146] *Id.* art. 1, 1249 U.N.T.S. at 16.
[147] *Id.* art. 3, 1249 U.N.T.S. at 16.
[148] *Id.* art. 4, 1249 U.N.T.S. at 16.
[149] *Id.* art. 5, 1249 U.N.T.S. at 17.
[150] *Id.*, Reservations and Declarations Made Upon Signature, 1249 U.N.T.S. at 121–42, *available at* http://untreaty.un.org/ENGLISH/bible/englishinternetbible/partI/chapterIV/treaty10.asp ("CEDAW Reservations") (listing further reservations occuring after printing of

30 • *Defending the Environment*

effectiveness of the CEDAW Convention, despite the provision in Article 28 that declares, "[a] reservation incompatible with the object and purpose of the present Convention shall not be permitted."[151] The 1993 Vienna World Conference on Human Rights called on the CEDAW to review the current reservations to the CEDAW Convention, and called on states to withdraw their reservations that were incompatible with the object and purpose of the CEDAW Convention,[152] giving a boost to efforts to get states to withdraw their reservations.

Under the CEDAW Convention, implementation is reviewed through submission of periodic reports by state parties to the CEDAW.[153] CEDAW consists of 23 members elected by the state parties to serve in their personal capacities.[154] CEDAW reviews the reports from the states and then reports on its findings to the state parties, the UN Commission on the Status of Women, and the UN General Assembly.[155] Under the CEDAW Convention, CEDAW "shall normally meet for a period of not more than two weeks annually in order to consider the reports submitted."[156] In 1996 the General Assembly authorized two annual sessions of three weeks each.[157] Because of significant time constraints, CEDAW does not have the power of many of the other UN treaty organs. The CEDAW Convention itself sets up neither an inter-state nor individual complaint system, which prevents the CEDAW from strengthening its authority.

Moreover, CEDAW allows for NGO input in several ways. First, Rule 47 of the Rules of Procedure allows NGO written submissions by invitation only.[158] Second, Rule 68(1) of the Rules of Procedure allows submissions "by others on behalf of an alleged victim where the alleged victim consents."[159] Third, Rule 83(3) of the Rules of Procedure allows the Committee to request additional information from, among others,

---

U.N.T.S. version). These Reservations generally involve three issues: those provisions in conflict with the laws of *Shariah Islam*; those provisions incompatible with national laws regarding succession to the throne; and those provisions of national law involving children taking the nationality of their mothers. *Id.*

[151] *Id.* art. 28(2), 1249 U.N.T.S. at 23.

[152] World Conf. on Hum. Rts., Vienna Declaration and Programme of Action, U.N. GAOR, art. II, ¶ 39, U.N. Doc. A/CONF.157/23 (1993).

[153] CEDAW, *supra* note 135, art. 17-18, 1249 U.N.T.S. at 21-22.

[154] *Id.* art. 17(1), 1249 U.N.T.S. at 21.

[155] *Id.* art. 21(1)-(2), 1249 U.N.T.S. at 22.

[156] *Id.* art. 20(1), 1249 U.N.T.S. at 22.

[157] Convention on the Elimination of All Forms of Discrimination against Women, G.A. Res. 51/68, U.N. GAOR, 51st Sess., Supp No. 49, at 198, U.N. Doc. A/Res/51/68 (1996).

[158] *Rules of Procedure of the Committee on the Elimination of Discrimination Against Women*, annex I, U.N. Doc. A/56/38(Supp), *reprinted in Compilation of Rules of Procedure Adopted by Human Rights Treaty Bodies*, U.N. Human Rights Instruments, addendum, ch. IV, U.N. Doc. HRI/GEN/3/Add.1 (2002), *available at* http://www.unhchr.ch/tbs/doc.nsf/ 898586b1dc764043c1256a450044f331/9430376abc72c30ec1256bcd00395ed9/$FILE/G0241183.pdf.

[159] *Id.* at Rule 68(1).

NGOs.[160] Through these three avenues, NGOs may be able to submit an *amicus* brief, among other courses of action.

Article 29(1) of the CEDAW Convention gives jurisdiction to the ICJ for disputes between the state parties regarding the interpretation or application of the CEDAW Convention.[161] However, Article 29(2) allows states to opt out of Article 29(1) and decline to accept the ICJ's jurisdiction.[162] Many of the state parties that have made reservations incompatible with the goals of the CEDAW Convention have opted out of the ICJ's jurisdiction, making it difficult for other states to challenge the reservations.[163]

On December 22, 2000, an Optional Protocol authorized the Committee to allow individuals or groups of individuals to submit complaints against a state party to the Protocol.[164] The confidential process gives a responding state six months to provide a written response to the views of the Committee.[165] In addition, under Article 8, a confidential inquiry can be conducted by one of the Committee members when it receives reliable information of "grave or systematic violations."[166]

5. Committee on the Rights of the Child[167]

The Convention on the Rights of the Child ("CRC Convention"), the most widely adopted human rights treaty, entered into force on September 2, 1990.[168] For the purposes of the CRC Convention, a child is understood to be "every human being below the age of eighteen years unless under the law applicable to the child, majority is attained earlier."[169] The CRC Convention was the first time many of the international civil, political, economic and social rights laid out in other human rights treaties were extended to children.[170]

---

160 *Id.* at Rule 83(3).
161 CEDAW, *supra* note 135, art. 29(1)-(2), 1249 U.N.T.S. at 23.
162 *Id.*
163 *See generally* CEDAW Reservations, *supra* note 142 (33 out of 97 signatory states to CEDAW opted out of Article 29(1)).
164 CEDAW, *supra* note 135, Optional Protocol, G.A. Res. 4, U.N. GAOR, 54th Sess., Agenda Item 109, Annex, art. 2, at 3, U.N. Doc. A/RES/54/4 (1999), *available at* http://www.un.org/womenwatch/daw/cedaw/protocol.op.pdf.
165 *Id.* art. 6, ¶¶ 1-2.
166 *Id.* art. 8, ¶ 1.
167 The official website for the Committee on the Rights of the Child may be found at http://www.unhchr.ch/html/menu2/6/crc/.
168 *See* Convention on the Rights of the Child, Nov. 20, 1989, 1577 U.N.T.S. 3 ("CRC").
169 *Id.* art. 1, 1577 U.N.T.S. at 46.
170 Nigel Cantwell, *The Origins, Development and Significance of the United Nations Convention on the Rights of the Child, in* THE UNITED NATIONS CONVENTION ON THE RIGHTS OF THE CHILD: A GUIDE TO THE 'TRAVAUX PREPARATOIRES' 19 (S. Detrick ed., 1992) *reprinted in* INTERNATIONAL HUMAN RIGHTS IN CONTEXT: LAW, POLITICS, MORALS 512, 516 (Philip Alston & Henry J. Steiner eds., 2d ed. 2000).

The Convention also establishes the Committee on the Rights of the Child ("CRC"), whose task it is to review the reports on implementation which state parties are obliged to submit.[171] The CRC does not, however, have any power to receive inter-state or individual complaints.[172] However, Article 45 of the Convention and Rule 70(2) of the Rules of Procedure allows the Committee to request expert advice from any body it deems competent.[173]

6. Commission on Human Rights and UN Special Rapporteurs[174]

The Commission on Human Rights ("CHR"), created by ECOSOC in 1946 pursuant to its mandate to create "commissions in economic and social fields . . . for the promotion of human rights,"[175] allows NGOs the opportunity to make written and oral statements on environmental human rights issues arguably within the scope of any item appearing on the agenda for the CHR's annual meeting.[176] Expanded from its initial 18 members to its current 53 member states, the CHR meets annually every spring to implement existing human rights treaties.[177] In the January prior to the CHR's session, NGOs can submit written comments on any matter within the scope of the CHR's broad agenda;[178] in addition, at the session, the practice of the CHR is to invite these NGOs at the start of each new agenda item to make short oral statements in support of those submitted comments.[179] NGO participation helps to focus part of the CHR sessions on otherwise unaddressed, current environmental human rights abuses.

---

[171] CRC, *supra* note 160, art. 38, 1577 U.N.T.S. at 56.

[172] *Id.* arts. 44–45, 1577 U.N.T.S. at 59–60.

[173] *Id.* art. 45, 1577 U.N.T.S. at 59–60; Provisional Rules of Procedure, U.N. Comm. on the Rts. of the Child (CRC/C/R), at Rule 70(2), U.N. Doc. CRC/C/4 (1991), *available at* http://193.194.138.190/tbs/doc.nsf/(Symbol)/CRC.C.4.En?OpenDocument.

[174] The official website for the Commission on Human Rights may be found at http://www.unhchr.ch/html/menu2/2/chr.htm. The Committee also publishes General Comments of the Convention, General Recommendations on thematic issues and its methods of work, and holds public discussions on particular issues. *Id.*

[175] U.N. CHARTER, art. 68.

[176] *See* Earthjustice Legal Defense Fund, *Issue Paper: Human Rights and the Environment*, submitted to the 57th Session of the U.N. Comm. on Hum. Rts. (CHR) (2001), *available at* http://www.earthjustice.org/regional/international/2001_human_rights_issue_paper.pdf; Earthjustice Legal Defense Fund, *Spraying Toxic Herbicides on Rural Colombian and Ecuadorian Communities*, U.N. Doc. E/CN.4/2002/NGO/36 (2002), *available at* http://www.unhchr.ch/Huridocda/Huridoca.nsf/TestFrame/dac6aff3c94f3067c1256b5d005bcd57?Opendocument. *See also* Alston & Steiner, *supra* note 87, at 620.

[177] *See* Introduction to the Human Rights Committee *available at* http://193.194.138.190/html/menu2/6/a/introhrc.htm.

[178] *See generally* E.S.C. Res. 1996/31, U.N. ESCOR, 49th plen. mtg. (1996), *available at* http://www.un.org/documents/ecosoc/res/1996/eres1996-31.htm.

[179] *Id.*

Exercising Environmental Human Rights and Remedies • 33

In 2003, as a consequence of the 2002 World Summit on Sustainable Development, the Commission on Human Rights began asking that the UN High Commissioner for Human Rights and the UN Environmental Program build capacity on the link between human rights and the environment in the context of sustainable development, and that the UN Secretary-General issue an annual report on the subject.[180] Those reports have included information and comments from nongovernmental organizations submitted to the international organizations working on them.[181]

In designating member states, the ECOSOC utilizes a formula to ensure equitable distribution of representation across the different regions of the world.[182] These representatives do not serve in their individual capacity, but rather as instructed government delegates.[183]

The CHR was created to draft treaties implementing Articles 55 and 56 of the UN Charter.[184] While early in its existence it was actually barred from taking actions on specific charges, the CHR did act in a promotional capacity and was responsible for drafting the Universal Declaration of Human Rights, the ICCPR, and the ICESCR.[185] Beginning in the late 1960s, however, human rights concerns began to play a larger role in the formation of the UN's political agenda.[186] Then, the 1980s and 1990s saw both an increased willingness on the part of the member states to accept UN intervention in these issues and an explosion in the number of human

---

[180] *See* Resolution 2003/71 (2003), *available at* http://www.unhchr.ch/Huridocda/Huridoca.nsf/(Symbol)/E.CN.4.RES.2003.71.En?Opendocument, at ¶¶ 10–11 (requesting that the United Nations High Commissioner for Human Rights and the United Nations Environment Program coordinate their efforts in capacity-building activities for the judiciary and that the UN Secretary-General prepare a report on the consideration being given to the possible relationship between the environment and human rights, taking into account the contributions that concerned international organizations and bodies have made.); Decision 2004/119, U.N. CHR, 60th Session, at 1, U.N. Doc. E/CN.4/2004/L.104 (2004), *available at* http://ap.ohchr.org/documents/E/CHR/decisions/E-CN_4-DEC-2004-119.doc (calling on the UN Secretary-General to update the report on the consideration being given to the relationship between the environment and human rights as part of sustainable development).

[181] *See* Report of the Secretary-General, Human rights and the environment as part of sustainable development, UN Doc. E/CN.4/2005/96 (Jan. 19, 2005), *available at* http://www.ohchr.org/english/bodies/chr/docs/61chr/E.CN.4.2005.96.doc; Report of the Secretary-General, Human rights and the environment as part of sustainable development, UN Doc. E/CN.4/2004/87 (Feb. 6, 2004), *available at* http://www.unhchr.ch/Huridocda/Huridoca.nsf/(Symbol)/E.CN.4.2004.87.En?Opendocument.

[182] Economic and Social Council website, *available at* http://www.un.org/esa/coordination/ecosoc/sub_bodies.htm.

[183] *See* CHR, Membership, *available at* http://www.unhchr.ch/html/menu2/2/chrmem.htm (Listing members by nation only, not by individual representative).

[184] U.N. CHARTER, arts. 55, 56.

[185] *See* Earth Summit 2002, *Toolkit for Women, Commission on Human Rights*, *available at* http://www.earthsummit2002.org/toolkits/women/un-doku/un-comm/chr/commissi5.htm.

[186] *See id.*

rights issues brought before the UN.[187] As a result, today the CHR's jurisdiction has expanded to such a degree in the areas of promotion and protection of human rights that few subjects relating to human rights are not brought before it. Together with the UN Human Rights Center, the Commission coordinates the many UN human rights institutions and is the principal political body addressing charges of human rights violations.

A key mechanism for accomplishing this goal has been the appointment of and reports from experts known as Special Rapporteurs. These individuals provide an informal outlet for NGOs to present written and oral submission on human rights concerns including environmental issues. Tables B and C in Part VIII of this Chapter provide further details on appropriate Special Rapporteurs for environmental human rights. Moreover, Table A cites several reports from Special Rapporteurs related to environmental human rights issues.

The political nature of the representation on the Commission unfortunately does tend to politicize the treatment of alleged human rights violations. Still, even in the face of the limitations posed by the political maneuverings of the representatives, the Commission has succeeded in bringing human rights issues to the fore as a major component of the UN agenda.

7. *Subcommission on Promotion and Protection of Human Rights*[188]

This Subcommission, formerly the Subcommission on the Prevention of Discrimination and Protection of Minorities, was established in 1947 as a subsidiary organ of the CHR.[189] It consists of 26 members elected by the CHR from nominees selected by the member states.[190] In contrast to the CHR, the members of the Subcommission serve in their individual capacities.[191] No doubt this has in some part contributed to the common conception that of all the human rights institutions, it is the most sympathetic to the human rights cause.

The Subcommission is charged with undertaking studies and making recommendations to the CHR concerning "the prevention of discrimination of any kind relating to human rights and fundamental freedoms and the protection of racial, national, religious, and linguistic minorities."[192] This mandate has been interpreted broadly, allowing the Subcommission to deal

---

[187] *Id.*

[188] The official website of the Subcommission on Promotion and Protection of Human Rights may be found at http://www.unhchr.ch/html/menu2/2/sc.htm.

[189] *See id.*

[190] *Id.*

[191] *Id.*

[192] *Id.*

with the whole spectrum of human rights issues that are presented to the UN.[193] Not only has the Subcommission undertaken a wide variety of studies and reports and participated in the drafting of human rights instruments, but also it recently has been heavily involved in examination of human rights violations.[194] In fact, it has been instrumental in pressing the UN to strengthen the complaint procedures. The Subcommission has also played an influential role in getting issues relating to minorities, indigenous peoples, slavery and disappearances on the UN agenda.[195] Recently, out of concern for the effect of rising sea levels and other harm from global warming, the Commission on Human Rights has urgently called upon the Subcommission on the Promotion and Protection of Human Rights to prepare a report on the legal implications of the disappearance of States for environmental reasons and to focus on human rights implication for affected residents, particularly indigenous peoples.[196] The Subcommission has acted similarly.[197]

NGOs have contributed to the environmental human rights work of the Subcommission by participating in working groups such as one focused on transnational corporations[198] and by submitting written comments on agenda items.[199] As with the CHR, such participation helps the Subcommission focus on current, otherwise unaddressed, environmental human rights concerns.

---

[193] See *Subcommission on Prevention of Discrimination and Protection of Minorities Meets in Geneva from 1 to 26 August*, U.N. Info. Serv., U.N. Doc. HR/CN/57 (July 29, 1994), available at http://nativenet.uthscsa.edu/archive/nl/9408/0017.html.

[194] See id.

[195] Id.

[196] See Decision 2004/122, U.N. CHR, 60th Session, at 1, U.N. Doc. E/CN.4/2004/L.49 (2004), available at http://ap.ohchr.org/documents/E/CHR/decisions/E-CN_4-DEC-2004-122.doc.

[197] See Report of the Sub-Commission on the Promotion and Protection of Human Rights on its 55th Session, U.N. Sub-Commission on the Promotion and Protection of Human Rights, 55th Sess., at 17, U.N. Doc. E/CN.4/2004/2, E/CN.4/Sub.2/2003/43 (2003), at 13, available at http://www.unhchr.ch/Huridocda/Huridoca.nsf/(Symbol)/E.CN.4.2004.2, E.CN.4.Sub.2.2003.43.En?Opendocument.

[198] *Report of the Sessional Working Group on the Working Methods and Activities of Transnational Corporations on its Fourth Session*, U.N. ESCOR, 54th Sess. Agenda Item 4, U.N. Doc. E/CN.4/Sub.2/2002/13 (2002), available at http://www.unhchr.ch/Huridocda/Huridoca.nsf/TestFrame/971d73502dd31b7bc1256c1e00533042?Opendocument; see also Press Release, Sub-Commission on the Promotion and Protection of Human Rights, Sub-Commission Begins Review of Agenda Item on Prevention on Discrimination; Expert Presents Report on Affirmative Action (Aug. 8, 2002), available at http://www.unhchr.ch/huricane/huricane.nsf/view01/7F2A67CF9BE4B670C1256C0F0055982D?opendocument.

[199] E.S.C. Res. 31, U.N. ESCOR, 49th plen. mtg. (1996), available at http://www.un.org/documents/ecosoc/res/1996/eres1996-31.htm.

8. Commission on the Status of Women

The Commission on the Status of Women was established in 1946 to study, report on, and make recommendations concerning human rights and related issues as they affect women.[200] Its 45 members are elected as state representatives under a system of regional representation similar to that of the CHR.[201] In the first few decades of its existence the Commission was dedicated to initiating programs to eliminate discrimination against women and was involved in the drafting of the principal treaties dealing with women's rights.[202] The political influence of the Commission has grown in recent years as the UN world conferences on women's rights have gained a higher profile.[203]

The Commission has not been able to do much in the way of acting on specific violations of women's rights. Although in the early 1980s the ECOSOC empowered the Commission to review complaints, the Commission still mostly engages in promotional activities.[204] Currently, their limited capacity to review communications serves more as a source of information for their studies than as an instrument of force, and there is an ongoing effort to expand the Commission's enforcement authority. One current avenue for NGOs is the ability to submit a complaint or petition to the UN Division for the Advancement of Women for advisory purposes.[205]

9. The 1235 and 1503 Procedures for Dealing with Gross Human Rights Violations

This discussion of the 1235 and 1503 procedures is included primarily for the sake of completeness. Resistance in international human rights law to the recognition of environmental human rights claims as gross violations of human rights at this time makes challenging the use of these procedures to remedy such harms.

From the very beginning, the UN has been inundated with petitions concerning human rights violations from individuals and NGOs. In 1947,

---

[200] E.S.C. Res. 11, U.N. ESCOR, 2d Sess. (1946), *expanded by* E.S.C. Res. 22, U.N. ESCOR (1987). *See also* U.N. Office of the High Comm'r for Hum. Rts., Comm. on the Status of Women, *available at* http://193.194.138.190/html/menu2/2/cswomen.htm; U.N. Comm. on the Status of Women, *available at* http://www.un.org/womenwatch/daw/csw ("CSW").

[201] CSW, *supra* note 188.

[202] *Id.*

[203] *Id.*

[204] *Id.*; *see also* Gender Mainstreaming, Extract from Report of the Economic and Social Council for 1997, at 1, U.N. Doc. A/52/3, *available at* http://www.un.org/womenwatch/daw/csw/GMS.PDF (stating the goal of "mainstreaming the gender perspective into all policies and programmes of the United Nations system").

[205] *See generally* CSW, *supra* note 188.

however, the CHR declared itself to have no authority to take action with regard to any of these communications.[206] The ECOSOC confirmed that opinion with Resolution 75(V) later that year.[207] The Resolution also established a system of classification for petitions and restricted access to information on the petitions to such a degree that the CHR was unable to access information contained in them, even to take action on specific cases.[208] Despite efforts to reverse this decision and empower the CHR to act on communications, in July 1959, ECOSOC Resolution 728(F) again reaffirmed the CHR's opinion that it had no power to act on human rights complaints.[209] In general, the Commission still has no power to act on human rights abuses, but two ECOSOC resolutions have created notable exceptions to this general rule.

Resolution 1235 allows the CHR and the Subcommission on Promotion and Protection of Human Rights to examine "gross violations of human rights and fundamental freedoms."[210] If, upon examination, the CHR discovers a consistent pattern of discrimination and violations of human rights, the CHR is authorized to conduct a thorough study and make a report to the ECOSOC.[211] While the language of Resolution 1235 makes specific reference to policies of "apartheid as practiced in the Republic of South Africa and in the Territory of South West Africa" and to "racial discrimination as practiced notably in Southern Rhodesia," it is generally understood that 1235 procedures apply to any large-scale violation of human rights.[212] The CHR's power to establish working groups and the rapporteur system for reporting on violations is derived from its 1235 powers.[213] In addition, UN members may also place items falling under 1235 directly on the CHR's agenda without first having them reviewed by the Subcommission.[214]

The 1503 procedure was revised in 2000 under ECOSOC Resolution 2000/3 to improve upon its effectiveness.[215] Resolution 1503 authorizes

---

[206] *Report to the Economic and Social Council on the First Session of the Commission*, U.N. CHR, U.N. ESCOR, 4th Sess., Supp. No. 1, at 6, U.N. Doc. E/259 (1947).

[207] E.S.C. Res. 75(V), U.N. ESCOR, *reprinted in* 1947–48 U.N.Y.B. 579.

[208] *Id.*

[209] *Report of the Commission on Human Rights*, U.N. ESCOR, 28th Sess., Annex, Agenda Item 10, at 2, U.N. Doc. E/3285 (1959).

[210] *Question of the Violation of Human Rights and Fundamental Freedoms, Including Policies of Racial Discrimination and Segregation and of Apartheid, in All Countries, with Particular Reference to Colonial and Other Dependent Countries and Territories*, U.N. ESCOR, 42d Sess., Supp. No. 1, at 17, U.N. Doc. E/4393 (1967). See E.S.C. Res. 1235, *supra* note 44.

[211] *Id.* at 18.

[212] *Id.* at 17.

[213] *Id.*

[214] *Id.*

[215] *See generally* Procedure for Dealing with Communications Concerning Human Rights, E.S.C. Res. 3, U.N. ESCOR, Supp. No. 1, at 24, U.N. Doc. E/RES/2000/3 (2000), *available*

the Subcommission to designate a working group, known as the Working Group on Communications, to examine communications received by the UN and to bring to the attention of the Working Group on Situations any communication that might "reveal a consistent pattern of gross and reliably attested violations of human rights and fundamental freedoms."[216] Under Resolution 1503 all proceedings must still be kept confidential.[217] The Subcommission adheres so closely to this confidentiality directive that petitioners are not even kept abreast of the status of their complaint beyond acknowledgment of its receipt.[218]

After the Working Group on Situations reviews a petition it may refer the petition back to the Subcommission with comments. The Subcommission in turn reviews the communications and relevant government responses and comments and decides whether to refer the petitions to the CHR for further investigation.[219] The CHR's own working group will screen the petitions before the petitions will be accepted by the Commission.[220] If a petition is referred to the CHR, the CHR will then decide whether to undertake a thorough study of the situation[221] or to establish an *ad hoc* committee to investigate the complaint.[222] Investigative action by an *ad hoc* committee can only be undertaken with the consent of the states involved.[223] Proceedings in the CHR ad hoc committee will take place in closed sessions[224] but the Commission will reveal the identities of the countries whose conduct is being treated under the 1503 procedures.[225] The CHR will make a finding and decide whether to refer the situation to the ECOSOC,[226] who may along with the General Assembly adopt resolutions calling for remedies to the violations.[227] Obviously, at this point the

---

at http://www.unhchr.ch/huridoca.nsf/(Symbol)/E.RES.2000.3.En?OpenDocument; Office of the High Commissioner for Human Rights, *The Revised 1503 Procedure*, available at http://www.unhchr.ch/html/menu2/8/1503.htm. For text of Resolution 1503, *see* E.S.C. Res. 1503, U.N. ESCOR, 49th Sess., Supp. No.1A, at 8, U.N. Doc. E/4832/Add.1 (1970), *available at* http://www.oup.co.uk/pdf/bt/cassese/cases/part3/ch16/1603.pdf.

[216] *Procedure for Dealing With Communications Relating to Violations of Human Rights and Fundamental Freedoms*, U.N. ESCOR, 49th Sess., Supp. No. 1A, at 8, U.N. Doc. E/4832/Add.1 (1970) ("*Procedure for Communications*").

[217] *Id.*

[218] UNITED NATIONS, FACT SHEET NO. 7 (REV. 1), COMPLAINT PROCEDURES, pt. II, *available at* http://www.unhchr.ch/html/menu6/2/fs7.htm.

[219] *Procedure for Communications, supra* note 204.

[220] *Id.*

[221] E.S.C. Res. 1503, *supra* note 203, ¶ 6(a).

[222] *Id.* ¶ 6(b).

[223] *Id.* ¶ 7.

[224] *Id.* ¶ 7(c).

[225] E.S.C. Res. 3, *supra* note 203, ¶ 7(c).

[226] E.S.C. Res. 1503, *supra* note 203, ¶ 8.

[227] U.N. CHARTER, art. 14.

debate becomes public. The Assembly's power extends beyond condemnation; in some cases it may call for member states to participate in voluntary sanctions.[228]

The Commission may also choose to turn a 1503 proceeding into a 1235 proceeding, effectively circumventing the confidentiality requirements of 1503.[229] In such a case, the CHR can still act on a situation without being bound to confidentiality.[230] The CHR used this arrangement in its 1993 actions against Sudan and Zaire.[231]

It is important to note that under 1235 and 1503 procedures individuals do have standing to file, but that this standing does not, in a strict sense, stem from a violation of any one person's individual rights. Rather, their standing is established by virtue of the violation being part of a "consistent pattern of gross and reliably attested violations of human rights and fundamental freedoms."[232] Further, as long as the petitioner has "direct and reliable knowledge" of violations, the petitioner need not be an actual victim of the violation.[233] It is also incumbent upon the petitioner to demonstrate that all domestic remedies have been exhausted, unless it can be shown that domestic remedies would be inadequate or unreasonably delayed.[234]

These human rights resolutions and the implementing organs that deal with human rights violations are effectively working under the principle that any gross violation of the rights laid out in the Universal Declaration or the Conventions is ultimately a failure to fulfill member state obligations as described in Articles 55 and 56 of the UN Charter.[235] As such, the UN is authorized to intervene in matters that otherwise might be deemed the states' domestic jurisdiction, notwithstanding the prohibition of Article 2(7) on domestic intervention.[236] Although currently the idea of "gross violations" is identified mainly with violations of the most basic civil and political rights laid out in the Universal Declaration, there is nothing to prohibit international opinion from broadening the definition of what

---

[228] *Id.* art. 41.
[229] E.S.C. Res. 3, *supra* note 203, ¶ 7(d)(iv).
[230] *Id.*
[231] *See* Clarence J. Dias, *Part I: Human Rights-Based Approach to Development, in* OCCASIONAL PAPER 21—HUMAN DEVELOPMENT AND SHELTER: A HUMAN RIGHTS PERSPECTIVE (Clarence J. Dias & Scott Leckie eds., 1996) *available at* http://hdr.undp.org/docs/publications/ocational_papers/oc21b.htm.
[232] E.S.C. Res. 1503, *supra* note 203, ¶ 1.
[233] Sub-Comm. on Prevention of Discrimination and Prot. of Minorities Res. 1, U.N. ESCOR, 24th Sess., at 50-51, U.N. Doc. E/CN.4/1070 (1971), *available at* http://www.umn.edu/humanrts/demo/1503Resolution1.html.
[234] *Id.*
[235] U.N. CHARTER arts. 55, 56.
[236] *Id.* art. 2, para. 7.

constitutes a fundamental right and thereby recognizing expanded authority to intervene.

10. UNESCO[237]

UNESCO is a specialized UN agency that has been active in the area of developing human rights law and that may provide an additional dispute resolution process for environmental human rights claims.

The Council of UNESCO is composed of 54 members, who are elected by the General Assembly to serve three-year terms.[238] The Council has one substantive meeting per year, lasting for about five weeks and alternating between New York and Geneva, Switzerland.[239] Commissions and committees who report back to the Council conduct the year-around work of UNESCO.[240] The Council is charged with "mak[ing] or initiat[ing] studies and reports with respect to international economic, social, cultural, educational, health, and related matters and may make recommendations" about these matters to the General Assembly.[241] The Council also may "make recommendations for the purpose of promoting respect for, and observance of, human rights and fundamental freedoms for all."[242] Furthermore, the Council is authorized to establish relations with, and regulate the activities of, specialized agencies and to set up commissions for the promotion of human rights.[243]

UNESCO has set up a confidential procedure for human rights complaints in its fields of education, science, culture, and information, under 104 Ex/Decision 3.3 of the Executive Board.[244] The procedure is implemented by a subcommittee of UNESCO's Executive Board, namely the Committee on Conventions and Recommendations.[245] Individuals, groups of individuals, and NGOs may submit communications to UNESCO if victims of violations or if they have "reliable knowledge" of such violations.[246] Communications are sent to the government concerned and the Committee on Conventions. The Committee examines communications twice yearly in private session.[247] The

---

[237] The official website of UNESCO may be found at http://www.unesco.org/.
[238] U.N. CHARTER art. 61, ¶¶ 1–2.
[239] U.N. ESCOR, *What ECOSOC Does, available at* http://www.un.org/esa/coordination/ecosoc/about.htm.
[240] *Id.*
[241] U.N. CHARTER art. 62, ¶ 1.
[242] *Id.* art. 62, ¶ 2.
[243] *Id.* arts. 63 & 68.
[244] *Decision Adopted by the Executive Board*, U.N. ESCOR, 104th Sess., Agenda Item 3.3, at 12–15, U.N. Doc. EX/Decisions (1977), *available at* http://unesdoc.unesco.org/images/0002/000284/028409E.pdf.
[245] *Id.* at 13.
[246] *Id.*
[247] *Id.* at 14.

petitioning party and government concerned are informed of the Committee's decision on the substance of the communication.[248] Any additional enforcement action is dependent upon the Director-General of UNESCO who, under 19C/Resolution 12.1, may make humanitarian representations on behalf of victims of human rights violations whose cases call for urgent consideration.[249] When denial of environmental protection is tied to rights of education, sharing in scientific advancement, participating freely in cultural life, and the right to information under Articles 26, 27, and 19 of the Universal Declaration of Human Rights, the UNESCO procedure may be available as yet another alternative forum.[250]

11. International Labor Organization[251]

Like UNESCO, the International Labor Organization ("ILO") is another UN specialized agency with a potential dispute resolution process available to handle environmental human rights claims, albeit only for indigenous and tribal peoples at this time. Although the ILO's work predominantly focuses on labor rights, not environmental rights, at least one opportunity exists at the ILO to protect environmental human rights, limited to indigenous and tribal peoples. The ILO Convention 169: Indigenous and Tribal Peoples Convention of 1989[252] ("ILO 169") sets forth several different human rights obligations of ILO members who have ratified it.[253] Among those duties, state parties must:

a. adopt special measures to safeguard the environment of indigenous and tribal peoples;[254]
b. assess environmental impacts to indigenous and tribal peoples from any development activities and consult with such peoples on such assessments;[255]

---

[248] *Id.* at 15.

[249] *The Protection of the Rights of Minorities*, Pamphlet No. 11, U.N. ESCOR, at 9, *available at* http://193.194.138.190/html/racism/minorpam11.doc.

[250] *See* U.N. ESCOR, *Complaints Concerning Violations of Human Rights in UNESCO's Fields of Competence*, *available at* http://www.unesco.org/general/eng/legal/hrights/.

[251] For general information about ILO human rights strategies, *see* Lee Swepston, *Human Rights Complaint Procedures of the International Labour Organization*, *in* HURST HANNUM, GUIDE TO INTERNATIONAL HUMAN RIGHTS PRACTICE 104 (2d ed. 1992).

[252] Indigenous and Tribal Peoples Convention of 1989, *entered into force* Sept. 5, 1991, 72 ILO Official Bull. 59, *available at* http://www.ilo.org/ilolex/english/convdisp1.htm ("ILO 169").

[253] To date, Argentina, Bolivia, Brazil, Colombia, Costa Rica, Denmark, Dominica, Ecuador, Fiji, Guatemala, Honduras, Mexico, Netherlands, Norway, Paraguay, Peru, Venezuela have ratified ILO 169. *See* ILOLEX, *Ratifications, available at* http://ilolex.ilo.ch:1567/cgi-lex/ratifice.pl?C169.

[254] ILO 169, *supra* note 240, art. 4(1).

[255] *Id.* art. 7(3).

c. protect and preserve the environment of indigenous and tribal territories;[256]

d. safeguard the right of indigenous and tribal peoples to participate in the use, management, and conservation of natural resources on or beneath their land[257]; and

e. consult with indigenous and tribal peoples regarding their relocation in light of development activities and safeguard their right to return after the development activity ends.[258]

Whenever a state party to ILO 169 fails to adhere to these standards, then an industrial association of employers or workers on behalf of indigenous and tribal individuals and groups (but not those individuals or groups themselves)[259] can pursue a two-part strategy against the state party. That two-part strategy is set forth in Articles 24 to 34 of the ILO Constitution[260] and summarized below.

Although the number of ILO members bound by ILO 169 is small, the list includes many countries that have permitted and/or will permit within their borders major development projects that advance the interests of multinational corporate and financial institutions at the expense of certain environmental human rights of indigenous and tribal peoples. Consequently, the two-step strategy to enforce ILO 169 obligations is an important accountability mechanism for such development. Moreover, because the strategy has not been used frequently, particularly in the case of ILO 169,[261] the door is wide open to shape this area of international environmental law enforcement.

The first step involves submitting a representation of non-observance of ILO 169.[262] An industrial association of employers or workers on behalf of indigenous and tribal individuals or groups (but not an individual or group itself) can present to the ILO's International Labor Office a representation that a state party "has failed to secure in any respect the effective observance within its jurisdiction of [ILO 169]."[263]

The representations must:

---

[256] *Id.* art. 7(4).

[257] *Id.* art. 15.

[258] *Id.* art. 16.

[259] The ILO determines what constitutes an industrial association, of employers or workers. However, the more recognized the association, or the closer its interests are to the dispute, the more likely the ILO is to give its written submissions more weight. *See* Swepston, *supra* note 239, at 104.

[260] ILO CONSTITUTION, arts. 24–34, *available at* http://www.ilo.org/public/english/about/iloconst.htm.

[261] *See* ILO, *Use of Complaints Procedure, in Practice, available at* http://www.ilo.org/public/english/standards/norm/enforced/complnt/a26_use.htm (last modified Oct. 20, 2000) ("*Complaints Procedure*").

[262] *See* ILO, *Article 24 Representation Procedure, available at* http://www.ilo.org/public/english/standards/norm/enforced/reprsnt/index.htm (last modified Oct. 20, 2000).

[263] *See* ILO CONSTITUTION, *supra* note 248, art. 24.

Exercising Environmental Human Rights and Remedies • 43

a. be in writing;
b. come from an industrial association with proof of status where possible;
c. concern an ILO member state party to ILO 169;
d. include well-documented, well-substantiated, and complete allegations of how the state party has failed to observe ILO 169;
e. be in any language, but preferably English, French, Spanish (ILO official languages) or German, Russian, or Chinese (additional ILO working languages); and
f. be mailed to:
Director-General
International Labour Office
4, route des Morillons
CH-1211 Geneva 22
Switzerland
T: 41.22.799.6026 or 41.22.799.6111
F: 41.22.799.8533 or 41.22.798.8685
E: cabinet@ilo.org or ilo@ilo.org

The International Labor Office provides the representation to the ILO Governing Body.[264] After the ILO Governing Body declares the representation receivable as to form, an *ad hoc* committee appointed by the ILO Governing Body from among its members considers the substance of the representation.[265] The *ad hoc* committee asks the government for comments and may also ask the filing organization for additional information.[266] The *ad hoc* committee then reviews the materials and makes a recommendation to the ILO Governing Body.[267]

Based on the recommendation, the ILO Governing Body decides whether the government's response is satisfactory.[268] If the ILO Governing Body decides in favor of the government, the procedure is closed and the ILO Governing Body may publish the allegations and the government response.[269] If the ILO Governing Body decides against the government, the ILO Governing Body may decide to pursue a complaint against the government and on behalf of the filing organization under Article 26 of the ILO Constitution as discussed below.[270] In addition, the ILO Governing

---

[264] ILO, *Article 24 Representation Procedure, available at* http://www.ilo.org/public/english/standards/norm/enforced/reprsnt/index.htm (last modified Oct. 20, 2000); ILO, *Standing Orders: Representations, Articles 24 and 25 of the Constitution*, art. 2, *available at* http://www.ilo.org/public/english/standards/norm/enforced/reprsnt/art24.htm#comexam (last modified Oct. 20, 2000) ("*Representations*").
[265] *Representations, supra* note 252, art. 3(1).
[266] *Id.* art. 4.
[267] *Id.* art. 6.
[268] *Id.* art. 7.
[269] *Id.* art. 8.
[270] *Id.* art. 10.

44 • Defending the Environment

Body will still publish the allegations and the government response along with its own discussion of the case.[271]

Thus, the representation stage can result in a statement of whether the government is complying with ILO 169. Moreover, the publication of the allegations, government response, and ILO Governing Body discussion, if any, alerts other ILO offices to potential concerns regarding ILO 169 compliance in a given country. Once alerted, those ILO offices are likely to monitor the situation as part of their future agenda.

The second step involves submitting a complaint of non-observance of ILO 169.[272] Although neither an industrial association of employers or workers nor individuals or groups can submit a complaint, the ILO Governing Body can, if it decides that the government's response to a representation is not satisfactory.[273] Moreover, any other ILO government and any delegate attending the International Labor Conference can submit a complaint.[274] Thus, even if one government or delegate decides against submitting a representation or fails to do so adequately, other avenues exist for a filing organization to ask another government or International Labor Conference delegate to submit a complaint.

Similar to representations, complaints must:

a. come from the ILO Governing Body, a government, or Conference delegate;
b. be in writing;
c. demonstrate—with well-documented, well-substantiated and complete allegations—that a present or former member of the ILO is not "securing the effective observance of [ILO 169];"[275]
d. be in any language, but preferably English, French, Spanish (ILO official languages) or German, Russian, or Chinese (additional ILO working languages); and
e. be mailed to:
Director-General
International Labour Office
4, route des Morillons
CH-1211 Geneva 22
Switzerland
T: 41.22.799.6026 or 41.22.799.6111
F: 41.22.799.8533 or 41.22.798.8685
E: cabinet@ilo.org or ilo@ilo.org

---

[271] *Id.* art. 8.
[272] *See* ILO, *Article 26 Complaints Procedure, available at* http://www.ilo.org/public/english/standards/norm/enforced/complnt/index.htm (last modified Oct. 20, 2000).
[273] *Id.*
[274] *Id.*
[275] ILO CONSTITUTION, *supra* note 248, art. 26(1).

Exercising Environmental Human Rights and Remedies • 45

Just as with representations, the International Labor Office forwards materials to the ILO Governing Body which then forwards the complaint to the government for comments. The ILO Governing Body then establishes, at its discretion, a Commission of Inquiry.[276]

The Commission of Inquiry can establish its own rules and procedures but usually follows established practices.[277] Such practice includes requesting written submissions from both parties on the merits of the case.[278] Such submissions are usually shared among the parties and opportunities for responses are usually provided. The Commission of Inquiry also can request information from other governments or NGOs, hold a hearing with parties and witnesses, and conduct on-site visits.[279]

The Commission of Inquiry eventually produces a report in response to the complaint.[280] That report includes recommendations and timetables to assure compliance with the Convention at issue (*i.e.*, ILO 169). The Director-General communicates the report to the ILO Governing Body and the concerned government(s), and then publishes it.[281] Concerned governments have three months in which to decide to appeal the report to the International Court of Justice.[282]

Similar to the outcome from the filing of representation, publication of the Commission of Inquiry recommendation will alert other ILO offices that are likely to make the issue part of their future agenda. Moreover, if a government fails to comply with the Commission on Inquiry's recommendations within the specified time, or any decision from the International Court of Justice requiring compliance, then the ILO Governing Body may recommend certain actions to the entire ILO Conference and/or establish a subsequent Commission of Inquiry to verify compliance.[283]

As for case studies, the two-party strategy discussed in this part does not appear to have been used yet to challenge a lack of compliance with ILO 169. Thus, although one can refer to the list of ILO cases, no specific case studies concern ILO 169.[284]

B. African System

The human right standards for Africa center on the African Charter on Human and People's Rights ("African Charter")[285] and the Protocol to the

---

[276] *Representations, supra* note 252, art. 8.
[277] *See* ILO, *Explanation of Article 26 Complaints Practice, available at* http://www.ilo.org/public/english/standards/norm/enforced/complnt/art26_2.htm#rules (last modified Oct. 20, 2000).
[278] *Id.*
[279] *Id.*
[280] ILO CONSTITUTION, *supra* note 248, art. 28.
[281] *Id.* art. 29(1).
[282] *Id.* art. 29(2).
[283] *Id.* arts. 33–34.
[284] *See Complaints Procedure, supra* note 249.
[285] *See* African Charter, *supra* note 23.

African Charter on Human and Peoples' Rights ("African Protocol"),[286] both created under the auspices of the African Union, formerly known as the Organization of African Unity, the regional governmental organization for Africa.[287] Table A, in Part VIII of this Chapter, refers to the environmental human rights from these instruments, most important of which is the right to environmental protection in Article 24 of the African Charter.[288] Unique to the African system is the protection of the rights of peoples as well as individuals.

The African Charter also establishes the African Commission on Human and Peoples' Rights ("African Commission").[289] Located in Banjul, the Gambia, the African Commission has 11 members, each from different countries. The African Commission handles a myriad of regional human rights tasks including, but not limited to, consideration of communications presented by individuals and NGOs from the region on any human rights issue in the region, including acts or omissions of any member state of the African Union. Articles 55-59 of the African Charter and Rules 102-105 set forth governing principals and procedures, respectively, about the receipt of and response to such communications but not with the same detail found in other regional systems.

The African Protocol establishes the African Court on Human and Peoples' Rights. When it commences operation, the African Court will have 11 judges authorized to hear cases not only between member states of the African Union, but also those presented by the Commission, NGOs with observer status with the Commission, and individuals themselves.[290] However, as with the Commission, detailed procedures are currently lacking. Tables A, B, and C, in Part VIII of this Chapter, refer to the key aspects of the above-mentioned treaties and processes.

In addition to submitting a communication, NGOs may want to consider *amicus curiae* submissions or lobbying a sympathetic nation-state to make use of the inter-state machinery.[291]

As with the UN strategies, readers should be sure to consult appropriate individuals on the List of Practitioner Experts, in the appendix to this book, as you proceed with these strategies.

---

[286] *See* www.africa-union.org.

[287] *Id.*

[288] "All peoples shall have the right to a general satisfactory environment favourable to their development." African Charter, *available at* http://www.achpr.org/africancharter.doc, at art. 24.

[289] *See* African Charter, *available at* http://www.achpr.org/africancharter.doc, at arts. 30-44.

[290] *See* African Charter, *available at* http://www.achpr.org/Protocol_on_the_African_Court.doc, at art. 5.

[291] On *amicus curiae* submissions, *see generally* http://www.achpr.org/html/basicinstruments.html at art. 76 (allowing consultations between the African IACHR and NGOs). On inter-state machinery, *see* http://www.achpr.org/africancharter.doc 47-53.

1.3 Ogoniland

During the 30th Ordinary Session of the African Commission on Human and People's Rights, the Commission reviewed a communication submitted by the Nigerian-based Social and Economic Rights Action Center (SERAC) and the U.S.-based Center for Economic and Social Rights (CESR) that concerned environmental human rights violations in Ogoniland, Nigeria. SERAC and CESR alleged that the Nigerian National Petroleum Company (NNPC), a state-owned oil company in consortium with the Shell Petroleum Development Corporation (SPDC), engaged in oil extraction and pipeline construction in Ogoniland that resulted in environmental degradation and environmentally related health problems.[292] More specifically, the allegations included exploitation of oil reserves; violation of international environmental law regarding concern for health and environment; contamination of water, soil, and air leading to long-term health problems; refusal to allow studies on the health effects of the oil production; and attacks on the Ogoni people followed by little to no investigation by the Government of Nigeria.[293] In an effort to redress the human rights violations by the former military government, in November 2000 the new civilian administration of Nigeria admitted the complaints and began instituting remedial measures including establishment of a Federal Ministry of Environment and enacting a law that would lead to the establishment of the Niger Delta Development Commission (NDDC) with funding to address environmental and social problems of oil production in the Niger region.[294]

The Commission found the Government of Nigeria in violation of fundamental rights set down in the African Charter, including the right to health (Article 16), the right to a satisfactory environment (Article 24), the right to freely dispose of one's wealth and natural resources (Article 21), the right to property (Article 14), and the right to protection of the family unit (Article 18(1)).[295] Although the Commission recognized that the NNPC had the right to produce oil in order to produce income that would help Nigerians, such oil production could not occur at the expense of human rights.[296] The Commission also found that by failing to safeguard the human rights of the Ogoni people, the Government of Nigeria signaled to private companies that they also could disregard human rights.[297] The Commission found that

(continued)

---

[292] *Communication from the Social and Economic Rights Action Center and the Center for Economic and Social Rights, Nigeria.* 30th Ordinary Session (Banjul, The Gambia 2001), 15th Annual Activity Report of the African Commission on Human and People's Rights (2001-2002), at 31. A copy of the submission can be found at http://cesr.org/nigeria.
[293] *Id.* at 31-32.
[294] *Id.* at 34.
[295] *Id.* at 38-41.
[296] *Id.* at 39.
[297] *Id.* at 39.

1.3 Ogoniland *(continued)*

allowing foreign companies to extract natural resources at the expense of abusing the rights of local residents was a painful reminder of Africa's history of colonial exploitation, and Nigeria had a duty to protect its citizens from this kind of exploitation.[298]

To redress the violations, the Commission suggested that the Government of Nigeria take the following five actions: stop all attacks on the Ogoni communities, conduct an investigation into human rights violations in Ogoniland and prosecute those responsible, ensure adequate compensation to victims of human rights violations, ensure assessments of environmental and social risks are prepared prior to any new oil production, and provide health and social risk information to communities likely to be affected by oil production.[299] In addition to these steps, the Commission also expressed interest in monitoring the continuation of Nigeria's work with the Federal Ministry of Environment, the Niger Development Commission, and the Judicial Commission of Inquiry, established to investigate human rights violations.[300] At the time of the Commission, the Judicial Commission of Inquiry had given top priority to petitions submitted by the Ogoni people about the specific human rights violations discussed in the communication.[301] Although the Commission was mainly concerned with protecting the Ogonis from human rights abuses, the Commission recognized the economic hardship on Nigeria if foreign companies were to halt efforts to pay for opportunities to extract oil. The Commission made no clear indication, however, as to how Nigeria was to balance economic development with protection of human rights. Instead, the Commission commended the civilian administration's efforts to redress the wrongs of the previous military government.[302]

C. American System

The human right standards for the Americas center on the American Declaration of the Rights and Duties of Man,[303] the American Convention on Human Rights ("American Convention"),[304] and the Additional Protocol

---

[298] *Id.* at 40.
[299] *Id.* at 44.
[300] *Id.* at 44.
[301] *Id.* at 34.
[302] *Id.* at 43.
[303] American Declaration on the Rights and Duties of Man, *available at* http://www.cidh.org/ Basicos/basic2.htm.
[304] American Convention, *supra* note 23, *available at* http://www.cidh.org/Basicos/basic3.htm. The Convention went into force on July 18, 1978. The Convention has been ratified by 25 OAS member states, including: Argentina; Barbados; Bolivia; Brazil; Chile; Colombia;

to the American Convention ("Protocol of San Salvador").[305] Table A, in Part VIII of this Chapter, includes the environmental human rights set forth in these instruments, most important of which is the right to a healthy environment found in Article 11 of the Protocol of San Salvador.[306]

These human rights instruments grew out of the creation on April 30, 1948, of the Organization of American States ("OAS")[307] and the adoption of the OAS Charter that went into effect three years later.[308] Article 3(l) of the OAS Charter generally obligates the OAS member states to protect human rights. That prompted member states to pass the American Declaration, originally as a non-binding resolution but now enforceable by the IACHR proceedings, as discussed below.[309] Moreover, Article 106 of the OAS Charter calls for the creation of the Inter-American Commission on Human Rights and for the American Convention which spells out the workings of the Inter-American Commission on Human Rights in greater detail.[310]

Unique to the American system is the protection of both enumerated and unenumerated rights. Article 1(1) of the American Convention provides that "States Parties to this Convention undertake [not only] to respect the rights and freedoms recognized herein ... [but also] to ensure to all persons subject to their jurisdiction the free and full exercise of those rights and freedoms." Thus, an affirmative duty to not violate the rights enumerated within the Convention sits alongside an unenumerated duty to take whatever other unwritten measures are necessary to ensure free and full exercise of those rights. The American System includes two organs to

---

Costa Rica; Dominica; Dominican Republic; Ecuador; El Salvador; Grenada; Guatemala; Haiti; Honduras; Jamaica; Mexico; Nicaragua; Panama; Paraguay; Peru; Suriname; Trinidad and Tobago; Uruguay; and Venezuela. The United States signed the American Convention during the Carter Administration but has yet to ratify it.

[305] Protocol of San Salvador, *available at* http://www.cidh.org/Basicos/basic5.htm.

[306] "1. Everyone shall have the right to live in a healthy environment and to have access to basic public services. 2. The states parties shall promote the protection, preservation, and improvement of the environment." *Available at* http://www.cidh.org/Basicos/basic5.htm at art. 11.

[307] Since its inception, the OAS has expanded to include Canada and the nations of the Caribbean. The 21 original members of the OAS are Argentina, Bolivia, Brazil, Chile, Colombia, Costa Rica, Cuba (although the Castro government was expelled in 1962), Dominican Republic, Ecuador, El Salvador, Guatemala, Haiti, Honduras, Mexico, Nicaragua, Panama, Paraguay, Peru, United States, Uruguay, and Venezuela. Fourteen additional members have been added to the OAS since its inception in 1948: 1967: Barbados; Trinidad and Tobago; 1969: Jamaica; 1975: Grenada; 1977: Suriname; 1979: Dominica; Saint Lucia; 1981: Antigua and Barbuda; Saint Vincent and the Grenadines; 1982: The Bahamas; 1984: St. Kitts and Nevis; 1990: Canada; 1991: Belize; Guyana.

[308] OAS Charter, *available at* http://www.cidh.oas.org/Basicos/charter.htm.

[309] *See* text accompanying notes 300-301 *infra*.

[310] American Convention, *supra* note 23, at arts. 34-51.

safeguard these rights and duties—the Inter-American Commission on Human Rights ("IACHR") and the Inter-American Court of Human Rights ("IACt.HR").

1. Inter-American Commission on Human Rights[311]

As mentioned above, Article 106 of the OAS Charter generally calls for the creation of the Inter-American Commission on Human Rights. Articles 34–51 of the American Convention provide greater details about the structure of the IACHR. In addition, the IACHR subsequently has adopted a statute to set forth its scope of authority[312] and rules of procedure to govern its operations.[313]

Among the myriad functions of the IACHR is its competence to receive petitions from "[a]ny person or group of persons, or any nongovernmental entity legally recognized in one or more member states of the Organization . . . containing denunciations or complaints of violation of this Convention by a State Party."[314] The American Convention differs from other international human rights regimes by making the right of individual petition mandatory and inter-state petitions optional. If an OAS member has ratified the American Convention, then they have also acknowledged the authority of the IACHR to inspect any private petitions made against that OAS member.

In addition, the IACHR is entrusted with the authority to act not only on formal, individual petitions, but also on other inter-state communications.[315] The OAS member must not only have accepted IACHR membership but must also have specifically accepted the inter-state jurisdiction of the IACHR.[316]

What follows is a discussion of the scope of the IACHR's authority and the prerequisites to guide the reader on what to consider when preparing the petition, as well as a summary of the IACHR procedure for handling petitions so that the reader gains a general sense of what to expect through the process. Be sure to consult appropriate individuals on the List of Experts in the appendix to this book before submitting your petition.

---

[311] The official internet site for the IACHR can be found at http://www.cidh.org.
[312] American Convention, *available at* http://www.cidh.org/Basicos/basic15.htm.
[313] American Convention, *available at* http://www.cidh.org/Basicos/basic16.htm.
[314] American Convention, art. 44. Generally speaking, the IACHR plays two roles that includes the petition power. First, the IACHR oversees the human rights obligations of all OAS members under Article 41(a)–(e) and (g) of the American Convention. Second, the IACHR oversees the obligations of the Convention parties under articles 41(f), 44–51.
[315] American Convention, art. 45.
[316] *Id.*

a. Scope of Authority

i. Party to the American Convention

If the OAS member-state is a party to the American Convention, then the IACHR has the power, among other things, to receive and act on petitions and communications against that nation-state, to appear before the IACt.HR on such petitions and communications, and to request the IACt.HR to take provisional measures that it considers appropriate in serious and urgent matters not yet submitted to the IACt.HR yet necessary to prevent irreparable injury.[317] With respect to the petitions, "[t]he [IACHR] shall consider petitions regarding alleged violations of the human rights enshrined in the American Convention on Human Rights and other applicable instruments, with respect to the member states of the OAS, only when the petitions fulfill the requirements set forth in those instruments, in the Statute, and in these Rules of Procedure."[318]

For purposes of a petition concerning environmental human rights, the IACHR will consider violations of the American Declaration and the American Convention[319] but not violations of the environmental or health

---

[317] Statute of the IACHR, *available at* http://www.cidh.org/Basicos/basic15.htm, at art. 19.

[318] IACt.HR. *available at* http://www.cidh.org/Basicos/basic16.htm at art. 28. *See also* http://www.cidh.org/Basicos/basic16.htm, art. 23 ("Any person or group of persons or nongovernmental entity legally recognized in one or more of the member states of the OAS may submit petitions to the IACHR, on their own behalf or on behalf of third persons, concerning alleged violations of a human right recognized in, as the case may be, the American Declaration of the Rights and Duties of Man, the American Convention on Human Rights, the Additional Protocol in the Area of Economic, Social and Cultural Rights, the Protocol to Abolish the Death Penalty, the Inter-American Convention to Prevent and Punish Torture, the Inter-American Convention on Forced Disappearance of Persons, and/or the Inter-American Convention on the Prevention, Punishment and Eradication of Violence Against Women, in accordance with their respective provisions, the Statute of the IACHR, and these Rules of Procedure....")

[319] *See* American Convention, art. 29:
No provision of this Convention shall be interpreted as:
a. permitting any State Party, group, or person to suppress the enjoyment or exercise of the rights and freedoms recognized in this Convention or to restrict them to a greater extent than is provided for herein;
b. restricting the enjoyment or exercise of any right or freedom recognized by virtue of the laws of any State Party or by virtue of another convention to which one of the said states is a party;
c. precluding other rights or guarantees that are inherent in the human personality or derived from representative democracy as a form of government; or
d. excluding or limiting the effect that the American Declaration of the Rights and Duties of Man and other international acts of the same nature may have.

52 • *Defending the Environment*

rights enshrined in the Protocol of San Salvador.[320] In addition, the combination of Article 29 of the American Convention[321] and the Inter-American Court's decision in *"Other Treaties" Subject to the Consultative Jurisdiction of the Court* about Article 64 of the American Convention[322] together support consideration of human rights instruments outside the American System. Therefore, a petition to the IACHR can and should refer to the same environmental human right found in other human rights instruments and systems.

ii. Non-Party to the American Convention

If the OAS member state is not a party to the American Convention, then the IACHR is limited to receiving and acting on communications or petitions but cannot refer the matter to the IACt.HR to review the status of the implementation of the IACHR recommendations and render a decision and judgment.[323] "The [IACHR] shall receive and examine any petition that contains a denunciation of alleged violations of the human rights set forth in the American Declaration of the Rights and Duties of Man in

---

[320] Protocol of San Salvador, art. 19(6):
Any instance in which the rights established in paragraph a) of Article 8 and in Article 13 are violated by action directly attributable to a State Party to this Protocol may give rise, through participation of the Inter-American IACHR on Human Rights and, when applicable, of the Inter-American Court of Human Rights, to application of the system of individual petitions governed by Article 44 through 51 and 61 through 69 of the American Convention on Human Rights.

[321] No provision of this Convention shall be interpreted as:
a. permitting any State Party, group, or person to suppress the enjoyment or exercise of the rights and freedoms recognized in this Convention or to restrict them to a greater extent than is provided for herein;
b. restricting the enjoyment or exercise of any right or freedom recognized by virtue of the laws of any State Party or by virtue of another convention to which one of the said states is a party;
c. precluding other rights or guarantees that are inherent in the human personality or derived from representative democracy as a form of government; or
d. excluding or limiting the effect that the American Declaration of the Rights and Duties of Man and other international acts of the same nature may have.

[322] Advisory Opinion OC-1/82, September 24, 1982, Inter-Am. Ct. H.R. (Ser. A) No. 1 (1982) *available at* http://www1.umn.edu/humanrts/iachr/b_11_4a.htm.

[323] Statute of the IACHR, *available at* http://www.cidh.org/Basicos/basic15.htm, at art. 20. *See, e.g.*, Case No. 10,675 v. United States. Admissibility: Report No. 28/93, *available at* http://www.oas.org/cidh/ annualrep/93eng/USA.10675.htm (Oct. 1993). Merits: Report No. 51/96, *available at* http://www.oas.org/ cidh/annualrep/96eng/USA10675.htm (Mar. 1997).

relation to the member states of the Organization that are not parties to the American Convention on Human Rights."[324]

Separate and apart from the above, Article 18 of the IACHR Statute outlines the authority of the IACHR applicable regardless of whether the OAS member is a party to the American Convention.[325] Key among these is the power "to conduct on-site observations in a state, with the consent or at the invitation of the government in question."[326]

b. Prerequisites

The only difference between the prerequisites for petitions lodged against parties to the American Convention and petitions lodged against non-parties is that the IACHR Rules of Procedures for referring a petition to the IACt.HR and for handling communications between two or more OAS members do not apply to the latter.[327] Otherwise, the prerequisites for petitions are repeated in Articles 46 and 47 of the American Convention, and 28 to 37 of IACHR Rules of Procedure.

For the IACHR to admit a petition, there must be a *prima facie* case[328] and the following requirements must be met:[329]

(1) that the remedies under domestic law have been pursued and exhausted in accordance with generally recognized principles of international law;
(2) that the petition or communication is lodged within a period of six months from the date on which the party alleging violation of his rights was notified of the final judgment;

---

[324] American Convention, *available at* http://www.cidh.org/Basicos/basic16.htm, at art. 49. *See also* http://www.cidh. org/Basicos/basic16.htm, art. 23 ("Any person or group of persons or nongovernmental entity legally recognized in one or more of the member states of the OAS may submit petitions to the IACHR, on their own behalf or on behalf of third persons, concerning alleged violations of a human right recognized in, as the case may be, the American Declaration of the Rights and Duties of Man, the American Convention on Human Rights, the Additional Protocol in the Area of Economic, Social and Cultural Rights, the Protocol to Abolish the Death Penalty, the Inter-American Convention to Prevent and Punish Torture, the Inter-American Convention on Forced Disappearance of Persons, and/or the Inter-American Convention on the Prevention, Punishment and Eradication of Violence Against Women, in accordance with their respective provisions, the Statute of the IACHR, and these Rules of Procedure....").

[325] *Icl* at art. 18 http://www.cidh.org/Basicos/basic16.htm.

[326] *Icl* at art.18(f) http://www.cidh.org/Basicos/basic16.htm.

[327] *Icl* at art. 50 http://www.cidh.org/Basicos/basic16htm ("The procedure applicable to petitions concerning member states of the OAS that are not parties to the American Convention shall be that provided for in the general provisions included in Chapter I of Title II; in Articles 28 to 43 and 45 to 47 of these Rules of Procedure [but not Article 44 on the IACt.HR and Article 48 on inter-State communications].").

[328] American Convention, art.47; IACHR Rules of Procedure, arts. 30-34.

[329] American Convention, art. 46(1); IACHR Rules of Procedure, arts. 29-30, 31(1), 32-33.

54 · Defending the Environment

(3) that the subject of the petition or communication is not pending in another international proceeding for settlement; and
(4) that, in the case of Article 44, the petition contains the name, nationality, profession, domicile, and signature of the person or persons or of the legal representative of the entity lodging the petition.

However, the above limitations are not applicable in the following conditions:[330]

(1) the domestic legislation of the state concerned does not afford due process of law for the protection of the right or rights that have allegedly been violated;
(2) the party alleging violation of his rights has been denied access to the remedies under domestic law or has been prevented from exhausting them; or
(3) there has been unwarranted delay in rendering a final judgment under the aforementioned remedies.

c. Procedure

After deciding which petitions are admissible,[331] the IACHR must then begin the process of examining the allegations. To do so, the IACHR will request information from the government of the state against which the petition was made.[332] If the IACHR, after receiving the requested information, decides that there is no ground for the petition, the IACHR will order the petition record closed.[333] If the investigation proceeds, the IACHR may hold hearings, receive oral and written statements, and will also, "place itself at the disposal of the parties concerned with a view to reaching a friendly settlement of the matter on the basis of respect for the human rights recognized in this Convention."[334] If a friendly settlement is reached, then the IACHR will draw up a report, transmit it to the petitioner and to the state members, and communicate the settlement to the Secretary General of the OAS.[335] If a settlement is not reached, the IACHR will still draw up their report containing both findings and conclusions, and will transmit this to the "concerned states."[336] Any member of the IACHR may attach a separate opinion to the IACHR report.[337] The final step in the

---

[330] American Convention, art. 46(2); IACHR Rules of Procedure, art. 31(2).
[331] IACHR Rules of Procedure, arts. 36-37.
[332] American Convention, art. 48(1)(a); IACHR Rules of Procedure, arts. 38-43, 45-47.
[333] American Convention, art. 48(1)(b); IACHR Rules of Procedure, arts. 38-43, 45-47.
[334] American Convention, art. 48(1)(f); IACHR Rules of Procedure, arts. 38-43, 45-47.
[335] American Convention, art. 49; IACHR Rules of Procedure, arts. 38-43, 45-47.
[336] American Convention, art. 50(2); IACHR Rules of Procedure, arts. 38-43, 45-47.
[337] American Convention, art. 50(1); IACHR Rules of Procedure, arts. 38-43, 45-47.

process is the vote of the IACHR in the case of an unresolved dispute: "If, within a period of three months from the date of the transmittal of the report of the [IACHR] to the states concerned, the matter has not either been settled or submitted by the [IACHR] or by the state concerned to the Court and its jurisdiction accepted, the [IACHR] may, by the vote of an absolute majority of its members, set forth its opinion and conclusions concerning the question submitted for its consideration."[338] The IACHR then will outline recommendations and set a timeline for the necessary measures to be taken.[339]

1.4 San Mateo de Huanchor

On February 28, 2003, in response to toxic contamination of their community by waste sludge containing heavy metals such as arsenic, lead, mercury, and cadmium from a nearby mine, the residents of San Mateo de Huanchor, Peru sought relief from the Inter-American Commission on Human Rights claiming that the Peruvian government had violated their human rights by failing to prevent the pollution.[340] In December 2003, the Center for International Environmental Law, a U.S.-based nongovernmental organization, became a copetitioner.[341]

Because of the imminent harm to the right to life, the petitioners then requested precautionary measures in June 2003 to have the local Peruvian State and/or the national Peruvian Government remove the sludge.[342] On August 17, 2004, the IACHR issued an order that Peru take precautionary measures to safeguard the lives and personal security of the San Mateo de Huanchor community. Recognizing the link between human rights and the environment in the impacts from pollution on human health, the Commission specifically requested that Peru undertake the following:
- Start up a health assistance and care program for the population of San Mateo de Huanchor, especially its children, in order to identify those persons who might have been affected by the pollution so that they can be given relevant medical care.
- Draw up as quickly as possible an environmental impact assessment study required for removing the sludge containing the toxic waste, which is located in the vicinity of the town of San Mateo de Huanchor.

(continued)

---

[338] American Convention, art. 51; *see also* IACHR Rules of Procedure, arts. 38–43, 45–47.
[339] American Convention, art. 51(2); IACHR Rules of Procedure, arts. 38–43, 45–47.
[340] *Community of San Mateo de Huanchor and its members v. Peru*, Case 504/03, Report No. 69/04, Inter-Am. C.H.R., OEA/Ser.L/V/II.122 Doc. 5 rev. 1 at 487 (2004), *available at* http://www.cidh.oas.org/annualrep/2004eng/Peru.504.03eng.htm.
[341] *Id.* at ¶ 7.
[342] *Id.* at ¶ 8.

1.4 San Mateo de Huanchor *(continued)*

- Once the environmental impact assessment study has been completed, the work required to treat and transfer the sludge to a safe site, where it will not produce pollution, in line with the technical conditions set forth in the above-mentioned study, shall start up.
- Draw up a timetable of activities to monitor compliance with the measure adopted by IACHR.[343]

On October 15, 2004, following the ordering of precautionary measures, the IACHR decided that the petition on the merits was admissible over objections from the Peruvian Government.[344] The Commission continues to analyze the case on its merits.[345]

1.5 Belize-Maya

In the Belize–Maya Case petitioners contended that the State of Belize violated the rights of the Maya people under Article XXIII of the American Declaration by granting logging concessions and oil concessions on Maya lands in the Toledo District without meaningful consultations with the Maya people, and in a manner that has caused substantial environmental harm and threatens long term and irreversible damage to the natural environment upon which the Maya depend.[346]

Concerning logging concessions, the Petitioners argued that since 1993, the Ministry of Natural Resources of Belize had granted numerous concessions for logging on a total of over half a million acres of land in the Toledo District.[347] The Petitioners claim that logging under these concessions is ongoing or imminent and that the areas of ten of the concessions include reservation and non-reservation lands that are traditionally used and occupied by the Maya people.[348] More particularly, the petition states that the logging concessions cover areas of land that include critical parts of the natural environment upon which the Maya people depend for subsistence, including vulnerable soils, primary forest growth, and important watersheds.[349] The Petitioners also claim that the logging activities have affected essential water supplies, disrupted plant and animal life, and, accordingly, affected Maya hunting, fishing, and gathering practices, which are essential to Maya cultural and physical survival.[350]

---

[343] *Id.* at ¶ 12.
[344] *Id.* at ¶¶ 42–68.
[345] *Id.* at Decision, ¶ 3.
[346] Case 12.053, Inter-Am. C.H.R. at 19, *available at* http://www.cidh.oas.org.
[347] *Id.* at 28.
[348] *Id.*
[349] *Id.*
[350] *Id.*

1.5 Belize-Maya *(continued)*

With respect to the concessions for oil development, the petitioners claimed that in late 1997, they learned that the Ministry of Energy, Science, Technology and Transportation of Belize had approved an application by a company to engage in oil exploration activities in oil development Block 12, which would include 749,222 acres of land in the Toledo District.[351] The area covered by the permit is said to include land used and occupied by the Maya and to encompass most, if not all, of the Maya villages in the Toledo District.[352]

In the report, having examined the evidence and arguments presented on behalf of the parties, the Commission concluded that the State of Belize violated the right to property enshrined in Article XXIII of the American Declaration, to the detriment of the Maya people, by failing to take effective measures to delimit, demarcate, and officially recognize their communal property right to the lands that they have traditionally occupied and used, and by granting logging and oil concessions to third parties without consultations with and the informed consent of the Maya people.[353]

Based upon these findings, the Commission recommended that the State provide the Maya people with an effective remedy, which includes recognizing their communal property right to the lands that they have traditionally occupied and used, without detriment to other indigenous communities, and delimit, demarcate, and title the territory in which this communal property right exists, in accordance with the customary land use practices of the Maya people.[354] The Commission also recommended that the State abstain from any acts that might lead the agents of the State itself, or third parties acting with its acquiescence or its tolerance, to affect the existence, value, use, or enjoyment of the property located in the geographic area occupied and used by the Maya people until their territory is properly delimited, demarcated and titled.[355] Finally, the Commission ordered the state to repair the environmental damage resulting from the logging and oil development concessions.[356]

2. *Inter-American Court of Human Rights*[357]

Articles 52–69 of the American Convention establish the Inter-American Court of Human Rights. In addition, the IACt.HR subsequently has adopted a statute to set forth its scope of authority[358] and rules of procedure to

---

[351] *Id.* at 30.
[352] *Id.*
[353] *Id.* at 193–94.
[354] *Id.* at 197.
[355] *Id.*
[356] *Id.*
[357] The official internet site for the IACt.HR can be found at http://www.corteidh.or.cr/index-ingles.html.
[358] *See* http://www.cidh.org/Basicos/basic17.htm *or* http://www.corteidh.or.cr/docs_basicos/Corte_Estat.html (Spanish only).

govern its operations.[359] The IACt.HR has both adjudicatory (*i.e.*, contentious) jurisdiction set forth in Articles 61–63 of the American Convention and advisory jurisdiction set forth in Article 64 of the American Convention.[360]

The Court is composed of seven judges elected by state parties to the American Convention to six-year, once-renewable terms.[361] The judges are not elected by the OAS General Assembly because the Court was not established under the OAS Charter, as was the IACHR.

a. Eligibility to File Cases

Only state parties and the IACHR are eligible to bring cases before the IACt.HR, regardless of whether the case invokes the IACt.HR's contentious or advisory jurisdiction. At times, however, the IACt.HR has allowed the individual, group, and/or NGO lodging the petition for the IACHR to present the case to the IACt.HR instead of the IACHR.[362] Otherwise, the IACHR can bring before the IACt.HR usually only cases that were originally lodged against OAS members who are parties to the American Convention.[363] Moreover, regardless of whether a state party or IACHR initiates the case, both the American Convention and the IACt.HR Statute require the IACHR to appear in all adjudicatory cases before the Court.[364] Moreover, under IACHR rules which took effect in 2001, it must refer all cases to the Court unless the IACHR votes otherwise by an absolute majority.[365]

b. Contentious Jurisdiction[366]

Under its contentious jurisdiction, the Court has authority to decide claims that a state party violated rights guaranteed by the American Convention. Contentious jurisdiction is optional and cases may be filed by or against only those states which have accepted such jurisdiction.

Article 62 of the American Convention addresses the IACt.HR's contentious jurisdiction:

---

[359] See http://www.cidh.org/Basicos/basic18.htm or http://www.corteidh.or.cr/info_general/Indicereg.html (Spanish only).

[360] IACt.HR Statute, *available at* http://www.cidh.org/Basicos/basic17.htm, at art. 2.

[361] American Convention, arts. 52, 54; IACt.HR Statute, *available at* http://www.cidh.org/Basicos/ basic17.htm, arts. 4–11.

[362] *See, e.g., The Mayagna (Sumo) Indigenous Community of Awas Tingni v. the Republic of Nicaragua*, issued Aug. 31, 2001, *available at* http://www1.umn.edu/humanrts/iachr/AwasTingnicase.html.

[363] IACHR Rules of Procedure 50.

[364] American Convention, art. 57; IACt.HR Statute, http://www.cidh.org/Basicos/basic17.htm, art. 28.

[365] See http://www.oas.org/cidh/Basicos/basic18.htm.

[366] *See generally* IACt.HR Rules of Procedure, *available at* http://www.oas.org/cidh/Basicos/ basic18.htm arts. 11–58, for the written, oral, evidentiary and operating procedures for contentious cases.

1. A State Party may, upon depositing its instrument of ratification or adherence to this Convention, or at any subsequent time, declare that it recognizes as binding, ipso facto, and not requiring special agreement, the jurisdiction of the Court on all matters relating to the interpretation or application of this Convention.

2. Such declaration may be made unconditionally, on the condition of reciprocity, for a specified period, or for specific cases. It shall be presented to the Secretary General of the organization, who shall transmit copies thereof to the other member states of the organization and to the Secretary of the Court.

3. The jurisdiction of the Court shall comprise all cases concerning the interpretation and application of the provisions of this Convention that are submitted to it, provided that the states parties to the case recognize or have recognized such jurisdiction, whether by special declaration pursuant to the preceding paragraphs, or by a special agreement.

When the Court finds that there has indeed been a violation of the Convention, the Court will mandate that the injured party be ensured the right of which s/he was deprived. Moreover, in certain situations, the Court also has the power to assess a remedy that is fair compensation.[367]

For each judgment made by the Court, the Court must outline its reasons for that decision.[368] However, once the Court has ruled, "[t]he judgment of the Court shall be final and not subject to appeal."[369] Member states must comply with the judgment of the Court.[370]

Each year, at the General Assembly meeting of the OAS, the Court reports on the cases it has tried in the previous year, including instances where states have not complied with Convention guidelines, and have also failed to comply with Court orders. The Court then makes recommendations to the OAS as how to best proceed in these situations.[371]

A separate and important aspect the IACt.HR's contentious jurisdiction is the authority to issue the equivalent of temporary restraining orders in emergency situations, even before or despite the filing of a case with the IACt.HR. Known as provisional measures, they are authorized in Article 63(2) of the American Convention:

> In cases of extreme gravity and urgency, and when necessary to avoid irreparable damage to persons, the Court shall adopt such

---

[367] American Convention, art. 63.
[368] *Id.*, art. 66(1).
[369] *Id.*, art. 67.
[370] *Id.*, art. 68.
[371] *Id.*, art. 65.

provisional measures as it deems pertinent in matters it has under consideration. With respect to a case not yet submitted to the Court, it may act at the request of the IACHR.

Meanwhile, Article 25 of the IACt.HR Rules explains the procedure by which the IACt.HR will exercise this authority.

> 1. At any stage of the proceedings involving cases of extreme gravity and urgency, and when necessary to avoid irreparable damage to persons, the Court may, at the request of a party or on its own motion, order such provisional measures as it deems pertinent, pursuant to Article 63(2) of the Convention.
>
> 2. With respect to matters not yet submitted to it, the Court may act at the request of the IACHR.
>
> 3. The request may be made to the President, to any judge of the Court, or to the Secretariat, by any means of communication. In every case, the recipient of the request shall immediately bring it to the President's attention.
>
> 4. If the Court is not sitting, the President, in consultation with the Permanent IACHR and, if possible, with the other judges, shall call upon the government concerned to adopt such urgent measures as may be necessary to ensure the effectiveness of any provisional measures that may be ordered by the Court at its next session.
>
> 5. The Court, or its President if the Court is not sitting, may convoke the parties to a public hearing on provisional measures.
>
> 6. In its Annual Report to the General Assembly, the Court shall include a statement concerning the provisional measures ordered during the period covered by the report. If those measures have not been duly implemented, the Court shall make such recommendations as it deems appropriate.

The authority to issue provisional measures brings greater legitimacy to the power of the IACt.HR.

c. Advisory Jurisdiction[372]

The IACt.HR's authority is broader under its advisory jurisdiction than under its contentious jurisdiction. It may render opinions interpreting not only the American Convention but also other human rights treaties of the

---

[372] *See generally* IACt.HR Rules of Procedure, *available at* http://www.oas.org/cidh/Basicos/ basic18.htm, arts. 59-64.

inter-American regime.[373] All OAS member states and all OAS organs may invoke the advisory jurisdiction of the court pursuant to Article 64:

> The member states of the Organization may consult the Court regarding the interpretation of this Convention or of other treaties concerning the protection of human rights in the American states. Within their spheres of competence, the organs listed in Chapter X of the Charter of the Organization of American States, as amended by the Protocol of Buenos Aires, may in like manner consult the Court.

The Court, at the request of a member state of the Organization, may provide that state with opinions regarding the compatibility of any of its domestic laws with the aforesaid international instruments. In contrast to the contentious jurisdiction cases, under advisory jurisdiction, the opinion of the Court is not binding.

If there is a general question with respect to an environmental human right issue that concerns an individual, group, and/or NGO, one may want to lobby OAS members to request an advisory opinion. As with others, this strategy should not be undertaken without consulting the appropriate experts listed in the appendix to this book.

1.6 Sarayacu

On December 19, 2003, the Kichwa peoples of the Sarayaku Community in Ecuador lodged a petition with the Inter-American Commission on Human Rights alleging that Ecuador, among other things, "is responsible for a series of acts and omissions harming [them] because [Ecuador] has allowed an oil company [CGC of Argentina] to carry out activities on the ancestral lands of the Sarayaku community without its consent, it has persecuted community leaders, and has denied judicial protection and legal due process to the Sarayaku community."[374]

In advance of lodging the petition, the Kichwa peoples sought precautionary measures from the IACHR in March 2003,[375] and in May 2003, the IACHR found in favor of the community, ordering Ecuador to adopt all measures necessary to secure the life and physical integrity of various protestors, adopt measures necessary to protect the special relationship that the community has with its territory, and investigate certain events in January 2003 against the community and prosecute accordingly.[376]

(continued)

---

[373] *See Other Treaties Subject to the Consultative Jurisdiction of the Court (Art. 64 of the American Convention on Human Rights)*, Advisory Opinion OC-1/82, Sept. 24, 1982, Inter-Am. Ct. H.R. (Ser.A) No. 1 (1982), *at* http://www1.umn.edu/humanrts/iachr/b_11_4a.htm.

[374] *The Kichwa Peoples of the Sarayaku Community v. Ecuador*, Inter-Am. C.H.R., Report No. 64/05, Petition No. 167/03, (2004), *available at* http://www.cidh.oas.org/annualrep/2004eng/Ecuador.167.03eng.htm, ¶ 2.

[375] *Id.* at ¶ 7.

[376] *Id.* at ¶ 9.

1.6 Sarayacu *(continued)*

When Ecuador failed to comply, the IACHR sought provisional measures from the Inter-American Court in June 2004 to help enforce its precautionary measures.[377] On July 6, 2004, the Court ordered Ecuador:

to adopt, without delay, all measures necessary to protect the life and personal integrity of the members of the Kichwa indigenous peoples of Sarayaku and those defending them in the required procedures before the authorities, to guarantee the right to freedom of movement of the members of the Sarayaku community, and to investigate the events giving rise to the adoption of provisional measures, so as to identify those responsible and impose corresponding sanctions.[378]

To date, Ecuador has refused to comply with the Court's order; the Court may have referred to the provisional measures and lack of compliance in its most recent Annual Report to the General Assembly of the Organization of American States.[379] Therefore, under the Court's Rules of Procedure, at this point the Court could "make such recommendations as it deems appropriate."[380] Given that Ecuador is a member of the OAS subject to the Court's jurisdiction, the Court may recommend sanctions of some kind when its term resumes in Fall 2005.

Separate and apart from the provisional measures issue, the merits of the Kichwa's petition moved one step forward when the IACHR ruled on October 13, 2004, that the petition was admissible.[381] A decision on the merits is expected during the IACHR's 2005 to 2006 term.

3. Additional Strategies

In addition to the aforementioned strategies—lodging petitions before the IACHR, awaiting decisions from IACt.HR contentious cases, or lobbying an OAS member to pursue an advisory opinion—two additional strategies relevant to both the IACHR and the IACt.HR are *amicus curiae* submissions and lobbying sympathetic OAS members to pursue a matter under the interstate machinery available before both the IACHR and the IACt.HR.

---

[377] *Id.* at ¶ 17. *See also* Rules of Procedure of the Inter-American Court of Human Rights, Art. 25(2), *available at* http://www.cidh.oas.org/Basicos/basic18.htm.

[378] *Id.* at ¶ 18. *See also Case of the Sarayaku Indigenous Community. Provisional Measures,* Order of the Inter-American Court of Human Rights of July 6, 2004, *available at* http://www.corteidh.or.cr/seriee/sarayaku_se_01.doc or http://www.corteidh.or.cr/serieepdf/sarayaku_se_01.pdf.

[379] *See* http://www.sarayacu.com/oil/news050624.html#eng.

[380] Rules of Procedure of the Inter-American Court of Human Rights, Art. 25(8), *available at* http://www.cidh.oas.org/Basicos/basic18.htm.

[381] *The Kichwa Peoples of the Sarayaku Community v. Ecuador,* Inter-Am. C.H.R., Report No. 64/05, Petition No. 167/03, (2004), *available at* http://www.cidh.oas.org/annualrep/2004eng/Ecuador.167.03eng.htm.

a. *Amicus Curiae*

Similar to the UN system, an *amicus curiae* submission to either the IACHR or the IACt.HR should: (1) explain how the case relates to the work of the NGO or community group filing it; (2) elaborate on legal arguments not adequately addressed in the petition; and (3) provide additional, supportive factual information not presented in the petition. As discussed earlier, in *Association of Lhaka Honhat Aboriginal Communities (Nuestra Tierra/Our Land) v. the State of Argentina, Precautionary Measures Request*,[382] filed with the Inter-American IACHR on Human Rights, two NGOs—the Center for Human Rights and the Environment in Cordoba, Argentina[383] and the Center for International Environmental Law in Washington, D.C.[384]—jointly filed an *amicus curiae* brief[385] to support the petitioner's claim that Argentina's plan to cut through the center of the protected land of the indigenous Wichi, Chorote, Chulupi, Toba, and Tapiete peoples to build a transnational road through Argentina linking Brazil to Chile would violate their right to life and their right to a clean and healthy environment.[386] This same strategy can also be undertaken before the Inter-American Court.[387] One should consult an appropriate expert in the Appendix to this book before pursuing this strategy.

b. Lobbying OAS Members to Pursue Inter-State Mechanisms

Articles 45 and 62 of the American Convention provide inter-state dispute resolution mechanisms between qualified OAS members before the IACHR and the IACt.HR, respectively. An individual, group, and/or NGO

---

[382] Brief of Amici Curiae Center for Human Rights and the Environment and Center for International Environmental Law, *Ass'n of Lhaka Honhat Aboriginal Communities (Nuestra Tierra/Our Land) v. Argentina*, Precautionary Measures Request, Inter-Am. Ct. H.R. (2000) (No. P12.094), *available at* http://www.ciel.org/Publications/WichiAmiciCuriae2.pdf.

[383] The Center for Human Rights and the Environment ("CEDHA") is a non-profit organization promoting sustainable development through the promotion of the symbiotic relationship existing between the environment and people, and striving to build awareness of the importance of addressing human rights and environmental protection in all development processes. *See* CEDHA, About CEDHA, *available at* http://www.cedha.org.ar/cedha.htm.

[384] The Center for International Environmental Law ("CIEL") is a public interest, not-for-profit environmental law firm founded in 1989 to strengthen international and comparative environmental law and policy around the world. *See* CIEL, CIEL's Goals, *available at* http://www.ciel.org/reciel.html.

[385] Brief of Amici Curiae CEDHA and CIEL, *Ass'n of Lhaka Honhat Aboriginal Communities* (No. P12.094).

[386] *See id.*

[387] *See amicus curiae* submission from CIEL and International Human Rights Law Group in *The Mayagna (Sumo) Indigenous Community of Awas Tingni v. the Republic of Nicaragua*, *available at* http://www.ciel.org/Publications/awastingnibrief.pdf (May 31, 1999).

64 • Defending the Environment

concerned about a human rights violation that an individual petition somehow is inadequate or unable to address could consider lobbying a sympathetic OAS member to initiate such a dispute on the matter before the IACHR or the IACt.HR. Again, one should consult an appropriate expert in the appendix to this book before pursuing this strategy.

D. European System

The longest standing and most well developed regional system of human rights law is in Europe. Much of that law is found in the European Convention for the Protection of Human Rights and Fundamental Freedoms as Amended by Protocol No. 11 (the "ECHR"),[388] the European Social Charter (the "ESC"),[389] and the Charter of Fundamental Rights of the European Union. The former two sources were created under the auspices of the Council of Europe,[390] while the latter was authored by the European Union (the "Charter").[391]

The ECHR and ESC are similar in organization and content to the International Covenant on Civil and Political Rights and the International Covenant on Economic, Social and Cultural Rights, respectively. However, the ECHR includes adjudicatory machinery that the ESC lacks (relying instead on a reporting system). In addition, the Petition Committee of the European Parliament handles dispute resolution in connection with the Charter.

1. European Commission

Originally, the European System included a Commission created by the ECHR[392] that considered petitions presented by non-state actors against those European members that had accepted the jurisdiction of the Commission.[393] Such petitions charged the member state with violations of the ECHR. The Commission sought friendly settlement among the disputing parties. However, if the Commission could not resolve the dispute,

---

[388] Entered into force 1953, *available at* http://conventions.coe.int/treaty/en/Treaties/Html/ 005.htm.

[389] European Social Charter, Oct. 18, 1961, art. 20, Europ.T.S. No. 35 (rev'd 1996), *available at* http://conventions.coe.int/treaty/en/treaties/html/163.htm.

[390] Article 3 of the Statute of the Council of Europe requires "[e]very member of the Council of Europe must accept the principles of the rule of law and of the enjoyment by all persons within its jurisdiction of human rights and fundamental freedoms ..." *available at* http://conventions.coe.int/Treaty/en/Treaties/Html/001.htm.

[391] Charter of Fundamental Rights, *availlable at* http://www.europarl.eu.int/comparl/libe/elsj/charter/default_en.htm.

[392] *See* http://www.pfc.org.uk/legal/echrtext.htm, art. 19.

[393] *Id.*, arts. 20–37 (European IACHR), particularly article 25.

and the Commission determined that the member state was violating or had violated the ECHR, the petition would be presented to the European Court.[394] The European Court would eventually enter a judgment that member states obligated themselves to follow and that the Committee of Ministers was expected to supervise.

However, in 1998, the adoption of Protocol No. 11 to the ECHR terminated the Commission and provided non-state actors with direct access to the European Court.[395] Consequently, only the procedure of that institution now controls the resolution of environmental human rights matters in Europe.

1.7 European Commission

Numerous examples exist in 2004 of the European Commission taking steps to enforce environmental laws of the European Union and subsequent judgments from the EU's European Court of Justice against member states that fail to comply. Against Greece, the Commission has brought numerous actions for, among other things, failure to phase out electrical equipment containing polychlorinated biphenyls (PCBs), which are now known carcinogens, unsafe handling of sludge from a waste water plant in the area of Athens, an illegal landfill on Crete, and the failure to protect a rare viper species on Milos.[396] Against Luxembourg, the Commission challenged gaps in legislation covering industrial accidents, inadequate treatment of urban wastewater, problems with integrated water management, and failure to create an air quality improvement plan.[397] Against Spain, the Commission challenged issues relating to waste disposal, urban wastewater, and construction projects that pose a threat to human health and the environment.[398] Against Austria, the Commission

(continued)

---

[394] See http://www.pfc.org.uk/legal/echrtext.htm, arts. 38–56 (European Court), particularly article 48.

[395] See http://conventions.coe.int/treaty/en/Treaties/Html/005.htm, art. 34.

[396] See European Commission, *Greece: Commission pursues legal action in nine cases for breach of EU environmental law* (July 20, 2004), available at http://europa.eu.int/rapid/pressReleasesAction.do?reference=IP/04/977&format=HTML&aged=1&language=EN&guiLanguage=en.

[397] See European Commission, *Luxembourg: Commission pursues legal action in six cases of breaches of EU environmental law* (July 20, 2004), available at http://europa.eu.int/rapid/pressReleasesAction.do?reference=IP/04/976&format=HTML&aged=1&language=EN&guiLanguage=en.

[398] See European Commission, *Spain: Commission pursues legal action over breaches of EU environmental law* (July 20, 2004), available at http://europa.eu.int/rapid/pressReleasesAction.do?reference=IP/04/973&format=HTML&aged=1&language=EN&guiLanguage=en.

> **1.7 European Commission** *(continued)*
>
> has challenged gaps in its nature protection legislation, failure to take action to improve air quality, and improper compliance with EU laws on prevention of major industrial accidents and on car recycling.[399] Finally, against Germany, the Commission has criticized incomplete legislation on car recycling, water management issues, missing plans for air quality improvement in some regions, and insufficient regulation of ozone-depleting substances.[400]

2. European Court

The newly constituted European Court of Human Rights that was established pursuant to Protocol 11 is located in Strasbourg, France, and operates full-time. It is the first permanent, full-time human rights court. It comprises a number of members equal to the membership of the Council of Europe.[401]

The Court has jurisdiction to decide contentious cases between a non-state actor and a member state, to decide contentious cases between member states, and/or provide advisory opinions.[402] For contentious cases submitted by non-state actors, a chamber of the Court will register the application, the Registry of the Court will contact the non-state actor if more information is need, and the submission will be assigned to a judge-rapporteur.[403] The judge-rapporteur may refer the application to a three-judge committee, which may include the judge-rapporteur, to determine whether the application is inadmissible. If the three-judge committee unanimously decides that the application is inadmissible, the application is dismissed. The committee's decision is final. If the committee does not

---

[399] *See* European Commission, *Austria: Commission pursues legal action for breaches of environmental legislation* (July 16, 2004), *available at* http://europa.eu.int/rapid/pressReleasesAction.do?reference=IP/04/942&format=HTML&aged=1&language=EN&guiLanguage=en.

[400] *See* European Commission, *Germany: Commission pursues legal action for breaches of EU environmental law* (July 16, 2004), *available at* http://europa.eu.int/rapid/pressReleasesAction.do?reference=IP/04/941&format=HTML&aged=1&language=EN&guiLanguage=en.

[401] *See* http://conventions.coe.int/treaty/en/Treaties/Html/005.htm, art. 20.

[402] *See* http://conventions.coe.int/treaty/en/Treaties/Html/005.htm, arts. 33, 34, and 47.

[403] The Registry of the Court has provided a suggested format and submission instructions for applications, *available at* http://www.echr.coe.int/BilingualDocuments/ApplicantInformation.htm.

unanimously decide that the application is inadmissible, the application is referred to a seven-judge chamber. If the judge-rapporteur believes that the application is admissible in that it raises a question of principle, then the application is referred to a seven-judge chamber. The seven-judge chamber will decide on the merits of the application and, if necessary, determine its competency to hear the case. The Court can award damages in contentious cases. Moreover, the Committee of Ministers oversees the execution of the Court's judgment.

Consequently, the key strategy for addressing environmental human rights matters is to make a submission to the European Court. Consult appropriate individuals on the List of Practitioner Experts in the appendix to this book to assist with the submission.

Additionally, one can submit *amicus curiae* petitions in support of an inter-state case or an individual application case to the President of the Court. ECHR Article 36(b) provides that "[t]he President of the Court may, in the interest of the proper administration of justice, invite ... any person concerned who is not the applicant to submit written comments or take part in hearings."[404] Moreover, the Rules of Court provide that "[i]n accordance with Article 36 § 2 of the Convention, the President of the Chamber may, in the interests of the proper administration of justice, invite or grant leave to ... any person concerned who is not the applicant, to submit written comments or, in exceptional cases, to take part in a hearing."[405] One should contact the President of the Court at:

European Court of Human Rights
Council of Europe
F - 67075 Strasbourg-Cedex
T: 33 (0)3 88 41 20 18
F: 33 (0)3 88 41 27 30
E: webmaster@echr.coe

Lastly, one can pursue asking member states to request an advisory opinion on a particular environmental human rights issue or to initiate an inter-state dispute on a particular problem. However, given the openness of the Court to non-state actors, these alternatives are likely not to advance one's issue in a possible way.

---

[404] *See* http://conventions.coe.int/treaty/en/Treaties/Html/005.htm, art. 36(b).
[405] Rules of Court (Oct. 2002), *available at* http://www.echr.coe.int/Eng/EDocs/RulesofCourt2002.htm, art. 61(3).

1.8 Taskin

"In 1992 the limited company E.M. Eurogold Madencilik (which subsequently became known as Normandy Madencilik A.Ş.) obtained the right to prospect for gold. The permit was valid for ten years and also authorized use of the cyanide leaching process for gold extraction. In 1994, on the basis of an environmental-impact report, the Ministry of the Environment gave the company a permit to operate the goldmine at Ovacık."[406] The company planned to mine in Ovacik in the district of Bergama.[407]

Several Turkish nationals from Bergama lodged a petition with the European Commission in September 1998 that was subsequently transferred to the European Court in November 1998.[408] The petition claimed that the granting of the permit violated their right to respect for private and family life under Article 8 of the European Convention because of the adverse impact that the cyanide leaching process would have on the environment.[409] With the cloud of a European Court decision looming, the Turkish court continually stayed efforts by the Turkish government to allow operations to go forward.[410] Finally, when the Ministry of Environmental and Forestry expressing a favorable opinion on the company's August 2004 final impact study, the European Court ruled.[411]

On November 10, 2004, the European Court found in favor of the petitioners.[412]

In its decision, the Court noted that the mine's operating permit did not serve the public interest and negatively impacted the "applicants' effective enjoyment of the right to life and to a healthy environment."[413]

3. Dispute Resolution Under the European Social Charter

The only relevant environmental human right in the ESC is the right to health in Article 11.[414] Although the ESC does not provide for resolution of disputes concerning Article 11, the treaty does establish a reportorial process though which awareness about environmental health issues can

---

[406] European Court of Human Rights, *Press Release: Grand Chamber Judgment in the Case of Taskin and Others v. Turkey* (Nov. 10, 2004), *available at* http://www.echr.coe.int/Eng/Press/2004/Nov/ChamberjudgmentTaskin&OthersvTurkey101104.htm.
[407] *Id.*
[408] *Id.*
[409] *Id.*
[410] *Id.*
[411] *Id.*
[412] *Taskin and Others v. Turkey*, Eur. Ct. H.R., No. 46117/99 (2004), *available at* http://echr.coe.int/Eng/judgments.htm.
[413] *Id.*
[414] *See* http://conventions.coe.int/treaty/en/treaties/html/163.htm, at art. 11.

be raised.[415] State parties "undertake to consider the economic, social and cultural rights enumerated [in the ESC]" and to pursue such aims with appropriate measures. States report on their progress in biennial reports submitted to the Council of Europe's Secretary General. The reports are examined by the Committee of Experts; then passed on with the Committee of Experts' conclusions to the Governmental Social Committee and finally to the Council's Consultative Assembly. The Committee of Ministers may, on the basis of reports and consultation with the foregoing bodies, make necessary recommendations to the state. Thus, the strategy for safeguarding the ESC's health right is to challenge inaccuracies in these reports.

4. European Parliament and the Charter

The European Parliament is the governing body for the European Union. With its adoption of the Charter of Fundamental Rights of the European Union, the European Parliament's Committee on Petitions now entertains submissions concerning environmental human rights problems in EU member states. Step-by-step procedures governing such submissions as well as a model application can be found on the European Parliament's website.[416] Although the European Parliament reminds applicants that it is not a judicial body, raising awareness with the European Parliament by making a submission may still contribute greatly to resolving an environmental human rights problem existing in the Europe System.

Moreover, separate and apart from considering environmental issues in the context of human rights, the European Parliament also considers environmental protection issues directly.[417]

V. NEWLY EMERGING RIGHTS AND FUNDAMENTAL RIGHTS RECOGNIZED AS CUSTOMARY INTERNATIONAL LAW

Customary international law results from "a general and consistent practice of states followed by them from a sense of legal obligation" and results in all nation-states being bound to such law without any kind of signature or ratification.[418] Whether the right to environmental protection or to a clean and healthy environment has yet risen to the level of customary international law is highly controversial. However, many of the human rights categorized in this chapter as environmental human rights are customary, so inclusion of this source of law is crucial to any NGO arguments made.

---

[415] *See* http://conventions.coe.int/treaty/en/treaties/html/035.htm, at arts. 21–29.
[416] *See* http://www.europarl.eu.int/petition/help_en.htm.
[417] *See generally* http://www.europarl.eu.int/petition/help_en.htm.
[418] RESTATEMENT (THIRD) OF THE FOREIGN RELATIONS LAW OF THE UNITED STATES ("RESTATEMENT"), § 102(2).

Quoted below, Section 702 of the Third Restatement of the Foreign Relations Law of the United States ("Restatement") gives examples of those human rights that have crystallized into customary international law. Although most environmental issues are probably not severe enough to fall in any of these categories (albeit some argue that certain environmental harms to indigenous communities is akin to cultural genocide), there are other environmental human rights such as the right to life and right to property that are also generally accepted as customary law.[419] The Restatement comments that the list in Section 702 is neither complete nor closed, and that other rights may have also reached the status of customary law.[420]

A state violates international law if, as a matter of state policy, it practices, encourages, or condones

a. genocide;
b. slavery or slave trade;
c. the murder or causing the disappearance of individuals;
d. torture or other cruel, inhuman or degrading treatment or punishment;
e. prolonged arbitrary detention;
f. systematic racial discrimination; or
g. a consistent pattern of gross violations of internationally recognized human rights.[421]

The process by which human rights become widely accepted in international customary law is somewhat unique, at least according to the Restatement's comments. The reporters' notes to Section 701 suggest that customary human rights law is established in a manner different from other customary law because, historically, human rights have been a matter between a state and its own inhabitants.[422] According to the notes, customary human rights law may be established through: virtually universal adherence to the UN Charter; virtually universal adherence to the Universal Declaration of Human Rights; widespread participation of states in preparation and adoption of international human rights agreements; widespread support for UN General Assembly resolutions applying international human rights principles; and frequent invocation and application of international human rights principles in both domestic practice and diplomatic practice.[423]

Thus, human rights law is constantly evolving in a multitude of sources and fora, from recognition of rights in treaties, UN resolutions, and domes-

---

[419] RESTATEMENT, § 702 cmt. a (1986).
[420] *Id.*
[421] *Id.* § 702.
[422] *See id.* §701 n.2.
[423] *Id.*

tic state practice, to the level of custom and *jus cogens*. Many protections originate in internal domestic law, with gradual recognition as general principles of international law if common to most legal systems. Such is arguably becoming the case for inclusion of freedom from environmental degradation among existing human rights, as well as the addition of new human rights focused solely on the environment.[424] Moreover, even as these environmental rights evolve, many existing human rights that include environmental protection within their scope are also evolving into or have crystallized into customary international law. Therefore, as mentioned at the outset of this section, an argument about customary international law is essential to a persuasive environmental human rights submission.

VI. SEEKING ENFORCEMENT IF A CLAIM PREVAILS AND A NATION-STATE FAILS TO COMPLY

In some cases, a petitioner will bring a human rights claim in one of the above UN or regional human rights bodies against a nation-state and prevail, but the nation-state will fail to comply with the ordered remedy. When a state fails to comply with the decision of a UN or regional human rights body, several additional steps may be necessary and/or possible to obtain enforcement of the decision. Although some measures have rarely, if ever, been invoked to date, their availability and potential use should not be overlooked. Again, consulting appropriate individuals listed in the appendix to this book is recommended.

A. United Nations System

1. Notify the UN High Commissioner for Human Rights

If the human rights body rendering the decisions fails to do so within a reasonable amount of time, the petitioner or, where appropriate, the *amicus curiae*, should notify the Office of the UN High Commission for Human Rights ("OHCHR") of a state's failure to comply with a decision.[425]

The position of High Commissioner on Human Rights ("HCHR") was established under UN General Assembly Resolution 48/141 of December 20, 1993.[426] The HCHR has an official position with the principal responsibility for UN human rights activities under the direction of the Secretary

---

[424] *See* sources cited for "Right to the Environment" in Table A in Part VIII of this chapter.

[425] The High Commissioner for Human Rights at the UN may be contacted through the UN website at http://www.unhchr.ch./html/hchr.htm.

[426] G.A. Res. 48/141, U.N. GAOR, 48th Sess., Supp. No. 49, at 261, U.N. Doc. A/Res/48/141 (1993).

General.[427] The HCHR's most important function is to "play an active role in removing the current obstacles and in meeting the challenges to the full realization of all the human rights and in preventing the continuation of human rights violations throughout the world."[428] The broad language allows the HCHR to be actively engaged in efforts to prevent human rights violations around the world and to address any modern human rights problem.

The HCHR has the rank of an Under-Secretary General of the UN.[429] S/he is charged with the supervision of the Human Rights Center, the human rights secretariat of the UN, and with the coordination of the UN's promotional and protection activities.[430] The HCHR is appointed by the Secretary General with the approval of the General Assembly for a term of four years, with a possible renewal of another four years.[431] In making the appointments, the Secretary General pays attention to geographic rotation.[432]

2. Encourage the HCHR to Notify the UN Secretary General

After the petitioner and/or *amicus curiae* notifies the HCHR of a nation-state's failure to comply with a human rights decision, the petitioner or *amicus curiae* should confirm with the HCHR when the HCHR notifies the UN Secretary General. The UN Secretary General is authorized pursuant to Article 99 of the UN Charter, if a nation-state's failure to abide by a decision causes a breach of international peace and security, to appeal to the UN Security Council to take measures to enforce such human rights decisions.[433]

3. Encourage the UN Security Council to Take Enforcement Action

The UN Security Council can take one of several measures to compel a nation-state to comply with a decision of a human rights body that is legally binding. Failure to comply can lead to ongoing negotiations between the violating state and the UN Secretary General to reach a diplomatic solution, the imposition of economic sanctions against the violating nation, and even the threat of undertaking military force if the human rights violation is not remedied.[434]

---

[427] *Id.*
[428] *Id.*
[429] *Id.*
[430] *Id.*
[431] *Id.*
[432] *See* UN High Commissioner of Human Rights, *available at* http://www.unhchr.ch/html/hchr/hchrbio.htm.
[433] U.N. CHARTER art. 99.
[434] *Id.* arts. 39–45. For a hypothetical scenario in which Security Council enforcement action might be appropriate and necessary in response to an environmental disaster, *see* Linda A. Malone, *Discussion in the Security Council on Environmental Intervention in the Ukraine*, 27 LOY. L.A. L. REV. 893 (1994).

B. African System

In July 2000, the Organization of African Unity reconstituted itself as the African Union ("AU") and adopted the Constitutive Act of the African Union to set forth the organization and power of the AU.[435] Two years later, the AU adopted the Protocol Relating to the Establishment of the Peace and Security Council of the African Union ("PSC")[436] modeled on the United Nations Security Council.

Although the AU is relatively new (the predecessor OAU had existed since 1963) and not much public information is readily accessible to confirm whether the AU Protocol has yet entered into force or what is the scope of the authority of each AU organ, the text of the AU Constitutive Act and the AU Protocol together indicate that the Assembly has both a sanctioning authority[437] and the ability to bring human rights situations to the attention of the PSC for further action.[438] Moreover, the AU Protocol states repeatedly that the PSC's mandate includes human rights issues[439] and that AU member states will follow the decisions of the PSC.[440] Therefore, perhaps the Assembly and/or the PSC could help enforce human rights decisions of the African Court on Human Rights (or even the African Commission on Human Rights) where the defending nation-state fails to comply with the decision. Individuals or groups who have received a ruling in their favor from either human rights body could perhaps contact the Assembly or the PSC directly or call upon the Commission, the administrative secretariat for the African Union, to raise the issue with either organ.

All three of these bodies are located in Addis Ababa in Ethiopia.
Contact the AU at:

African Union Headquarters
P.O. Box 3243
Roosevelt Street (Old Airport Area)
W21K19 Addis Ababa Ethiopia
T: (251) 1-51-77-00
F: (251) 1-51-78-44
W: www.africa-union.org

In addition, the Office of the Legal Counsel can be reached at olc@africa-union.org.

---

[435] See http://www.au2002.gov.za/docs/key_oau/au_act.htm ("AU Constitutive Act").
[436] See http://www.au2002.gov.za/docs/summit_council/secprot.htm ("AU Protocol").
[437] See http://www.au2002.gov.za/docs/key_oau/au_act.htm, art. 23.
[438] See http://www.au2002.gov.za/docs/summit_council/secprot.htm, art. 6(g).
[439] See http://www.au2002.gov.za/docs/summit_council/secprot.htm, arts. 5(2)(g), 7(1)(m).
[440] See http://www.au2002.gov.za/docs/summit_council/secprot.htm, art. 7(3).

C. Inter-American System

Article 30 of the IACt.HR Statute provides that "[t]he Court shall submit a report on its work of the previous year to each regular session of the OAS General Assembly. It shall indicate those cases in which a state has failed to comply with the Court's ruling." The OAS Permanent Council also considers the report.[441]

If the Court's report alone does not result in action on the part of the OAS General Assembly and/or the OAS Permanent Council to take steps to persuade the non-complying OAS member to comply, then the individual, group, and/or NGO that lodged the petition may want to lobby the OAS Permanent Council about the non-compliance. The OAS Permanent Council appears to have primary jurisdiction over matters of peace and security and related emergencies[442] and seems to have greater enforcement authority than the OAS General Assembly at least with respect to such matters.[443] Although one could probably lobby the OAS Permanent Council directly, better protocol would be to raise the issue with the OAS General Secretariat or OAS General Assembly that, pursuant to Articles 110 and 82, respectively, have the ability to have their concerns considered by the Permanent Council.

Contact these organs through the OAS at:

Organization of American States
17th Street & Constitution Ave., N.W.
Washington, D.C. 20006, USA
T: (202) 458-3000
W: www.oas.org

D. European System

1. Council of Europe

Article 46 of the ECHR provides that "[t]he High Contracting Parties undertake to abide by the final judgment of the Court in any case to which they are parties" and that "[t]he final judgment of the Court shall be transmitted to the Committee of Ministers, which shall supervise its execution." Composed of the foreign ministers of the Council of Europe members, the Committee of Ministers meets on a regular basis to consider the progress of compliance with the Court's decisions.[444] The Committee's involvement appears sufficient to ensure enforcement of the Court's decisions.

---

[441] OAS Charter, *available at* http://www.cidh.org/Basicos/charter.htm, art. 91(f).
[442] OAS Charter, *available at* http://www.cidh.org/Basicos/charter.htm, art. 84.
[443] *Compare* OAS Charter, *available at* http://www.cidh.org/Basicos/charter.htm, arts. 54–60 *with* OAS Charter, *available at* http://www.cidh.org/Basicos/charter.htm, arts. 80–92.
[444] *See* http://www.coe.int/t/E/Committee_of_Ministers/Home/General_Information/Execution_of_judgments_of_the_Court_of_Human_Rights/01_intro.asp#TopOfPage.

However, were an individual or group not satisfied with such compliance, they should raise that concern with the newly created Commissioner for Human Rights, a separate organ within the Council of Europe established specifically to act as an ombudsmen with respect to human rights problems. One can contact the Commissioner through Gregory Mathieu, the Communications Officer, at:

> Office of the Commissioner for Human Rights
> Council of Europe
> F-67075 STRASBOURG CEDEX
> T: 33 (0)3 88 41 39 15
> M: 33 (0)632 64 58 75
> F: 33 (0) 3 90 21 50 53
> E: commissiner.humanrights@coe.int

As for matters concerning environmental health issues under Article 11 of the European Social Charter that are not within the jurisdiction of the Court or the Committee of Ministers, the member states of the Council of Europe are not bound to that provision unless they choose to be.[445] Consequently, no enforcement option exists with respect to any report that a member state's compliance with the right to health in connection with an environmental problem is inadequate.

2. *European Parliament*

The concept of enforcing a judicial or quasi-judicial judgment or decision is not relevant to the environmental human rights set forth in the Charter of Fundamental Rights of the European Union because the Committee on Petitions of the European Parliament ("Petitions Committee") that handles citizen submissions concerning violations of those environmental human rights is not a judicial or quasi-judicial body that renders enforceable judgments, opinions or decisions. Instead, to encourage citizens to submit environmental human rights matters, among others, the Petitions Committee has pledged to review these petitions and then refer them to the appropriate European Parliament committees for further action.[446] In addition, the Committee may draft an opinion in response to a submission and present that opinion to the President of the European Parliament to forward to the Council and/or European Commission for action.[447]

---

[445] *See* http://conventions.coe.int/treaty/en/treaties/html/035.htm, art. 20(1).
[446] *See* http://www.europarl.eu.int/petition/help_en.htm, para. 9.
[447] *See* http://www.europarl.eu.int/petition/help_en.htm, para. 9.

VII. CONCLUSION

This Chapter has provided a comprehensive array of fora and approaches by which environmental degradation may be challenged in the UN system and regional human rights systems as a violation of human rights. As the analysis indicates, these avenues of enforcement vary widely in the extent to which they have been used and may be used effectively for these type of claims. The challenges and obstacles to enforcement of international environmental law may be more familiar to lawyers and other advocates of public international law than to those who are more grounded in domestic environmental law. Among lawyers and other advocates of public international law, the fora for the environmental human rights claims outlined in this Chapter may be more familiar to human rights lawyers and advocates than to those specializing in international environmental law. Consequently, progressive enforcement of international environmental law may well depend upon drawing lessons from the advances in human rights enforcement in domestic courts, use of the more expansive supranational fora available for human rights claims, and greater recognition of the substantive relationship between environmental degradation and human rights violations. A necessary first step is for environmental lawyers and advocates to join forces with human rights lawyers and advocates so as to improve familiarity with the fora and approaches in the Chapter.

Despite the relative weakness and challenges to some of these methods, there is a need to use them in order to strengthen them. If strengthened, they have the potential to be powerful tools not merely for public recognition of environmental degradation throughout the globe as human rights problems, but for remedial measures and sanctions as well. The purpose of this Chapter is to encourage and enable such use by advocates to lay the groundwork for more meaningful, expanded protection of the environment and human rights.

VIII: TABLES

Table A: Sources of International Law Applicable to Environmental Human Rights[1]

RIGHT	TREATY PROVISIONS[2]	DECLARATION PROVISIONS[3]	RESOLUTIONS, DECISIONS, AND REPORTS[4]	INTERNATIONAL COURT DECISIONS[5]	DOMESTIC CONSTITUTIONAL PROVISIONS[6]
Environment; Clean Environment; Healthy Environment; Environmental Protection	Additional Protocol to the American Convention on Human Rights in the Area of Economic, Social and Cultural Rights, http://www.cidh.oas.org/Basicos/basic5.htm ("PSS"), art. 11.	Stockholm Declaration on the Human Environment, http://www.unep.org/Documents/Default.asp?DocumentID=97&ArticleID=1501, particularly Principle 1.	Report of the Secretary-General, Human rights and the environment as part of sustainable development, UN Doc. E/CN.4/2005/96 (Jan. 19, 2005), available at http://www.ohchr.org/english/bodies/chr/docs/61chr/E.CN.4.2005.96.doc.	Decision regarding Communication No. 155/96 (Social and Economic Rights Action Center/Center for Economic and Social Rights v. Nigeria), Case No. ACHPR/comm/A044/1 (May 27, 2002) at http://www.umn.edu/humanrts/africa/comcases/allcases.html.	See generally Robert L. CONSTITUTIONS OF THE WORLD (Congressional Quarterly Inc. (2001)) (including constitutions of the world that may contain this right). See also Constitutions of the States of Montana and Pennsylvania in the United States.

[1] Please note that the information listed in this chart is not exhaustive but instead suggests some of the leading sources that support each of these environmental human rights. For an excellent discussion of these sources as well as others, see "Human Rights and the Environment," Chapter 15 of A. Kiss and D. Shelton, INTERNATIONAL ENVIRONMENTAL LAW (3d ed. 2004).

[2] Treaties are akin to international conventions which are a source of international law. See Statute of the International Court of Justice, June 26, 1945, art. 38(1)(a), 59 Stat. 1031, 1060, T.S. No. 993, http://www.icj-cij.org/icjwww/ibasicdocuments/Basetext/istatute.htm ("international conventions, whether general or particular, establishing rules expressly recognized by the contesting states").

[3] Declarations comprise part of international custom which is a source of international law. See Statute of the International Court of Justice, June 26, 1945, art. 38(1)(b), 59 Stat. 1031, 1060, T.S. No. 993, http://www.icj-cij.org/icjwww/ibasicdocuments/Basetext/istatute.htm ("international custom, as evidence of a general practice accepted as law").

[4] Resolutions, decisions, and reports are evidence of international custom which is a source of international law. See Statute of the International Court of Justice, June 26, 1945, art. 38(1)(b), 59 Stat. 1031, 1060, T.S. No. 993, http://www.icj-cij.org/icjwww/ibasicdocuments/Basetext/istatute.htm ("international custom, as evidence of a general practice accepted as law"). Please note that many of the institutions included in this table annually repeat and at times expand the scope of these instruments.

[5] Judicial decisions are a source of international law. See Statute of the International Court of Justice, June 26, 1945, art. 38(1)(b), 59 Stat. 1031, 1060, T.S. No. 993, http://www.icj-cij.org/icjwww/ibasicdocuments/Basetext/istatute.htm ("judicial decisions . . . as subsidiary means for the determination of rules of law").

[6] When a sufficient number of domestic constitutions recognize the same right, then the right can be considered a general principle of law recognized by civilized nations which is a source of international law. See Statute of the International Court of Justice, June 26, 1945, art. 38(1)(C), 59 Stat. 1031, 1060, T.S. No. 993, http://www.icj-cij.org/icjwww/ibasicdocuments/Basetext/istatute.htm ("general practice of law recognized by civilized nations").

RIGHT	TREATY PROVISIONS	DECLARATION PROVISION	RESOLUTIONS, DECISIONS, AND REPORTS	INTERNATIONAL COURT DECISIONS	DOMESTIC CONSTITUTIONAL PROVISIONS
Environment, cont'd	African Convention on Conservation of Nature and Natural Resources, http://www.dfa.gov.za/for-relations/multilateral/treaties/nature.htm, ("ACCNNR"), art. II. Indigenous and Tribal Peoples Convention, International Labor Convention No. 169 (1989) http://www.ilolex.ilo.ch:1567/cgi_lex/convde.pl?C169 ("ILO 169"), arts. 4(1), 7(3), 7(4), 15, and 16.	Draft Declaration of Principles on Human Rights and the Environment, Annex I to Final Report, Human Rights and the Environment, prepared by Mrs. Fatma Zohra Ksentini, Special Rapporteur on Human Rights and the Environment, UN Doc. E/CN.4/Sub.2/1994/9 (1994), available at http://www.193.194.138.190/Huridocda/Huridoca.nsf/TestFrame/eeab2b6937bccaa18025675c005779c3?Opendocument.	Report of the Secretary-General, Human rights and the environment as part of sustainable development, UN Doc. E/CN.4/2004/87 (Feb. 6, 2004), available at http://www.unhchr.ch/Huridocda/Huridoca.nsf/(Symbol)/E.CN.4.2004.87.En?Opendocument. "Adverse effects of the illicit movement and dumping of toxic and dangerous products and wastes on the enjoyment of human rights," Resolution 2004/17, U.N. CHR, 60th Session,		Part III ("Developments at the National Level") of the Report of the Secretary-General, Human rights and the environment as part of sustainable development, UN Doc. E/CN.4/2005/96 (Jan. 19, 2005), available at http://www.ohchr.org/english/bodies/chr/docs/61chr/E.CN.4.2005.96.doc. Report of the Secretary-General, Human rights and the environment as part of sustainable development, UN Doc. E/CN.4/2004/87 (Feb. 6, 2004),

Exercising Environmental Human Rights and Remedies • 79

RIGHT	TREATY PROVISIONS	DECLARATION PROVISION	RESOLUTIONS, DECISIONS, AND REPORTS	INTERNATIONAL COURT DECISIONS	DOMESTIC CONSTITUTIONAL PROVISIONS
Environment, cont'd	African Charter on Human and Peoples' Rights, http://www.achpr.org/africancharter.doc ("ACHPR"), art. 24. Charter of Fundamental Rights of the European Union, http://www.europarl.eu.int/charter/pdf/text_en.pdf, ("EU Charter"), art. 37.	Draft Principles Relating to the Human Rights Conduct of Companies, Annex I to *Principles relating to the human rights conduct of companies*, UN Doc. E/CN.4/Sub.2/2000/WG.2/WP.1 (2000), Annex 1, ¶¶ 33–35.	at 2, U.N. Doc. E/CN.4/2004/L.18 (2004), available at http://ap.ohchr.org/documents/E/CHR/resolutions/E-CN_4-RES-2004-17.doc (promoting the right to life and health in the prevention of illicit movement and dumping of environmentally harmful toxics). *n.b.* the Special Rapporteur usually submits this report annually. "Adverse effects of the illicit movement and dumping of toxic and dangerous products and wastes on the enjoyment of		*available at* http://www.unhchr.ch/Huridocda/Huridoca.nsf/(Symbol)/E.CN.4.2004.87.En?Opendocument.

RIGHT	TREATY PROVISIONS	DECLARATION PROVISION	RESOLUTIONS, DECISIONS, AND REPORTS	INTERNATIONAL COURT DECISIONS	DOMESTIC CONSTITUTIONAL PROVISIONS
Environment, cont'd			human rights," Resolution 2003/20, UN Doc. No. E/CN.4/RES/2003/20, available at http://www.unhchr.ch/Huridocda/docansf/(Symbol)/E.CN.4.RES.2003.20.En?Opendocument. "Adverse effects of the illicit movement and dumping of toxic and dangerous products and wastes on the enjoyment of human rights," Report of the Special Rapporteur, UN Doc. No. E/CN.4/2004/46/Add.1 and Corr.1,		

RIGHT	TREATY PROVISIONS	DECLARATION PROVISION	RESOLUTIONS, DECISIONS, AND REPORTS	INTERNATIONAL COURT DECISIONS	DOMESTIC CONSTITUTIONAL PROVISIONS
Environment, cont'd			available at http://www.unhchr.ch/Huridocda/Huridoca.nsf/(Symbol)/E.CN.4.2004.46.Add.1+and+Corr.1.En?Opendocument. Report of the Sessional Working Group on the Working Methods and Activities of Transnational Corporations on its Fifth Session, U.N. Subcommission on the Promotion and Protection of Human Rights, U.N. Doc. E/CN.4/Sub.2/2003/13 (2003), at ¶ 32, available at http://www.unhchr.ch/Huridocda/Huridoca.nsf/(Symbol)/E.CN.4.Sub.2.2003.13.En?Opendocument.		

RIGHT	TREATY PROVISIONS	DECLARATION PROVISION	RESOLUTIONS, DECISIONS, AND REPORTS	INTERNATIONAL COURT DECISIONS	DOMESTIC CONSTITUTIONAL PROVISIONS
Environment, cont'd			Concluding observations of the Committee on Economic, Social and Cultural Rights: Ecuador, U.N. Doc. E/C.12/1/Add.100 (June7, 2004), ¶ 12, available at http://www.unhchr.ch/tbs/doc.nsf/(Symbol)/E.C.12.1.Add.100.En?Opendocument (voicing concerns "about the negative health and environmental impacts of natural resource extracting companiesí activities" on the exercise of land and culture rights by the affected indigenous communities and the equilibrium of the ecosystem).		

RIGHT	TREATY PROVISIONS	DECLARATION PROVISION	RESOLUTIONS, DECISIONS, AND REPORTS	INTERNATIONAL COURT DECISIONS	DOMESTIC CONSTITUTIONAL PROVISIONS
Environment, cont'd			World Health Organization, Human Rights, Health & Environmental Protection: Linkages in Law & Practice by Dinah Shelton, *available at* http://www.who.int/hhr/information/en/Series_1%20%20Human Rights_Health_Environmental%20Protection_Shelton.pdf. *Final Report, Human Rights and the Environment,* prepared by Mrs. Fatma Zohra Ksentini, Special Rapporteur on Human Rights and the Environment,		

RIGHT	TREATY PROVISIONS	DECLARATION PROVISION	RESOLUTIONS, DECISIONS, AND REPORTS	INTERNATIONAL COURT DECISIONS	DOMESTIC CONSTITUTIONAL PROVISIONS
Environment cont'd			UN Doc. E/CN.4/Sub.2/1994/9 (1994), available at http://www.193.194.138.190/Huridoca/Huridoca.nsf/TestFrame/eeab2b6937bccaa1802567 5c005779c3?Opendocument. The Realization of Economic, Social and Cultural Rights: The Question of Transnational Corporations, Report of the Sessional Working Group on the Working Methods and Activities of Transnational Corporations on its First Session. UN Doc. E/CN.4/Sub.2/1999/9		

RIGHT	TREATY PROVISIONS	DECLARATION PROVISION	RESOLUTIONS, DECISIONS, AND REPORTS	INTERNATIONAL COURT DECISIONS	DOMESTIC CONSTITUTIONAL PROVISIONS
Environment cont'd			(1999) at ¶ 9(6) (calling on future work to focus on the impacts of transnational corporations on "the right to healthy environment"). *Promotion of a democratic and equitable international order*, Res. 2001/65. U.N. Comm'n on Hum. Rts. 57th Sess., para. 3k. n.b. The UN Commission on Human Rights usually passes this resolution annually.		

RIGHT	TREATY PROVISIONS	DECLARATION PROVISION	RESOLUTIONS, DECISIONS, AND REPORTS	INTERNATIONAL COURT DECISIONS	DOMESTIC CONSTITUTIONAL PROVISIONS
Water	International Covenant on Economic, Social and Cultural Rights, http://www.unhchr.ch/html/menu3/b/a_cescr.htm, ("ICESCR"), art. 11(1), 12(1). Convention on the Elimination of Discrimination Against Women, unhchr.ch/html/menu3/b/elcedaw.htm ("CEDAW"), art. 14(2)(h). Convention on the Rights of the Child, http://www.unhchr.ch/html/menu3/b/k2crc.htm ("CRC"), art. 24(2)(c). General Comment No. 15, note 5.	Universal Declaration of Human Rights http://www.un.org/Overview/rights.html ("UDHR"), arts. 1, 3 (considered in General Comment 15 along with ICESCR arts. 11 and a right to water).	*The Right to Water*, UN Committee on Economic, Social and Cultural Rights ("CESCR") General Comment 15. UN Doc. E/C.12/2002/11 (2002), http://www.unhchr.ch/html/menu2/6/gc15.doc ("General Comment No. 15") (interpreting IESCR arts. 11 and 12 to include a right to water). Resolution 2004/6, UN Sub-Commission on the Promotion and Protection of Human Rights, Fifty-Sixth Session, at 21, UN Doc.		*See generally* Robert L. Maddex, CONSTITUTIONS OF THE WORLD (Congressional Quarterly Inc. (2001) (including constitutions of the world that may contain this right).

RIGHT	TREATY PROVISIONS	DECLARATION PROVISION	RESOLUTIONS, DECISIONS, AND REPORTS	INTERNATIONAL COURT DECISIONS	DOMESTIC CONSTITUTIONAL PROVISIONS
Water cont'd			E/CN.4/Sub.2/2004/L.20 (2004), Resolution 2003/1, in Report of the Sub-Commission on the Promotion and Protection of Human Rights on its Fifty-Fifth Session, U.N. Sub-Commission on the Promotion and Protection of Human Rights, 55th Sess., at 1, U.N. Doc. E/CN.4/2004/2, E/CN.4/Sub.2/2003/43 (2003), at 17–18, available at http://www.unhchr.ch/Huridocda/Huridoca.nsf/(Symbol)/E.CN.4.2004.2.E.CN.4.		

RIGHT	TREATY PROVISIONS	DECLARATION PROVISION	RESOLUTIONS, DECISIONS, AND REPORTS	INTERNATIONAL COURT DECISIONS	DOMESTIC CONSTITUTIONAL PROVISIONS
Water cont'd			Sub.2.2003.43.En? Opendocument. World Health Organization, Issue No. 3, The Right to Water, available at http://www.who.int/docstore/water_sanitation_health/Documents/righttowater/righttowater.htm		

RIGHT	TREATY PROVISIONS	DECLARATION PROVISION	RESOLUTIONS, DECISIONS, AND REPORTS	INTERNATIONAL COURT DECISIONS	DOMESTIC CONSTITUTIONAL PROVISIONS
Life	ICCPR, art. 6. CRC, art. 6. ACHR, art. 4. ECHR, art. 2. EU Charter, art. 2. ACHPR, art. 4.	UDHR, art. 3. AD, art. I.	See Adverse Effects from Toxics Resolution, *supra*.	*Huorani v. Ecuador*, Report on the Situation of Human Rights in Ecuador, Inter-Am. C.H.R., OEA/ser. L./V./II.96, doc. 10 rev. 1 (Apr. 24, 1997), at http://www.cidh.oas.org/countryrep/ecuador-eng/index%20-%20ecuador.htm. *Yanomami*, Res. 12/85, Case 7615, Inter-Am. C.H.R., OEA/ser. L./V./II.66, doc. 10 rev. 1 (Mar. 5, 1985), *reprinted in* 1985 Inter-Am. Y.B. on H.R. (Inter-Am. C.H.R.) 264, 272–76, available at http://www/cidhoas.org/Indigenas/Annex1.htm. Communication No.67/1980 *EHP v. Canada*, 2 Selected Decisions of the Human Rights Committee 20 (1990).	*See generally* Robert L. Maddex, CONSTITUTIONS OF THE WORLD (Congressional Quarterly Inc. (2001)) (including constitutions of the world that may contain this right).

RIGHT	TREATY PROVISIONS	DECLARATION PROVISION	RESOLUTIONS, DECISIONS, AND REPORTS	INTERNATIONAL COURT DECISIONS	DOMESTIC CONSTITUTIONAL PROVISIONS
Health	European Social Charter, http://conventions.coe.int/Treaty/EN/cadreListeTraites.htm, art. 11. ICESCR, art. 12. CRC, art. 24. ACHPR, art. 16. EU Charter, art. 35. PSS, art. 10.	UDHR, art. 25. Declaration of the Rights of the Child, http://www.unhchr.ch/html/menu3/b/k2crc.htm ("DRC"), Principle 2. American Declaration on the Rights and Duties of Man, http://www.cidh.org/Basicos/basic2.htm ("AD"), art. XI.	The Right to the Highest Attainable Standard of Health, CESCR General Comment 14. UN Doc. E/C.12/2000/4 (2000), at, inter alia, ¶¶ 4, 15, http://193.194.138.190/tbs/doc.nsf/(symbol)/E.C.12.2000.4.+CESCR+General+comment+14.En?OpenDocument. Resolution 2004/27, U.N. CHR, 60th Session, at 3, U.N. Doc. E/CN.4/2004/L.41 (2004), available at http://ap.ohchr.org/documents/E/CHR/resolutions/E-CN_4-RES-2004-27.doc. CRC Concluding Observations: each year, the CRC prepares several concluding	Yanomami v. Brazil, Res. 12/85, Case 7615, Inter-Am. C.H.R., OEA/ser. L./V/II.66, doc. 10 rev. 1 (Mar. 5, 1985), reprinted in 1985 Inter-Am. Y.B. on H.R. (Inter-Am. C.H.R.) 264, , 272–76 available at http://www/cidhoas.org/Indigenas/Annex1.htm. Communications 25/89, 47/90, 56/91, 100/93 against Zaire, African Commission on Human and Peoples' Rights.	See generally Robert L. Maddex, CONSTITUTIONS OF THE WORLD (Congressional Quarterly Inc. (2001)) (including constitutions of the world that may contain this right).

RIGHT	TREATY PROVISIONS	DECLARATION PROVISION	RESOLUTIONS, DECISIONS, AND REPORTS	INTERNATIONAL COURT DECISIONS	DOMESTIC CONSTITUTIONAL PROVISIONS
Health cont'd			observations that call for the country in question to combat environmental degradation as one means for assuring the health of its children. *See e.g.*, CRC Concluding observations: Jamaica (April 7, 2003), U.N. Doc. CRC/C/15/Add.210, *available at* http://www.unhchr.ch/tbs/doc.nsf/(Symbol)/CRC.C.15.Add.210.En?OpenDocument; CRC Concluding observations on the second periodic report of the Czech Republic, U.N. Doc. CRC/C/15/ Add.201 (Jan. 31, 2003), *available at* http://www.unhchr.ch/html/menu2/6/crc/doc/co/co-czech-2.pdf.		

RIGHT	TREATY PROVISIONS	DECLARATION PROVISION	RESOLUTIONS, DECISIONS, AND REPORTS	INTERNATIONAL COURT DECISIONS	DOMESTIC CONSTITUTIONAL PROVISIONS
Health cont'd			See Adverse Effects from Toxics Resolution, supra.		
Privacy; Inviolability of Home and Family cont'd	European Convention for the Protection of Human Rights, http://conventions.cor.int/Treaty/EN/cadrelistetraites.htm, art. 8. African Charter on the Rights and Welfare of the Child, http://www1.umn.edu/hhumanrts/africa/afchild.htm, art. 10. ICCPR, art. 17. CRC, art. 16. ACHR, EU Charter, art. 7	UDHR, art. 12. AD, arts. IX, X.	Resolution 2003/17, in Report of the Sub-Commission on the Promotion and Protection of Human Rights on its Fifty-Fifth Session, U.N. Sub-Commission on the Promotion and Protection of Human Rights, 55th Sess., at 17, U.N. Doc. E/CN.4/2004/2, E/CN.4/Sub.2/2003/43 (2003), at 55, *available at* http://www.unhchr.ch/Huridocda/Huridoca.nsf/(Symbol)/E.CN.4.2004.2.E.CN.4.Sub.2.2003.43.En?Opendocument (forced evictions).	*Lopez Ostra v. Spain*, App. No. 16798/90, 20 Eur. H.R. Rep. 277 (Judgment of Dec. 4, 1994); *Guerra and Others v. Italy* (Judgment of Feb. 19, 1998); *Hatton & Others v. U. K.*, Application No. 36022/97 (Judgment of Feb. 10, 2001), http://www.echr.coe.int/.	*See generally* Robert L. Maddex, CONSTITUTIONS OF THE WORLD (Congressional Quarterly Inc. (2001)) (including constitutions of the world that may contain this right).

RIGHT	TREATY PROVISIONS	DECLARATION PROVISION	RESOLUTIONS, DECISIONS, AND REPORTS	INTERNATIONAL COURT DECISIONS	DOMESTIC CONSTITUTIONAL PROVISIONS
Residence	International Convention on Civil and Political Rights, http://www.unhchr.ch/html/menu3/b/a_ccpr.htm ("ICCPR"), art. 12. American Convention on Human Rights, http://www.cigh.org/Basicos/basic3.htm ("ACHR"), art. 22. ACHPR, art. 12. EU Charter, art. 45.	AD, art. VIII.			*See generally* Robert L. Maddex, Constitutions of the World (Congressional Quarterly Inc. (2001)) (including constitutions of the world that may contain this right).
Food	ICESCR, art. 11. CRC, art. 24. ACHR, art. 12 CEDAW, art. 14	UDHR, art. 25. AD, art. XI.	*Economic, Social and Cultural Rights: The Right to Food*, Report submitted by the Special Rapporteur on the Right to Food, UN Doc. E/CN.4/2003/54		*See generally* Robert L. Maddex, Constitutions of the World (Congressional Quarterly Inc. (2001)) (including constitutions of the world that may contain this right).

RIGHT	TREATY PROVISIONS	DECLARATION PROVISION	RESOLUTIONS, DECISIONS, AND REPORTS	INTERNATIONAL COURT DECISIONS	DOMESTIC CONSTITUTIONAL PROVISIONS
Food cont'd			(Jan. 10, 2003) available at http://www.unhchr.ch/Huridocda/Huridoca.nsf/(Symbol)/E.CN.4.2003.54.En?Opendocument (focusing as well on the right to water). Resolution 2004/19, U.N. CHR, 60th Session, at 2, U.N. Doc. E/CN.4/2004/L.24 (2004), available at http://ap.ohchr.org/documents/E/CHR/resolutions/E-CN_4-RES-2004-19.doc. Resolution 2003/9, in Report of the Sub-Commission on the Promotion and Protection of Human Rights on its Fifty-Fifth		

RIGHT	TREATY PROVISIONS	DECLARATION PROVISION	RESOLUTIONS, DECISIONS, AND REPORTS	INTERNATIONAL COURT DECISIONS	DOMESTIC CONSTITUTIONAL PROVISIONS
Food cont'd			Session, U.N. Sub-Commission on the Promotion and Protection of Human Rights, 55th Sess., at 17, U.N. Doc. E/CN.4/2004/2, E/CN.4/Sub.2/2003/43 (2003), at 36, *available at* http://www.unhchr.ch/Huridocda/Huridoca.nsf/(Symbol)/E.CN.4.2004.2.E.CN.4.Sub.2.2003.43.En?Opendocument. The Right to Adequate Food, CESCR General Comment 12, UN Doc. E/C.12/1999/5, (1999). http://www.unhchr.ch/tbs/doc.nsf.Johannesburg Summit Plan of Implementation, Chptr. X (2002).		

RIGHT	TREATY PROVISIONS	DECLARATION PROVISION	RESOLUTIONS, DECISIONS, AND REPORTS	INTERNATIONAL COURT DECISIONS	DOMESTIC CONSTITUTIONAL PROVISIONS
Sustenance	ICESCR, art. 11. CRC, art. 27. CEDAW, art. 14	UDHR, art. 25. DRC, Principle 6.			See generally Robert L. Maddex, CONSTITUTIONS OF THE WORLD (Congressional Quarterly Inc. (2001)) (including constitutions of the world that may contain this right).
Property	ILO 169, arts. 4(1), 7(3), 7(4), 15, and 16. ACHR, art. 21. ECHR, Protocol I, art. 1. EU Charter, art. 17.	UDHR, art.17. AD, art. XXIII.		*Pialopoulos and Others v. Greece*, Feb. 15, 2001 (Eur. Ct. Hum. Rts., 2001 Reports of Judgments and Decisions). *The Mayagna (Sumo) Awas Tingni Community Case*, Inter-Am. Ct. H.R., Case No. 11.557 (filed Oct. 2, 1995), Judgment of Feb. 1, 2000, available at http://www1.umn.edu/humanrts/iachr/series_D.html.	See generally Robert L. Maddex, CONSTITUTIONS OF THE WORLD (Congressional Quarterly Inc. (2001)) (including constitutions of the world that may contain this right).

RIGHT	TREATY PROVISIONS	DECLARATION PROVISION	RESOLUTIONS, DECISIONS, AND REPORTS	INTERNATIONAL COURT DECISIONS	DOMESTIC CONSTITUTIONAL PROVISIONS
Information	Aarhus Convention on Access to Information, Public Participation in Decision-Making and Access to Justice in Environmental Matters, http://www.unece.org/env/pp/documents/cep43e.pdf ("Aarhus Convention"), arts. 4–5. United Nations Framework Convention on Climate Change, http://www.unfccc.int/resource/docs/convkp/conveng.pdf ("UNFCCC"), art. 6. Convention on Biological Diversity, http://www.biodiv.org/doc/legal/cbd-en.pdf ("CBD"), art. 13.	Rio Declaration on Environment and Development, UN Doc. A/CONF.151/26, Annex I, http://www.un.org/documents/ga/conf151/aconf15126-1annex1.htm ("Rio Declaration"), Principle 10. Johannesburg Declaration on Sustainable Development, para. 25 (2002). UDHR, art. 21 AD, arts. IV, XXIV.	Johannesburg Summit Plan of Implementation, para. 128 (2002).	Huorani v. Ecuador, Report on the Situation of Human Rights in Ecuador, Inter-Am. C.H.R., OEA/ser. L/V/II.96, doc. 10 rev. 1 (Apr. 24, 1997), at http://www.cidh.oas.org/countryrep/ecuador-eng/index%20-%20ecuador.htm.	See generally Robert L. Maddex, CONSTITUTIONS OF THE WORLD (Congressional Quarterly Inc. (2001)) (including constitutions of the world that may contain this right).

RIGHT	TREATY PROVISIONS	DECLARATION PROVISION	RESOLUTIONS, DECISIONS, AND REPORTS	INTERNATIONAL COURT DECISIONS	DOMESTIC CONSTITUTIONAL PROVISIONS
Information cont'd	Rotterdam Convention on Prior Informed Consent Procedure for Certain Hazardous Chemicals and Pesticides in International Trade, http://www.pic.int ("PIC"), art. 15. ICCPR, art. 19. ACHR, art. 13. ACHPR, art. 9. EU Charter, arts. 11, 42. Protocol on Strategic Environ-mental Assess-ment to the Convention on Environmental Impact Assessment in a Transboundary Context, available at http://www.unece.org/env/eia/documents/protocolenglish.pdf ("Sea"), art. 8. Protocol on Pollutant Release and Transfer Reg-isters, http://www.				

RIGHT	TREATY PROVISIONS	DECLARATION PROVISION	RESOLUTIONS, DECISIONS, AND REPORTS	INTERNATIONAL COURT DECISIONS	DOMESTIC CONSTITUTIONAL PROVISIONS
Information cont'd	unecer.org/env/pp/ prtr/docs/PRTR %20 Protocol %20 English.pdf ("PRTR"), art.11.				
Public Participation	United Nations Convention to Combat Desertification, http://www. unccd/irt/convention/ text/co nvention. php, arts. 3, 10, 13, 14, 19, 25,UNFCCC, art. 4 CBD, art. 14 ICCPR, art. 19. EU Charter, arts. 41, 44. Aarhus Convention, art. 6–8. ACHR, art. 23. ACHPR, arts. 9, 13. SEA, art. 8. PRTR, art. 13.	UDHR, art 21 Rio Declaration, Principle 10. AD, art. XX.		*Huorani v. Ecuador,* Report on the Situation of Human Rights in Ecuador, Inter-Am. C.H.R., OEA/ser. L./V./II.96, doc. 10 rev. 1 (Apr. 24, (1997), *available at* http://www.cidh.oas. org/countryrep/ ecuador-eng/index %20-%20ecuador. htm.	*See generally* Robert L. Maddex, CONSTITUTIONS OF THE WORLD (Congressional Quarterly Inc. (2001) (including constitutions of the world that may contain this right).

RIGHT	TREATY PROVISIONS	DECLARATION PROVISION	RESOLUTIONS, DECISIONS, AND REPORTS	INTERNATIONAL COURT DECISIONS	DOMESTIC CONSTITUTIONAL PROVISIONS
Expression; Association	ICCPR, arts. 19, 22. CRC, art. 13, 15. ACHR, arts. 13, 16. ECHR, arts. 10, 11. ACHPR, arts. 9, 10. ACRNC, arts. 7, 8. EU Charter, arts. 11, 12.	UDHR, arts. 19, 20. AD, arts. IV, XXII.	Report of the Special Rapporteur, The Right to Freedom of Opinion and Expression, U.N. Doc. E/CN.4/2004/62, ¶ 61, available at http://www.unhchr.ch/Huridocda/Huridoca.nsf/(Symbol)/E.CN.4.2004.62.En?Opendocument (conveying appreciation "projects designed to facilitate monitoring of the implementation of the right to information, . . . some [of which] focus . . . on . . . environmental information/sustainable development fields").		See generally Robert L. Maddex, CONSTITUTIONS OF THE WORLD (Congressional Quarterly Inc. (2001)) (including constitutions of the world that may contain this right).

RIGHT	TREATY PROVISIONS	DECLARATION PROVISION	RESOLUTIONS, DECISIONS, AND REPORTS	INTERNATIONAL COURT DECISIONS	DOMESTIC CONSTITUTIONAL PROVISIONS
Vote	ICCPR, art. 25. ACHPR, art. 13. EU Charter, arts. 39, 40. ACHR, art. 23. ECHR, Protocol I, art. 3.	UDHR, art. 21. AD, art. XXXIII.		Chassagnou and Others v. France, April 29, 1999 (Eur. Ct. Hum. Rts., 1999-III Reports of Judgments and Decisions). Bladet Tromsø et Stensaas v. Norway, May 20, 1999 (Eur. Ct. Hum. Rts., 1999-III Reports of Judgments and Decisions).	See generally Robert L. Maddex, CONSTITUTIONS OF THE WORLD (Congressional Quarterly Inc. (2001)) (including constitutions of the world that may contain this right).
Liberty or Security of Person	ICCPR, art. 9. CRC, art. 37. ACHR, art. 7. ECHR, art. 5. EU Charter, art. 6. ACHPR, art. 6.	UDHR, art. 3. AD, art. I.	Concluding observations of the Human Rights Committee: Russian Federation, U.N. Doc. CCPR/CO/ 79/RUS, available at http://www.unhchr.ch/tbs/doc.nsf/0/622c5ddc8c476dc4c1256e0c003c9758?Opendocument (expressing concern about the conviction of environmental activists on treason charges).		See generally Robert L. Maddex, CONSTITUTIONS OF THE WORLD (Congressional Quarterly Inc. (2001)) (including constitutions of the world that may contain this right).

RIGHT	TREATY PROVISIONS	DECLARATION PROVISION	RESOLUTIONS, DECISIONS, AND REPORTS	INTERNATIONAL COURT DECISIONS	DOMESTIC CONSTITUTIONAL PROVISIONS
Humane Treatment	ICCPR, art. 7. CRC, art. 37. ACHR, art. 5. ACHPR, art. 4. ECHR, art. 3.	UDHR, art. 5. DRC, Principle 9. AD, art. I.	Promotion and Protection of Human Rights Defenders, U.N. Doc. E/CN.4/2003/104/Add.1, appendix (Feb. 20, 2003), available at http://www.unhchr.ch/Huridocda/Huridoca.nsf/0/69f5d61900b8f5b7c1256cf4004eae6c?Opendocument (restating that the ambit of the mandate for the Special Rapporteur on Human Right Defenders was "broad enough to include . . . those defending the right to a healthy environment [or] promoting the rights of indigenous peoples" (E/CN.4/2003/104/Add.1, appendix).		*See generally* Robert L. Maddex, CONSTITUTIONS OF THE WORLD (Congressional Quarterly Inc. (2001)) (including constitutions of the world that may contain this right).

RIGHT	TREATY PROVISIONS	DECLARATION PROVISION	RESOLUTIONS, DECISIONS, AND REPORTS	INTERNATIONAL COURT DECISIONS	DOMESTIC CONSTITUTIONAL PROVISIONS
Equal Protection	Convention on the Elimination of Racial Discrimination, http://www.unhchr.ch/html/menu3/b/d_icerd.htm, at preamble, art. 5. CEDAW, preamble. ICCPR, art. 26. ACHR, art. 24. EU Charter, art. 20. ACHPR, art. 3.	Declaration on the Elimination of Racial Discrimination http://www.unhchr.ch/html/menu3/b/9.htm, at art. 7. Declaration of the Elimination of Discrimination Against Women, http://www.unhchr.ch/html/menu3/b.21.htm, at pmble. UDHR, art. 7. AD, art. II.	UN Committee on the Elimination of Discrimination Against Women ("CEDAW Comm."): Summaries of Concluding Observations GA Res. 34/180, UN GAOR, Supp. No. 46, at 193, UN Doc. A/34/180 (1981), http://www.un.org/documents/ga/res/34/a34res180.pdf; Concluding Observations on Romania, CEDAW Comm., UN Doc. CEDAW/C/2000/II/Add.7	*The Lubicon Lake Band v. Canada*, Human Rights Committee, Communication No. 167/1984, CCPR/C/38/D/167/1984 (28 Mar. 1990), *available at* http://unhchr.ch/tbs/doc.nsf/(Symbol)/c3166b134879a76fc125696.	*See generally* Robert L. Maddex, CONSTITUTIONS OF THE WORLD (Congressional Quarterly Inc. (2001)) (including constitutions of the world that may contain this right).

RIGHT	TREATY PROVISIONS	DECLARATION PROVISION	RESOLUTIONS, DECISIONS, AND REPORTS	INTERNATIONAL COURT DECISIONS	DOMESTIC CONSTITUTIONAL PROVISIONS
Equal Protection cont'd			at ¶ 38 (2000), http://www.un.org/womenwatch/daw/cedaw/committee.htm.		
Culture	ICCPR, art. 27 ICESCR, art. 15. CRC, art. 30. ACHR, art. 14. EU Charter, art. 22. ACHPR, art. 22.	UDHR, art. 27. AD, art. XIII.	Resolution 2003/14, in Report of the Sub-Commission on the Promotion and Protection of Human Rights on its Fifty-Fifth Session, U.N. Sub-Commission on the Promotion and Protection of Human Rights, 55th Sess., at 17, U.N. Doc. E/CN.4/2004/2, E/CN.4/Sub.2/2003/43 (2003), at 47, available at http://www.unhchr.ch/Huridocda/Huridoca.nsf/(Symbol)/E.CN.4.2004.2.E.CN.4.Sub.2.2003.43.En?Opendocument.	The Lubicon Lake Band v. Canada, Human Rights Committee, Communication No. 167/1984, CCPR/C/38/D/167/1984 (28 Mar. 1990), available at http://unhchr.ch/tbs/doc.nsf/(Symbol)/c3166b134879a76fc125696; Kitok v. Sweden, Communication No. 197/1985, UN Doc. CCPR/7/Add. 1 at 442; Apirana Mahuika et al. v. New Zealand, Communication No. 547/1992, UN Doc. CCPR/6/70/D/547/1993.	See generally Robert L. Maddex, CONSTITUTIONS OF THE WORLD (Congressional Quarterly Inc. (2001)) (including constitutions of the world that may contain this right).

RIGHT	TREATY PROVISIONS	DECLARATION PROVISION	RESOLUTIONS, DECISIONS, AND REPORTS	INTERNATIONAL COURT DECISIONS	DOMESTIC CONSTITUTIONAL PROVISIONS
Indigenous Peoples			Indigenous Peoples' Permanent Sovereignty over Natural Resources, Preliminary Report of the Special Rapporteur, Erica-Irene A. Daes, 55th Session at 1, U.N. Doc. E/CN.4/Sub.2/2003/20 (2003) at 2, available at http://www.unhchr.ch/Huridocda/Huridoca.nsf/(Symbol)/E.CN.4.Sub.2.2003.20.En?Opendocument. Concluding observations of the Human Rights Committee: Suriname. (April 4, 2004), available at http://www.unhchr.ch/tbs/doc.nsf/		

RIGHT	TREATY PROVISIONS	DECLARATION PROVISION	RESOLUTIONS, DECISIONS, AND REPORTS	INTERNATIONAL COURT DECISIONS	DOMESTIC CONSTITUTIONAL PROVISIONS
Indigenous Peoples cont'd			(Symbol)/CCPR.CO.80.SUR.En?Opendocument, ¶ 21 (noting that release of mercury into the environment in the vicinity of indigenous communities "continues to threaten the life, health, and environment of indigenous and tribal peoples").		

Table B: Jurisdiction of Human Rights Body Over the Claim

HUMAN RIGHTS BODIES/PROCESSES	INSTRUMENT CREATING BODY/PROCESS	ENVIRONMENTAL HUMAN RIGHTS	NATION-STATES SUBJECT TO BODY OR TREATY[1]
UN Human Rights Committee http://www.unhchr.ch/html/menu2/6/hrc.htm.	International Covenant on Civil and Political Rights, Dec. 16, 1966, 999 U.N.T.S. 171 http://www.unhchr.ch/html/menu3/b/a_ccpr.htm.	Association Equal protection Freedom from inhumane treatment Information Inviolability of home and family Liberty and security of person Life Privacy	See http://www.unhchr.ch/tbs/doc.nsf/Statusfrset?OpenFrameSet

[1] An "(s)" after the name of the nation-state listed in the table indictes that the state is only a signatory to the treaty and not yet a state party. All other state names listed are parties to the treaty. For a comprehensive listing of ratifications of the principle human rights treaties, *see* Status of Ratifications of the Principle International Human Rights Treaties, at http://193.194.138.190/pdf/report.pdf.

HUMAN RIGHTS BODIES/PROCESSES	INSTRUMENT CREATING BODY/PROCESS	ENVIRONMENTAL HUMAN RIGHTS	NATION-STATES SUBJECT TO BODY OR TREATY
UN Human Rights Committee, cont'd		Property	See http://www.unhchr.ch/tbs/doc.nsf/Statusfrset?OpenFrameSet
		Public participation	
		Residence	
		Speech or expression	
		Vote	
UN Committee on Economic, Social and Cultural Rights http://www.unhchr.ch/html/menu2/6/cescr.htm.	International Covenant on Economic, Social and Cultural Rights, Dec. 16, 1966, 993 U.N.T.S. 3 http://www.unhchr.ch/html/menu3/b/a_cescr.htm.	Culture	See http://www.unhchr.ch/tbs/doc.nsf/Statusfrset?OpenFrameSet
		Food	
		Health	
		Housing	
		Sustenance	
		Water	

HUMAN RIGHTS BODIES/PROCESSES	INSTRUMENT CREATING BODY/PROCESS	ENVIRONMENTAL HUMAN RIGHTS	NATION-STATES SUBJECT TO BODY OR TREATY
UN Committee on the Elimination of Racial Discrimination http://www.unhchr.ch/html/menu2/6/cerd.htm.	International Convention on the Elimination of All Forms of Racial Discrimination, Mar. 7, 1966, 660 U.N.T.S. 195 http://www.unhchr.ch/html/menu3/b/d_icerd.htm.	Environmental human rights deprived on the basis of race	See http://www.unhchr.ch/tbs/doc.nsf/Statusfrset?OpenFrameSet
UN Committee on the Elimination of Discrimination against Women http://www.unhchr.ch/html/menu2/6/cedw.htm.	Convention on the Elimination of Discrimination against Women http://www.unhchr.ch/html/menu3/b/e1cedaw.htm.	Environmental human rights deprived on the basis of gender	See http://www.unhchr.ch/tbs/doc.nsf/Statusfrset?OpenFrameSet
Convention on the Rights of the Child http://www.unhchr.ch/html/menu2/6/crc.htm.	Convention on the Rights of the Child, Nov. 20, 1989, 1577 U.N.T.S. 3 http://www.unhchr.ch/html/menu3/b/k2crc.htm.	Environmental human rights deprived of children	See http://www.unhchr.ch/tbs/doc.nsf/Statusfrset?OpenFrameSet

HUMAN RIGHTS BODIES/PROCESSES	INSTRUMENT CREATING BODY/PROCESS	ENVIRONMENTAL HUMAN RIGHTS	NATION-STATES SUBJECT TO BODY OR TREATY
UN Permanent Forum on Indigenous Issues http://www.unhchr.ch/indigenous/forum.htm.	UN ECOSOC Resolution 2000/22 http://www.193.194.138.190/huridocda/huridoca.nsf/(Symbol)/E.RES 2000.22.En?Opendocument.	Environmental human rights deprived of indigenous peoples. See Draft United Nations Declaration on the Rights of Indigenous Peoples, United Nations Sub-Commission on Prevention of Discrimination and Rights of Minorities, 46th Sess., Resolution 1994/45, UN Doc. E/CN.4/Sub.2/1994/56 (1994), http://www.unhchr.ch/huridocda/huridoca.nsf/2848af408d01ec0ac1256609004e770b/e4fc6deeafb3b06c802566cf003bea67?OpenDocument#res45. (outlining those rights).	All current United Nations member states, http://www.un.org/Overview/unmember.html.

HUMAN RIGHTS BODIES/PROCESSES	INSTRUMENT CREATING BODY/PROCESS	ENVIRONMENTAL HUMAN RIGHTS	NATION-STATES SUBJECT TO BODY OR TREATY
UN Human Rights Special Rapporteurs http://www.unhchr.ch/html/menu2/7/b/tm.htm. —Special Rapporteur on the right of everyone to the enjoyment of the highest attainable standard of physical and mental health http://www.unhchr.ch/html/menu2/7/b/mmen.htm. —Special Rapporteur of the Commission on Human Rights on the situation of human rights and fundamental freedoms of indigenous people http://www.unhchr.ch/html/menu2/7/b/mindp.htm.	Various resolutions of the UN Commission on Human Rights and UN Sub-Commission on the Promotion and Protection of Human Rights, themselves created pursuant to UN Charter, art 68.	Rights within the scope of the title of the given Rapporteur as further detailed in the resolution creating that Rapporteur's mandate.	All current United Nations member states, http://www.un.org/Overview/unmember.html.

HUMAN RIGHTS BODIES/PROCESSES	INSTRUMENT CREATING BODY/PROCESS	ENVIRONMENTAL HUMAN RIGHTS	NATION-STATES SUBJECT TO BODY OR TREATY
UN Human Rights Special Rapporteurs cont'd —Special Rapporteur of the Commission on Human Rights on the adverse effects of the illicit movement and dumping of toxic and dangerous products and wastes on the enjoyment of human rights http://www.unhchr.ch/html/menu2/7/b/mtow.htm. —Special Rapporteur of the Commission on Human Rights on violence against women, its causes and consequences http://www.unhchr.ch/html/menu2/7/b/mwom.htm.			

HUMAN RIGHTS BODIES/PROCESSES	INSTRUMENT CREATING BODY/PROCESS	ENVIRONMENTAL HUMAN RIGHTS	NATION-STATES SUBJECT TO BODY OR TREATY
UN Human Rights Special Rapporteurs cont'd —Special Rapporteur of the Commission on Human Rights on the independence of judges and lawyers http://www.unhchr.ch/html/menu2/7/b/mijl.htm. —Special Rapporteur of the Commission on Human Rights on the right food http://www.unhchr.ch/html/menu2/7/b/mfood.htm. —Special Representative of the Secretary General on the situation of human rights defenders http://www.unhchr.ch/html/menu2/7/b/mdef.htm.			

HUMAN RIGHTS BODIES/PROCESSES	INSTRUMENT CREATING BODY/PROCESS	ENVIRONMENTAL HUMAN RIGHTS	NATION-STATES SUBJECT TO BODY OR TREATY
UN Human Rights Special Rapporteurs cont'd —Special Representative of the Commission on Human Rights on contemporary forms of racism, racial discrimination, xenophopia and related intolerance http://www.unhchr.ch/html/menu2/7/b/mrad.htm.			
Economic and Social Council 1503 Procedure http://www.unhchr.ch/html/menu2/8/1503.htm.	Procedure for dealing with communications relating to violations of human rights and fundamental freedoms, ECOSOC Resolution 1503, http://www.unhchr.ch/huridocda/huridoca.nsf/(Symbol)/1970.1503.En?Open Document.	Protection from gross and consistent pattern of violations in various areas, including environmental law	All current United Nations member states, http://www.un.org/Overview/unmember.html.

HUMAN RIGHTS BODIES/PROCESSES	INSTRUMENT CREATING BODY/PROCESS	ENVIRONMENTAL HUMAN RIGHTS	NATION-STATES SUBJECT TO BODY OR TREATY
Economic and Social Council 1503 Procedure cont'd	Revised by: Procedure for dealing with communications concerning human rights, ECOSOC Resolution 2000/3, http://www.unhchr.ch/huridocda/huridoca.nsf/(Symbol)E.RES.2000.3.En?Open Document.		All current United Nations member states, http://www.un.org/Overview/unmember.html.
Commission on the Status of Women http://www.un.org/womenwathc/daw/csw/	Economic and Social Council Resolutions 76 (V) of 5 August 1947, 304 I (XI) of 14 and 17 July 1950, 1983/27 of 26 May 1983, 1992/19 of 30 July 1992 and 1993/11 of 27 July 1993.	Environmental human rights related to women See generally Political Declaration, UN GA Resolution S-23/2, http://www.un.org/womenwatch/daw/followup/ress232e.pdf.	
United Nations Education, Scientific and Cultural Organization (UNESCO) Complaint Procedure.	See text of Chapter.	See text of Chapter.	See http://www.unesco.org/general/eng/about/members.shtml.

HUMAN RIGHTS BODIES/PROCESSES	INSTRUMENT CREATING BODY/PROCESS	ENVIRONMENTAL HUMAN RIGHTS	NATION-STATES SUBJECT TO BODY OR TREATY
International Labor Organization (ILO): compliance with Indigenous and Tribal Peoples Convention of 1989 (ILO Convention No. 169) http://www.ilo.org/ilolex/english/convdisp2.htm.	Representations: ILO Constitution, http://www.ilo.org/public/english/about/iloconst.htm, arts. 24–25 Complaints: ILO Constitution, http://www.ilo.org/public/english/about/iloconst.htm, arts. 26–34.	Environmental human rights deprived of indigenous and tribal peoples. See Indigenous and Tribal Peoples Convention No. 169, http://www.ilo.org/ilolex/english/convdisp2.htm, arts. 4(1), 7(3), 7(4), 15 and 16.	Argentina, Bolivia, Brazil, Colombia, Costa Rica, Denmark, Dominica, Ecuador, Fiji, Guatemala, Honduras, Mexico, Netherlands, Paraguay, Peru, Venezuela have ratified. See http://www.ilo.org/ilolex/english/newratframeE.htm.
African Commission on Human and Peoples' Rights, http://www.achpr.org/html/africancommission human.html.	African Charter on Human and Peoples' Rights, http://www.achpr.org/html/basicinstruments.html#1.	Association Culture Equal protection Environment Freedom from inhumane treatment Health	Algeria, Angola, Benin, Botswana, Burkina Faso, Burundi, Cameroon, Cape Verde, Central African Republic, Chad, Comoros, Congo, Congo (RD), Côte d'Ivoire, Djibouti, Egypt, Equatorial Guinea, Eritrea, Ethiopia, Gabon, Gambia, Ghana, Guinea, Guinea Bissau, Kenya, Lesotho, Liberia, Libya, Madagascar, Malawi, Mali, Mauritania, Mauritius, Mozambique, Namibia, Niger, Nigeria, Uganda, Rwanda, Sahrawi Arab Democratic Republic, Sao Tome & Principe, Senegal, Seychelles, Sierra Leone, Somalia, South Africa, Sudan, Swaziland, Tanzania, Togo, Tunisia, Zambia, Zimbabwe.

HUMAN RIGHTS BODIES/PROCESSES	INSTRUMENT CREATING BODY/PROCESS	ENVIRONMENTAL HUMAN RIGHTS	NATION-STATES SUBJECT TO BODY OR TREATY
African Commission on Human and Peoples' Rights cont'd		Information	
		Liberty and security of person	
		Life	
		Public participation	
		Residence	
		Speech or expression	
		Vote	
African Court on Human and Peoples' Rights	Protocol to the African Charter on Human and Peoples' Rights.	Association	Algeria, Angola, Benin, Botswana, Burkina Faso, Burundi, Cameroon, Cape Verde, Central African Republic, Comoros, Congo, Congo (RD), Côte d'Ivoire, Djibouti, Egypt, Equatorial Guinea, Eritrea, Ethiopia, Gabon, Gambia, Ghana, Guinea, Guinea Bissau, Kenya, Lesotho, Liberia, Libya, Madagascar, Malawi, Mali, Mauritania, Mauritius, Mozambique, Namibia, Niger, Nigeria, Uganda, Rwanda, Sahrawi Arab Democratic Republic, Sao Tome and Principe, Senegal, Seychelles, Sierra Leone, Somalia, South Africa, Sudan, Swaziland, Tanzania, Chad, Togo, Tunisia, Zambia, Zimbabwe.
		Culture	
		Equal protection	
		Environment	
		Freedom from inhumane treatment	
		Health	

HUMAN RIGHTS BODIES/PROCESSES	INSTRUMENT CREATING BODY/PROCESS	ENVIRONMENTAL HUMAN RIGHTS	NATION-STATES SUBJECT TO BODY OR TREATY
African Court on Human and Peoples' Rights, cont'd		Information Liberty and security of person Life Public participation Residence Speech or expression Vote	
Inter-American Commission on Human Rights http://www.cidh.org tates(s), www.cidh.org/Basicos/basic2.htm.	American Convention on Human Rights	Association Culture Equal protection Environment Food Freedom from inhumane treatment Health	Argentina, Barbados, Bolivia, Brazil, Chile, Colombia, Costa Rica, Dominica, Dominican Republic, Ecuador, El Salvador, Grenada, Guatemala, Haiti, Honduras, Jamaica, Mexico, Nicaragua, Panama, Paraguay, Peru, Suriname, Trinidad and Tobago, Uruguay, United States, Venezuela. *n.b.* OAS members are subject to IACHR even if non-party to Convention (*e.g.*, Canada)

HUMAN RIGHTS BODIES/PROCESSES	INSTRUMENT CREATING BODY/PROCESS	ENVIRONMENTAL HUMAN RIGHTS	NATION-STATES SUBJECT TO BODY OR TREATY
Inter-American Commission on Human Rights cont'd		Information	
		Inviolability of the home and family	
		Liberty and security of person	
		Life	
		Privacy	
		Public participation	
		Residence	
		Speech or expression	
		Vote	
Inter-American Court of Human Rights http://www.corteidh.org.cr.	American Convention on Human Rights www.cidh.org/Basicos/basic2.htm.	Association	Argentina, Barbados, Bolivia, Brazil, Chile, Colombia, Costa Rica, Dominican Republic, Ecuador, El Salvador, Guatemala, Haiti, Honduras, Jamaica, Mexico, Nicaragua, Panama, Paraguay, Peru, Suriname, Trinidad y Tobago, Uruguay, Venezuela.
		Culture	
		Equal protection	
		Environment	
		Food	

HUMAN RIGHTS BODIES/PROCESSES	INSTRUMENT CREATING BODY/PROCESS	ENVIRONMENTAL HUMAN RIGHTS	NATION-STATES SUBJECT TO BODY OR TREATY
Inter-American Court of Human Rights cont'd		Freedom from inhumane treatment Health Information Inviolability of the home and family Liberty and security of person Life Privacy Property Public participation Residence Vote	
European Court on Human Rights http://www.echr.coe.int/.	European Convention on the Protection of Human Rights, and Its Five Protocols	Association Culture Equal protection	Albania, Andorra, Armenia, Austria, Azerbaijan, Belgium, Bosnia and Herzegovina, Bulgaria, Croatia, Cyprus, Czech Republic, Denmark, Estonia, Finland, France, Georgia, Germany, Greece, Hungary, Iceland, Ireland, Italy, Latvia, Liechtenstein, Lithuania,

HUMAN RIGHTS BODIES/PROCESSES	INSTRUMENT CREATING BODY/PROCESS	ENVIRONMENTAL HUMAN RIGHTS	NATION-STATES SUBJECT TO BODY OR TREATY
European Court on Human Rights cont'd	http://www.conventions.coe.int/Treaty/EN/CadreListeTraites.htm.	Environment Freedom from inhumane treatment Health Information Inviolability of the home and family Liberty and security of person Life Privacy Property Public participation Residence Speech or expression Vote	Luxembourg, Malta, Moldova, Netherlands, Norway, Poland, Portugal, Romania, Russia, San Marino, Serbia and Montenegro (has signed but has not ratified), Slovakia, Slovenia, Spain, Sweden, Switzerland, the former Yugoslav Republic of Macedonia, Turkey, Ukraine, United Kingdom.

HUMAN RIGHTS BODIES/PROCESSES	INSTRUMENT CREATING BODY/PROCESS	ENVIRONMENTAL HUMAN RIGHTS	NATION-STATES SUBJECT TO BODY OR TREATY
European Parliament, Committee on Petitions http://www.europarl.eu.int/committees/peti_home.htm.	Charter of Fundamental Rights of the European Union http://www.europarl.eu.int/charter/default_en.htm.	Association Culture Environment Equal Protection Health Information Inviolability of the home and family Liberty Life Privacy Property Public participation Residence Speech Vote	Austria, Belgium, Denmark, Finland, France, Germany, Greece, Ireland, Italy, Luxembourg, Netherlands, Portugal, Sweden, United Kingdom.

HUMAN RIGHTS BODIES/PROCESSES	INSTRUMENT CREATING BODY/PROCESS	ENVIRONMENTAL HUMAN RIGHTS	NATION-STATES SUBJECT TO BODY OR TREATY
Secretary General of the European Social Charter.	European Social Charter http://conventions.coe.int/Treaty/EN/Cadre ListeTraites.htm.	Health	Albania, Andorra, Armenia, Austria, Azerbaijan, Belgium, Bosnia and Herzegovina, Bulgaria, Croatia, Cyprus, Czech Republic, Denmark, Estonia, Finland, France, Georgia, Germany, Greece, Hungary, Iceland, Ireland, Italy, Latvia, Liechtenstein, Lithuania, Luxembourg, Malta, Moldova, Netherlands, Norway, Poland, Portugal, Romania, Russia, San Marino, Serbia and Montenegro (has signed but has not ratified), Slovakia, Slovenia, Spain, Sweden, Switzerland, the former Yugoslav Republic of Macedonia, Turkey, Ukraine, United Kingdom.

Table C: Private Rights of Action Available

See generally Fact Sheet No. 7/Rev. 1, Complaint Procedures, Office of the High Commissioner for Human Rights, http://www.unhchr.ch/html/menu6/2/fs7.htm.

HUMAN RIGHTS BODIES	TYPE OF PRIVATE RIGHT OF ACTION	SIGNIFICANT LIMITATIONS
UN Human Rights Committee http://www.unhchr.ch/html/menu2/6/hrc.htm.	Complaint/Petition	To submit complaint/petition against particular nation-state, that nation-state must be party to the Optional Protocol
	Critique of reports submitted by treaty parties	Exhaustion of domestic remedies
	Informal written and/or oral advocacy	No related proceeding in another formal international or regional dispute resolution forum
	Amicus curiae submissions	
UN Committee on Economic, Social and Cultural Rights http://www.unhchr.ch/html/menu2/6/cescr.htm.	Written statement	No individual complaint/petition procedure yet in existence
	Oral statements	
	Critique of reports	
UN Committee on the Elimination of Racial Discrimination http://www.unhchr.ch/html/menu2/6/cerd.htm.	Complaint/Petition	To submit complaint/petition against particular nation-state, that nation-state must recognize competence of the Committee
	Critique of reports submitted by treaty parties	Exhaustion of domestic remedies
	Informal written and/or oral advocacy	

HUMAN RIGHTS BODIES	TYPE OF PRIVATE RIGHT OF ACTION	SIGNIFICANT LIMITATIONS
UN Committee on the Elimination of Discrimination against Women http://www.unhchr.ch/html/menu2/6/cedw.htm.	Complaint/Petition Critique of reports submitted by treaty parties Informal written and/or oral advocacy Amicus curiae submissions	To submit complaint/petition against particular nation-state, that nation-state must be party to the Optional Protocol Exhaustion of domestic remedies No related proceeding in another formal international or regional dispute resolution forum
UN Committee on the Rights of the Child http://www.unhchr.ch/html/menu2/6/crc.htm.	Critique of reports submitted by treaty parties Informal written and/or oral advocacy	No individual complaint/petition procedure yet in existence
UN Permanent Forum on Indigenous Issues http://www.unhchr.ch/indigenous/forum.htm.	Informal written and/or oral advocacy	No individual complaint/petition procedure yet in existence
Special Rapporteur on the right of everyone to the enjoyment of the highest attainable standard of physical and mental health http://www.unhchr.ch/html/menu2/7/b/mmen.htm.	Written statement Informal oral statement when visit made to nation-state where problem exists	No individual complaint/petition procedure yet in existence

HUMAN RIGHTS BODIES	TYPE OF PRIVATE RIGHT OF ACTION	SIGNIFICANT LIMITATIONS
Special Rapporteur on the Commission on Human Rights on the situation of human rights and fundamental freedoms of indigenous people http://www.unhchr.ch/html/menu2/7/b/mindp.htm.	Written statement Informal oral statement when visit made to nation-state where problem exists	No individual complaint/petition procedure yet in existence
Special Rapporteur of the Commission on Human Rights on the adverse effects of the illicit movement and dumping of toxic and dangerous products and wastes on the enjoyment of human rights http://www.unhchr.ch/html/menu2/7/b/mtow.htm.	Written statement Informal oral statement when visit made to nation-state where problem exists	No individual complaint/petition procedure yet in existence
Special Rapporteur of the Commission on Human Rights on violence against women, its causes and consequences http://www.unhchr.ch/html/menu2/7/b/mwom.htm	Written statement Informal oral statement when visit made to nation-state where problem exists	No individual complaint/petition procedure yet in existence
Special Rapporteur of the Commission on Human Rights on the independence of judges and lawyers http://www.unhchr.ch/html/menu2/7/b/mijl.htm.	Written statement Informal oral statement when visit made to nation-state where problem exists	No individual complaint/petition procedure yet in existence

HUMAN RIGHTS BODIES	TYPE OF PRIVATE RIGHT OF ACTION	SIGNIFICANT LIMITATIONS
Special Rapporteur of the Commission on Human Rights on the right to food http://www.unhchr.ch/html/menu2/7/b/mfood.htm.	Written statement Informal oral statement when visit made to nation-state where problem exists	No individual complaint/petition procedure yet in existence
Special Representative of the Secretary-General on the situation of human rights defenders http://www.unhchr.ch/html/menu2/7/b/mdef.htm.	Written statement Informal oral statement when visit made to nation-state where problem exists	No individual complaint/petition procedure yet in existence
Special Representative of the Commission on Human Rights on contemporary forms of racism, racial discrimination, xenophobia, and related intolerance http://www.unhchr.ch/html/menu2/7/b/mrad.htm.	Written statement Informal oral statement when visit made to nation-state where problem exists	No individual complaint/petition procedure yet in existence
UN Commission on Human Rights http://www.unhchr.ch/html/menu2/2/chr.htm.	Written statement/Issue statement Oral statement Critique of reports submitted by UN member states *Ad hoc* advocacy to expand scope of mandates of UN Special Rapporteurs	No individual complaint/petition procedure yet in existence

HUMAN RIGHTS BODIES	TYPE OF PRIVATE RIGHT OF ACTION	SIGNIFICANT LIMITATIONS
UN Sub-Commission on the Promotion and Protection of Human Rights http://www.unhchr.ch/html/menu2/2/sc.htm.	Written statement, including statements particularly directed to Working Group on Transnational Corporations to continue to pressure corporations to adhere to environmental human rights standards *Ad hoc* advocacy to expand scope of mandates of UN Special Rapporteurs *Ad hoc* advocacy to Working Group on Transnational Corporations to continue to pressure corporations to adhere to environmental human rights standards	No individual complaint/petition procedure yet in existence
UN Commission on Human Rights, including the Economic and Social Council 1503 Procedure http://www.unhchr.ch/huridocda.nsf/(Symbol)/E.RES.2000.3.En??Open Document.	Complaint/Petition submitted to UN Office of High Commissioner for Human Rights	High threshold for consideration of complaint/petition: a consistent pattern of gross and reliably attested violations of human rights and fundamental freedoms occurring in any country of the world
UN Commission on the Status of Women http://www.un.org/womenwatch/daw/csw/. African Commission on Human and Peoples' Rights http://www.achpr.org/html/africancommissiononhuman.html.	Complaint/Petition submitted care of the UN Division for the Advancement of Women for advisory purposes Complaint/Petition Critique of reports submitted by treaty parties *Amicus curiae* submissions	Exhaustion of domestic remedies No related proceeding in another formal international or regional dispute resolution forum

HUMAN RIGHTS BODIES	TYPE OF PRIVATE RIGHT OF ACTION	SIGNIFICANT LIMITATIONS
African Court on Human and Peoples' Rights	Complaint/Petition for NGOs having observer status with the African Commission on Human Rights Amicus curiae submissions	Case first presented to the African Commission on Human Rights, unless an inter-state dispute
Inter-American Commission on Human Rights http://www.cidh.org.	Complaint/Petition Critique of reports submitted by treaty parties Amicus curiae submissions	Exhaustion of domestic remedies No related proceeding in another formal international or regional dispute resolution forum
Inter-American Court of Human Rights http://www.coreidh.org.cr.	Interaction with the Commission if the Commission submits one's case to the Court Amicus curiae submissions	Case first presented to the Inter-American Commission on Human Rights, unless inter-state dispute
European Court on Human Rights http://www.echr.coe.int/.	Complaint/Petition Amicus curiae submissions Lobbying member states to commence request for advisory opinion	To submit complaint/petition against particular nation-state, that nation-state must be party to the Optional Protocol Exhaustion of domestic remedies No related proceeding in another formal international or regional dispute resolution forum
European Parliament, Committee on Petitions http://www.europarl.eu.int/committees/peti_home.htm.	Petition	Against member of European Parliament only
Secretary General, European Social Charter	Critique of reports submitted by treaty parties	

CHAPTER 2

ADVOCATING FOR INTERNATIONAL FINANCE AND TRADE INSTITUTIONS TO ADHERE TO ENVIRONMENTAL AND PUBLIC HEALTH STANDARDS

I. INTRODUCTION

Another outlet for the enforcement of international environmental law is advocating for international finance and trade institutions to adhere to environmental and public health standards. Many international financial institutions provide dispute resolution processes for concerned citizens to claim that a particular project funded by that institution has failed to comply with an environmental or public health standard created by and/or required of that institution. In addition, some international trade institutions have created fact-finding bodies to investigate whether a member state has failed to comply with its environmental laws.

The prerequisites for filing claims before these environmental dispute resolution processes appear less complicated and more straightforward than those for environmental human rights claims filed with a human rights forum. Matters presented to international financial institution dispute resolution bodies must simply involve a project that the particular international financial institution is funding. Matters presented to international trade dispute resolution bodies must simply involve an existing domestic environmental law that one of the member states has failed to enforce.

However, whether enforcement before these fora leads to a more effective remedy than enforcement before human rights fora is not at all clear. Decisions from the environmental dispute resolution processes of finance and trade bodies do not usually give rise to a loud, public shaming like those from human rights bodies but instead lead to a quiet, subtle reform of how a particular project moves forward. Moreover, although environmental dispute resolution processes at finance and trade organizations have shorter dockets and better funding, there is rarely a formal appeals process to a judicial body as there can be with human rights fora.

Below is a discussion of several dispute resolution processes available in international finance and trade institutions where one can request enforcement of environmental and public health standards created by these institutions and/or their members. The discussion overviews each process and then explains who can, and how to make. a submission.

There are two important items to note in review of this chapter. First, even if a party is ineligible or uninterested in making a submission to any of the bodies discussed below, such a party may want to submit information even as a non-party. From time to time, the discussion below indicates that a particular decision maker is allowed to consider additional information besides that provided from the submitting party, the member state, and/or the international institution; even if not explicitly stated, a decision maker will likely accept and review such a submission. But one should provide the decision maker with additional information that the parties probably will not submit, and/or additional perspectives on the materials already provided, and/or additional reasoning with respect to the applicable law. Second, many of the financial inspection mechanisms share a similar format and may very well be modeled on one another.

Lastly, as with the environmental human rights strategies in Chapter 1, one should contact appropriate individuals on the List of Practitioner Experts, in the appendix to this book, to assist.

II. WORLD BANK INSPECTION PANEL

1818 H St. NW
Washington, D.C. 20433, USA
T: (202) 458-5200
F: (202) 522-0916
E: ipanel@worldbank.org
W: www.inspectionpanel.org

A. Overview

"The Inspection Panel is a three-member body created in 1993 to provide an independent forum to private citizens who believe that they or their interests have been or could be directly harmed by a project financed by the World Bank."[1] More specifically, communities and/or individuals affected by a development project funded by the International Bank for Reconstruction and Development ("IBRD") or the International Development Association ("IDA" and together with the IBRD, the "Bank")—the two World Bank Group organizations that provide loans to governments—can make a written request that the World Bank Inspection Panel

---

[1] See http://wbln0018.worldbank.org/ipn/ipnweb.nsf/WOverview/overview?opendocument.

Advocating for Adherence by Financial and Trade Institutions • 133

("Panel") investigate whether these bodies have complied with World Bank operational policies, including environmental and public health ones. Alternatively, the community can designate a representative to handle the matter for it. The World Bank Group sets forth its operational policies (known as "OPs" and distinguishable from bank policies known as "BPs") in the World Bank Operation Manual for the Inspection Panel.[2] The OPs that concern the environment include:

> Volume I. Strategies
>   Section 4.02 — Environmental Action Plans
>   Section 4.03 — Water Resources Management
> Volume II. Project Requirements
>   Section 4.01 — Environmental Assessment
>   Section 4.04 — Natural Habitats
>   Section 4.20 — Indigenous Peoples
>   Section 4.36 — Forestry
>   Section 4.37 — Safety of Dams
>   Section 7.5 — Projects on International Waterways[3]

The Center for International Environmental Law in Washington, D.C. has prepared an extremely helpful Citizen's Guide to the World Bank Inspection Panel and translated it into several languages.[4]

B. Eligibility to Submit a Request

Where an IBRD or IDA project exists that adversely impacts a community, then a group of private citizens from that community or an organization on behalf of those private citizens (but not single individuals) can submit a request. The request must demonstrate to the Inspection Panel that:

[1] [submitter's] rights or interests have been or are likely to be directly affected by
[2] an action or omission of the Bank
[3] as a result of a failure of the Bank to follow its [OPs]
[4] with respect to the design, appraisal and/or implementation of a project financed by the Bank (including situations where the Bank is alleged to have failed in its follow-up on the borrower's obligations under loan agreements with respect to such policies and procedures)

---

2   *See* http://wbln0018.worldbank.org/institutional/manuals/opmanual.nsf.
3   *Id.*
4   *See* http://www.ciel.org/Publications/citizensguide.pdf.

134 • Defending the Environment

[5] provided in all cases that such failure has had, or threatens to have, a material adverse effect.[5]

The request must further demonstrate to the Inspection Panel that:

[1] the subject matter of the request has been dealt with by the Management of the Bank;
[2] Management has failed to demonstrate that it has followed, or is taking adequate steps to follow the Bank's policies and procedures; [and]
[3] the alleged violation of the Bank's policies and procedures is of a serious character.[6]

Finally, the request must not be:

[1] Complaints with respect to actions which are the responsibility of other parties, such as a borrower, or potential borrower, and which do not involve any action or omission on the part of the Bank.[7]
[2] Complaints against procurement decisions by Bank borrowers from suppliers of goods and services financed or expected to be financed by the Bank under a loan agreement, or from losing tenderers for the supply of any such goods and services, which will continue to be addressed by staff under existing procedures.[8]
[3] Requests filed after the Closing Date of the loan financing the project with respect to which the request is filed or after the loan financing the project has been substantially disbursed.[9]
[4] Requests related to a particular matter or matters over which the Panel has already made its recommendation upon having received a prior request, unless justified by new evidence or circumstances not known at the time of the prior request.[10]

C. Submitting the Request

Once private citizens satisfy the above set of requirements, then they can submit a Request for Inspection. Such request must:

1. be in writing;
2. state all relevant facts, including, in the case of a request by an

---

[5] IBRD Res. 93-10, IDA Res. 93-6 (Sept. 22, 1993), http://wbln0018.worldbank.org/IPN/ipnweb.nsf/WRelease/A31199D3A1AFBC0E85256900006 82B79 ("IBRD/IDA Res."), at ¶ 12.
[6] Id. ¶ 13.
[7] Id. ¶ 14.
[8] Id.
[9] Id.
[10] Id.

Advocating for Adherence by Financial and Trade Institutions • 135

affected party, the harm suffered by or threatened to such party or parties by the alleged action or omission of the Bank;[11]
3. explain the steps already taken to deal with the issue, as well as the nature of the alleged actions or omissions and shall specify the actions taken to bring the issue to the attention of Management, and Management's response to such action;[12] and
4. be mailed, hand-delivered, faxed, or e-mailed to the address stated above.

D. Decision Making

After the request is submitted, the Panel obtains a response from the Management of the Bank on how the Bank complied with Bank Policies and Procedures and determines in a written Report and Recommendation whether the Board of Executive Directors (the "Board") should recommend that the Panel undertake an investigation.[13] If the Board agrees with the Panel, then the Panel undertakes a thorough investigation and submits its finished findings to the Board.[14] Management then has six weeks to respond to the Board on those findings.[15] The Board then considers the Panel's findings and Management's response at the time that the project is submitted to the Board for financing. Two weeks after the Board announces its decision, the Panel makes the decision public.[16]

E. Locating Requests for Inspection, Inspection Panel Reports, and Management Responses

The Inspection Panel maintains a publicly available register of all documents received and generated throughout an investigation. Reviewing these materials can tremendously help your own submissions.

For the Panel Register for each project, *see* http://wbln0018.worldbank.org/ipn/ipnweb.nsf/WRegister?openview&count=500000.

For the Requests for Inspection submitted by affected communities for each project, *see* http://wbln0018.worldbank.org/ipn/ipnweb.nsf/WRequest?openview&count=500000.

For the Inspection Panel Reports & Recommendations requesting permission from the Board to conduct an investigation and for subsequent Investigation Reports generated after such investigations, *see* http://wbln0018.worldbank.org/ipn/ipnweb.nsf/WReport?openview&count=500000.

---

[11] *Id.* ¶ 16.
[12] *Id.*
[13] *Id.* at ¶¶ 17-18.
[14] *Id.* at ¶¶ 19-22.
[15] *Id.* at ¶ 23.
[16] *Id.* at ¶ 23.

For a summary of Management Responses and Board Decisions with respect to each Investigation Report, see http://wbln0018.worldbank.org/ipn/ipnweb.nsf/WRelease?openview&count=500000.

2.1 Pakistan

On September 10, 2004, the Inspection Panel received a Request for Inspection related to the National Drainage Program Project (NDP) in Pakistan. The original purpose of the Project was to restore "environmentally-sound irrigated agriculture" through the minimization and eventual evacuation of saline drainable surplus.[17] The Request was submitted by seven individuals on their own behalf and on behalf of others who live in the area known as district Badin, Sindh Pakistan, in the Indus River Basin.

According to the Request, more than fifty villages in the district would suffer the permanent threat of flooding if the Project were allowed to proceed in the disposal of all saline effluents from upcountry into the existing faulty Left Bank Outfall Drain (LBOD) system.[18] Additionally, the Requesters indicated that during the 2003 rains, thirty people died, thousands of houses were damaged, and thousands of acres used for agriculture were destroyed due to overflowing and breaches from the Project. Furthermore, the Project did not take into consideration the large-scale displacement of people that would result when the drainage system overflowed during monsoon seasons.[19] Due to the seeping of drainage effluents containing saline, pesticides, fertilizers, and industrial waste, the remaining freshwater source in the Indus Delta could be destroyed, leading to the destruction marine fisheries and mangrove forests.[20] The Requesters also claimed that the NDP would cause the destruction of two *dhands* (coastal wetlands) that are protected by the Ramsar Convention on Wetlands of International Importance. Lastly, the Requesters claimed that the local communities, and especially the affected people of the coastal belt, had not been kept adequately informed as to project plans and environmental assessments.

Before the Inspection Panel could make a decision on the request for an investigation, Bank Management was supposed to provide evidence that it had complied or would comply with procedures and policies related to the Project.[21] The Management's response indicated that although poverty-targeted intervention was needed in the affected area, the NDP was not the mechanism to

---

[17] Excerpted from The Inspection Panel, World Bank Group, Notice of Registration Re: Request for Inspection, Pakistan: National Drainage Program Project (Sept. 17, 2004), *available at* http://wbln0018.worldbank.org/IPN/ipnweb.nsf.(attachmentweb)/PAKNoticeofRegistration/$File/PAKNoticeofRegistration.pdf (last visited June 6, 2005).

[18] Request for Inspection, Pakistan National Drainage Program Project (Sept. 9, 2004), *available at* http://siteresources.worldbank.org/EXTINSPECTIONPANEL/Resources/PAKRequestforinspection.pdf (last visited June 16, 2005).

[19] *Id.*

[20] *Id.*

[21] Notice of Registration, *supra* at note 1, at 4.

2.1 Pakistan *(continued)*

address this problem, and that the Project had not worsened the living conditions of the people living in the region. Management then indicated several projects at work in the area with which they would continue to be involved including the National Rural Support Program, with resources from the Pakistan Poverty Alleviation Fund (PPAF), which worked on infrastructure construction in the region, and the Government of Sindh High-Level Technical Committee, which worked to outline improvements to the areas prone to flooding in lower Badin.[22] Although Management said they would pursue the issues raised in the request with the Borrowers, Management did not believe that the Requesters' rights would be adversely affected by the Project.

Following the Management's Response, the Inspection Panel filed a Report and Recommendation on the Request for Inspection. The Panel found substantial contradictions between what the Requesters claimed and what Management asserted that were not easily reconciled. The Panel also received evidence that before filing an official Request for Inspection, the Requesters had tried to raise concerns over the Project with Bank Management. The Requesters wrote several letters to Bank Management, but they received no response and at one point a demonstration against the Project took place outside the Bank's office in Islamabad.[23] The Panel indicated that only an investigation could determine whether the Bank had followed procedures and whether the Project was the cause of the flooding in lower Badin.[24] On December 8, 2004, the World Bank Board of Executive Directors authorized an official investigation specifically looking at the Bank's actions or omissions.[25]

III. THE INTERNATIONAL FINANCE CORPORATION—COMPLIANCE ADVISOR OMBUDSMAN

2121 Pennsylvania Ave. NW
Washington, D.C. 20433, USA
T: (202) 458-1973
F: (202) 522-7400
E: cao-compliance@ifc.org
W: www.ifc.org/cao or http://www.miga.org/screens/about/cao.htm

---

[22] Bank Management Response to Request for Inspection Panel Review of the Pakistan National Drainage Program Project, (Oct. 19, 2004), *available at* http://siteresources.worldbank.org/EXTINSPECTIONPANEL/Resources/MGMTRESPFULL.pdf (last visited June 16, 2005).

[23] Excerpted from The Inspection Panel, Report and Recommendation on Request for Inspection, *available at* http://siteresources.worldbank.org/EXTINSPECTIONPANEL/Resources/EligibilityReport.pdf (last listed June 16, 2005), at 23–24.

[24] *Id.* at 24.

[25] Press Release: World Bank Board of Executive Directors authorizes Inspection Panel to conduct investigation (Dec. 15, 2004), *available at* http://siteresources.worldbank.org/EXTINSPECTIONPANEL/News%20And%20Events/20307398/R&R%20Press%20Release.pdf (last visited June 16, 2005).

A. Overview

The Compliance Advisor Ombudsman ("CAO") is to the International Finance Corporation and the Multilateral Investment Guarantee Agency ("MIGA") of the World Bank Group what the Inspection Panel is to the International Bank for Reconstruction and Development and the International Development Association, only with less structure and power. Communities and/or individuals affected by a development project funded by the International Finance Corporation and the Multilateral Investment Guarantee Agency—the two World Bank Group organizations that provide loans to private, non-governmental parties—can make a written request that the World Bank Office of the Compliance Advisor Ombudsman investigate whether these bodies have complied with World Bank operational policies, including environmental and public health ones. Alternatively, the community can designate a representative to handle the matter for them.

The CAO performs ombudsman, advisory and compliance roles in accordance with the Operational Guidelines of IFC/MIGA (April 2000) ("OGs").[26] This section discusses only the CAO's ombudsman role because that is the only role that involves "responding to Complaints by persons who are affected by projects and attempting to resolve the issues raised using a flexible, problem solving approach."[27] The OG provides a flowchart summarizing the complaint process.[28]

An additional, very reliable source for CAO information is *A Handbook on the Office of the Compliance Advisor Ombudsman of the International Finance Corporation and Multilateral Investment Guarantee Agency* prepared by the Center for International Environmental Law.[29]

B. Eligibility to Submit a Complaint[30]

1. Who can file?
   a. Any person, group or community affected by, or likely to be affected by, a project; or
   b. A representative on behalf of such a group, community or person, provided that the complaint shows that the group, community or person has authorized the representative to file on its behalf.

---

[26] See http://www.cao-ombudsman.org/file_download.php/FINAL+CAO+GUIDE-LINES++IN+ENGLISH+%2809-20-00%29.doc?URL_ID=1265&filename=10378105840FINAL_CAO_GUIDELINES_IN_ENGLI SH_%2809-20-00%29.doc&filetype=application%2Fmsword&filesize=173568&name=FINAL+CAO+GUIDE LINES++IN+ENGLISH+%2809-20-00%29.doc&location=user-S/.

[27] See OG § 1.1.2(1), *supra* note 22.

[28] See OG, Annex 1, at 24, *supra* note 22.

[29] See http://www.ciel.org/Publications/CAOhandbook.pdf.

[30] See OG § 2.2, *supra* note 22.

n.b. The complaint can be filed confidentially so that only the staff of the Office of the CAO know the contents.
2. When to file?
Filing can be made anytime during the project process, even if the IFC or MIGA has not yet approved the project. However, filing before the IFC has provided its loan or MIGA has provided its guarantee better enables those organizations to change the behavior of the project sponsor. Unfortunately, becoming aware of a project during the early phases is extremely difficult as most discussions at that point are confidential.
3. Conditions precedent
Affected parties must demonstrate prior engagement through meetings, e-mails, letters, or telephone calls with the IFC or MIGA regarding their concerns with the project.

C. Submitting the Complaint[31]

The CAO provides a model complaint form on its website.[32] The complaint should:

1. relate to any aspect of the planning, implementation or impact of a project, but need not address a violation of an IFC or MIGA policies, guidelines, or procedures because CAO's authority not limited to such violation and such policies are difficult to obtain outside the internet or in languages other than English;
2. be in writing;
3. include name, address and other contact information of the person bringing the complaint and, in the case of a representative, also identify the people on whose behalf the complaint is being brought;
4. request and give reasons for confidential treatment, if any, although the act itself of filing cannot be kept confidential;
5. identify and describe the nature of the project;
6. state factual information about the project including, but not limited to, the stage of implementation, the name the corporate sponsor, whether an IFC project or a MIGA project, and the identity of any known personnel involved;
7. state clearly how the project has impacted the complainant including, but not limited to, a description of all the issues and problems that the complainants would like the CAO to address, the number of people affected, the threat of irreversible harm, the seriousness of the issues or policy, and the violations alleged;

---

[31] See OG §§ 2.3-2.5, *supra* note 22.
[32] See OG, Annex 2, at 25-26, *supra* note 22.

8. state what the complainant has done to attempt to resolve the problem, including specifically any contact with IFC or MIGA personnel, the sponsor or host government;
9. state what aspects remain unresolved if the action has been partly resolved;
10. state precisely the most desirable outcome of the process;
11. include any other relevant facts;
12. include copies of prior correspondence with the IFC or MIGA, and any other relevant documents; and
13. be mailed, hand delivered, faxed, or e-mailed to the address stated above.

D. Response[33]

Usually within five days, the CAO will acknowledge receipt of the complaint. Usually within 15 days, the CAO will decide whether the complaint falls within its mandate and can be accepted or whether it does not and must be rejected. Usually within 30 days, the CAO will complete a preliminary investigation to determine pursuant to criteria set forth in OG § 3.3.6, whether the CAO should handle the complaint within its ombudsman capacity.[34]

Unless the complaint is to be kept confidential, CAO also will refer any accepted complaint to IFC/MIGA management who should respond within 20 days. In addition, the CAO is also required to notify the member state project sponsor.

E. Results[35]

Although the CAO does not have authority to stop a project, it can still play several roles to help make the project comply with IFC/MIGA environmental standards. If the CAO decides to consider the complaint in its ombudsman capacity, then the CAO can take steps to help the member state and affected parties negotiate a solution. First, the CAO can facilitate dialogue between the affected party and the responsible member state. Second, the CAO can conciliate and/or mediate the matter. Third, the CAO can foster a settlement agreement.

Should a negotiated outcome initially fail, the CAO then conducts a further investigation of the dispute. The investigation can involve research, meetings, site visits, public hearings, and/or the hiring of experts. The results of such investigation may suggest new approaches for dialogue, conciliation, or mediation which the CAO can then commence again. Further investigation may also enable the CAO to generate recommendations for the President of the World Bank Group to discuss with IFC/MIGA management. Such discussion can encourage those entities to play a role as well in help-

---

[33] See OG §§ 3-4 at 13-19 and Annex 1, at 24, *supra* note 22.
[34] See OG §§ 3.3.4-3.3.6, at 14, *supra* note 22.
[35] See OG §§ 4-6, at 15-23, *supra* note 22.

Advocating for Adherence by Financial and Trade Institutions • *141*

ing to resolve the conflict. Where IFC/MIGA management and the concerned member state reach an agreement, then the CAO plays a monitoring and follow-up role.

Where an ombudsman investigation yields concerning results, the CAO may decide to conduct a compliance audit. Such an audit is separate and apart from the CAO's ombudsman role and the complaint. Nevertheless the pressure and exposure resulting from the audit might cause the complainant, the President and/or IFC/MIGA staff to revisit their negotiation efforts.

Lastly, the CAO on it own initiative or at the request of the President or the IFC/MIGA management may play an advisory role instead of an ombudsman or audit role to help find further ways to negotiate a solution.

F. CAO and the Panel

When a World Bank project includes funding from the IBRD and/or IDA as well as the IFC or MIGA, any challenge by an affected party would likely result in the CAO working cooperatively with the Panel to resolve the dispute. Usually the CAO defers to the Panel and plays only a role of assistance.

2.2 Brazil

In November 2004, the Executive Vice President of the International Finance Corporation (IFC) requested that the CAO prepare an audit of the IFC's categorization of the Amaggi Expansion Project in Brazil. The project involved the expansion of Amaggi's soy agricultural operations.[36] The Executive Vice President, who was strongly pressured by NGOs to examine the project,[37] raised two questions: (1) whether IFC followed its own procedures for categorization; and (2) whether IFC's categorization of the project as a Category B project was justified.[38] Categorization is used by the IFC to determine the scope of an environmental assessment ("EA") for a project. Projects categorized as Category A are likely to have significant impact on the environment and call for a full EA whereas Category B projects have a potential environmental impact less adverse than a Category A project. Category B projects are not given the same level of environmental assessment.[39]

CAO found that IFC had followed its own procedures for categorization but that the procedures were not clearly defined and there were no rules

(continued)

---

[36] Final Report, CAO Audit of IFC's Environmental and Social Categorization of the Amaggi Expansion Project (May 2005), *available at* http://www.cao-ombudsman.org/pdfs/AmaggiFinal_Editedversion_05-26-05.pdf (last visited June 17, 2005).

[37] *See id.* at 15, Office Memorandum, Request for an Independent Audit of the Environmental Categorization of the Amaggi Project (Nov. 1, 2004).

[38] *Id.* at 1.

[39] *Id.* at 3.

2.2 Brazil (continued)

on disclosing categorization decisions to the public. Furthermore, CAO found that the categorization of the project as Category B was unjustified due to three factors: (1) the IFC failed to assure that the Environmental and Social Management System (ESMS) set up by the Amaggi would afford adequate environmental and social protection; (2) the IFC did not evaluate the ESMS before granting the Amaggi a second loan; and (3) the IFC did not clearly define to the Amaggi the level of environmental assessment that was necessary.[40] CAO recommended that IFC prepare and publicly disclose the actions they will take in response to CAO's findings.[41]

2.3 Kazakstan

In October 2004, the Office of Compliance Advisor/Ombudsman (CAO) received a complaint about the Lukoil Overseas Project, an IFC investment in the Karachaganak Oil and Gas Condensate Field (KOGCF) in Western Kazakhstan. KOGCP is one of the largest gas-oil condensate fields in the world, and oil reserves are estimated at 1.9 billion barrels.[42] The complaint alleged three main problems with the Project: (1) the KOGCF's proximity to the town of Berezovka exposed inhabitants to adverse health impacts; (2) the KOGCF operations deteriorated economic circumstances in Berezovka; and (3) a reduction in the Sanitary Protection Zone was unjustified.[43]

The Complainants alleged that Berezovka's proximity to KOGCF and its emissions had caused residents to suffer health problems, including upper respiratory tract and cardiovascular disorders, allergies, and memory loss.[44] The CAO found that the Government of Kazakhstan and the Karachaganak Petroleum Operation (KPO) had both conducted health studies about the impact of KOGCF's emission levels, but it was unclear why the results of these studies had not been made available to the residents of Berezovka. CAO indicated that Western Kazakhstan was suffering from a pervasive decline in health and, therefore, it was unclear whether it was KOGCF that was causing the adverse health effects or other factors such as alcohol consumption, smoking, access to medical care, or genetics.[45] CAO did recommend, however, that KPO give the Complainants access to the health

---

[40] *Id.* at 4
[41] *Id.* at 14.
[42] Assessment Report, Complaint Regarding the Lukoil Overseas Project (Karachaganak Oil and Gas Field_ Burlinsky District, Western Kazakhstan Oblast, Kazakhstan (April 15, 2005) *available at* http://www.cao-ombudsman.org/pdfs/Karachaganak_Assessment_Report%2004-14-05.pdf (last visited June 17, 2005).
[43] *Id.*
[44] *Id.* at 7.
[45] *Id.* at 9.

2.3 Kazakstan *(continued)*

studies, continue appointing independent reviewers to evaluate environmental health aspects, and revise procedures for disclosing environmental information to the public.[46]

The CAO found no evidence of economic deterioration in Berezovka as a result of the Project and it actually found some improvements to the town including road repairs and improved drinking water quality. CAO found that the deterioration in socioeconomic conditions was due to the collapse of the Soviet Union, not KOGCF operations.[47] The CAO recommended that KPO work within local infrastructure to strengthen social investment and to make all investments known to the public.[48] Furthermore, the CAO also found that the Complainants' request for a resettlement plan because of the reduction in the Sanitary Protection Zone should be handled in public meetings between KPO and Berezovka residents. The meetings should make clear why the SPZ was moved and create a written agreement about resettlement plans for Berezovka.[49]

IV. INTER-AMERICAN DEVELOPMENT BANK—INDEPENDENT INVESTIGATION MECHANISM

1300 New York Ave., NW, Stop E-1217
Washington, D.C. 20577
T: (202) 623-3952
F: (202) 312-4057
E: investigation@iadb.org
W: http://www.iadb.org/cont/poli/investig/brochure.htm

A. Overview

Communities and/or individuals affected by a development project funded by the Inter-American Development Bank ("IDB") can make a written request that the IDB Independent Investigation Mechanism investigate whether the IDB complied with its operational procedures, including environmental and public health ones. Alternatively, the community can designate a representative to handle the matter for it.

The IDB's Independent Investigation Mechanism (the "Mechanism"), established in 1994, provides to individuals and groups affected by IDB-financed projects a means to ensure that the IDB exercises due diligence—

---

[46] *Id.* at 10.
[47] *Id.* at 11.
[48] *Id.* at 12.
[49] *Id.* at 14.

including environmental and public health—in the design, analysis and negotiation of those projects. Affected populations or eligible representatives of those populations submit a Request for Investigation to the IDB to determine whether the IDB has violated its operational policies during the preparation and implementation of projects. The procedure for how the IDB handles that Request for Investigation is summarized below.[50]

Similar to the World Bank's Operational Policies pertaining to the environment, the IDB Operational Policies ("IDB-OP") require that "in all projects financed by the [IDB,] environmental aspects are considered and that appropriate measures are taken to avoid adverse environmental impact, with due attention to economic and social costs and benefits."[51]

In addition, the IDB has included the environment among its key mandates and is in the process of developing training programs and guidelines to enable its member states to conduct proper environmental assessments of domestic projects and undertake more effective domestic environmental and public health protection.[52]

B. Preliminaries

Prior to submitting a formal Request for Investigations, affected groups and individuals should register a written complaint with the relevant IDB operational departments, the relevant IDB country office, or the Office of External Relations.[53] Affected groups and individuals will need to report the outcome of this preliminary inquiry in their Request for Investigation.

C. Eligibility to Submit a Request[54]

1. Who can file?
    a. Affected parties, defined as a community of persons such as an organization, association, society or other grouping of individuals; or
    b. Representatives of affected parties who demonstrate that the affected parties authorized such representatives to file on their behalf.
2. Requests for investigation do not qualify if they:
    a. do not involve an IDB action or omission;
    b. are covered by another procedure or related to matter where recommendation already made; or
    c. are filed after approximately 95 percent of the loan is distributed.

---

[50] See http://www.iadb.org/cont/poli/mecanism.pdf for a detailed copy of IDB policies and procedures.
[51] IDB-UP 703, *at* http://www.iadb.org/cont/poli/OP-703E.htm.
[52] See http://www.iadb.org/sds/env/index_env_e.htm.
[53] Note different contact information from that provided at the start of Section IV. E: pic@iadb.org, F: (202) 623-1403, T: (202) 623-1397.
[54] See http://www.iadb.org/cont/poli/mecanism.pdf at Section 3.

D. Submitting the Request[55]

Requests for investigation must:

1. Be in writing;
2. Claim that the IDB has failed in the design, analysis or implementation of proposed or ongoing operations to follow its own established operational policies (including environmental and public health ones), or norms formally adopted for the execution of those policies;
3. Include reasonable evidence that the rights or interests of the affected party have been or are likely to be directly and materially affected by such IDB failure;
4. State all relevant facts, and annex any evidence possessed by the complaining party of the validity of its allegations, or indicate where such evidence may be obtained;
5. Indicate the steps already taken to bring the allegations to the attention of the IDB's Management and the response received.

E. Deciding Whether to Authorize an Investigation[56]

1. Eligibility Determination

After an affected party or representative submits a request, the Coordinator of the Independent Investigation Mechanism (the "Coordinator") and the Legal Department will determine whether the request complies with eligibility requirements. If not in compliance, the request will be denied.

2. Frivolity Determination

If eligible, the Coordinator asks the IDB President to appoint an individual from an existing roster to serve as a consultant (the "Consultant"). The Consultant reviews the request to determine whether it is frivolous or non-substantive. If frivolous, the IDB Board of Executive Directors ("Board") must concur and, then, the request is denied.

3. Management Response

If non-frivolous, the Consultant prepares an explanatory statement that the Coordinator submits to the Board and the President together with the request and supporting documentation. The President, in turn, submits information to IDB's Management to respond within 30 calendar days.

---

[55] *See* http://www.iadb.org/cont/poli/mecanism.pdf at Sections 4.1 and 4.2.
[56] *See* http://www.iadb.org/cont/poli/mecanism.pdf at Sections 4.3–4.9.

4. Investigation Authorization

The Coordinator then forwards Management's response to the Consultant. The Consultant then reviews the response along with the original request to determine whether the Board should authorize investigation. The Consultant may ask the requester and/or Management for additional information. The Coordinator submits the Consultant's recommendation to the Board to consider and notifies the requester that the Board is now considering whether to authorize an investigation. Once the Board decides, the President then meets with the Board to discuss the decision. In addition, the Coordinator will notify the requesting party within 15 days of such Board determination as to whether an investigation will proceed.

5. Exception

In exceptional circumstances, when a serious violation of the Bank's operational policies or norms may have occurred, a director may request that the Board convene a Panel for the purpose of conducting an investigation without the necessity of a request from outside the Bank. The determination by the Board as to whether an investigation should proceed based on such request will be made following receipt of a response from Management.[57]

F. Investigation and Reports[58]

1. Panel Investigation Report

If the Board determines that investigation is warranted, the Board names a panel of three or more rosters of independent experts, each of different nationalities, who qualify ("Panel").[59] The Panel will determine the investigating procedures necessary to arrive at a finding on the request presented. The Panel can rely upon outside technical experts. The Panel must obtain the consent of the borrower nation before conducting any investigations within that country.

The Panel will submit to the Board and the President findings of any IDB violations and Panel recommendations ("Panel Investigation Report"). The Panel Investigation Report will be made publicly available within 90 days following the Board's Report and Response described below.

2. Management Reply

Management will submit a reply to the Panel Investigation Report within 30 days. The IDB will make the reply publicly available within 90 days following the Board's Report and Response described below.

---

[57] See http://www.iadb.org/cont/poli/mecanism.pdf at Section 4.9.
[58] See http://www.iadb.org/cont/poli/mecanism.pdf at Sections 5-8.
[59] See http://www.iadb.org/cont/poli/mecanism.pdf at Section 2.

3. Board's Report and Response

On the basis of the Panel's investigation and Management's reply, the Board will determine what preventive or corrective action, if any, should be taken. Management will then implement the decision and report on the implementation with a time period designated by the Board. Upon request from the public, the Board will make its Report and Response available within 15 days of such request.

The Coordinator will also organize release of annual reports following up on the matter.

V. ASIAN DEVELOPMENT BANK—ACCOUNTABILITY MECHANISM

6 ADB Avenue
Mandaluyong City
0401 Metro Manila, Philippines

Special Project Facilitator
T: (63-2) 632-4825
F: (63-2) 636-2490
E: spf@adb.org
W: http://www.adb.org/SPF/default.asp

Secretary, Compliance Review Panel
T: (63-2) 632 4149
F: (63-2) 636 2088
E: crp@adb.org
W: http://compliance.adb.org/

A. Overview

The Asian Development Bank ("ADB") created the Accountability Mechanism in May 2003 "to provide better access for people adversely affected by ADB-assisted projects to voice and seek solutions to their problems and also report alleged violations of ADB's operational policies and procedures."[60] Taking effect on December 12, 2003, the Accountability Mechanism replaced the Inspection Function in an effort to streamline the former process and make it more effective. The Accountability Mechanism involves two phases—consultation and compliance. The steps are summarized well in an online brochure prepared by the ADB.[61]

---

[60] See http://www.adb.org/Accountability-Mechanism/default.asp.
[61] See http://www.compliance.adb.org/dir0035p.nsf/attachments/ADB-AccountabilityMechanismBrochure.pdf/$FILE/ADB-AccountabilityMechanismBrochure.pdf.

B. Consultation Phase

The Consultation Phase is designed "to assist people who are adversely affected by ADB-assisted projects to find solutions to their problems" and is led by the ADB's special project facilitator.[62]

The ADB has created a straightforward guide to explain the phase to affected communities and has included a sample complaint letter. Review this pamphlet before filing a complaint, as it discusses steps one must take prior to filing, eligibility, and how to draft a complaint.[63]

The Consultation Phase is implemented by the Office of the Special Project Facilitator ("OSPF") and involves the following steps:

Timeline	Event
	Complaintant files complaint
7 days from filing of complaint	Registration and acknowledgement of complaint
21 days from filing of complaint	Determination of eligibility of complaint
49 days from filing of complaint	Review and assessment of complaint—results in findings
7 days from report of findings	Complainant decides whether to proceed or file a request with the OSPF for compliance review—if at any time, complainant finds remainder of process not purposeful, complainant can request compliance review
14 days from notification	Comments on findings by the Operations Department and the complainant; recommendations by OSPF
7 days from comments and recommendations	Implementation of course of action in consultation process

Termination of consultation option to proceed with compliance review if consultation has been abandoned

---

[62] *See* http://www.adb.org/Accountability-Mechanism/default.aspb.
[63] *See* http://www.adb.org/SPF/Documents/information-guide.pdf.

Advocating for Adherence by Financial and Trade Institutions • *149*

C. Compliance Review

The Compliance Review is designed to "establish ADB's accountability in its operations by providing a forum in which project-affected people (and in special circumstances, any ADB Board member) can file requests for compliance review."[64] This phase is handled by the Compliance Review Panel ("CRP") in accordance with operating procedures approved on June 5, 2004.[65]

The CRP includes three members, one of whom serves as chair. Two members must come from regional countries, one of which is developing, and the third must come from a nonregional country.[66] In addition, the CRP receives Secretariat support from the Office of Compliance Review Panel.[67]

1. Filing Compliance Review Requests

The procedures for filing compliance review requests are discussed in detail in Part II of the Operating Procedures for the CRP.[68] Below is a summary of some of these procedures so be sure to consult the online information before filing. Moreover, Appendix I to the operating procedures provides a helpful sample form of a compliance review request provided for guidance even though no particular form is required.

The statute of limitations for commencing either consultation or compliance review is two years after a project is completed. Completion is measured either from when the ADB issues a project completion report, when physical completion ends and operation begins, or at final disbursement or termination of ADB's involvement in the project, whichever occurs earliest.[69]

Compliance review usually commences after consultation has occurred but when it has not resolved a matter. "In cases where the complainant files a request for compliance review, the S[pecial] P[rocedure] F[acilitator] will share with C[ompliance] R[eview] P[anel] documents and information relating to eligibility and fact-finding gathered under the consultation phase with CRP. If the SPF has rejected the eligibility of the complaint, CRP will determine independently whether in its judgment the request for compliance review meets CRP's eligibility criteria."[70]

---

[64] *See* http://www.adb.org/Accountability-Mechanism/default.asp.
[65] *See* http://compliance.adb.org/dir0035p.nsf/attachments/CRP%20Final%20Op%20Procedures-7Jun04.pdf/$FILE/CRP%20Final%20Op%20Procedures-7Jun04.pdf.
[66] *Id.* at ¶ 5.
[67] *Id.* at ¶ 4.
[68] *See* http://compliance.adb.org/dir0035p.nsf/attachments/CRP%20Final%20Op%20Procedures-7Jun04.pdf/$FILE/CRP%20Final%20Op%20Procedures-7Jun04.pdf, at ¶¶ 16–27.
[69] *See id.* at 6, note 2.
[70] *See* http://compliance.adb.org/dir0035p.nsf/attachments/CRP%20Final%20Op%20Procedures-7Jun04.pdf/$FILE/CRP%20Final%20Op%20Procedures-7Jun04.pdf, at ¶ 15.

150 • Defending the Environment

Similar to the consultation process, only the following can file a request for compliance review:

(i) any group of two or more people in a borrowing country where an ADB-assisted project is located or in a member country adjacent to the borrowing country;
(ii) a local representative of the affected group;
(iii) a non-local representative, in exceptional cases where local representation cannot be found and CRP agrees; or
(iv) any one or more members of the Board, after raising their concerns first with Management, in special cases involving allegations of serious violations of ADB's operational policies and procedures relating to an ongoing ADB-assisted project that have or are likely to have a direct, material, and adverse effect on a community or other grouping of individuals residing in the country where the project is being implemented or residing in a member country adjacent to the borrowing country.[71]

Identity of requesters is kept confidential if requested but anonymous requests are not accepted.[72]

Furthermore, requests must be:

(i) in writing:
(ii) addressed to:
Secretary, Compliance Review Panel
Asian Development Bank
6 ADB Avenue
Mandaluyong City
1550 Metro Manila, Philippines
(iii) mailed, faxed, e-mailed, or hand-delivered either to ADB headquarters or ADB representative office:

ADB headquarters:
T: 63-2 632 4149
F: 63-2 636 2088
E: crp@adb.org

If faxed or e-mailed, send paper copy by mail in English or any official or national language of ADB developing member countries if an English translation cannot be provided (but note that requests send in other languages may take more time).[73]

---

[71] *Id.* at ¶ 16.
[72] *Id.* at ¶ 18.
[73] *Id.* at ¶¶ 19-22.

Advocating for Adherence by Financial and Trade Institutions • *151*

As for the content of the request, not only do the Operating Procedures provide a sample at Appendix A, but also the OCRP is available to provide advice and guidance by telephone or e-mail.[74] The following must be included, the absence of which may cause the CRP to request such information, thereby delaying review:

(i) that the requester is, or is likely to be, directly affected materially and adversely by the ADB-assisted project;

(ii) that the requester claims that the direct and material harm is, or will be, the result of an act or omission of ADB's alleged failure to follow its operational polices and procedures (specified or otherwise) in the course of the formulation, processing, or implementation of the ADB-assisted project;

(iii) a description of the direct and material harm, *i.e.*, the rights and interests that have been, or are likely to be, directly affected materially and adversely by the ADB-assisted project;

(iv) the identification of the requester and contact information, with a request for confidentiality if required;

(v) if a request is made through a representative, identification of the project-affected people on whose behalf the request is made and evidence of authority to represent them;

(vi) a brief description of the ADB-assisted project, including its name and location;

(vii) the desired outcome or remedies that the project-affected people believe ADB should provide through the compliance review phase;

(viii) an explanation of the results of the requester's efforts to address the complaint first to SPF (or if the SPF has rejected the complaint as ineligible, an explanation of why the request should still be considered for compliance review);

(ix) an explanation of why any of the above information cannot be provided; and

(x) any other directly relevant matters or facts with supporting documents.[75]

Apart from the above eligibility requirements, the following requests are *prima facie* ineligible:

(i) not related to ADB's actions or omissions in the course of the formulation, processing, or implementation of ADB-assisted projects;

---

[74] *Id.* at ¶ 23.
[75] *Id.* at ¶ 24.

152 • *Defending the Environment*

(ii) about decisions made by ADB, the borrower, the executing agency, or the private project sponsor, relating to procurement of goods and services, including consulting services (addressed by a different body);
(iii) about allegations of fraud or corruption in ADB-assisted projects and by ADB staff (addressed by a different body);
(iv) about an ADB-assisted project for which a project completion report has been issued;
(v) relating to matters already considered under the previous inspection function or by CRP unless there is significant new evidence presented that was not known at the time of the original complaint or unless the subsequent complaint can be readily consolidated with the earlier complaint;
(vi) about the adequacy or suitability of ADB's existing policies and procedures;
(vii) that are considered by CRP to be frivolous, malicious, trivial, or generated to gain competitive advantage;
(viii) within the jurisdiction of ADB's Appeals Committee or ADB's Administrative Tribunal or relating to ADB personnel matters (addressed by a different body);
(ix) relating to actions that are the responsibility of other parties, such as a borrower, executing agency, or potential borrower, unless the conduct of these other parties is directly relevant to an assessment of ADB's compliance with its operational policies and procedures;
(x) relating to matters that otherwise do not involve an action or omission as a result of ADB's failure to follow its operational policies and procedures;
(xi) relating to the laws, policies, and regulations of the executing agency or DMC government concerned unless they directly relate to ADB's compliance with its operational policies and procedures;
(xii) relating to a private sector project that received concept clearance before May 29, 2003; and/or
(xiii) when a corresponding complaint has not first been filed with the SPF.[76]

2. Compliance Review Process

The following table summarizes the review process, which is detailed in Part III of the Operating Procedures.[77]

---

[76] *Id.* at ¶ 26.
[77] *Id.* at ¶¶ 28–45.

Advocating for Adherence by Financial and Trade Institutions • 153

Timeline	Event
	Compliance review request filed with Compliance Review Panel ("CRP")
7 days from receipt of request	Registration and acknowledgement of request
14 days from registration of request (or 21 days from registration if SPF has determined complaint ineligible)	Determination of eligibility of request —if CRP finds ineligible, CRP informs Board —if CRP finds eligible, CRP asks Board to authorize compliance review
21 days from receipt of CRP's recommendation	Board authorizes compliance review on a no-objection basis
7 days from receipt of Board's decision	Requester informed of Board's decision
14 days from receipt of Board's authorization for compliance review	CRP will clear with Board's Compliance Review Committee the CRP's its terms of reference for compliance review and then release those terms along with the CRP's methodology
	CRP then conducts review
No timetable	CRP issues draft report with findings and recommendations to ADB Management and requester for comments
30 days from receipt of CRP's draft report	ADB Management and requester provide comments
14 days from receipt of responses from ADB Management and requester	CRP reviews comments before presenting final report with findings to the Board along with recommendations to ensure compliance
21 days from receipt of CRP's final report	The Board will consider CRP's final report and make the final decision regarding any recommendations on how to bring the project into compliance and/or mitigate any harm, if appropriate
7 days from Board's decision	Board's decision and CRP's final report released to requester
	Board approves the Monitoring of Implementation of Remedial Actions

3. Remedial Actions

These procedures are detailed at Part IV of the Operating Procedures.[78] Generally, CRP will monitor remedial actions in accordance with applicable ADB procedures (sometimes requiring consent of the borrower or grant recipient) within a period of five years, reporting annually to the Board, unless the Board specifies otherwise. The methodology for monitoring may include consultations, document review, site visits receipt of information from the requester or the public, or similar steps.

The goal of remediation is for CRP to prepare a monitoring report. CRP will usually first provide the draft report to the Board's Compliance Review Committee to review and comment before making the final report available to the requester. That final report will include:

(i) a summary of the original request and any original Board decision on that request;
(ii) a summary of any information provided by the requester(s), the concerned stakeholders, and any other interested parties;
(iii) CRP's findings regarding the current status of implementation of the Board's decision; and
(iv) any further recommendations by CRP as necessary to bring the project into compliance.[79]

4. Requester and Third Party Participation

Part V of the Operation Procedures sets forth terms for requester and third party participation.[80] These rules generally encourage the requester and third party stakeholders to provide the CRP with new evidence and supplemental information during and following compliance review so that the CRP can then revise its review and implementation process as necessary.

2.4 Chasma Right Bank Irrigation Project

In November 2002, a Request for Inspection of the Chashma Right Bank Irrigation Project was submitted on behalf of those affected by the Project. The Request alleged that the Project contained design-related social and environmental problems, induced flooding, lacked proper resettlement and compensation plans, and lacked information-sharing or consultation with the affected parties.[81] The Board of Directors of the Asian Development Bank (ADB) approved inspection of the Project in April 2003. Following the inspection, the

---

[78] *Id.* at ¶¶ 46-49.
[79] *Id.* at ¶ 49.
[80] *Id.* at ¶¶ 50-52.
[81] Report and Recommendation of the Board Inspection Committee to the Board of Directors on the Request for Inspection on Chashma Right Bank Irrigation Project (July 2004), *available at* http://www.adb.org/documents/inspection/pak/chashma_irrigation/text.pdf (last visited June 22, 2004).

2.4 Chasma Right Bank Irrigation Project *(continued)*

Panel submitted a report to the Board Inspection Committee (BIC) for its consideration in making a final recommendation to the Board of Directors.

The Panel found several breaches of ADB policy and procedures which had detrimental environmental effects on the Requesters including: poorly timed response to flooding, interference with traditional irrigation systems, reduced access to grazing land and woods, and violation of the rights of the affected persons to gain access to information or participate in decision-making.[82] The Panel recommended five steps for Management to address the Project's issues: (1) that ADB discuss extending the completion date with the Government of Pakistan to allow time to address the remaining problems; (2) that ADB discuss funding of a long-term environmental management plan with the Government of Pakistan; (3) that ADB formulate legally binding agreements based on the two suggestions above; (4) that ADB assure transparency in other large-scale irrigation projects; and (5) that ADB adequately compensate and resettle affected persons.[83] In response to the Panel's report, Management contended that although some of the environmental issues listed had arisen during the project, that were not a result of any breach of ADB's policies and procedures. Management did admit to poorly supervised resettlement and flooding plans due to a lack of continuity in supervisors and a lack of resources.[84]

The BIC approved the Panel's findings in BIC's recommendations to the Board, acknowledging that some of the Panel's suggestions were already underway, including discussions with the Government of Pakistan for additional time and a long-term environmental management plan. BIC also noted that in following the procedures of the Accountability Mechanism, it was necessary that the Compliance Review Panel (CRP) monitor ADB to assure that the Panel's recommendations were being implemented.[85]

VI. EUROPEAN BANK FOR RECONSTRUCTION AND DEVELOPMENT—INDEPENDENT RECOURSE MECHANISM

One Exchange Square
London EC 2A 2JN
United Kingdom
T: 44 20 7338 6868
F: 44 20 7338 6102
E: ngo@ebrd.com
W: www.ebrd.com

---

[82] *Id.* at 6.
[83] *See* the Panel's Recommendation, *available at* http://www.adb.org/Inspection/projects/chashma_right.asp (last visited June 24, 2005).
[84] Report and Recommendation, *supra* at note 24, at 6.
[85] *Id.* at 11.

156 • Defending the Environment

Established in London in April 1991 pursuant to the Agreement Establishing the European Bank for Reconstruction and Development signed in May 1990 ("EBRD Agreement"), the European Bank for Reconstruction and Development is the first multilateral development bank to have an explicit environmental mandate in its founding charter. Article 2 of the EBRD Agreement states that the EBRD shall pass measures "to promote in the full range of its activities environmentally sound and sustainable development."[86] Moreover, Article 11 of the EBRD Agreement provides that the EBRD make loans available for environmental programs, and Article 35 of the EBRD Agreement requires the EBRD to report annually on the environmental and public health impacts of its activities.[87]

On April 29, 2003, the EBRD Board of Directors approved new Environmental Policies and new Environmental Procedures for the EBRD.[88] The Environmental Policy provides an Independent Recourse Mechanism ("IRM") "to provide a venue for complaints and grievances from people who are, or are likely to be, directly and adversely affected by an EBRD-financed project to determine where there has been material non-compliance by the Bank with specified policies, such as the Environmental Policy."[89] The mechanism will determine whether the EBRD should conduct fact-finding, mediation, conciliation, or other methods to resolve these complaints.[90] However, the full scope of the IRM and the submission process are still being developed as of the time of this writing.

In addition, the EBRD Environmental Procedures include a public consultation process that requires the EBRD and/or project sponsors to inform affected communities and concerned NGOs of projects and provide documents where appropriate.[91]

VII. EUROPEAN PARLIAMENT—COMMITTEE ON PETITIONS

Members Activities Division
L-2929 Luxembourg
T: (352) 43 00-1
F: (352) 43 00 294 94, (352) 43 293 93, (352) 43 292 92
E: www.europarl.eu.int/petition/petition_en.htm
W: www.europarl.eu.int/committees/peti_home.htm
—or— www.europarl.eu.int/petition/help_en.htm

---

[86] See http://www.ebrd.com/about/index.htm.
[87] See http://www.ebrd.com/about/index.htm, arts. 17 and 35.
[88] See http://www.ebrd.com/enviro/index.htm, http://www.ebrd.com/about/policies/enviro/policy/policy.pdf (Environmental Policy), and http://www.ebrd.com/about/policies/enviro/procedur/procedur.pdf (Environmental Procedures).
[89] See http://www.ebrd.com/about/policies/enviro/policy/policy.pdf at ¶ 32.
[90] See http://www.ebrd.com/about/policies/enviro/policy/policy.pdf at ¶ 32.
[91] See http://www.ebrd.com/about/policies/enviro/procedur/procedur.pdf at § 2.3.4. See also THE EUROPEAN BANK FOR RECONSTRUCTION AND DEVELOPMENT: AN ENVIRONMENTAL PROGRESS REPORT prepared by the Center for International Environmental Law, at http://www.ciel.org/Publications/summary1.html.

Advocating for Adherence by Financial and Trade Institutions • 157

The European Parliament is the legislative arm of the European Union, which is predominantly a trade institution. With the European Parliament's adoption of the Charter of Fundamental Rights of the European Union, the Committee on Petitions entertains submissions concerning environmental protection issues in EU member states.[92] Again, step-by-step procedures governing submissions about environmental problems as well as a model application can be found on the European Parliament's website.[93] Although the European Parliament reminds applicants that it is not a judicial body, the ability to raise the European Parliament's awareness of an environmental problem may still contribute to the resolution of an environmental protection problem in Europe.

VIII. AFRICAN DEVELOPMENT BANK GROUP—INDEPENDENT REVIEW MECHANISM

Headquarters
Rue Joseph Anoma
01 BP 1387 Abidjan 01
Côte d'Ivoire
T: (225) 20.20.44.44
F: (225) 20.20.49.59
E: afdb@afdb.org
W: www.afdb.org

Temporary Relocation
Avenue du Ghana, Rue Pierre de Coubertin, Rue Hedi Nouira
BP. 323 1002
Tunis Belvedére
Tunisia
T: (+216) 71 333 511 / 7110 3450
F: (+216) 71 351 933
E : afdb@afdb.org
W: www.afdb.org

Consisting of an African Development Bank and an African Development Fund, the African Development Bank Group came into force in 1964 pursuant to the Agreement Establishing the African Development Bank that was signed in 1963.[94]

On June 30, 2004, the African Development Bank Group decided to establish an Independent Review Mechanism composed of a Compliance Review and Mediation Unit and an independent Roster of Experts. The

---

[92] Chapter 1 discussed the Committee's role in considering environmental human rights issues.
[93] See http://www.europarl.eu.int/petition/help_en.htm.
[94] See http://www.afdb.org/pls/portal/docs/PAGE/ADB_ADMIN_PG/DOCUMENTS/ LEGALINFORMATION/AGREEMENT_ESTABLISHING_ADB_JULY2002_EN.DOC.

mechanism is not yet operating but is anticipated to possess many of the attributes summarized in "Proposal on the Establishment of an Inspection Fund for the African Development Bank Group."[95]

Part of the process involves creation of a Roster of Experts from which Compliance Review Panels would be constituted. Upon recommendation from the President, the Board of Directors would appoint three experts to the Roster every five years for a single term, staggering the first three experts at three, four, and five years to ensure continuity.[96] "The[se] experts would be drawn from persons who are nationals of member states of the Bank Group, possessing the expertise, experience and integrity to act independently and who are professionally qualified in their chosen fields."[97]

There also would be a Director to administer the Compliance Review Unit with assistance from a Compliance Officer and staff.[98]

The mechanism would receive and review any requests arising from the African Development Bank Group's operational policies and procedures "including requests concerning . . . environmental compliance with respect to private sector and/or non-sovereign guaranteed projects financed by the Bank."[99]

Requests would be received only from groups of two or more individuals with a common interest. "A local representative would be permitted to file a request for review on behalf of affected persons. A foreign representative would only be permitted to file a request for review on behalf of affected persons in exceptional circumstances to be defined in the mechanism's operating rules and procedures."[100]

Eligibility[101] requirements for requests would include:

- Good faith effort to resolve the issue through mediation with the relevant Bank department.
- Requester would be "directly and adversely affected by a Bank Group-financed project."
- Request does not pertain to an excluded category:
  - procurement;
  - fraud and corruption—separate process being created
  - matter before the administrative tribunal

---

[95] *See* http://www.afdb.org/pls/portal/docs/PAGE/ADB_ADMIN_PG/DOCUMENTS/LEGALINFORMATION/ADB_INSPECTION_FUNCTION_BOARD_EN.DOC.
[96] *Id.* at Section 3.20.
[97] *Id.* at Section 3.21.
[98] *Id.* at Sections 3.23–3.27.
[99] *Id.* at Section 3.28.
[100] *Id.* at Section 3.33.
[101] *Id.* at Sections 3.31 and 3.35.

- matter pending before another judicial body
- frivolous and malicious requests
- matter motivated by intention to gain competitive advantage
- previously decided matters
- completed projects (12 months after physical completion)
- requests concerning private sector or other nonsovereign guaranteed projects except with respect to social and environmental compliance;
- adequacy of suitability of a Bank policy (because that review if for the Board alone to undertake)
* Director approves
* The end result: "The CRMU would, to the extent practicable and as directed by the President or the Boards, as the case may be, monitor the implementation of approved recommendations and submit monitoring reports to the competent authority. The CRMU would also include in its annual report a section on such implementation." The CRMU would, to the extent practicable and as directed by the President or the Boards, as the case may be, monitor the implementation of approved recommendations and submit monitoring reports to the competent authority. The CRMU would also include in its annual report a section on such implementation.[102]

IX. NORTH AMERICAN COMMISSION ON ENVIRONMENTAL COOPERATION

393 Rue St-Jacques Ouest
Bureau 200
Montréal (Québec), H2Y 1N9 Canada
T: (514) 350-4300
F: (514) 350-4314
E: info@ccemtl.org
W: www.cec.org

A. Overview

The North American Agreement on Environmental Cooperation ("NAAEC")—more commonly known as the NAFTA environmental side agreement—has created a process in which non-state actors from Canada, Mexico, or the United States (each a "Party") can make a submission to the Secretariat of the North American Commission on Environmental Cooperation ("CEC Secretariat"). The submission must allege that one of these

---

[102] *Id.* at Sections 3.36.

governments is failing or has failed to effectively enforce an existing environmental law. Such submissions can result in a factual record prepared by the CEC Secretariat with the permission of two members of the three-member CEC Council of Environmental Ministers (the "Council"). The factual record discusses the environmental degradation and the defending government's ineffective response. After the Council reviews and comments on the draft factual record prepared for a particular matter, then the CEC Secretariat can make the final factual record public with the Council's approval. Such factual records can be powerful tools for future domestic administrative, legislative, and judicial proceedings or media campaigns focused on the issue discussed in the record.

B. Eligibility

Any non-governmental organization or person residing or established in Canada, Mexico, or the United States is eligible. Article 45(1) of the NAAEC defines non-governmental organization as "any scientific, professional, business, non-profit, or public interest organization or association which is neither affiliated with, nor under the direction of, a government."

C. Making a Submission[103]

1. The submission must:
   a. be 15 letter-size typed pages or less, excluding supporting materials;
   b. be in English, French, or Spanish;
   c. include a copy on diskette if at all possible;
   d. clearly identify the person or organization making the submission and provide contact information (address, telephone, e-mail);
   e. provide sufficient information to allow the Secretariat to review the submission, including any documentary evidence on which the submission may be based;
   f. appear to be aimed at promoting enforcement rather than at harassing industry;
   g. be mailed (not faxed and not e-mailed) to:
   North American Commission on Environmental Cooperation
   393 Rue St-Jacques Ouest
   Bureau 200
   Montréal (Québec), H2Y 1N9
   Canada

---

[103] For important additional details, see Article 14 of the NAAEC, http://www.cec.org/pubs_info_resources/law_treat_agree/naaec/naaec05.cfm?varlan=english#14; CEC Council Resolution 99-06 (June 29, 2001) (provides guidelines), http://www.cec.org/citizen/guide_submit/index.cfm?varlan=english; *Bringing the Facts to Life*, CEC Secretariat (provides step-by-step procedures for making a submission), http://www.cec.org/files/PDF/SEM/Bringing Facts.pdf at 9–22.

Advocating for Adherence by Financial and Trade Institutions • 161

2. In addition, the submitter must communicate the matter in writing to the relevant authorities of the Party and indicate such communication and response in its submission.
3. Moreover, the Secretariat will consider the following factors to determine whether to request a response from the Party so submitters may want to address them where applicable:
   a. whether the submission alleges harm to the person or organization making the submission;
   b. whether the submission, alone or in combination with other submissions, raises matters whose further study in this process would advance the goals of the NAAEC;
   c. whether the submitter pursued private remedies available under the Party's law; and
   d. whether the submission is drawn exclusively from NACEC mass media reports.

D. Decision Making

If the Secretariat finds that the submission qualifies, then it determines whether to request a response from the Party. If the Secretariat determines that a request is warranted, the Party has 30 days from the date it receives a copy of the submission from the Secretariat to provide its response. Such response includes whether a pending judicial or administrative proceeding is currently considering the same matter, in which case the Secretariat will not proceed any further.[104]

After receiving a response from the Party, the Secretariat decides whether a factual record is warranted. If so, the Secretariat seeks permission of two-thirds of the three-person Council. The Secretariat "shall consider any information furnished by a Party and may consider any relevant technical, scientific or other information that is: (a) publicly available; (b) submitted by interested non-governmental organizations or persons; (c) submitted by the Joint Public Advisory Committee; or (d) developed by the Secretariat or by independent experts."[105] The Secretariat then submits a draft of the factual record to the Council for any Party, not just the Party against whom the submission is alleged, to review and comment. The Secretariat then finalizes the factual record, incorporating appropriate comments. The Council can then vote to make the final factual record publicly available.[106]

---

[104] See Article 14(3) of the NAAEC, http://www.cec.org/pubs_info_resources/law_treat_agree/naaec/naaec05.cfm?varlan=english#14.

[105] See Article 15 of the NAAEC, http://www.cec.org/pubs_info_resources/law_treat_agree/naaec/naaec05.cfm?varlan=english#15.

[106] Id.

2.5 CEC—Coal Fired Power Plants

In September 2004, the Secretariat received a submission from a coalition of American and Canadian environmental groups, claiming that the United States is failing to enforce effectively the federal Clean Water Act against coal-fired power plants for mercury emissions that are contaminating thousands of rivers, lakes, and other bodies of water throughout the United States and across the border in Canada.[107] According to the petitioners, since 1993, the number of fish consumption advisories for mercury has risen from 899 to 2347. They also allege that the U.S. Environmental Protection Agency "is allowing both nonpoint and point source discharges of mercury from coal-fired power plants that are contributing to a steady degradation of the nation's waterways as evidenced by increasing mercury fish advisories and the effective withdrawal of existing uses (fishable) of many of these water bodies."[108] In April 2005, the Secretariat accepted a response from the U.S. government contending that steps have been taken to remedy the mercury emissions and the Secretariat will now determine if an investigation is warranted.[109]

2.6 CEC—Montreal Technoparc[110]

This submission, filed by several Canadian and United States environmental NGOs, asserts that Canada is failing to enforce effectively the Canadian Fisheries Act against the City of Montreal with regard to discharge of toxic pollutants from the city's Technoparc site into the St. Lawrence River.[111] The submitters cited information on the adverse effects of the discharges on human health and aquatic ecosystems.[112] The Secretariat determined that a factual record was necessary, it formulated a work plan, and, in February 2005, the Secretariat requested information relevant to the factual record via its public website.[113]

---

[107] *See* NACEC, Coal-Fired Power Plants, Submission ID SEM-04-005, *available at* http://www.cec.org/citizen/submissions/details/index.cfm?varlan=english&ID=103 (last visited June 8, 2005).

[108] *Id.*

[109] *Id.*

[110] This development is an update to a development that was included in the issue paper prepared for the Commission's 60th Session.

[111] *See* NACEC, Montreal Technoparc, Submission ID SEM-03-005, *available at* http://www.cec.org/citizen/submissions/details/index.cfm?varlan=english&ID=94 (last visited June 8, 2005).

[112] *Id.*

[113] *Id.*

X. CANADA-CHILE COMMISSION ON ENVIRONMENTAL COOPERATION

A. Overview

The Canada-Chile Agreement on Environmental Cooperation ("CCAEC") is the environmental side agreement to the Canada-Chile Free Trade Agreement ("CCFTA"). The CCFTA resulted from the inability of Canada, Mexico, and the United States collectively to permit Chile to join the North American Free Trade Agreement ("NAFTA"). Consequently, Canada and Chile pursued a bilateral free trade agreement modeled on NAFTA with a core trade text, a labor side agreement, and an environmental side agreement. The resulting CCAEC is modeled on the NAAEC and provides for a similar citizen submission process.

Again, non-state actors from Canada or Chile can allege that either of these governments is failing or has failed to effectively enforce an existing environmental law. Such submissions can result in a factual record prepared by the Joint Submission Committee with the permission of the government concerned. The factual record discusses the environmental degradation and the defending government's ineffective response. After the Council reviews and comments on the draft factual record prepared for a particular matter, the Secretariat can make the final factual record public with the Council's approval. Such factual records can be powerful tools for future domestic administrative, legislative, and judicial proceedings or media campaigns focused on the issue discussed in the record.

B. Eligibility

Any non-governmental organization or person residing or established in Chile or Canada is eligible. Article 44(1) of the CCAEC defines a non-governmental organization as "any scientific, professional, business, non-profit, or public interest organization or association which is neither affiliated with, nor under the direction of, a government."[114]

C. Making a Submission[115]

1. The submission must:
   a. be 15 letter-size typed pages or less, excluding supporting materials;
   b. be in English, French, or Spanish;

---

[114] See http://can-chil.gc.ca/English/Resource/Agrements/Aeccc/AECCC-2.cfm#article44.

[115] For important additional details, see Article 14 of the CCAEC, http://can-chil.gc.ca/English/Resource/Agreements/AECCC/AECCC_2.cfm#article14; Guidelines, http://can-chil.gc.ca/English/Profile/JSC/Registry/guide.cfm.

c. include a copy on diskette if at all possible;
   d. clearly identify the person or organization making the submission and provide contact information (address, telephone, e-mail);
   e. provide sufficient information to allow the Secretariat to review the submission, including any documentary evidence on which the submission may be based;
   f. appear to be aimed at promoting enforcement rather than at harassing industry;
   g. include, in the case of submissions sent by a person or organization residing or established in the territory of Canada, a declaration to the effect that the matter will not subsequently be submitted to the Secretariat of the Commission for Environmental Cooperation under the North American Agreement on Environmental Cooperation, with a view to avoiding duplication in the handling of submissions;
   h. be mailed (not faxed and not e-mailed) to:
      Canada-Chile Commission for Environmental Cooperation
      National Secretariat of Canada
      Environment Canada
      10 Wellington Street, 23rd Floor
      Hull, Quebec
      Canada K1A 0H3
      www.can-chil.gc.ca
      — or —
      Canada-Chile Commission for Environmental Cooperation
      National Secretariat of Chile
      National Commission for the Environment (CONAMA)
      Obispo Donoso 6, Providencia
      Santiago, Chile
2. In addition, the submitter must communicate the matter in writing to the relevant authorities of the Party and indicate such communication and response in its submission.
3. Moreover, the Joint Submission Committee will consider the following factors to determine whether to request a response from the Party so submitters may want to address them where applicable:
   a. whether the submission alleges harm to the person or organization making the submission;
   b. whether the submission, alone or in combination with other submissions, raises matters whose further study in this process would advance the goals of the CCAEC;
   c. whether the submitter pursued private remedies available under the Party's law; and
   d. whether the submission is drawn exclusively from mass media reports.

D. Decision Making

If the Joint Submission Committee finds that a submission qualifies, then it determines whether to request a response from the Party. If the Joint Submission Committee determines that a request is warranted, the Party has 30 days from the date it receives a copy of the submission from the Joint Submission Committee to provide its response. Such response includes whether a pending judicial or administrative proceeding is currently considering the same matter, in which case the Joint Submission Committee will not proceed any further.[116]

After receiving a response from the Party, the Joint Submission Committee decides whether a factual record is warranted. If so, the Joint Submission Committee seeks permission of two-thirds of the three-person Council. The Joint Submission Committee "shall consider any information furnished by a Party and may consider any relevant technical, scientific or other information that is: (a) publicly available; (b) submitted by interested non-governmental organizations or persons; (c) submitted by the Joint Public Advisory Committee; or (d) developed by the Joint Submissions Committee or by independent experts."[117] The Joint Submission Committee then submits a draft of the factual record to the Council for both Parties to review and comment. The Joint Submission Committee then finalizes the factual record, incorporating appropriate comments. The Council can then vote to make the final factual record publicly available.[118]

2.7 Cascada-Chile Project[119]

On June 27, 2000, three non-governmental organizations—Comité Nacional Pro-Defensa de la Fauna y Flora, Sociedades Sustentables Red Nacional de Acción Ecológica, and Instituto de Ecología Politica—represented by Fiscalía del Medio Ambiente, a Chilean public interest environmental law organization, filed the first citizen submission to the Canada-Chile Commission on Environmental Cooperation. The organizations challenged the Chilean government's failure to require an adequate environmental assessment from the Cascada-Chile wood chip and structural panel manufacturing plant. With the help of the Sierra Legal of Canada and the Interamerican Association for Environmental Defense (AIDA), FIMA argued that the Chilean government

(continued)

---

[116] See Article 14(3) of the CCAEC, http://can-chil.gc.ca/English/Resource/Agreements/AECCC/AECCC_2.cfm#article14.

[117] See Article 15 of the CCAEC, http://can-chil.gc.ca/English/Resource/Agreements/AECCC/AECCC_2.cfm#article15 (Article 15).

[118] Id.

[119] Submission No. A14-2000-01. For a copy of the petition, see http://can-chil.gc.ca/English/Profile/JSC/Registry/Registry.cfm (Submission No. A14-2000-01) or www.aida2.org.

> **2.7 Cascada-Chile Project** *(continued)*
>
> had looked only at the environmental impact from the construction of the manufacturing facility itself without also considering the harm to 5,000 hectares of old-growth forest that would occur each year when the plant began producing wood chips.
>
> On August 2, 2000, the National Secretariats notified the submitters that their submission met Article 14(1) criteria. The submission was then forwarded to the Joint Submission Committee to decide whether the submission merits requesting a response from the government of Chile. On November 28, 2000, the Joint Submission Committee requested a response from the government of Chile in accordance with Article 14(2). The following January, the Chilean government submitted its response. Soon thereafter the U.S. partner in the Cascada-Chile venture—Boise Cascade—ended the project. Coincidently (if not consequently), by April 2001, the Joint Submission Committee decided not to develop a factual record.

XI. CONCLUSION

Environmental review of the acts of international and regional financial institutions is a promising development for the future. With regular challenges by civil society through inspection panel and ombudsmen mechanisms, these institutions will take increasingly more seriously their commitment to development in a manner protective of the environment and public health. Moreover, such enforcement actions may help to strengthen some of the weaker mechanisms as they realize that taking the initiative themselves rather than constantly defending against civil society complaints is a more effective and positive use of resources.

CHAPTER 3

PREVENTING NEW INTERNATIONAL TRADE AND INVESTMENT DISPUTE RESOLUTION MECHANISMS FROM UNDERMINING CURRENT ENVIRONMENTAL AND PUBLIC HEALTH REGULATIONS

I. INTRODUCTION

This chapter focuses on strategies to prevent adverse impacts to the environment and public health from investment and trade decisions of international finance and trade dispute settlement processes. Although these strategies involve some of the same institutions discussed in Chapter 2, they are different. The strategies in that chapter involve initiating submissions to international finance and trade dispute resolution bodies to advocate for environmental and public health issues. Strategies in this chapter involve responding to submissions initiated by nation-states and investors to protect and promote international investment and trade (*i.e.*, globalization) at the expense of environmental and public health regulations.

A. The Impact of Increased Globalization on Environmental and Public Health Regulations

The creation of the European Union ("Eu") on November 1, 1993,[1] the implementation of the North American Free Trade Agreement ("NAFTA") on January 1, 1994,[2] and the establishment of the World Trade Organization ("WTO") on January 1, 1995[3] have ushered in an era of globalization in the aftermath of the Cold War. New trade institutions have emerged and existing financial institutions have been reinvigorated. The international agreements

---

[1] See http://europa.eu.int/abc/history/1993/1993_en.htm.
[2] 19 U.S.C. §§ 3301 *et seq.*
[3] See http://www.wto.org/english/thewto_e/whatis_e/whatis_e.htm.

giving birth to these new and reinvigorated institutions include efficient and effective dispute resolution mechanisms such as the WTO Dispute Settlement Body and NAFTA Chapter 11 tribunals that issue binding judgments. Such binding judgments are often enforceable by trade sanctions that these tribunals can impose or through subsequent domestic action. Moreover, these binding judgments tend to protect and promote trade or investment at the expense of domestic environmental or public health regulations. Consequently, an indirect manner in which to enforce international environmental law is to prevent investment and trade dispute settlement from undermining vital environmental and public health protections.

Over the past several years, nation-states and investors—the only entities eligible to appear before these dispute resolution bodies—have filed claims alleging that certain domestic environmental and/or public health regulations conflict with the terms of these trade and investment provisions. These claims call upon the nation-state enforcing such regulations to stop enforcing the law, change the law, and/or pay compensation to the allegedly aggrieved nation-state or investor.

For example, in the WTO dispute *United States—Import Prohibition of Certain Shrimp and Shrimp Products*[4] the nation-states of India, Malaysia, Pakistan, and Thailand claimed that a U.S. federal law banning imports of shrimp and shrimp products from countries that harvested such shrimp in a manner adversely affecting sea turtles[5] constituted unfair trade in violation of Articles XI:1 and XIII:1 the General Agreement on Tariffs and Trade ("GATT 1947").[6] They argued that the restriction was greater than necessary, that it benefited U.S. shrimp harvesters not subject to the restriction, and that it did not qualify for the environmental exceptions in Article XX of GATT 1947[7] because the restriction was a trade measure in disguise. However, the U.S. Congress had passed the law as part of a larger turtle protection and conservation effort,[8] not to level the playing field for U.S. fisheries. The WTO ruled that the United States needed to enforce the law in a less restrictive manner or pay compensation.[9] The U.S. Department of State complied by relaxing its guidelines that implement the statutory provision.[10] Similar concerns have been raised in connection with investor-

---

[4] *See* WTO Official Record WT/DS58/R, WTO Doc. No. 98-1710 (May 15, 1998), http://www.sice.oas.org/DISPUTE/wto/58r00/shrius.asp ("Decision").

[5] Section 609 of Pub. L. 101-162. *See* 16 U.S.C. § 1537note, *available at* http://www4.law.cornell.edu/uscode/16/1537.notes.html.

[6] *See* WTO Official Record LT/UR/A-1A/1/GATT/2, WTO Doc. No. (Apr. 15, 1994), http://docsonline.wto.org/gen_browseDetail.asp?preprog=3, at arts. XI:1 and XIII:1. *See also* Decision, *supra* note 4, at ¶¶ 3.135-3.143 and ¶¶ 7.11-7.23.

[7] *See* WTO Official Record LT/UR/A-1A/1/GATT/2, WTO Doc. No. (Apr. 15, 1994), http://docsonline.wto.org/gen_browseDetail.asp?preprog=3, at art. XX(b), XX(g) and XX: chapeau. *See also* Decision, *supra* note 4, at ¶¶ 3.144-3.296 and ¶¶ 7.24-7.63.

[8] *See* 16 U.S.C. § 1537 note, *at* http://www4.law.cornell.edu/uscode/16/1537.html.

[9] *See* Decision, *supra* note 4, at ¶¶ 8.1-8.2.

[10] *Compare* Revised Notice of Guidelines for Determining Comparability of Foreign

Preventing Adverse Impacts from Investment and Trade Decisions • 169

state arbitrations under NAFTA as well as other investment and trade dispute resolution processes.[11]

Despite the emergence of dispute resolution processes in trade regimes that pose a threat to the environment and public health, civil society succeeded in the late 1990s in preventing the Organization for Economic Cooperation and Development ("OECD"), an economic development international organization with members primarily from Europe and North America, from launching an effort to create a multilateral investment treaty that would compliment the General Agreement on Tariffs and Trade and related agreements collectively administered by the World Trade Organization. Initially, civil society demanded inclusion of environmental and labor standards and then sought to oppose its completion without such additions. In fact, the inability of OECD members to achieve a global investment agreement complete with a dispute resolution process likely led these members, in their capacity as members of regional trade organizations like NAFTA and the European Union, to incorporate investment sections into trade treaties and provide non-state investors with alternative dispute resolution in order to encourage foreign investment. One particular new development to watch is the negotiation of the Free Trade Agreement for the Americas ("FTAA") modeled heavily on NAFTA.[12] Consequently, dispute resolution initiated by multinational corporations has begun posing a threat to the environment, public health, and safety, thereby necessitating the use of strategies mentioned in this chapter.

In sum, international investment and trade dispute resolution bodies are capable of issuing binding decisions that can undermine domestic environmental and public health regulations. Consequently, environmentalists must go beyond just advocating for international investment and finance bodies to adhere to their own environmental and public health standards or seeking to enforce obligations set forth in Multilateral Environmental Agreements ("MEAs"). Instead, NGOs and community groups need to monitor and intervene directly in international trade and investment dispute settlement to minimize the impact on domestic environmental and public health regulations.

Programs for the Protection of Sea Turtles in Shrimp Trawl Fishing Operations, 63 Fed. Reg. 46094 (Aug. 28, 1998), *with* Revised Notice of Guidelines for Determining Comparability of Foreign Programs for the Protection of Sea Turtles in Shrimp Trawl Fishing Operations, 64 Fed. Reg. 36946 (July 8, 1999).

[11] *See* documents pertaining to *In the Arbitration under Chapter 11 of the North American Free Trade Agreement and the UNCITRAL Arbitration Rules between Methanex Corporation and the United States of America*, *at* http://www.state.gov/s/l/c5818.htm.

[12] *See* http://www.ftaa-alca.org.

B. Strategically Targeting Globalization Processes

This chapter suggests three strategies to help minimize the impact of international trade and investment dispute settlement on environmental and public health regulations. The first strategy involves non-state actors appearing as *amicus curiae* in trade and investment disputes and then asserting relevant environmental and public health positions for decision makers to consider. The second strategy involves non-state actors requesting that their government bring environmental or public health claims before these trade and investment bodies to advance their interests. The third strategy involves submitting public comments to domestic governmental officials with respect to environmental reviews of trade and investment treaties. A fourth strategy—discussed in a latter chapter on domestic strategies rather than in this chapter—involves non-state actors demanding transparency and public participation from their governments with respect to existing and future trade and investment treaties and institutions. Non-state actors can request government information about a trade and investment matter that is (or could be) adversely affecting the environment and public health and safety and file court actions if the government denies such requests. Connected to this fourth strategy, non-state actors also can ask environmentalists to serve on government advisory committees addressing trade and investment issues and file court actions if the government refuses.

C. Why New Strategies?

One may ask why the approach of intervening in investment and trade disputes is necessary to protect domestic environmental and public health regulations. After all, fora already exist in international finance and trade bodies and in connection with MEAs to address such concerns separately, and strategies for those processes are provided in other chapters. Moreover, some of the finance and trade treaties that create the very dispute resolution processes addressed in this chapter also contain provisions calling for the protection of the environment and public health.

The reason for proposing the strategies in this chapter is that these strategies provide a more direct manner in which to counter the impact of international trade and investment on the environment and public health. Such directness is required because an imbalance currently exists between the level of protection for investment and trade provided by trade dispute resolution processes and the level of protection for the environment and public health provided by finance and trade dispute resolution process and/or MEAs. Neither of these latter two avenues results in binding judgments enforced by trade sanctions; however, the former avenue—trade dispute resolution processes—usually does.[13] Furthermore, even when the

---

[13] For example, *compare* NAFTA, art. 1135, *at* http://www.nafta-sec-alena.org/english/index.htm (enforcement provision for investment disputes) *with* NAAEC, arts. 14–15, *at* http://www.cec.org/pubs_info_resources/law_treat_agree/naaec/index.cfm?varlan=english.

International Court of Justice ("ICJ") can provide even secondary enforcement,[14] the voluntary nature of nation-state personal jurisdiction before the ICJ makes this enforcement avenue unappealing at best, and, more often, unavailable.

Moreover, in the case of MEAs, the dispute resolution provisions are much weaker than trade dispute resolution even if the environmental obligations in MEAs are as strong as the investment and trade obligations in trade treaties.[15] First, the subject matter jurisdiction of *ad hoc* MEA arbitral bodies are more limited in scope.[16] Second, political decisions are often necessary before rulings from these MEA bodies can be properly enforced but not so for rulings from investment and trade bodies.[17] Third, the requirement that parties agree to the jurisdiction of the ICJ on a dispute-by-

---

[14] Oftentimes, treaty provisions pertaining to dispute resolution allow the parties to bring the dispute itself or a decision from such dispute before the International Court of Justice for resolution. *See, e.g.*, Convention on Biological Diversity, http://www.biodiv.org/convention/articles.asp, art. 27(3)(b).

[15] *Compare* Convention on the Conservation of Migratory Species and Wild Animals, June 23, 1979, art. 3, sec. 5, 19 I.L.M. 11, 19, *at* http://www.wcmc.org.uk/cms/ ("Parties that are Range States of a migratory species listed in Appendix I shall prohibit the taking of animals belonging to such species") *with* Article I(1) of the General Agreement on Tariffs and Trade, Oct. 30, 1947, 61 Stat. A-11, 55 U.N.T.S. 187, *at* http://www.wto.org/english/docs_e/legal_e/gatt47_e.doc ("With respect to customs duties and charges of any kind imposed on or in connection with importation or exportation or imposed on the international transfer of payments for imports or exports, and with respect to the method of levying such duties and charges, and with respect to all rules and formalities in connection with importation and exportation, and with respect to all matters referred to in paragraphs 2 and 4 of Article III, any advantage, favour, privilege or immunity granted by any contracting party to any product originating in or destined for any other country shall be accorded immediately and unconditionally to the like product originating in or destined for the territories of all other contracting parties.").

[16] *Compare* Convention on Migratory Species, art. XIII, Convention on the Conservation of Migratory Species and Wild Animals, June 23, 1979, art. 13, 19 I.L.M. 11, 26, *at* http://www.wcmc.org.uk/cms/ ("1. Any dispute which may arise between two or more Parties with respect to the interpretation or application of the provisions of this Convention shall be subject to negotiation between the Parties involved in the dispute. 2. If the dispute cannot be resolved in accordance with paragraph 1 of this Article, the Parties may, by mutual consent, submit the dispute to arbitration, in particular that of the Permanent Court of Arbitration at The Hague, and the Parties submitting the dispute shall be bound by the arbitral decision.") *with* the Dispute Settlement Understanding of the World Trade Organization, http://www.wto.org/english/tratop_e/dispu_e/dispu_e.htm.

[17] Even if the ICJ were to provide further enforcement, as discussed above, the prevailing party must often call upon the UN Security Council, a political party, to take steps to compel compliance with the ICJ's judgment. *See* U.N. CHARTER, art. 94(2). Similarly, the factual records from the North American Commission on Environmental Cooperation—which are not even legal judgments—require the political approval of two of the three environmental ministers before they take effect. *See* North American Agreement for Environmental Cooperation, Aug., 1993, art. 15(2), *at* http://www.cec.org/pubs_info_resources/law_treat_agree/naaec/index.cfm?varlan=english ("2. The Secretariat shall prepare a factual record if the Council, by a two-thirds vote, instructs it to do so."). No similar political limitations exist for the trade and investment dispute resolution mechanisms.

dispute basis again makes that alternative unappealing at best, and, more often, unavailable.

As long as the above imbalances continue, the following strategies—designed to inject environmental and public health concerns directly into international investment and trade disputes—remain necessary. When pursuing these strategies, again, be sure to contact appropriate individuals on the List of Practitioner Experts, in the appendix to this book, for assistance.

II. STRATEGY NO. 1: *AMICUS CURIAE* SUBMISSIONS TO TRADE AND INVESTMENT BODIES

A. Strategy Summary

When a trade or investment dispute resolution process considers a matter that may adversely impact the environment or public health, often that dispute resolution process does not provide a private right of action for non-state actors. In such situations, filing an *amicus curiae* submission to the tribunal may be an effective alternative mechanism for alerting the decision maker to those harms and minimizing the detrimental effects. Moreover, such a filing provides a strong basis for publicity that can help make the general public aware of the problem and persuade it to call upon its government to change the overall process.

Although international trade and investment dispute resolution processes are either closed to non-state actors or only open to certain types of non-state actors—namely for-profit foreign investors—the treaty provisions that frame the dispute resolution processes and/or the rules of procedure that govern them may explicitly or implicitly authorize the tribunal to allow *amicus curiae* participation. Below is a list of most international trade and investment dispute resolution processes and an assessment of whether *amicus curiae* participation may be allowed. Each entry provides the text creating and governing the process and discusses whether *amicus curiae* appearances have been sought successfully or could probably be pursued successfully.

B. Bodies to Whom Such Submission May Be Made

1. *World Trade Organization*

Centre William Rappard
Rue de Lausanne 154
CH-1211 Geneva 21
Switzerland

T: 44-22-739-51-11
F: 44-22-731-42-06
E: enquiries@wto.org
W: www.wto.org/english/tratop_e/dispu_e/dispu_e.htm

Preventing Adverse Impacts from Investment and Trade Decisions • 173

The WTO Understanding on Rules and Procedures Governing the Settlement of Disputes ("DSU")[18] establishes a process for resolving disputes between WTO members. It includes conciliation and mediation conducted by the permanent Dispute Settlement Body ("DSB") followed by an arbitration undertaken by *ad hoc* Dispute Resolution Panels (the "Panels"), the decision from which can be appealed to a permanent Appellate Body ("AB").

Whether the Panels and/or the AB allow *amicus curiae* submissions remains in flux. The Panels and the AB have accepted *amicus curiae* submissions in prior cases and have defended such acceptances as according with the DSU and/or the Working Procedures for Appellate Review (WPAW).[19] Although, many of the WTO member states expressed serious reservations at the November 22, 2000, meeting of the WTO General Council about whether the DSU or the WPAW allows either the Panels or the AB to accept *amicus curiae* submissions,[20] the ability to make *amicus curiae* submissions to the DSB panels and the AB was recognized by the WTO Director-General as recently as June 2003.[21] Moreover, in 2002, the United States Trade Representative

---

[18] See Annex 2 to the Agreement establishing the World Trade Organization 33 I.L.M. 1125 (1994), *at* http://www.wto.org/english/docs_e/legal_e/28-dsu.wpf.

[19] Regarding the Panels, the Appellate Body found in *United States—Import Prohibition of Certain Shrimp and Shrimp Products* that, among other things, the clause "[e]ach panel shall have the right to seek information" in Article 13 of the Dispute Settlement Understanding, WTO B.I.S.D., 1994, 33 I.L.M. 1125, 1234, *at* http://www.wto.org/english/docs_e/legal_e/28-dsu.doc (1994) allows the Panel to accept *amicus curiae* submission from non-WTO member states. *See United States—Import Prohibition of Certain Shrimp and Shrimp Products* WT/DS58/AB/R, Doc. No. 98-3899, ¶¶ 99–110 (Oct. 12, 1998). *See also* GATT Appellate Body Report on U.S.—Imposition of Countervailing Duties on Certain Hot Rolled Lead and Bismuth Carbon Steel Prods. Originating in the U.K., WT/DS138/AB/R ¶ 39 (May 10, 2000), *available at* 2000 WL 569563 ("Therefore, we are of the opinion that as long as we act consistently with the provisions of the DSU and the covered agreements, we have the legal authority to decide whether or not to accept and consider any information that we believe is pertinent and useful in an appeal.").

Moreover, even after WTO members have sought to create new policies to reverse this determination, the Appellate Body still is willing to receive and, where appropriate, review *amicus* submissions. *See United States—Import Prohibition of Certain Shrimp and Shrimp Products—Recourse to Article 21.5 of the DSU by Malaysia*, AB-2001-4, WT/DS58/AB/RW, Doc. No. 01-5166 (Oct. 22, 2001), ¶¶ 75–78, *at* http://www.wto.org/english/tratop_e/dispu_e/distabase_e.htm (click Appellate Body 2001); *United States—Import Prohibition of Certain Shrimp and Shrimp Products*, AB-1998-4, WT/DS58/AB/R, Doc. No. 98-3899 (Oct. 12, 1998), ¶¶ 79–91, *at* http://www.wto.org/english/tratop_e/dispu_e/distabase_e.htm (click Appellate Body 1998). Report of the Appellate Body 79 24, Appellate Body Report, WT/DS58/AB/R, *adopted* Nov. 6, 1998, ¶ 89.

[20] *See* WT/GC/M/60, at ¶ 76 (Jan. 23, 2001) (noting that the United States was the only Member State that spoke strongly in support of the authority of the Panels and the Appellate Body to accept *amicus curiae*).

[21] *See* "Comments by the Director-General to US NGO's," *available at* http://www.wto.org/english/forums_e/ngo_e/ngospe_e.htm ("[T]he issue of amicus briefs to Panels was addressed in the ruling of the Appellate Body on Shrimps and Sea-turtles. It is now clear that panels should accept amicus briefs and then decide how to treat this information.").

sought to formalize the submission process with a written proposal that has not yet been acted upon.[22] Thus, for now, one can still participate as *amicus curiae*.

2. NAFTA

www.nafta-sec-alena.org/DefaultSite/contact/index-e.aspx?categoryID=5

The North America Free Trade Agreement ("NAFTA") contains three different dispute resolution processes that may be able to accept *amicus curiae* submissions. This book will treat only the two that appear relevant to environmental issues—investor-state disputes pursuant to NAFTA Chapter 11 and state-to-state disputes concerning the interpretation and/or application of the NAFTA provisions pursuant to Chapter 20. The third forum is also state-to-state and hears anti-dumping and countervailing duty disputes pursuant to NAFTA Chapter 19.

a. NAFTA Chapter 11

NAFTA Chapter 11 tribunals[23] decide matters between non-state actors that qualify as foreign investors in a given NAFTA nation and the member state that hosts the foreign investor regarding certain investment-related claims set forth in NAFTA Chapter 11. Article 1120 of NAFTA Chapter 11 provides that disputes under this chapter are governed by the United Nations Commission on International Trade Law ("UNCITRAL") Arbitration Rules, the International Center for the Settlement of Investment Disputes at the World Bank ("ICSID") Convention, or the Additional Facility Rules of ICSID.[24]

Each of these sets of rules seems to authorize the tribunal to receive *amicus* submissions. For disputes governed by the UNCITRAL Arbitration Rules,[25] Article 15(1) of the UNCITRAL Arbitration Rules states, "subject to these Rules, the arbitral tribunal may conduct the arbitration in such manner as it considers appropriate, provided the parties are treated with equality and that at any stage of the proceedings each party is given a full opportunity of presenting his case." In the NAFTA Chapter 11 dispute of *Methanex Corporation v. United States of America*, the tribunal so far has decided that "pursuant to Article 15(1) of the UNCITRAL Arbitration Rules, . . . [the tribunal] has the power to accept *amicus* written submissions . . ." but not to allow the *amicus* petitioners to argue orally, attend hearings, or receive documents.[26]

---

[22] See "United States Proposes Greater Openness for WTO Disputes," available at http://www.ustr.gov/Document_Library/Press_Releases/2002/August/United_States_Proposes_Greater_Openness_for_WTO_Disputes.html?ht=amicus%20.

[23] See http://www.nafta-sec-alena.org/english/nafta/chap-111.htm, http://www.state.gov/s/l/c3439.htm.

[24] See http://www.nafta-sec-alena.org/english/nafta/chap-111.htm#A1120.

[25] See http://www.uncitral.org/en-index.htm (click "Adopted Text" and "International Commercial Arbitration and Conciliation").

[26] See Decision of the Tribunal on Petitions from Third Persons to Intervene as *"Amici Curiae,"* available at http://www.state.gov/documents/organization/6039.pdf.

Preventing Adverse Impacts from Investment and Trade Decisions • *175*

For disputes governed by the ICSID Convention,[27] the ICSID Convention and the ICSID Arbitration Rules contain provisions similar to, but narrower than UNCITRAL. Article 41(1) of the ICSID Convention states that, "[t]he Tribunal shall be the judge of its own competence."[28] ICSID Rule 19 states, "[t]he Tribunal shall make the orders required for the conduct of the proceeding."[29] Despite the absence here of further authority to confirm the intent of the drafters of these provisions, a tribunal governed by these rules likely would have sufficient authority to accept *amicus* submissions.

For disputes governed by the ICSID Additional Facility Rules,[30] these rules contain the same provision found in the ICSID Arbitration Rules, namely that "[t]he Tribunal shall make the orders required for the conduct of the proceeding."[31] Again, despite the absence here of further authority to confirm the intent of the drafters of these provisions, a tribunal governed by these rules likely would have sufficient authority to accept *amicus* submissions.

Following from the decision that the *Methanex* tribunal made to accept *amicus* submissions from Earthjustice and the International Institute of Sustainable Development, the NAFTA Free Trade Comission ("FTC") subsequently adopted at its annual meeting in 2003 a more general statement on nondisputing party participation in NAFTA Chapter 11 tribunals.[32]

That statement found that "no provision of the North American Free Trade Agreement ('NAFTA') limits a Tribunal's discretion to accept written submissions from a person or entity that is not a disputing party (a 'non-disputing party')"[33] and acknowledged "that written submissions by non-disputing parties in arbitrations under Section B of Chapter 11 of NAFTA may affect the operation of the Chapter."[34]

Consequently, "any non-disputing party that is a person of a Party, or that has a significant presence in the territory of a Party" can file a written submission with the Tribunal provided that the application for leave to file and the submission itself accord with the following.

---

[27] *See* http://www.worldbank.org/icsid/basicdoc/9.htm (Convention); http://www.worldbank.org/icsid/basicdoc/63.htm (Rules).

[28] International Center for Settlement of Investment Disputes, Mar. 18, 1965, part A, sec. 3, art.41, sec. 1, at 22, *at* http://www.worldbank.org/icsid/basicdoc/22.htm.

[29] International Center for Settlement of Investment Disputes, Mar. 18, 1965, part D, chp. 3, rule 19, at 20, http://www.worldbank.org/icsid/basicdoc/73.htm.

[30] *See* http://www.worldbank.org/icsid/facility/1.htm.

[31] ICSID Additional Facility Rules Governing the Additional Facility for the Administration of Proceedings by the Secretariat of the International Centre for Settlement of Investment Disputes ("ICSID Additional Facility Rules"), Schedule C—Arbitration Rules, Article 27, at 43, http://www.worldbank.org/icsid/facility/43.htm.

[32] *See* http://www.ustr.gov/Document_Library/Press_Releases/2003/October/NAFTA_Commission_Announces_New_Transparency_Measures.html.

[33] *See* http://www.ustr.gov/assets/Trade_Agreements/Regional/NAFTA/asset_upload_file660_6893.pdf.

[34] *Id.*

The application for leave to file must:
- (a) "be made in writing, dated, and signed by the person filing the application, and include the address and other contact details of the applicant;
- (b) be no longer than five typed pages;
- (c) describe the applicant, including, where relevant, its membership and legal status (*e.g.*, company, trade association or other non-governmental organization), its general objectives, the nature of its activities, and any parent organization (including any organization that directly or indirectly controls the applicant);
- (d) disclose whether or not the applicant has any affiliation, direct or indirect, with any disputing party;
- (e) identify any government, person, or organization that has provided any financial or other assistance in preparing the submission;
- (f) specify the nature of the interest that the applicant has in the arbitration;
- (g) identify the specific issues of fact or law in the arbitration that the applicant has addressed in its written submission;
- (h) explain, by reference to the factors specified in paragraph 6, why the Tribunal should accept the submission; and
- (i) be made in a language of the arbitration.[35]

The application itself must:

- (a) be dated and signed by the person filing the submission;
- (b) be concise, and in no case longer than 20 typed pages, including any appendices;
- (c) set out a precise statement supporting the applicant's position on the issues; and
- (d) only address matters within the scope of the dispute.[36]

Finally, the nondisputing party must file and serve the application for leave and the application with the Tribunal and all parties. Following filing and serving, "[t]he Tribunal will set an appropriate date by which the disputing parties may comment on the application for leave to file a non-disputing party submission."[37]

The Tribunal will then determine whether to grant leave by considering, "among other things, the extent to which:
- (a) the non-disputing party submission would assist the Tribunal in the determination of a factual or legal issue related to the arbitration by bringing a perspective, particular knowledge or insight that is different from that of the disputing parties;

---

[35] *Id.*
[36] *Id.*
[37] *Id.*

(b) the non-disputing party submission would address matters within the scope of the dispute;
(c) the non-disputing party has a significant interest in the arbitration; and
(d) there is a public interest in the subject-matter of the arbitration."[38]

At the same time, "[t]he Tribunal will ensure that:

(a) any non-disputing party submission avoids disrupting the proceedings; and
(b) neither disputing party is unduly burdened or unfairly prejudiced by such submissions."[39]

At that point, "[t]he Tribunal will render a decision on whether to grant leave to file a non-disputing party submission. If leave to file a non-disputing party submission is granted, the Tribunal will set an appropriate date by which the disputing parties may respond in writing to the nondisputing party submission. By that date, nondisputing NAFTA Parties may, pursuant to Article 1128, address any issues of interpretation of the Agreement presented in the nondisputing party submission."[40]

b. NAFTA Chapter 20

NAFTA Chapter 20 tribunals decide matters among Canada, Mexico, and/or the United States "regarding the interpretation or application of [NAFTA] or wherever a Party considers that an actual or proposed measure of another Party is or would be inconsistent with the obligations of this Agreement or cause nullification or impairment...."[41]

Article 2012(2) of NAFTA provides that "[u]nless the disputing Parties otherwise agree, the panel shall conduct its proceedings in accordance with the Model Rules of Procedure."[42] Similar to UNCITRAL and ICSID, Article 17 of the Model Rules states, "Where a procedural question arises that is not covered by these rules, a panel may adopt an appropriate procedure that is not inconsistent with the Agreement."[43] Again, despite the absence here of further authority to confirm the intent of the drafters of this provision, a tribunal governed by these rules likely would have sufficient authority to accept *amicus* submissions.

---

[38] *Id.*
[39] *Id.*
[40] *Id.*
[41] See www.nafta-sec-alena.org/english/rules/ch20/ch20p.htm.
[42] See http://www.nafta-sec-alena.org/english/index.htm (click NAFTA).
[43] Model Rules of Procedure for Chapter Twenty of NAFTA, http://www.nafta-sec-alena.org/english/index.htm (click "Rules"), art. 17.

3.1 Methanex

In 1999, Methanex Corporation initiated arbitration before an international investment tribunal under Chapter XI, Section B of the North American Free Trade Agreement ("NAFTA").[44] Methanex alleged that the United States breached its obligations under Chapter XI, Section A—including the Minimum Standard of Treatment provision in Article 1105 and the Expropriation and Compensation provision in Article 1110—when California's governor issued an Executive Order to ban methyl tertiary-butyl ether (MTBE).[45] Methanex supplied methanol to MTBE producers, some of whom were located in California, and said the Executive Order would result in a loss of profits. Several environmental organizations sought to obtain *amicus curiae* status before the tribunal asserting an important environmental step in protecting groundwater was at risk. Their attempt to participate led to the NAFTA Free Trade Commission's Statement of the Free Trade Commission on Non-Disputing Party Participation.[46]

On August 25, 2000, the Canadian-based International Institute for Sustainable Development ("IISD") requested permission to submit an *amicus curiae* brief, arguing its participation was necessary because the outcome of the case would affect how and whether governments continue to issue environmental regulations.[47] IISD expressed concern that constitutional issues, such as the government's authority to regulate for the public interest, were at stake. IISD argued its expertise in both investment and environmental policies would ensure that the tribunal considers sustainable development principles.[48] At the time of its *amicus curiae* application, NAFTA did not have a provision that allowed the participation of non-disputing parties. IISD argued, however, that the tribunal has the authority to accept *amicus* briefs because the UNCITAL grants it the authority to conduct arbitration proceedings in any way it sees appropriate.[49]

In October 2000, Earthjustice represented non-profit organizations, California-based Bluewater Network, Communities for a Better Environment, and the Center for International Environmental Law in applying for leave to submit an *amicus* brief. To convince the tribunal that their participation

(continued)

---

[44] Notice of Arbitration, *available at* http://www.naftaclaims.com/disputes_us_6.htm (last visited June 28, 2005).
[45] Notice of Arbitration, *supra* note 1 at "General Nature of Claim."
[46] NAFTA Free Trade Commission, Statement of the Free Trade Commission on Non-Disputing Party Participation, para. B ("Statement"), *available at* http://www.ustr.gov/assets/Trade_Agreements/Regional/NAFTA/asset_upload_file660_6893.pdf (last visited June 23, 2005).
[47] Petition to the Arbitral Tribunal from International Institute for Sustainable Development ("IISD Petition"), *available at* http://www.naftaclaims.com/disputes_us/disputes_us_6.htm (last visited June 23, 2005).
[48] IISD Petition, *Id.* ¶ 3.6.
[49] IISD Petition, *Id.* ¶¶ 4.1, 4.6.

3.1 Methanex *(continued)*

would help the proceedings, these non-profit organizations argued that their knowledge of MTBE would be used to show why California required such a ban in order to protect the groundwater.[50] Additionally, these groups contended they should be allowed to participate because the outcome would affect governmental authority and the public interest.

On January 15, 2001, the tribunal issued a decision on whether it had the authority to accept *amicus* submissions. The tribunal could not establish whether allowing these parties to participate would help the proceedings, but said it had to assume it would.[51] While the tribunal held that it had the authority to accept *amicus* submissions, it did not formally allow these particular *amici* to submit written briefs until January 2004 when the tribunal issued a press release, after IISD and Earthjustice had reiterated their interest in being *amici*.[52] Subsequently, IISD submitted its precedent-setting *amicus curiae* brief on March 9, 2004. When hearings were held in June 2004, it was the first time an international investment arbitration was open to the public. After the hearings on June 29, 2004, Earthjustice and IISD jointly petitioned for the right to submit a posthearing submission because the United States did not argue the MTBE ban was an environmental measure in addition to a public health measure.[53] The two groups wanted to submit this information to ensure that both public health and environmental measures were protected from investment arbitration. The tribunal denied the petition to submit because the disputing parties could not agree on whether to allow participation by non-disputing parties.[54]

3. Canada-Chile Free Trade Agreement

www.sice.oas.org/trade/chican_e/chcatoc.asp

The text of the Canada-Chile Free Trade Agreement ("CCFTA") is nearly identical to that of NAFTA. Therefore the same opportunities for *amicus* submissions likely exist. Similar to NAFTA Chapter 11, CCFTA Chapter G on investment incorporates by reference the ICSID Arbitration Rules,

---

[50] Application for Standing from Communities for a Better Environment, The Bluewater Network of Earth Island Institute, and the Center for International Environmental Law ("Application for Standing"), ¶ 2, *available at* http://www.naftaclaims.com/disputes_us/disputes_us_6.htm (last visited June 23, 2005).

[51] Decision, on Authority to Accept Amicus Submissions, ¶ 49, *available at* http://www.naftaclaims.com/disputes_us/disputes_us_6.htm (last visited June 23, 2005).

[52] A backgrounder on the controversial case under NAFTA's Chapter 11, and on IISD's Involvement *available at* http://www.iisd.org/investment/methanex_background.asp (last visited June 29, 2005).

[53] *Id.*

[54] Summary of *Methanex v. the United States of America, available at* http://www.iisd.org/investment/methanex.asp.

Additional Facility Rules of ICSID, and UNCITRAL Arbitration Rules.[55] Similar to NAFTA Chapter 20, CCFTA Chapter N on dispute settlement incorporates by reference Model Rules of Procedure.[56] Among those rules is Rule 17 which enables the arbitration panel to consider acceptance of *amicus* submissions.[57]

4. Court of Justice of the Andean Community

Calle Roca 450
Quito
Ecuador

T: (00593-2) 529990 / 529998
F: (00593-2) 565007 / 554533
E: tjca@tribunalandino.org.ec
W: www.tribunalandino.org.ec

The Court of Justice has broad authority to handle arbitrations between private parties on trade contracts or similar agreements.[58] It is not clear whether the Court also would have the authority to allow a third party to intervene in such an arbitration were the matter being decided to have adverse environmental or public health effects.

5. EU Court of Justice and Court of First Instance

L-2925 Luxembourg

T: 352-4303-1
F: 352-4337-66
E: ECJ.Registry@curia.eu.int -or- CFI.Registry@curia.eu.int
W: www.curia.eu.int/index.htm

Article 37 of the European Union Statute of the Court of Justice allows intervention by "any ... person establishing an interest in the result of any case submitted to the Court, save in cases between Member States, between institutions of the Community or between Member States and institutions of the Community...."[59] Article 93 of the Rules of Procedure details the process for intervening.[60]

---

[55] See art. G-21, http://www.sice.oas.org/trade/chican_e/Chca07be.asp#G-21.
[56] See art. N-12, http://www.sice.oas.org/trade/chican_e/Chca14e.asp#N-12.
[57] See http://www.dfait-maeci.gc.ca/tna-nac/ccfta_model-en.asp at Rule 17 ("Where a procedural question arises that is not addressed by these rules, a panel may adopt an appropriate procedure that is not inconsistent with the Agreement.").
[58] Arts. 38 and 39.
[59] See http://www.curia.eu.int/en/txts/acting/statut.htm.
[60] See http://www.curia.eu.int/en/txts/acting/txt5.pdf. For more information, *see* Chapter 5 *infra*.

6. Common Market for Eastern and Southern Africa (COMESA)

W: http://www.comesa.int (click "Contacting COMESA")

Rule 84 of the Rules of Procedure of the COMESA Court of Justice empowers the court to "make Rules of Court which shall, subject to the provisions of this Treaty, regulate the detailed conduct of business of the Court." Therefore, one could potentially intervene in matters pertaining to the Treaty that are presented to the Court and that could adversely impact the environment or public health.

7. East African Community Court of Justice (EAC)

Registrar of the Court of Justice
Arusha International Conference Center (AICC) Building
Kilimanjaro Wing
5th Floor
P.O. Box 1096
Arusha
Tanzania

T: 255-27-2504253/4/6/7/8
F: 255-27-2504255 / 2504481
E: eac@eachq.org
W: www.eachq.org

Article 40 of the Statute of the EAC Court of Justice states that "a resident of a Partner State who is not a party to a case before the Court may, with leave of the Court, intervene in that case, but the submissions of the intervening party shall be limited to evidence supporting or opposing the arguments of a party to the case."[61] Therefore, one could potentially intervene in matters that are presented to the Court that could adversely impact the environment or public health.

8. Economic Community of Western African States (ECOWAS)

W: www.ecowas.int

Article 22 of the ECOWAS Treaty authorizes the presiding arbitrator of any dispute settlement process to settle all questions of procedure.[62] Presumably, the president arbitrator could resolve the issue of whether *amicus* submissions could be made with respect to matters adversely impacting the environment or public health.

---

[61] See http://www.eachq.org/Treaty/eac-TheTreaty08.htm.
[62] See http://www.ecowas.int/sitecedeao/english/ap011184.htm.

9. Others (APEC, OECS, Mercosur, BITs)

At the time of this writing, limited information exists to demonstrate whether the Asian Pacific Economic Community (APEC),[63] Organization of Eastern Caribbean States (OECS),[64] and, for the eastern part of South America, Mercosur[65] have similar processes to which an *amicus* submission could be made.

In addition to investment dispute resolution processes in trade agreements that allow non-state investors to challenge governments that allegedly interfere with investment through environmental, public health, and safety rules, these non-state investors are also making use of bilateral investment treaties to accomplish the same goals. Numerous bilateral investment treaties ("BITs") and bilateral free trade agreements exist that provide for dispute settlement modeled on the aforementioned multilateral treaties.[66] Therefore, *amicus curiae* submissions may likely be accepted in these processes as well.

Such BIT arbitrations are becoming routine. A March 17, 2003, article in the National Law Journal pointed to the following examples where the environment and public health are at risk if the defending governnment submits to the corporate actor's demands:

> —The tiny country of Costa Rica is facing a $57 billion arbitration claim from Houston-based Harken Energy Corp. because the country's Ministry of Environment and Energy allegedly blocked Harken from exercising its contractual right to drill for oil off the nation's Caribbean coast.

> —Bolivia is fighting an arbitration claim of $25 million, and far more could be at stake. The complainant, an international consortium headed by San Francisco-based Bechtel Corp., has argued that Bolivia wrongfully cancelled the consortium's concession to provide water to the country's third-largest city, Cochabamba, and expropriated the consortium's water-system assets. The $25 million listed in the arbitration papers covers only the money that the consortium put into Cochabamba's water system, according to Bechtel spokesman Jeff Berger. It does not include lost profits, which the consortium may also seek to recover in the arbitration.

---

[63] *See* http://arbitration.co.nz/apec/.
[64] *See* http://www.oecs.org.
[65] *See* http://www.mercosur.org.uy/pagina1esp.htm.
[66] For general information about BITs, *see* http://www.worldbank.org/icsid/treaties/main.htm *or* http://www.sice.oas.org/bitse.asp. For general information about the U.S. and BITs, *see* http://www.ustr.gov/agreements/bit.pdf. For general information about Inter-American bilateral free trade agreements, *see* http://www.ftaa-alca.oas.org/publications/inw10c3e.doc.

Preventing Adverse Impacts from Investment and Trade Decisions • 183

—Ecuador has been fighting in its courts to keep $180 million in taxes collected from EnCana, Occidental Petroleum, and other foreign oil companies working in the country. The companies have claimed they are entitled to the same tax rebate given to exporters in order to promote overseas sales, but Ecuador's tax authorities said that all applicable tax rebates are already included in contracts with the oil companies.[67]

Ordinarily, obtaining publicly available information about the existence of disputes is extremely limited. Nevertheless, if your organization wants to make a submission to such BIT proceedings, you may want to contact ICSID at the World Bank in Washington, D.C. to learn where and when the arbitration is taking or will take place and where you might be able to obtain documents pertaining to the dispute. Contact information for ICSID is:

1818 H Street, NW
Washington, D.C. 20433
T: (202) 458-1534
F: (202) 522-2615

In addition, work with the appropriate List of Experts in the appendix to make sure your submission is as effective as possible.

C. Preparing and Filing Your *Amicus Curiae* Brief

As indicated in Section III.F. of the Introduction, *amicus curiae* briefs must be well written and convincing. They require accurate recitation of the facts and precise application of the law to those facts and should include relevant documentary and/or testimonial evidence where possible. As you prepare your submission, consult the appropriate individuals in the List of Practitioner Experts listed in the appendix to this book.

In the case of the submitting such brief to a tribunal deciding an international trade or investment dispute, the issues in the dispute ought to concern adverse impact to the environment or public health that pertain to the work of your organization. Generally speaking, the goal of your submission should be:

1. to provide the dispute resolution body with information that it would otherwise not receive from either party or that might be distorted by either party; and/or

---

[67] Steve Seidenberg, *Legal Business Tangles in Latin America: Governments Are Facing Big Arbitration Claims*, NAT'L L.J., Mar. 17, 2003, *available at* http://www.nlj.com/business/032403bizlede.shtml.

2. to inform the dispute resolution body of the perspective on the dispute that it otherwise would not be asked to consider by the parties.

As for the actual brief, a few additional guidelines include:

1. Draft a petition addressed to the tribunal that asks to appear as *amicus curiae* and that explains why the tribunal has authority to accept your submission. Use the information above to structure your argument.
2. Draft your submission and attach it to the petition. Keep your submission to a reasonable length, usually fewer than 25 pages.
3. Send these materials, with a cover letter, to the appropriate body. See the addresses and websites listed above.
4. Send copies of the above documents to each of the parties in the dispute.

III. STRATEGY NO 2: PERSUADING A DOMESTIC GOVERNMENT TO FILE A TRADE OR INVESTMENT DISPUTE TO PREVENT THE WEAKENING OF ENVIRONMENTAL OR PUBLIC HEALTH LAWS

As the above discussion concerning *amicus curiae* submissions indicate, many of the dispute resolution processes affecting environmental or public health regulations are available only for nation-states to bring claims against other nation-states. Sometimes, however, a nation-state files trade and investment claims against other nation-states on behalf of a particular domestic industry. The industry may have requested and encouraged the government to take such action to safeguard that industry from a law or claim in the other nation-state that undermines the ability of that industry to compete well in that other nation-state.

For example, the United States Mission to the European Union filed a dispute with the WTO in 1996 on behalf of the U.S. beef industry when the European Union implemented a ban on imports of red meat from animals treated with six growth promotants, both natural and synthetic.[68] The ban adversely impacted the U.S. beef industry. The U.S. devoted resources to the arbitration for more than three years.

Similarly, NGOs ought to request and encourage sympathetic governments, not necessarily their own, to file claims on behalf of such NGOs against nation-states that maintain a law or practice that harms the environment or public health. Attempts will be far more difficult for NGOs than for-profit industries. However, a nation-state might be persuaded that a clean and healthy environment is as much a beneficial commodity as prof-

---

[68] *See* http://www.useu.be/AGRI/ban.html#background.

Preventing Adverse Impacts from Investment and Trade Decisions • 185

its or that a weakening of regulations to protect the environment and public health actually subsidizes those industries that were previously required to comply with such regulations.

In the United States, consider contacting:

1. Office of the General Counsel
   Office of the U.S. Trade Representative
   600 17th Street, NW
   Washington, D.C. 20508
   T: (202) 395-3150
   W: http://www.ustr.gov
2. Office of the General Counsel
   U.S. Department of Commerce
   1401 Constitution Avenue, NW
   Washington, D.C. 20230
   W: http://www.doc.gov
3. Office of the General Counsel
   U.S. Department of Treasury
   1500 Pennsylvania Avenue, NW
   Washington, D.C. 20220
   T:(202) 622-2000
   W: http://www.ustreas.gov
4. Environmental and Natural Resources Division
   U.S. Department of Justice
   950 Pennsylvania Avenue, NW
   Washington, D.C. 20530-0001
   T:(202) 514-2701
   W: http://www.usdoj.gov

IV. STRATEGY NO. 3: SUBMITTING PUBLIC COMMENTS TO ENVIRONMENTAL REVIEWS OF TRADE AND INVESTMENT AGREEMENTS

Because of mounting public concerns over the impact of investment and trade agreements on the environment and public health, the Office of the United States Trade Representative ("USTR") and the Council on Environmental Quality ("CEQ") are now required to assess and consider the environmental impacts of each new treaty and, in most cases, draft a written environmental review.[69] Before USTR and CEQ can finalize the writ-

---

[69] *See* Environmental Review of Trade Agreements, Executive Order 13141, 64 Fed. Reg. 63169 (Nov. 18, 1999), *at* http://ceq.eh.doe.gov/nepa/regs/eos/eo13141.html (ordering environmental review of trade agreements). *See also* United States Trade Representative and Council on Environmental Quality, Guidelines for Implementation of Executive Order 13141: Environmental Review of Trade Agreements, 65 Fed. Reg. 79442 (Dec. 19, 2000), *at* http://www.ustr.gov/releases/2000/12/guides.pdf (implementing Executive Order 13141).

ten environmental reviews, they must publish them and then invite and consider public comments. Consequently, the public can obtain copies of such drafts in the Federal Register and on the USTR website.[70]

Submitting public comments on these draft environmental reviews is an important way to minimize the impact of globalization on the environment, at least in the United States. Sometimes, the USTR and CEQ do not adequately assess all environmental and public health impacts. However, only a handful of NGOs and individuals regularly comment. Perhaps more comments from more NGOs and individuals would improve the likelihood that the USTR and CEQ would reconsider its positions with respect to a particular trade agreement.

To use this strategy, constantly watch the USTR website for the posting of draft environmental reviews or ask USTR to send copies when they are posted. Then, prepare written comments similar to those routinely provided to U.S. agencies. Be sure to consult NGOs and individuals who regularly comment. Again, helpful contacts appear in the appendix to this book.

Although this strategy is domestic rather than international, the authors include it in this chapter because it relates directly to the topic of minimizing the impact of investment and trade treaties on environmental and public health regulations. Most other domestic strategies in this area are less direct, focusing primarily on transparency. Therefore, the authors have included those strategies in the domestic chapter (Chapter 6).

A similar process may exist in other countries but is beyond the scope of this book.

V. STRATEGY NO. 4: DEMANDING TRANSPARENCY AND PUBLIC PARTICIPATION FROM DOMESTIC GOVERNMENTS ON TRADE AND INVESTMENT ISSUES ADVERSELY AFFECTING THE ENVIRONMENT AND PUBLIC HEALTH

Another means for combating the impact of trade and investment dispute settlement on environmental and public health regulation is to obtain information about trade and investment matters and design responsive campaigns. Relevant strategies are covered in Chapter 6: Enforcing International Environmental Law Through Domestic Law Mechanism Problems Abroad.

---

[70] *See* http://www.ustr.gov/.

3.2 FTAA

In April 1998, thirty-four North, Central, and South American democracies began negotiating a Free Trade Area of the Americas (FTAA) " . . . to unite the economies of the Americas into a single free trade area" by gradually lowering trade and investment barriers.[71] By March 2004, negotiations had been suspended, largely as a result of growing opposition throughout the Americas, and the arrival of more progressive governments in South America.[72] Although it is unclear if or when negotiations will resume, the January deadline for signing the treaty has passed—a day FTAA opponents say "should be remembered in history as the day the social movements of the hemisphere achieved one of [their] greatest triumphs."[73]

U.S.-based Public Citizen's Global Trade Watch, Stop the FTAA Coalition, and the internationally based Global Exchange oppose FTAA, arguing its policies are an expansion of NAFTA in that they will lead to environmental degradation and give corporations the power to overturn environmental regulations.[74] Social mobilization against FTAA is an international unified effort. National coalitions, with a range of labor and environmental objectives, have formed a Hemispheric Social Alliance, which mobilizes rallies, educates the public about the FTAA, pressures local and state officials, and organizes Congressional opposition.[75] In Brazil, localized social movements organized a plebiscite, in which 10 million people voted to reject the FTAA. For this strategy to succeed in other locations, it requires a strong mass-based social movement.[76]

In 1998, the Hemispheric Social Alliance produced an alternative to FTAA that does not ignore environmental, human rights, or labor concerns for the sake of trade. The Alternatives for the Americas laid out Environmental Guiding Principles, which required corporations to be held to high environmental standards, and uphold strong environmental laws.[77]

(continued)

---

[71] Free Trade Area of the Americas, *Antecedents of the FTAA Process, available at* http://www.ftaa-alca.org/view_e.asp (last updated June 21, 2005) ("Antecedents of FTAA").

[72] Global Exchange, "What is the Current Status of the FTAA Negotiations," *available at* http://www.globalexchange.org/campaigns/ftaa/faq.html#10 (last updated April 1, 2005) ("Current Status"). The progressive governments in South America have led to the original countries differing on issues that they once agreed upon.

[73] Deborah James, *A Decade's Struggle Ends in Victory*, Global Exchange (May 15, 2005), *available at* http://www.globalexchange.org/campaigns/ftaa/3070.html.pf.

[74] Aurita Withers, *The FTAA and the Environmental Destruction—How It Happens*, Stop the FTAA, *available at* http://www.stopftaa.org/article.php?id=39 (last visited June 26, 2005).

[75] James, *supra* note 3.

[76] James, *supra*, note 3.

[77] Alternatives for the Americas, Environment section, *available at* http://www.web.net/comfront/alts4americas/eng./eng.html (last visited June 21, 2005).

> **3.2 FTAA** *(continued)*
>
> As this book goes to press, recent efforts in Fall 2005 by the United States to revise FTA talks and move closer to completion have not yet succeeded and continue to meet with oposition.

VI. CONCLUSION

As more trade and investment agreements appear and existing ones strengthen, more foreign investors and nations may turn to the dispute resolution processes provided in these agreements to challenge environmental, health and safety regulations as unfair trade restrictions. Civil society must continue to insert itself into these processes by filing *amicus curiae* petitions and continue to call for environmental reviews of new trade and investment treaties. The more that civil society scrutinizes these process, the less damage they will be able to do away from the public eye.

CHAPTER 4

ENCOURAGING SECRETARIATS OF MULTILATERAL ENVIRONMENTAL AND PUBLIC HEALTH AGREEMENTS TO ENFORCE CURRENT INTERNATIONAL ENVIRONMENTAL STANDARDS

I. INTRODUCTION

Recognizing the inter-state nature of environmental and public health harms, nations of the world have drafted, signed, and ratified numerous multilateral environmental agreements ("MEAs"). MEAs usually protect the atmosphere, lithosphere, hydrosphere, or biosphere. They often contain provisions that create secretariats and inter-state dispute resolution processes, each of which gives rise to NGO strategies.

This chapter presents three such strategies. First, NGOs can submit petitions to MEA treaty secretariats calling on those bodies to take steps to resolve a particular environmental and public health harm that is not receiving adequate attention but is occurring within a member nation-state. Second, NGOs can encourage nation-states to initiate state-to-state dispute resolution under these MEAs to help resolve an environmental or public health problem. Detailed below, these strategies may help to strengthen the effectiveness of MEAs and better protect the environment and public health. Third, where the MEA allows, NGOs can participate at MEA Conferences of the Parties or appropriate bodies of charter-based institutions and lobby member states to take particular environmental action.

Using these strategies may compensate for the weak enforcement mechanisms found in MEAs. Such weak enforcement mechanisms have undermined the ability of MEAs to protect the environment and public health as effectively as perhaps intended, especially in the wake of competing political demands. Although the International Court of Justice ("ICJ") may provide effective secondary enforcement of MEA dispute resolution decisions, the voluntary nature of nation-state personal jurisdiction before the ICJ makes this enforcement avenue unappealing at best, and, more often, unavailable.[1]

Moreover, inequities between MEAs and international trade and investment treaties further weaken the ability of MEAs to protect the environment and public health because global commercial development bolstered by international trade and investment treaties often overtake such protections instead of being compelled to reconcile with them. First, MEA dispute resolution processes do not usually result in binding, enforceable decisions whereas trade and investment dispute resolution processes usually do. Second, the subject matter jurisdiction of *ad hoc* MEA arbitral bodies are more limited in scope than international trade and investment dispute resolution processes.[2] Third, political decisions are often necessary before rulings from these MEA bodies can be properly enforced but not so for rulings from investment and trade bodies.[3] Fourth, international trade and investment dispute bodies are not required to consider MEA obligations when rendering their decisions because their subject matter jurisdiction extends only to the obligations of the international trade or investment treaty that created them. Fifth, nations take a longer time to ratify MEAs and become subject to their dispute resolution processes. For

---

[1] Most MEA dispute resolution provisions allow a decision to be presented to the ICJ for enforcement. In addition, the Security Council can refer such a matter to the ICJ. *See* U.N. CHARTER, art. 94(2).

[2] *Compare* Article 27 of the Convention on Biological Diversity, www.biodiv.org/convention/articles.asp ("1. In the event of a dispute between Contracting Parties concerning the interpretation or application of this Convention, the parties concerned shall seek solution by negotiation. 2. If the parties concerned cannot reach agreement by negotiation, they may jointly seek the good offices of, or request mediation by, a third party. 3. When ratifying, accepting, approving or acceding to this Convention, or at any time thereafter, a State or regional economic integration organization may declare in writing to the Depositary that for a dispute not resolved in accordance with paragraph 1 or paragraph 2 above, it accepts one or both of the following means of dispute settlement as compulsory: (a) Arbitration in accordance with the procedure laid down in Part 1 of Annex II; (b) Submission of the dispute to the International Court of Justice. 4. If the parties to the dispute have not, in accordance with paragraph 3 above, accepted the same or any procedure, the dispute shall be submitted to conciliation in accordance with Part 2 of Annex II unless the parties otherwise agree. 5. The provisions of this Article shall apply with respect to any protocol except as otherwise provided in the protocol concerned.") *with* the entire Dispute Settlement Understanding of the World Trade Organization, at Annex 2 to the Agreement Establishing the World Trade Organization, *available at* http://www.wto.org/english/docs_e/legal_e/28-dsu.pdf.

[3] Many disputes brought under global environmental treaties can be referred to the International Court of Justice for resolution, but the prevailing party must often call upon the UN Security Council to enforce the ICJ's judgments. *See* U.N. CHARTER, art. 94(2). Similarly, the factual records from the North American Commission on Environmental Cooperation—which are not even legal judgments—require the political approval of two of the three environmental ministers before they take ef

example, the United States has not yet ratified the Convention on Biological Diversity that President Clinton signed in June 1993,[4] and has not even signed the Convention on Migratory Species that entered into force in November 1983.[5] However, the United States had ratified and fully implemented through domestic legislation both the NAFTA by 1994 and the World Trade Agreement by 1995.[6]

As a result of these inequities, no adequate international forum exists to address the adverse environmental and public health impacts from the increased manufacture and sale of goods and services that have resulted from these new trade and investment agreements regimes. Consequently, the strategies discussed that focus on strengthening MEAs may prove extremely helpful for the protection of the environment and public health.

As with other strategies in this book, individuals on the List of Practitioner Experts can assist in making your efforts as effective as possible. Lastly, as indicated in the introduction to this book, please note that some of the strategies in this chapter may also be appropriate for UN Specialized Agencies and UN Related Agencies. As these institutions and any of their dispute resolution fora are not addressed separately in this book, please consult http://www.un.or/aboutun/chart.html for more details on these entities.

II. STRATEGY NO. 1: MAKING SUBMISSIONS PURSUANT TO SPECIFIC MEA PROCESSES OPEN TO NON-PARTY PARTICIPATION

Few MEAs have explicit processes by which non-parties can make submissions. Several have evolved, however, in recent years in the treaties and protocols adopted by the United Nations Economic Commission for Europe ("UNECE").

First, in October 2002 at the Sixth Meeting of the Parties of the Convention on Access to Information, Public Participation in Decision-making and Access to Justice in Environmental Matters ("Aarhus Convention"),[7] the members adopted Decision I/7, which created a non-confrontational, non-judicial, consultative mechanism for reviewing compliance with the Aarhus Convention.[8] Called the "Compliance Commission," it was estab-

---

[4] See http://www.biodiv.org/world/parties.asp (last visited Nov. 24, 2002).
[5] See http://www.wcmc.org.uk/cms/wrd/en/Partylist_eng.doc (last visited Nov. 24, 2002).
[6] See U.S. Department of State, *Treaties in Force*, at 473-74 (Jan. 1, 2000), *available at* http://www.http://www.state.gov/s/l/c3431.htm (last visited Nov. 24, 2002).
[7] U.N. Doc. ECE/CEP/43 (June 25, 1998), *available at* http://www.unece.org/env/pp/documents/cep43e.pdf.
[8] U.N. Doc. ECE/MP.PP/2/Add.8 (April 2, 2004), *available at* http://www.unece.org/env/pp/documents/mop1/ece.mp.pp.2.add.8.e.pdf.

192 • *Defending the Environment*

lished pursuant to Article 15 of the Aarhus Convention.[9] Although it only has advisory powers, the Compliance Committee has a number of special features. Its members are experts serving in their personal capacity; it is able to undertake information-gathering visits within the territory of the party concerned (with the party's consent); and it is able to accept communications directly from the public.[10]

Paragraph 18 of Decision I/7 carves out a specific process by which non-state actors can communicate directly with the Compliance Commission, thereby obviating the need for employing the other strategies set forth in this chapter. That paragraph states:

> On the expiry of twelve months from either the date of adoption of this decision or from the date of the entry into force of the Convention with respect to a Party, whichever is the later, communications may be brought before the Committee by one or more members of the public concerning that Party's compliance with the Convention, unless that Party has notified the Depositary in writing by the end of the applicable period that it is unable to accept, for a period of not more than four years, the consideration of such communications by the Committee. The Depositary shall without delay notify all Parties of any such notification received. During the four-year period mentioned above, the Party may revoke its notification thereby accepting that, from that date, communications may be brought before the Committee by one or more members of the public concerning that Party's compliance with the Convention.[11]

To date, the Commission has received a number of communications.[12]

Second, the Protocol on Pollutant Release and Transfer Registers ("PRTR") to the Aarhus Convention provides safeguards similar to the U.S. Emergency Planning and Community Right to Know Act.[13] "The objective

---

[9] *See* http://www.unece.org/env/pp/documents/cep43e.pdf ("The Meeting of the Parties shall establish, on a consensus basis, optional arrangements of a non-confrontational, non-judicial and consultative nature for reviewing compliance with the provisions of this Convention. These arrangements shall allow for appropriate public involvement and may include the option of considering communications from members of the public on matters related to this Convention.")

[10] *See* http://www.unece.org/env/pp/documents/mop1/ece.mp.pp.2.add.8.e.pdf.

[11] Decision I/7, ¶ 18, U.N. Doc. ECE/MP.PP/2/Add.8 (April 2, 2004), *available at* http://www.unece.org/env/pp/documents/mop1/ece.mp.pp.2.add.8.e.pdf.

[12] *See* http://www.unece.org/env/pp/compliance.htm#sixthmeeting.

[13] *Compare* Protocol on Pollutant Release and Transfer Registers (Dec. 31, 2004), *available at* http://www.unece.org/env/pp/prtr/docs/PRTR%20Protocol%20English.pdf, *with* 42 U.S.C. § 11001 *et seq*. The PRTR was adopted at an extra-ordinary meeting of the Parties to the Aarhus Convention on May 21, 2003 in Kiev, Ukraine and has 36 signatories but is not yet in force. *See generally* http://www.unece.org/env/pp/welcome.html.

of this Protocol is to enhance public access to information through the establishment of coherent, integrated, nationwide pollutant release and transfer registers" to which national government must ensure the companies operating in their country adhere.[14] The protocol sets forth robust access to information and public participation provisions, while not yet establishing a process akin to the Compliance Committee for the Aarhus Convention itself.[15] Perhaps the Compliance Committee's jurisdiction will grow over time to include this protocol.

Third, the Protocol on Strategic Environmental Assessment ("SEA") to the UNECE's Convention on Environmental Impact Assessment in a Transboundary Context, also signed by numerous countries but not yet in force, provides for a public participation process similar to the PRTR that allows affected members of the public to review the plans and express their concerns.[16] The protocol requires parties to conduct environmental review and consultations for a number of different kinds of projects and activities undertaken at the national and local level, similar to the U.S. National Environmental Policy Act and U.S. state equivalents.[17] Its public participation process, although not yet as formal as the Aarhus Compliance Committee process, provides enough public participation tools to encourage non-party involvement.[18]

4.1 Aarhus Compliance Commission: Communication against Ukraine

This case concerns the process of approval undertaken by the government of Ukraine on a proposal made for the construction of a deepwater navigation canal on the Danube River delta.[19] The Charitable Foundation Ecopravo-Lviv, the communicant, claimed in a submission dated May 6, 2004, and supplemented on December 1, 2004, that Ukraine did not comply with its obligations under Article 6 of the Convention, in that it failed to allow proper public participation in the decision-making process, and it did not allow sufficient access to relevant documents involved in the approval process.[20]

The communicant first contacted the Ukrainian Ministry of Environment concerning the construction proposal with a letter dated April 30, 2003.[21]

(continued)

---

[14] *Id.* at art. 1.
[15] PRTR, *supra* note 6.7, at arts. 11 and 13.
[16] See Protocol on Strategic Environmental Assessment to the Convention on Environmental Impact Assessment in a Transboundary Context, *available at* http://www.unece.org/env/eia/documents/protocolenglish.pdf, art. 8. *See generally* http://www.unece.org/env/eia/sea_protocol.htm (status of ratifications).
[17] *Compare* SEA, *id.*, arts. 3, 4, Annexes I–III *with* 42 U.S.C. §§ 4321-43.
[18] See http://www.unece.org/env/eia/publicpart.html.
[19] Report on the Seventh Meeting, *available at* http://www.unece.org/env/pp/compliance/C2004-03/S01C03findings.pdf, at 12.
[20] *Id.* at 2.
[21] *Id.* at 14.

4.1 Aarhus Compliance Commission *(continued)*

Since that time the communicant made several requests to the Ministry of Environment for information regarding the proposal.[22] Each of these requests were denied.[23] On July 17, 2003 the Ministry of Environment approved the conclusions of the Ukraine's state environmental expert.[24] In response for a request of those conclusions made by the communicant, the Ministry cited technical reasons as to why it could not send the whole document.[25]

The Aarhus Committee determined that by failing to provide the relevant documents upon request, and by failing to involve the public, the government of Ukraine did not comply with its obligations under the Convention.[26] The Committee therefore found in favor of the applicant and further requested that Ukraine bring its legislation and practice into compliance with the Convention and that Ukraine submit a strategy, by the end of 2005, for transposing the Convention's provisions into national law.[27]

III. STRATEGY NO. 2: PETITIONING MEA SECRETARIATS

A. Strategy Summary

If the action or omission of a nation-state party to a particular MEA results in an environmental or public health harm that undermines the MEA, then an NGO can often informally submit a petition to the secretariat of that relevant MEA and call upon that secretariat to pressure the nation-state to change its behavior.

One of several different outcomes may result from such a petition. First, the state party may take action to resolve the environmental or public health problem. Second, the MEA secretariat may work with a state party to resolve the problem. Third, the petition may raise public awareness of a previously unknown concern.

Remember that because this strategy is new and innovative, concerns may exist among the NGO community that if a petition is not prepared properly, then MEA secretariats may decide never to consider petitions from any non-state actors in the future. Therefore, seeking assistance from individuals on the List of Practitioner Experts can help strengthen your petition or lead to alternative strategies to resolve your issue.

---

[22] *Id.* at 16.
[23] *Id.*
[24] *Id.* at 18.
[25] *Id.* at 19.
[26] *Id.* at 38–39.
[27] *Id.* at 41.

B. Creating the Petition

Preparing a petition involves several steps discussed below. Table A in Section VII of this chapter provides information from several key MEAs to help facilitate the creation and submission of petitions. The list is not exhaustive, as hundreds of MEAs exist.

1. Select a Treaty Secretariat

Selecting a treaty secretariat usually involves three steps. First, identify the environmental and/or public health harm. Second, try to determine the possible causes of that harm. Third, based on these determined harms, select the appropriate MEA. Table A in Section VII of this chapter briefly mentions the scope of several key MEAs. Consult the text of the MEA for further guidance.

2. Prepare an Argument on the MEA Secretariat's Authority

The first section of the petition (or the cover letter accompanying it) should explain to the MEA secretariat why it has authority to receive, review, and respond to the facts and the environmental or public health harm presented in the petition. The text of and materials for most MEAs do not explicitly provide the secretariat with such authority. Therefore, it will be necessary to persuade the MEA otherwise.

First, cite provisions that list the powers of the particular MEA secretariat and argue that the language is broad enough to allow the MEA secretariat to consider your petition. Table A provides those provisions for the MEAs listed.

Second, cite examples of tasks that the MEA secretariat has undertaken in the past that demonstrate sufficiently broad authority to consider your petition. Examples of tasks are found in the resolution, reports, and related documents of the MEA. These materials may be located on most MEA internet sites under "Documents."

Table A provides an example of such an argument to the secretariat for the Convention on Biological Diversity.

3. Present Your Case

The petition should include detailed, accurate facts that demonstrate the environmental or public health harm. Provide documents or other evidentiary materials where necessary. The petition should further explain how the MEA is designed to address such harms. Finally, it should suggest certain actions that the MEA secretariat could take to help resolve the harm presented and persuade the MEA secretariat to act.

IV. STRATEGY NO. 3: LOBBYING STATE PARTIES TO INITIATE DISPUTE RESOLUTION PROCEEDINGS

MEA dispute resolution processes are available only for nation-states to bring claims against nation-states concerning matters within the scope of the given MEA. Therefore, non-state actors, such as NGOs, can and ought to request and encourage sympathetic governments—not necessarily their own—to file claims on behalf of such NGOs against nation-states that maintain a law or practice that harms the protection of the environment within the scope of that MEA.

Such a dispute could result in several different outcomes, similar to what may result from NGOs petitioning secretariats. First, the state party may take action to resolve the environmental or public health problem. Second, the MEA secretariat may pressure a state party to resolve the problem. Third, the petition may raise public awareness of a previously unknown concern.

An NGO wanting to pursue this strategy should determine which entity within the government of the nation-state represents that nation-state at such dispute resolution proceedings. Once determined, the NGO should submit a written request or schedule an in-person meeting with that office.

In the United States, consider contacting the following federal government offices for the issue listed.

- *MEAs Conference of Parties / MEA Secretariats*
  U.S. Department of State
  Office of Assistant Legal Advisor for Oceans, International Environmental and Scientific Affairs (L/OES)
  Office of the Legal Advisor
  U.S. Department of State
  2201 C Street, NW, Room 6420
  Washington, D.C. 20006
  T: (202) 647-1370
- *Air, Water, Hazardous Waste*
  U.S. Environmental Protection Agency
  Office of International Environmental Law
  USEPA Headquarters
  Ariel Rios Building
  1200 Pennsylvania Avenue, NW
  Washington, D.C. 20460
  T: (202) 564-5406
- *Biodiversity, Wetlands, Land Protection, Desertification*
  U.S. Department of Interior
  Office of the Solicitor / Office of International Affairs
  U.S. Department of the Interior
  1849 C Street, NW

Washington, D.C. 20240
Telephone directory: http://www.doi.gov/sol/solphone.html
- *Marine Resources, Fisheries*
U.S. Department of Commerce
National Oceans and Atmosphere Administration (NOAA)
(in particular, National Marine Fisheries Service)
U.S. Department of Commerce
14th Street & Constitution Avenue, NW
Room 6217
Washington, D.C. 20230
T:(202) 482-6090
- *Forestry*
U.S. Department of Agriculture
Office of the General Counsel / International Affairs
U.S. Department of Agriculture
Washington, D.C. 20250
Telephone directory: http://dc-directory.hqnet.usda.gov/pdf/usda_dc_agency.pdf
- *Dispute Resolution*
U.S. Department of Justice
Environmental and Natural Resources
U.S. Department of Justice
950 Pennsylvania Avenue, NW
Washington, D.C. 20530-0001
T:(202) 514-2701

V. STRATEGY NO. 4: PARTICIPATING AT MEA CONFERENCES OF THE PARTIES OR IN APPROPRIATE BODIES OF CHARTER-BASED INSTITUTIONS

Most MEAs allow non-state actors to participate as observers at periodic meetings among the MEA members states known as the Conference of the Parties ("COPs") in the case of conventions and Meetings of the Parties ("MOPs") in the case of Protocols. These mandatory gatherings require member states to report on the status of the MEA and focus on how to improve it. Member state attendees of COPs include the key government employees within a given member state and the staff of the MEA secretariat who are often the most knowledgeable about that MEA, who are experts in the field related to the MEA, and who may be responsible for making important decisions for the given member state and/or the MEA secretariat with respect to the development of that MEA. Consequently, attending the COP affords an NGO tremendous access to those who may be able to improve the enforcement of a given MEA with respect to a particular environmental or public health issue of concern to the NGO. Moreover, observer NGOs can often lobby generally on an issue among an audience intimately involved and familiar with the MEA, even if the observer NGO cannot vote.

In addition to participating at MEA COPs, civil society also can obtain similar consultative status with charter-based international governmental organizations such as the United Nations or the Organization of American States. Generally speaking, such status enables NGOs to attend legislative sessions, submit written statements, and make oral statements on a periodic basis.

Undertaking the strategy of participating at MEA conferences involves a few straightforward steps. First, one must again determine the MEA most relevant to one's environmental or public health issue of concern. Second, one must assess whether one has expertise in the field related to the MEA as such expertise is often a prerequisite for obtaining observer status. Third, one must consult the text of the MEA to confirm that it allows NGOs to attend the COP and/or MOP as an observer. Most do. Table A in Section VII of this chapter lists these provisions for the treaties included in that table. Because the language is usually identical, a quick look at the provisions indicated in Table A will help one locate the same provision in treaties not included in Table A. Fourth, one should consult the internet site for the MEA's secretariat to locate the procedures for applying for observer status. Such status may be available permanently for all COPs and/or MOPs or only temporarily for one particular COP and/or MOP. Often applications must be submitted far in advance of the date of the COP and/or MOP. Fifth, once one obtains observer status, one should locate other NGOs with observer status and build a coalition of groups interested in one's issue prior to attending the COP and/or MOP. Most MEA internet sites list entities with observer status. Sixth, one should prepare to lobby just as one prepares to lobby in other arenas.

Apart from COP and MOP participation, civil society can also obtain consultative or observer status with charter-based international or regional organizations. Such status may vary with each institution. Below are comments about a select few with information easily available from the Internet. For most, however, possessing consultative status with the Economic and Social Council ("ECOSOC") of the United Nations is usually necessary and often sufficient for receiving such status. Below is a summary of the requirements for the consultative status with the United Nations Economic and Social Council, observer accreditation for the Governing Council of the United Nations Environmental Program, World Summit on Sustainable Development Partnerships organized by the United Nations Division for Sustainable Development, the United Nations Food and Agriculture Program, consultative and observer status with the United Nations Educational, Scientific and Cultural Organization, and similar status with the Organization of American States. To obtain similar status with other international and regional institutions, be sure to telephone or e-mail the organization's public affairs office for further information.

Encouraging Secretariats to Enforce Environmental Standards • 199

A. United Nations

Information about obtaining consultative status with the United Nations Economic and Social Council, which serves as the general civil society accreditation process for the entire United Nations system, can be found at http://www.un.org/esa/coordination/ngo/.

B. United Nations Environmental Program ("UNEP")

Information about obtaining observer accreditation with the UNEP Governing Council can be found at http://www.unep.org/dpdl/cso/Default. asp?src=New_files_under_guidelines/Rules_For_Civil_S ociety_eng.htm.

The United Nations Guidelines on Compliance with and Enforcement of Multilateral Environmental Agreements and the accompanying Draft Manual to these guidelines include provisions addressing citizen enforcement of, access to, and participation in MEAs. The Draft Manual includes not only the provisions themselves but also examples of the manners in which countries have implemented the provisions to the benefit of their citizens.

Section 41(i) of the UNEP Guidelines provides for public access to judicial procedures, specifically to challenge acts and/or omissions by government or corporations that violate national environmental law.[28] The Draft Manual explains that allowing public access to judicial action "can greatly enhance the strength of a country's environmental enforcement."[29] The need for citizen participation in enforcement of environmental law is especially important when an enforcement agency fails to properly monitor environmental conduct that violates national law. Principle 10 of the Rio Declaration articulates the need for citizens and NGOs to act as "watchdogs" especially when an environmental agency is unwilling to act.[30] It is also possible for citizens to access justice through administrative bodies which have quasi-judicial functions. Not every citizen or NGO with an interest in a particular legal issue, however, can bring a lawsuit to court. A citizen or NGO must have "standing," which in many countries means that the individual must prove harm by the environmental violation or a group must prove that its members have been harmed.[31] Laws regarding standing, however, are not the same in every country and many countries allow for law-

---

[28] Guidelines on Compliance with and Enforcement of Multilateral Environmental Agreements (2002), *available at* http://www.unep.org/DEPI/programmes/law_implementation.html, at 10 ("Guidelines").

[29] Draft Manual on Compliance with and Enforcement of Multilateral Environmental Agreements (November 2004), *available at* http://www.unep.org/DEPI/programmes/law_implementation.html, at 215 ("Draft Manual").

[30] *Id.* at 215.

[31] *Id.* at 217.

200 • *Defending the Environment*

suits on an environmental issue regardless of a citizen's or NGO's connection to the issue. Countries have chosen to implement section 41(i) in the following ways: in the Philippines, the Supreme Court characterized the right to a healthy environment as a "specific fundamental legal right" in *Oposa v. Factoran* (1993); in Ontario, Canada, the Environmental Bill of Rights provides the right to sue when harm is caused to a public resource in Ontario; in Mexico, the Constitution includes the right to a healthy environment and the right to sue if any constitutionally granted rights are violated.[32]

Section 41(j) provides for public access to environmental information held by governments and agencies providing that the access complies with international and national law regarding confidentiality, access, and transparency.[33] Allowing public access to environmental information expands the body from which law and policy can be developed and helps spread improvement of compliance and enforcement with environmental law.[34] The most widespread form of public access to information is through an environmental impact assessment (EIA). Many countries now require that an EIA be completed before final approval for a project is given. Public participation in EIAs can range from mere access to the information contained in the EIA to input in the creation of the EIA.[35] Countries have chosen to implement section 41(j) in the following ways: in Croatia, the Ministry of Environmental Protection Physical Planning and Construction maintains a website that disseminates information about environmental laws, regulations and planning; in Korea, the government regularly publishes water and air quality assessments; in Macedonia, the Public Relations Office was established to facilitate information flow between the Ministry of Environment and Physical Planning ("MOEPP") and the public.[36]

Section 41(k) provides for community participation in decisions and actions that contribute to the protection of the environment.[37] The UNEP NGO/Civil Society Unit in the Division of Policy Development and Law works with NGOs around the world to help improve their ability to address environmental issues and to help these groups participate in conferences and programs that will allow their environmental concerns to be heard. This two-fold approach is geared toward creating a congruous relationship with governments in order to best promote environmental protection and

---

[32] *Id.* at 216.
[33] Guidelines, *supra* note 28, at 10.
[34] Draft Manual, *supra* note 29, at 219.
[35] *Id.* at 219.
[36] *Id.* at 220–221.
[37] Guidelines, *supra* note 28, at 10.

enforcement.[38] Many MEAs also include national implementation plans or exercises that are most productive when public participation by those likely to be affected is involved. Some countries have chosen to implement provision 41(k) in the following ways: in the United States, through EPA telephone hotlines providing information to the public and a forum for the public to report environmental violations; in India, permanent tribunals to hear people's environmental concerns; in Mongolia, partnerships between governments and environmental NGOs; in Bulgaria, compulsory public participation in all stages of EIA development.[39]

C. United Nations Division for Sustainable Development

Among other things, the UN Division for Sustainable Development is charged with implementing the Plan of Implementation ("POI") from the recent World Summit on Sustainable Development held in August 2002 in Johannesburg, South Africa. The POI aims to advance development in developing countries in an environmentally conscience matter. However, to better assure this, civil society should involve itself in the post-summit partnerships being created between governments and the private sector to handle the day-to-day implementation of the POI. Information on participating in existing partnerships and creating new ones can be found at http://www.un.org/esa/sustdev/index.html by clicking "Partnerships" on the left side of the screen.

D. United Nations Food and Agriculture ("FAO")

Information about consultative or observer status may be found at http://www.fao.org by clicking "NGO's and civil society organizations" and then clicking "FAO-NGO/CSO cooperation." Further information about consultative and observer status can be obtained by telephoning or e-mailing the FAO.

E. United Nations Educational, Scientific, and Cultural Organization ("UNESCO")

Information about the Sector for External Relations and Cooperation which handles requests for consultative and observer status for NGOs can be found at http://www.unesco.org by clicking "UNESCO Partners" and then "NGO'S" and then "About Us." Further information can be obtained by telephoning or e-mailing UNESCO.

---

[38] Draft Manual, *supra* note 29, at 223.
[39] *Id.* at 226–228.

F. Organization of American States ("OAS")

Consultative or observer status can also be obtained from certain regional organizations such as the Organization of American States. To apply, send a letter and accompanying materials listed below to:

Dr. César Gaviria, Secretary General
Organization of American States
MNB-20
17th St. and Constitution Ave., NW
Washington, D.C. 20006
USA.

The letter must include the following information:

a. The official name, address, and date of establishment of the organization,
b. The names of directors and legal representatives,
c. The primary area of activity and areas of the OAS where the organization sees the most compatibility and potential for contribution to the work of the OAS,
d. Reasons why your organization believes its proposed contributions to OAS activities would be of interest to the OAS,
e. Identification of the OAS work areas in which your organization proposes to support ongoing activities or to make recommendations on the best way to achieve OAS objectives.

Accompanying materials include:

a. Annual Report,
b. Institutional Mission Statement,
c. Financial Statements for the previous fiscal year, including reference to public and private sources of financing. This information must include a listing of sources of financing and donations received, including, in particular, those originating from government sources. Those organizations that are not membership-based shall also provide a listing of sources of financing and any donations received, including in particular, those originating from government sources.

VI. CONCLUSION

Making multilateral environmental agreements more effective is arguably the most direct way in which to protect the global environment. Whereas human rights processes require reshaping the environmental issues as a human rights problem and international finance and trade mechanisms limit their review to environmental harms in connection with globalization activity, the MEAs address particular environmental issues *qua*

Encouraging Secretariats to Enforce Environmental Standards • 203

environmental issues. But the success of MEAs is often hindered by vague language, a lack of sufficient signatory or ratifying nation-state participation, and the absence of political will on the part of parties to uphold and enforce the obligations to which they have committed themselves. The more that civil society appeals to the ombudsmen nature of MEA secretariats either through the submission of petitions or participation as observers, the more likely that those entities will begin to take initiative to encourage solutions to environmental and public health problems.

4.2 World Heritage Petitions

PETITION FOR HUASCARAN NATIONAL PARK

In light of the environmental threat to the Huascaran National Park caused by climate change Foro Ecológico del Peru, along with other NGOs and environmental lawyers, petitioned the World Heritage Committee on November 17, 2004 to add the site to its list of World Heritage Sites in Danger.[40]

Situated in the Cordillera Blanca, the world's highest tropical mountain range, Mount Huascaran rises to 6,768 meters above sea level. Deep ravines, watered by numerous torrents, glacial lakes, and the variety of vegetation make it a site of spectacular beauty. Unfortunately, recent scientific studies identify climate change as a real and serious threat to the Huascaran National Park. Climate change is causing the melting of glaciers that eventually leads to glacier reduction, to the formation of glacial lakes or an increase in their size, and to changes in ecosystem composition. The glaciers of the Cordillera Blanca range in the Huascaran National Park have retreated 25 meters in the last 50 years.

The petition was accepted by the World Heritage Committee, and a decision is expected next year.

PETITION FOR BELIZE BARRIER REEF

In response to serious environmental threats facing the Belize Barrier Reef the Belize Institute of Environmental Law and Policy (BELPO), a NGO incorporated in Belize to promote the development and enforcement of environmental laws, petitioned the World Heritage Committee on November 15, 2004 to list the Belize Barrier Reef as a World Heritage in Danger Site.[41]

(continued)

---

[40] Petition for the Huascaran National Park, *available at* http://www.climatelaw.org/media/UNESCO.petitions.release/peru.huascaran.national.park.doc.

[41] Petition for the Belize Barrier Reef, *available at* http://www.climatelaw.org/media/UNESCO.petitions.release/belize.barrier.reef.doc.

4.2 World Heritage Petitions *(continued)*

The unique and diverse Belize Barrier Reef community is currently facing serious danger due to the effects of global climate change. The site faces additional threats, including pollution, coral disease, coastal development, increased tourism impacts, especially cruise ship tourism, and over fishing, all of which have weakened and will continue to further weaken the resiliency of the reef system. These threats compound the danger of global climate change by making the reef more vulnerable to its effects.

Global climate change is a real and serious threat, particularly to sensitive coral reef ecosystems like that of the Belize Barrier Reef. Climate change can cause a phenomenon known as coral bleaching that eventually leads to changes in ecosystem composition and mortality of corals. Coral bleaching has resulted in a 50 percent reduction in live coral cover in some areas at the Belize Barrier Reef.

The World Heritage Committee has accepted the petition. The item will be on the agenda for next year's meeting.

PETITION FOR SAGARMATHA NATIONAL PARK

Due to the serious dangers threatening the environment of the Sagarmatha National Park, the Forum for Protection of Public Interest petitioned the World Heritage Committee on November 15, 2004 to add the site to its list of World Heritage in Danger.[42]

Sagarmatha is an exceptional area with dramatic mountains, glaciers, and deep valleys, dominated by Mount Everest, the highest peak in the world (8,848 m). Several rare species, such as the snow leopard and the lesser panda, are found in the park. The presence of the Sherpas, with their unique culture, adds further interest to this site. Tragically, Sagarmatha is now threatened by the serious danger of climate change.

In the Nepal Himalayas, data from 49 monitoring stations reveal a clear increase in temperature since the mid-1970s, with the greatest increases at higher altitudes.

The increased temperatures are causing the glaciers of Sagarmatha National Park and the greater Himalayan region to retreat. The resulting long-term loss of natural freshwater storage has had and could continue to have devastating downstream effects. Futhermore, if the glaciers continue to retreat it could pose a serious threat to human life, agriculture, property, fisheries, and wildlife.

The World Heritage Committee accepted the petition, and a decision is expected sometime next year.

---

[42] Petition for the Sagarmatha National Park, *available at* http://www.climatelaw.org/media/UNESCO.petitions.release/nepal.sagarmatha.national.park.doc.

VI. TABLE–SAMPLE MEAS

TREATY	OBJECTIVE	SECRETARIAT WEBSITE (Text of treaty available through website)	SECRETARIAT PROVISION AND ADDRESS	STATE-TO-STATE DISPUTE RESOLUTION PROVISION	COP/MOP OBSERVER PROVISION
Convention on Biological Diversity; Cartagena Protocol on BioSafety	Convention: To conserve biological diversity, particularly through creation and maintenance of national parks. Protocol: To safeguard against potential risks posed by living modified organisms resulting from modern biotechnology.	www.biodiv.org	Article 24 (Convention) Article 31 (Protocol) World Trade Centre 393 St Jacques Street Office 300 Montréal, Québec, Canada H2Y 1N9 (514) 288-2220 (514) 288-6588 (Fax) secretariat@biodiv.org	Article 27 (Convention) Article 32 (Protocol)	Article 23(5) (Convention) Article 29(8) (Protocol)
Vienna Convention for the Protection of the Ozone Layer; Montreal Protocol on Substances that Deplete the Ozone Layer	To protect the ozone layer.	www.unep.org/ozone	Article 7 (Vienna) Article 12 (Montreal) Secretariat for the Vienna Convention and the Montreal Protocol P. O. Box 30552 Nairobi, Kenya (254-2) 62-3850/1234 (254-2) 62-3601/3913 (Fax)	Article 11 (Vienna)	Article 6(5) (Vienna) Article 11(5) (Montreal)

TREATY	OBJECTIVE	SECRETARIAT WEBSITE (Text of treaty available through website)	SECRETARIAT PROVISION AND ADDRESS	STATE-TO-STATE DISPUTE RESOLUTION PROVISION	COP/MOP OBSERVER PROVISION
United Nations Framework Convention on Climate Change; Kyoto Protocol to the UNFCCC	To stabilize greenhouse gas concentrations to prevent climate change.	www.unfccc.int	Article 8 (UNFCCC) Article 14 (Kyoto) Haus Carstanjen Martin-Luther-King-Strasse 8 D-53175 Bonn Germany (49-228) 815-1000 (49-228) 815-1999 (Fax) secretariat@unfccc.int	Article 14 (UNFCCC) Article 19 (Kyoto)	Article 7(6)
Convention on International Trade in Endangered Species	To combat trade in endangered species.	www.cites.org	Article XII CITES Secretariat International Environment House Chemin des Anémones CH-1219 Châtelaine Geneva Switzerland (4122) 917-8139/40 (4122) 797-3417 (Fax) cites@unep.ch	Article XVIII	Article XI(7)

TREATY	OBJECTIVE	SECRETARIAT WEBSITE (Text of treaty available through website)	SECRETARIAT PROVISION AND ADDRESS	STATE-TO-STATE DISPUTE RESOLUTION PROVISION	COP/MOP OBSERVER PROVISION
Ramsar Convention on Wetlands of International Importance especially as Waterfowl Habitat	To conserve wetlands.	www.ramsar.org	Article 8 Ramsar Convention Bureau Rue Mauverney 28 CH-1196 Switzerland (4122) 999 0170 (4122) 999 0160 (Fax) ramsar@ramsar.org	No provision	No provision
Convention on Migratory Species	To protect migratory species and their habitat.	http://www.wcmc.org.uk/cms/	Article IX UNEP/CMS Secretariat United Nations Premises in Bonn Martin-Luther-King-Str. 8 D-53175 Bonn, Germany (49 228) 815 2401/2 (49 228) 815 2449 (Fax) cms@unep.de	Article XIII	Article VII(9)

TREATY	OBJECTIVE	SECRETARIAT WEBSITE (Text of treaty available through website)	SECRETARIAT PROVISION AND ADDRESS	STATE-TO-STATE DISPUTE RESOLUTION PROVISION	COP/MOP OBSERVER PROVISION
Basel Convention on the Control of Transboundary Movements of Hazardous Waste and Their Disposal	To administer transboundary movement of hazardous waste.	www.basel.int	Article 16 Secretariat of the Basel Convention International Environment House 11-13 chemin des Anémones Building D 1219 Châtelaine Geneva, Switzerland (4122) 917 8218 (4122) 797 3454 (Fax) sbc@unep.ch	Article 20	Article 15(6)
United Nations Convention to Combat Desertification	To combat desertification and mitigate effects of drought.	www.unccd.int	Article 23 UNCCD Secretariat P.O. Box 260129 Haus Carstanjen D-53153 Bonn, Germany (49-228) 815-2800/2802 (49-228) 815-2898/99 (Fax) secretariat@unccd.int	Article 28	Article 22(7)

TREATY	OBJECTIVE	SECRETARIAT WEBSITE (Text of treaty available through website)	SECRETARIAT PROVISION AND ADDRESS	STATE-TO-STATE DISPUTE RESOLUTION PROVISION	COP/MOP OBSERVER PROVISION
Constitution of the Food and Agriculture Organization ("FAO Constitution")[1]	Includes fisheries and forestry.	www.fao.org	Articles VI (FAO Council), VII (Director-General), VIII (Director-General Staff), XIV (Treaties) Food and Agriculture Organization of the United Nations (FAO) Viale delle Terme di Caracalla, 00100 Rome, Italy 39-06-5705-1 39-06-5705-3152 (Fax) FAO-HQ@fao.org Key FAO Council Committees	Article XVII (for FAO Constitution); see similar provisions in each fisheries and/or forestry treaty at http://www.fao.org/Legal/default.htm	

[1] The FAO Constitution is not an MEA but instead the governing document for the Food and Agricultural Organization ("FAO"), a specialized agency of the United Nations. The FAO serves as administrator for numerous treaties and voluntary codes. Established pursuant to Article XIV of the FAO Constitution, these treaties pertain to fisheries and forestry issues, among others. Therefore, petitioning the FAO on fisheries and forestry issues is arguably identical to petitioning the relevant treaty secretariats. The FAO can direct the petition to the correct section handling administration of the particular treaty at issue. For a list of the fisheries and forestry treaties for which the FAO serves as administrator, see http://www.fao.org/Legal/default.htm (click "Treaties").

TREATY	OBJECTIVE	SECRETARIAT WEBSITE (Text of treaty available through website)	SECRETARIAT PROVISION AND ADDRESS	STATE-TO-STATE DISPUTE RESOLUTION PROVISION	COP/MOP OBSERVER PROVISION
Constitution of the Food and Agriculture Organization ("FAO Constitution"), cont'd			Committee on Fisheries (COFI) Benedict P. Satia (Ph.D.) Secretary of Committee on Fisheries (COFI) 39-06-5705-2847 39-06-5705-6500 (Fax) benedict.satia@fao.org Committee on Forestry (COFO) www.fao.org/forestry		

Encouraging Secretariats to Enforce Environmental Standards • 211

TREATY	OBJECTIVE	SECRETARIAT WEBSITE (Text of treaty available through website)	SECRETARIAT PROVISION AND ADDRESS	STATE-TO-STATE DISPUTE RESOLUTION PROVISION	COP/MOP OBSERVER PROVISION
United Nations Law of the Sea ("UNCLOS"), Part XII: Protection and Preservation of the Marine Environment (Arts. 192–237)	To protect the marine environment.	Division of Ocean Affairs and the Law of the Sea: http://www.un.org/Depts/los/index.htm Text of UNCLOS (including Parts XII (Protection and Preservation of the Marine Environment) and XV (Settlement of Disputes)): http://www.un.org/Depts/los/convention_agreements/texts/unclos/closindx.htm	Sections 7.1 and 7.20 of the Secretary-General's Bulletin ST/SGB/1997/8 (Organization of the Office of Legal Affairs) at http://www.un.org/Depts/los/doalos_activities/about_doalos.htm#Bulletin%20ST/SGB/1997/8 (click "Core Functions") (last visited Nov. 24, 2002) Director Division for Ocean Affairs and the Law of the Sea Office of Legal Affairs Room DC2-0450 United Nations New York, NY 10017 (212) 963-3950 (212) 963-5847 (Fax) doalos@un.org	UNCLOS, Part XV (Arts. 279–299)	

TREATY	OBJECTIVE	SECRETARIAT WEBSITE (Text of treaty available through website)	SECRETARIAT PROVISION AND ADDRESS	STATE-TO-STATE DISPUTE RESOLUTION PROVISION	COP/MOP OBSERVER PROVISION
Convention on Access to Information, Public Participation in Decision-making and Access to Justice in Environmental Matters ("Aarhus Convention"), http://www.unece.org/env/pp/treatytext.htm	To ensure transparency and access to justice for environmental matters among the European parties.	http://www.unece.org/env/pp/welcome.html	Article 12, *but see* Decision I/7 pursuant to Article 15 (U.N. Doc. ECE/MP.PP/2/Add.8 (April 2, 2004) http://www.unece.org/env/pp/documents/mop1/ece.mp.pp.2.add.8.e.pdf). Address submissions for this Article 15 consultative mechanism to Aarhus Convention Compliance Committee, c/o UN Economic Commission for Europe Information Service Palais des Nations, CH - 1211 Geneva 10 Switzerland T: 41 (0) 22 917 12 34 F:41 (0) 22 917 05 05	Article 16, *but see* Decision I/7, ¶ 18 pursuant to Article 15 (U.N. Doc. ECE/MP.PP/2/Add.8 (April 2, 2004) http://www.unece.org/env/pp/documents/mop1/ece.mp.pp.2.add.8.e.pdf) that creates a consultative mechanism for reviewing party compliance with the Convention pursuant to Article 15 that allows non-parties to submit communications.	Article 10, *but see* Decision I/7, ¶ 18 pursuant to Article 15 (U.N. Doc. ECE/MP.PP/2/Add.8 (April 2, 2004) http://www.unece.org/env/pp/documents/mop1/ece.mp.pp.2.add.8.e.pdf), which creates a consultative mechanism for reviewing party compliance with the Convention pursuant to Article 15 that allows non-parties to submit communications.

Exercising Environmental Human Rights and Remedies · 213

TREATY	OBJECTIVE	SECRETARIAT WEBSITE (Text of treaty available through website)	SECRETARIAT PROVISION AND ADDRESS	STATE-TO-STATE DISPUTE RESOLUTION PROVISION	COP/MOP OBSERVER PROVISION
Convention on Access to Information, Public Participation in Decision-making and Access to Justice in Environmental Matters ("Aarhus Convention"), http://www.unece.org/env/pp/treatytext.htm	To ensure transparency and access to justice for environmental matters among the European parties.	http://www.unece.org/env/pp/welcome.html	info.ece@unece.org. For submissions not related to the Article 15 consultative mechanism, just address to the UN Economic Commission for Europe.	Article 16, but see Decision I/7, ¶ 18 pursuant to Article 15 (U.N. Doc. ECE/MP.PP/2/Add.8 (April 2, 2004) http://www.unece.org/env/pp/documents/mop1/ece.mp.pp.2.add.8.e.pdf) that creates a consultative mechanism for reviewing party compliance with the Convention pursuant to Article 15 that allows non-parties to submit communications.	Article 10, but see Decision I/7, ¶ 18 pursuant to Article 15 (U.N. Doc. ECE/MP.PP/2/Add.8 (April 2, 2004) http://www.unece.org/env/pp/documents/mop1/ece.mp.pp.2.add.8.e.pdf), that creates a consultative mechanism for reviewing party compliance with the Convention pursuant to Article 15 that allows non-parties to submit communications.

TREATY	OBJECTIVE	SECRETARIAT WEBSITE (Text of treaty available through website)	SECRETARIAT PROVISION AND ADDRESS	STATE-TO-STATE DISPUTE RESOLUTION PROVISION	COP/MOP OBSERVER PROVISION
Protocol on Pollutant Release and Transfer Registers to the Aarhus Convention, http://www.unece.org /env/pp/prtr/docs/PRT R%20Protocol%20En glish.pdf (not yet in force).	To ensure access to information and public participation with respect to pollutant release and transfer registers for environmental impacts from companies within each European state party.	http://www.unece. org/env/pp/prtr.htm.	Article 21 Executive Secretary UN Economic Commission for Europe Information Service Palais des Nations CH - 1211 Geneva 10 Switzerland T: 41 (0) 22 917 12 34 F: 41 (0) 22 917 05 05 info.ece@unece.org	Article 23	Article 17
Protocol on Strategic Environmental Assessment to the Convention on Environmental Impact Assessment in a Transboundary Context,	To ensure access to information and public participation with respect to environmental assessments and consultations on various national	http://www.unece. org/env/eia/sea_ protocol.htm	Article 17 United Nations Economic Commission for Europe Environment and Human Settlements Division	Article 20	Article 14

TREATY	OBJECTIVE	SECRETARIAT WEBSITE (Text of treaty available through website)	SECRETARIAT PROVISION AND ADDRESS	STATE-TO-STATE DISPUTE RESOLUTION PROVISION	COP/MOP OBSERVER PROVISION
http://www.unece.org/env/eia/documents/protocolenglish.pdf (not yet in force).	and local projects and activities within each European state party.		Secretariat Palais des Nations 8-14, avenue de la Paix - 1211 Geneve 10 Switzerland T: 00 41 22 917 2448 F: 00 41 22 917 0107 E: eia.conv@unece.org		
World Heritage Convention	To designate and protect certain natural and cultural places of world heritage, including a special list of the places of world heritage in danger for which major operations are necessary. Non-state actors can petition state parties to list	http://whc.unesco.org/en/comittee/	Part III (Arts. 8–14) establishes the World Heritage Committee The World Heritage Centre UNESCO 7, Place de Fontenoy 75352 Paris 07 SP France T: 33-1-45 68 15 71 F: 33-1-45 68 55 70 E: wh-info@unesco.org	Not applicable	Not applicable

TREATY	OBJECTIVE	SECRETARIAT WEBSITE (Text of treaty available through website)	SECRETARIAT PROVISION AND ADDRESS	STATE-TO-STATE DISPUTE RESOLUTION PROVISION	COP/MOP OBSERVER PROVISION
	natural places to increase conservation efforts and to have them designated as in danger to afford greater protections.		Division of Ecological Sciences, Science Sector UNESCO 1, rue Miollis 75352 Paris, Cedex 15, France 33-1-45 68 40 67 33-1-45 68 58 04 Man and Biosphere Programme: mab@unesco.org http://www.unesco.org/mab		
Rotterdam Convention on the Prior Informed Consent Procedure for Certain Hazardous Chemicals and Pesticides in International Trade	Establishes prior consent and access to information procedures designed to limit risks associated with the international trade of certain hazardous chemicals and pesticides so as to pro-	http://www.pic.int/en/viewpage.asp?Id_Cat=76&mTitre=Secretariat	Article 19 Secretariat for the Rotterdam Convention United Nations Environment Programme (UNEP) 11-13 Chemin des Anèmones CH-1219 Châtelaine	Article 20	Article 18

TREATY	OBJECTIVE	SECRETARIAT WEBSITE (Text of treaty available through website)	SECRETARIAT PROVISION AND ADDRESS	STATE-TO-STATE DISPUTE RESOLUTION PROVISION	COP / MOP OBSERVER PROVISION
	tect human health and the environment from potential harm.		GE Switzerland 41 22 917 8296 41 22 797 3460 (fax) pic@unep.ch		
Stockholm Convention on Persistent Organic Pollutants	To protect human health and the environment from the harmful impact of persistent organic pollutants (POPs).	http://www.pops.int/documents/convtext/convtext_en.pdf	Article 20 Secretariat for the Stockholm Convention on Persistent Organic Pollutants 11-13 Chemin des Anémones 1219 Châtelaine Geneva Switzerland (41) 22 917 8191 (41) 22 797 3460	Article 18	Article 19

218 · Defending the Environment

TREATY	OBJECTIVE	SECRETARIAT WEBSITE (Text of treaty available through website)	SECRETARIAT PROVISION AND ADDRESS	STATE-TO-STATE DISPUTE RESOLUTION PROVISION	COP/MOP OBSERVER PROVISION
Environmental treaties under the auspices of the International Maritime Organization designed to safeguard the high seas from ship pollution, including International Convention for the Prevention of Pollution from Ships (MARPOL), International Convention on Oil Pollution Preparedness, Response and Co-operation (OPRC), and the International Convention on Civil Liability for Oil Pollution Damage.	The International Maritime Organization is the United Nations' specialized agency responsible for improving maritime safety and preventing pollution from ships.	Marine Environment Protection Committee, http://www.imo.org	Provision not applicable. International Maritime Organization Albert Embankment London SE1 7SR United Kingdom T: 44 (0)20 7735 7611 F: 44 (0)20 7587 3210 info@imo.org Instead of calling or writing, send all inquiries to the e-mail address above.	See various environmental treaties of the IMO on the Marine Environment page.	See various environmental treaties of the IMO on the Marine Environment page.

TREATY	OBJECTIVE	SECRETARIAT WEBSITE (Text of treaty available through website)	SECRETARIAT PROVISION AND ADDRESS	STATE-TO-STATE DISPUTE RESOLUTION PROVISION	COP/MOP OBSERVER PROVISION
The International Maritime Organization is the United Nations' specialized agency responsible for improving maritime safety and preventing pollution from ships.					

CHAPTER 5

ENFORCING INTERNATIONAL ENVIRONMENTAL LAW IN TRIBUNALS OF GENERAL JURISDICTION

I. INTRODUCTION

Nearly all of the fora presented in the earlier chapters of this book have limited subject matter jurisdiction. They usually can address only environmental issues that involve no more than one of the following links: (1) human rights, (2) a development project that depends on international financial institutions, (3) international trade and investment, or (4) a specific multilateral treaty. In addition to these more focused fora, however, are international and regional courts and tribunals of general jurisdiction. Such fora include the International Court of Justice, the Permanent Court on Arbitration, the International Criminal Court, the European Court of Justice, and the African Court of Justice. These fora are open to disputes about any civil or criminal matter, including environmental matters, but their jurisdiction over parties is often limited only to nation-states, unlike many of the fora mentioned in earlier chapters. Nevertheless, with perseverance and clever strategizing, non-state entities can succeed in having at least one of these bodies hear environmental claims.

II. INTERNATIONAL COURT OF JUSTICE

The International Court of Justice ("ICJ") is the principal judicial organ of the United Nations.[1] It is composed of 15 judges elected to nine-year terms and sits at The Hague. No more than one judge from a single country can serve on the ICJ, and the judges act as independent magistrates rather than representatives of any particular country. The official languages of the ICJ are French and English.

The Court proceedings include both written and oral phases with the judges deliberating *in camera* and delivering the judgment at a public sit-

---

[1] *See* UN Charter, http://un.org/aboutun/charter/, arts. 92–96.

ting. Decisions are based on law drawn from international treaties, custom, and general principles of law, as well as judicial decisions and scholarly writings as subsidiary sources.[2] ICJ judgments are final and cannot be appealed. The UN Security Council is authorized to enforce ICJ decisions,[3] but has yet to do so in large part due to the veto power.

Only states may bring cases before the ICJ. States may accept the Court's jurisdiction in one of three ways: by special agreement to submit the conflict to the Court by a treaty with a provision that directs disputes arising under the treaty to the Court, or by a general declaration agreeing to submit to the Court's compulsory jurisdiction (approximately 60 states have done so, many with provisions excluding certain categories of dispute). General declarations accepting the Court's compulsory jurisdiction are limited by the requirement of reciprocity—the defending state must not only accept the Court's compulsory jurisdiction, it is entitled to assert the petitioning states' reservations to compulsory jurisdiction as well as its own. In other words, the lowest common denominator of jurisdiction applies.

The ICJ may also render advisory opinions,[4] but only at the request of the five organs of the UN or one of the 16 specialized agencies of the UN.[5] The Court's advisory opinions are based on the information provided by the appropriate organizations and by application of the same sources of law as outlined above with the contentious decisions.[6]

Although the ICJ is competent to hear cases involving the environment, it has heard very few, and perhaps only one[7] that can be character-

---

[2] Statute of the International Court of Justice, http//www.icj-cij.org/icjwww/ibasicdocuments/ibasictext/ibasicstatute.htm ("ICJ Statute"), Art. 38.

[3] UN Charter, Art. 94.

[4] Id. Art. 96.

[5] In 1996, the ICJ rendered an advisory opinion for a request brought by the UN General Assembly on the Legality of the Threat or Use of Nuclear Weapons. 1996 I.C.J 226. In the opinion, the Court found that the use of nuclear weapons was not prohibited by international environmental laws, and that the law of war was a more appropriate source for answering the question of the legality of using nuclear weapons, in which case environmental concerns would be a factor in determining necessity and proportionality. Sean D. Murphy, *Does the World Need a New Environmental Court?*, 32 GEO. WASH. J. INT'L L. & ECON. 333, 335 (2000); *see* text accompanying notes 21-30 *infra*.

[6] *See* http://www.icj-cij.org for more general information about the ICJ.

[7] The Gabcikovo-Nagymaros Project case was the first environmental case decided by the ICJ. Hungary and Slovakia entered into a treaty for a project establishing a system of locks on the Danube River. Hungary abandoned the project alleging risk to the environment and Slovakia continued an alternative project that harmed Hungary's access to water from the river. The Court grounded its decision more on the law of treaties and international water courses than on more generally applicable rules of international environmental law. It concluded that Hungary had breached the treaty by suspending work on the project and that the breach was not justified under the treaty based on "ecological necessity." It also found, however, that Slovakia's modified continuation of the project wrongfully interfered with Hungary's rights under the law of international water courses. Both states were directed to

ized as primarily environmental. In 1993, the ICJ established a special seven-member Chamber for Environmental Matters ("CEM").[8] To date, no state has submitted a dispute to this chamber.[9] The non-use of the CEM may be explained by the fact that states have the option to form an *ad hoc* chamber when settling disputes before the ICJ. The formation of the *ad hoc* chamber takes the parties' views into account in formation of the chamber whereas the composition of the CEM is already established.[10]

Some scholars have suggested the non-use of the ICJ for bringing environmental disputes is because states fear counterclaims on environmental matters.[11] Others claim the lack of NGO and private party access to the ICJ deprives the Court of hearing cases by the most directly affected and most ardent supporters of the environment.[12] One author has advocated more utilization of the ICJ because "the protection of the environment is closely linked to international human rights law" and would therefore impose minimum standards on states for environmental protection for the sake of life.[13]

There are many political and procedural impediments to the use of the ICJ in environmental cases.[14] Many states are not willing to submit any

---

negotiate a good faith solution under the still valid treaty. *Case Concerning the Gabcikovo-Nagymaros Project (Hungary/Slovakia)*, 1997 I.C.J. 92.

The majority opinion's almost incidental acknowledgment of international environmental law did little to develop the law. Most helpful in this regard is Judge Weeramantry's separate opinion recognizing sustainable development as a legal principle. This opinion provides the strongest argument to date for expanded recognition by the ICJ of international environmental law. This opinion is also significant because the Court acknowledged that the concept of *jus cogens* extends to environmental norms. Eva M. Kornicker Uhlmann, *State Community Interests, Jus Cogens and Protection of the Global Environment: Developing Criteria for Peremptory Norms*, 11 GEO. INT'L ENVTL. L. REV. 101, 126 (1998).

[8] Article 26 of the Statute of the International Court of Justice authorizes the Court to establish chambers for "particular categories of cases."

[9] Peggy Rodgers Kalas, *International Environmental Dispute Resolution and the Need for Access by Non-state Entities*, 12 COLO. J. INT'L ENVTL. L. & POL'Y 191, 208 (2001).

[10] *Id.* at 209.

[11] Johanna Rinceanu, *Enforcement Mechanisms in International Environmental Law: Quo Vadunt? Homo Sanus in Natura Sana*, 15 J. ENVTL. L. & LITIG. 147, 155 (2000); Jeffrey L. Dunoff, *Institutional Misfits: the Gatt, the ICJ & Trade-environment Disputes*, 15 MICH. J. INT'L L. 1043, 1093 (1999).

[12] *See* Kalas, *supra* note 9, at 192, 208; Rinceanu, *supra* note 11, at 155. The ICJ has in only one instance allowed submission from an international nongovernmental organization. This occurred during the proceedings in its 1950 advisory opinion in *International Status of South-West Africa*. Amnesty International has attempted to build on that opportunity, and in 2001 submitted to the ICJ a memorandum on universal jurisdiction in the case of *Democratic Republic of Congo v. Belgium*. It is unclear, however, what if any use the judges officially made of the memorandum. *See* T. TREVES, M. DI RATTALMA, A. TANZI, A. FODELLA, C. PITEA, C. RAGNI, CIVIL SOCIETY, INTERNATIONAL COURTS AND COMPLIANCE BODIES 15 (2005).

[13] Uhlmann, *supra* note 7, at 135, *see generally* Chapter 1, *supra*.

[14] *See* Dunoff, *supra* note 11, at 1085-1111.

224 • *Defending the Environment*

disputes to the Court's jurisdiction, especially in matters of perceived "secondary importance."[15] Adjudication does not usually encourage a mutually beneficial compromise, and ICJ decisions retain a perceived "lack of bite" due to lack of enforceability.[16] Also, because private entities often are responsible for environmental damage, it is more difficult to demonstrate to what extent a state will be responsible for the acts of such entities.[17] Furthermore, many states are unfamiliar or uncomfortable with the law affecting international environmental cases and may avoid pursuing cases for which the outcome is perceived as more unpredictable than under state domestic law.[18] This uncertainty is self-perpetuating.[19]

The ICJ's jurisdictional requirements and its limitation to state parties significantly decrease the number of environmental cases it hears. Not only are interested and financially capable NGOs excluded from the Court, but states must struggle to demonstrate standing when their own territory is not directly injured (*e.g.*, the harm is inflicted upon a global environmental resource).[20]

In 1988, the International Physicians for the Prevention of Nuclear War ("IPPNW") endorsed the letter-writing campaign of Aotearoa/New Zealand retired judge Harold Evans to seek an advisory opinion from the ICJ addressing the use of nuclear arms.[21] In 1989, this letter writing campaign was endorsed by the International Peace Bureau ("IPB") and the International Association of Lawyers Against Nuclear Arms ("IALANA").[22] Collectively, the IPPNW, the IPB, and the IALANA joined to form the World Court Project in 1992.[23] The World Court Project played a key role in persuading the World Health Assembly, the governing body of the World Health Organization (WHO), to request an advisory opinion from the ICJ addressing the issue of nuclear weapons.[24] In 1993, the World Health Assembly asked the ICJ to address the question: "In view of the health and environmental effects, would the use of nuclear weapons by a state in war or other armed conflict be a breach of its obligations under international law includ-

---

[15] *Id.* at 1090.

[16] *Id.*

[17] *Id.* at 1096.

[18] *Id.* at 1091-93. The United Nations Environment Programme once declared that "'an obligation to protect the environment exist[s] in international law, but ... its content [is] not established.'" Dunoff, *supra* note 11, at 1094 (quoting Report of the Group of Experts in Liability for Pollution and Other Environmental Damage and Compensation for Such Damage, U.N. Doc. UNEP/WG.818, 4 (1977)).

[19] Dunoff, *supra* note 11, at 1097.

[20] *Id.* at 1098.

[21] *See* Kate Dewes & Robert Green, *The World Court Project: How a Citizen Network Can Influence the United Nations*, 7 PACIFICA REV. 22-25 (No. 2, 1995).

[22] JOHN BURROUGHS, THE (IL)LEGALITY OF THREAT OR USE OF NUCLEAR WEAPONS 10 (1997).

[23] *See id.*

[24] *See id.*

ing the WHO Constitution?"[25] Endorsements for the efforts of the World Court Project to seek the advisory opinion were received from more than 700 groups around the world.[26] Concerned citizens also signed individual declarations opposing nuclear weapons and, for the first time, signatures of nearly four million citizens were presented to the registrar of the ICJ.[27] IALANA lawyers also drafted the briefs that many countries used as models when making their own written submissions to the court.[28]

The Court declined to hear the WHO's question on the grounds that although the WHO had been authorized by the General Assembly to request advisory opinions on "legal questions arising within the scope of its competence," this particular issue was deemed to be outside of that scope.[29] Shortly after the WHO's request was denied, the General Assembly filed a request with the Court. Because the UN Charter expressly names the General Assembly as authorized to seek an advisory opinion on "any legal question," the Court clearly had the authority to reply to its request.[30] Although the Court refused to hear the WHO request, the initiative of IALANA was critical in commencing the process that eventually led to the Court's consideration of the legality of nuclear weapons.

Finally, in contentious proceedings, Article 34(2) and Article 69 in the Rules of Court allow international governmental organizations to provide information to the Court at its request. For now, however, non-governmental organizations may only be involved in contentious proceedings indirectly before the court by influencing states to commence proceedings or by influencing inter-governmental organizations in the observations or information they might provide under Articles 69(1) or (2) of the Rules of Court.

III. THE LAW OF THE SEA TREATY REGIME

In 1973 the third United Nations Convention on the Law of the Sea was convened, meeting for several months a year through 1982, before the Convention voted to adopt the United Nations Convention on the Law of the Sea ("UNCLOS").[31] The treaty was available for signature in Montego

---

[25] *See* World Health Assembly Resolution wha46.40, *adopted* May 14, 1993, Requesting Advisory Opinion.
[26] *See* BURROUGHS, *supra* note 22, at 9.
[27] *See id.* at 10.
[28] *See id.*
[29] *See Legality of the Use by a State of Nuclear Weapons in Armed Conflict*, General List No. 93 (Advisory Opinion of July 8, 1996).
[30] *See* BURROUGHS, *supra* note 22, at 9.
[31] RENATE PLATZODER, THIRD UNITED NATIONS CONFERENCE ON THE LAW OF THE SEA (1987) (17 vol. set). For an analysis and discussion of the content of these conferences, *see* Bernard H. Oxman, *The Third United Nations Conference on the Law of the Sea: Tenth Session*, 76 AM. J. INT'L L. 1 (1982).

Bay, Jamaica, on December 10, 1982.[32] In accordance with Article 308, which required 60 signatory states, the Convention entered into force on November 16, 1994.[33] A subsequent Agreement to the implementation procedures of Part XI of the Convention governing the deep seabed was adopted on July 28, 1994, entering into force on July 28, 2000.[34] The Convention applies to all states parties, with "'States Parties' mean[ing] States which have consented to be bound by this Convention and for which this Convention is in force."[35] Additionally, "[t]his Convention applies *mutatis mutandis* to the entities referred to in article 305 . . .[36] which become Parties to this Convention in accordance with the conditions relevant to each, and to that extent 'States Parties' refers to those entities."[37] There are currently 157 signatory states to the Convention, with 138 having ratified; 79 signatures to the Agreement relating to Part XI of the Convention, with 108 having ratified; and 59 signatory states to the Agreement for the implementation of the provisions of the Convention relating to the conservation and management of straddling fish stocks and highly migratory fish, with 32 having ratified.[38]

With 320 Articles and nine Annexes, the Convention on the Law of the Sea represents "the most comprehensive legal framework on the international environmental plane."[39] It provides a constitutional framework for the implementation and development of marine environmental law.[40] The Convention creates numerous state obligations for the protection of the marine environment, including broad requirements to minimize marine pollution, and to preserve and protect the marine environment, as well as more narrow requirements: to formulate environmental standards, to notify

---

[32] See id; see also P. Chandrasekhara Rao, *International Tribunal for the Law of the Sea: An Overview*, in THE INTERNATIONAL TRIBUNAL FOR THE LAW OF THE SEA: LAW AND PRACTICE 1 (P. Chandrasekhara Rao & Rahmatullah Khan eds., 2001) ("LAW AND PRACTICE").

[33] See United Nations Convention on the Law of the Sea of December 10, 1982: an Overview, *available at* http://www.un.org/Depts/los/convention_agreements/convention_overview_convention.htm.

[34] See Rao, *supra* note 32, at 1.

[35] UNCLOS, Art. 1(2)(1).

[36] Article 305 reads in relevant part "This Convention shall be open for signature by . . . (f) international organizations, in accordance with Annex IX." UNCLOS, Art. 305(1)(f).

[37] UNCLOS, Art. 1(2)(2).

[38] See Status of the United Nations Convention on the Law of the Sea, of the Agreement relating to the implementation of Part XI of the Convention and of the Agreement for the implementation of the provisions of the Convention relating to the conservation and management of straddling fish stocks and highly migratory fish, *available at* http://www.un.org/Depts/los/reference_files/status2002.pdf. This information is current as of October 21, 2002. See id.

[39] Johanna Rinceanu, *Enforcement Mechanisms in International Environmental Law: Quo Vadunt? Homo Sanus in Natura Sana*, 15 J. ENVTL. L. & LITIG. 147, 157 (2000).

[40] See Daniel Bodansky, *Protecting the Marine Environment from Vessel-Source Pollution: UNCLOS III and Beyond*, 18 ECOLOGY L.Q. 719, 721 (1991).

other states of "imminent danger" from pollution, to cooperate in scientific efforts, to provide assistance (both technical and scientific) to developing states, to formulate joint contingency plans in the event of a pollution spill, to perform environmental assessment reports, and to monitor the risks and effects associated with marine pollution.[41] "A state which fails to fulfill its obligations to protect and preserve the marine environment is liable in accordance with international law."[42] International law may require a state to terminate, reduce, or prevent any activity threatening or creating pollution, or to pay monetary damages for the injury caused.[43]

In structure, the Convention created a system that would protect and govern the entire sea, from the seabed and subsoil to the airspace above.[44] The Convention's enforcement provisions for protecting the marine environment are contained within Articles 213 to 222 and authorize enforcement by port states, coastal states, and flag states.[45] Article 213, "Enforcement with respect to pollution from land-based sources," requires states to enforce their laws and regulations in accordance with Article 207[46] and to modify their laws and regulations in accordance with the rules and standards set by competent international organizations or diplomatic conferences.[47] Article 214, "Enforcement with respect to pollution from sea-bed activities," requires states to enforce their laws and regulations in keeping with

---

[41] See id. at 721-22.
[42] LOUIS B. SOHN & KRISTEN GUSTAFSON, THE LAW OF THE SEA: IN A NUTSHELL 210 (1984); LOS Convention, Art. 235(1).
[43] See id.
[44] See Rinceanu, *supra* note 11, at 157.
[45] See id. The 1954 Conventions on the law of the sea did not include a separate treaty or subchapter specifically dedicated to preservation of the marine environment.
[46] Article 207 "Pollution from land-based sources" reads:
States shall adopt laws and regulations to prevent, reduce and control pollution of the marine environment from land-based sources . . . taking into account internationally agreed rules, standards and recommended practices and procedures; [and] States shall take other measures as may be necessary to prevent, reduce and control such pollution; [and] States shall endeavour to harmonize their policies in this connection at the appropriate regional level; [and] States, acting especially through competent international organizations or diplomatic conference, shall endeavour to establish global and regional rules, standards and recommended practices and procedures to prevent, reduce and control pollution of the marine environment from land-based sources, taking into account characteristic regional features, the economic capacity of developing States and their need for economic development. Such rules, standards and recommended practices and procedures shall be reexamined from time to time as necessary.
UNCLOS, Art. 207(1), (2), (3), (4).
[47] See id. art. 213.

Article 208,[48] with an emphasis on preventing, reducing and controlling marine pollution created by seabed activities.[49] Article 215, "Enforcement with respect to pollution from activities in the Area," requires that the enforcement of the international rules established under Part XI of the Convention, shall be governed by Part XI.[50] Article 216, "Enforcement with respect to pollution from dumping," requires the following states parties to enforce the provisions against dumping: the coastal state; the flag state; and any state in whose territory the dumping occurs, but notes that no state must instigate a proceeding if another has already done so.[51] Article 217, "Enforcement by flag States," requires flag states to ensure the compliance with the provisions of the Convention for all vessels flying their flag; if a violation is committed by any such vessel, the flag state is to conduct an immediate investigation thereof, and must inform the international organization of the action taken, at risk of penalty for failure to do so.[52]

Article 218, "Enforcement by port States," is noteworthy, as it entitles "harbor states to enforce the provisions against oil pollution even if such pollution occurs outside their territorial waters, regardless of the jurisdiction of the flag state's delinquent vessel or the damage suffered by the harbor itself."[53] Article 218 thereby establishes a common interest and responsibility for the preservation and enforcement of the Convention within the international community, ensuring that pollution will not go unpunished merely because another state has refused to fulfill its obligations (or, in the alternative, to sign the Convention).[54] The inclusion of Article 218 was an innovative step in the arena of international law, as it was "intended to protect the now-recognized public interest of the international community, not just individual state interests."[55]

Article 219, "Measures relating to seaworthiness of vessels to avoid pollution," requires that a state that becomes aware that one of their flag vessels is in violation of international rules, or at risk of being in violation, must take adequate administrative proceedings against that vessel to prevent it from sailing; at the most, the vessel may be permitted to sail to the nearest suitable repair yard.[56] Article 220, "Enforcement by coastal States,"

---

[48] Article 208 mirrors the language of Article 207 fairly closely, with an emphasis on pollution from seabed activities. *See* LOS Convention, art. 208.
[49] *See id.* art. 214.
[50] *See id.* art. 215.
[51] *See id.* art. 216.
[52] *See id.* art. 217.
[53] Jost Delbruck, *A More Effective International Law or New "World Law"?—Some Aspects of the Development of International Law in a Changing International System*, 68 IND. L.J. 705, 718 (1993).
[54] *Id.*
[55] *See* Rinceanu, *supra* note 11, at 158.
[56] *See* UNCLOS, art. 219.

gives coast states the right to investigate or detain vessels who are suspect of being in violation of the Convention, provided certain criteria are met; the criteria vary depending upon the location of the foreign vessel (at port, off-shore, in the territorial sea, or in the EEZ) at the time of violation.[57] Article 221,"Measure to avoid pollution arising from maritime casualties," gives states the right to take and enforce measures beyond the territorial sea in the event of a maritime casualty, in order to protect their own coastline or related interest.[58] Finally, Article 222, "Enforcement with respect to pollution from or through the atmosphere," requires states to help prevent, reduce and control pollution of the marine environment, from their flag vessels or vessels in their territory, which are threatening or causing pollution of the atmosphere.[59]

The Convention also establishes an International Tribunal for the Law of the Sea ("the Tribunal").[60] The United States prepared the first proposals for formulating a tribunal for the settlement of disputes arising under the Law of the Sea, and presented these to the Seabed Committee in 1973.[61] The disputes at issue related to seabed mining for which the actors might include not only states, but natural or juridical persons and international organizations.[62] Under the adopted Convention, the dispute settlement system was not optional, but rather an integral part of the Convention.[63] The Tribunal was central to the dispute settlement regime formed.[64] At the second meeting of states parties on August 1, 1996, in which 100 states parties participated by vote, 21 judges were elected to the Tribunal.[65] The Tribunal also consists of an independent executive arm, the secretariat or registry.[66] Two weeks after the Tribunal had adopted its rules in 1997, the first case was filed with the Court, concerning the release of the vessel M/V "Saiga."[67] Following this first case, nine more had been filed with the Tribunal by 2001.[68] The parties to the various cases have been as follows: Saint Vincent and the Grenadines versus Guinea (*M/V Saiga* case); Australia

---

[57] See *id*. art. 220.
[58] See *id*. art. 221.
[59] See *id*. art. 222.
[60] See generally Law and Practice, *supra* note 32; CURRENT MARINE ENVIRONMENTAL ISSUES AND THE INTERNATIONAL TRIBUNAL FOR THE LAW OF THE SEA (Myron H. Nordquist & John Norton Moore eds., 2001) ("CURRENT MARINE ENVIRONMENTAL ISSUES").
[61] See Hugo Caminos, *The Establishment of Specialized Courts*, *in* CURRENT MARINE ENVIRONMENTAL ISSUES, *supra* note 60, at 35; *see also* A/AC.138/97.
[62] See *id*.
[63] See Gritakumar E. Chitty, *A Brief History of the Post Conference Development of the Tribunal as an International Judicial Body*, *in* CURRENT MARINE ENVIRONMENTAL ISSUES, *supra* note 60, at 43.
[64] See *id*.
[65] See *id*. at 48. Each judge had to be elected by a two-thirds majority vote. *See id*.
[66] See *id*. at 49.
[67] See *id*. at 48.
[68] See *id*; ITLOS Proceedings & Judgments, *at* http://www.itlos.org/start2_en.html.

and New Zealand against Japan (*Southern Bluefin Tuna* case); Panama versus France (*Camouco* case); Seychelles versus France (*Confurco* case); Chile and the European Union (*Conservation and Sustainable Exploitation of Swordfish Stocks in the South-Eastern Pacific Ocean* case); Belize versus France (*Grand Prince* case); Panama versus Yemen (*Chaisiri Reefer 2* case); Ireland versus the United Kingdom (*MOX Plant* case).[69]

Although it might appear from the above list of parties that only state actors have utilized the Tribunal thus far, one international lawyer noted:

> [a]nother feature of many of these bodies [international tribunals] is that they are not all state-centered. Individuals, NGO's, corporations, and international organizations are now actively involved in cases before some of these bodies. In some cases, these new actors are formally involved. This can be as a party—for example in the presently suspended proceedings between Chile and the EU before this [LOS] Tribunal—or as an intervenor. And in other cases, even if they are not formally involved, these new actors are present behind the scenes, exerting their influence in numerous ways.[70]

The official webpage for ITLOS answers the question "Can only States Parties submit cases to the Tribunal?" with the following response:

> The Tribunal is also open to entities other than States Parties to the Convention in any case expressly provided for in Part XI of the Convention or in any case submitted pursuant to any other agreement conferring jurisdiction on the Tribunal which is accepted by all the parties to that case. In Part XI provision is made, for example, for private companies or individuals to bring cases to the Seabed Disputes Chamber in connection with activities in the Area.[71]

However, deciphering the rights of non-state entities to bring claims and/or be held responsible under the Convention has proven difficult, as com-

---

[69] See Shabati Rosenne, *The Case-Law of ITLOS (1997-2001): An Overview*, in CURRENT MARINE ENVIRONMENTAL ISSUES, *supra* note 60, at 127; ITLOS Proceedings & Judgments, *at* http://www.itlos.org/start2_en.html.

[70] Philippe Sands, *ITLOS: An International Lawyer's Perspective*, in CURRENT MARINE ENVIRONMENTAL ISSUES, *supra* note 60, at 142. The proceedings between Chile and the EU were suspended, after the countries entered into negotiations and reached an amicable settlement pursuant to their obligations under the World Trade Organization (WTO). *See* "EU and Chile Reach an Amicable Settlement to End WTO/ITLOS Swordfish Dispute," *at* http://europa.eu.int/comm/fisheries/news_corner/press/inf01_05_en.htm.

[71] ITLOS, Frequently Asked Questions, *at* http://www.itlos.org/start2_en.html (last visited Dec. 2, 2002).

ments by David R. Robinson, an international lawyer, demonstrate. In a fictional oil-spill example presented at a recent LOS colloquium, Robinson pondered how France could receive compensation under the Convention, when the primary responsible parties appeared to be non-state entities. As he noted, "International conventions generally create rights and obligations between States alone, and, thus, the legal adviser can only wonder how the LOS Convention would help France impose state-to-state liabilities in the fact pattern of the [fictional] *Erika* disaster."[72] As the fictional advisor to France begins to review Part XII of the Convention, dealing with the Protection and Preservation of the Marine Environment, he "[q]uickly realizes that the Convention may hint at answers but not in what appears to be a conclusive manner."[73] After an examination of whether France could impose civil liability upon the flag state, the practitioner considers other options.[74]

> [T]he only other useful step that the legal adviser and the specialist can visualize is a suggestion that the Minister of Justice of France consider ways of claiming French domestic courts against the owner of the vessel, the charterer, the owner of the cargo, the classification societies, and/or the international insurance companies. Any such advice goes against the legal adviser's grain as an international lawyer, and he is concerned that any such suggestion might be regarded by some international lawyers as overreaching. But with so few options available, it is simply unacceptable to the legal adviser that France not take every possible step in seeking to impose liability and to recover the costs of clean-up and compensation for other damages.[75]

There have been real-life cases, similar to the fictional situation described above by Robinson. In the decision of *In re: Oil Spill by Amoco Cadiz off the Coast of France* on March 16, 1978, the Seventh Circuit found jurisdiction in the claim brought by French citizens against various affiliates of Standard Oil Company (based in Indiana), including the owner of the vessel, Amoco Transport Company.[76] The court based its decision on the following reasoning: The true owner of the vessel was the American parent corporation,

---

[72] David R. Robinson, *Recourse Against Flag States for Breaches of Their International Obligations Under the 1982 Law of the Sea Convention*, in CURRENT MARINE ENVIRONMENTAL ISSUES, *supra* note 60, at 374.
[73] *Id.* at 375.
[74] *See id.* at 374–79.
[75] *Id.* at 379.
[76] *See* 699 F.2d 909 (7th Cir. 1983).

because there were no significant links between the vessel and the flag state.[77] Interestingly, the court also found jurisdiction over the shipbuilder, Astilleros Espanoles, S.H., a Spanish company, and a cross-claim for indemnification filed by Amoco Transport Company against Astilleros Espanoles.[78]

Article 63 of the Statute of the Court also allows for other parties to intervene in a case involving the interpretation of a treaty as a matter of right.[79] However, this intervention is granted only to "State Parties."[80] It has been noted that the term "state parties" is in accordance with Article 2, paragraph 1(g) of the Vienna Convention on the Law of Treaties, defined to mean "States which have consented to be bound by a treaty and for which the treaty is in force."[81] The Vienna Convention, however, included a specific definition for "international organizations," while Article 1 of the LOS Convention subsumes "international parties" within its definition of states parties. There is at least an argument to be made that the intent of the Convention was not to prevent "international parties" from intervening in cases as a matter of right.

Critiques of the ability of the state-centric LOS Convention and other multilateral environmental treaties (MEAs) to "ensure an effective international environmental legal system"[82] are plentiful. In a recent article by Peggy Kalas, she notes the following problems: (1) treaty ratification is voluntary, with some nations making reservations even when they do sign and inconsistent interpretations of treaty provisions between signatory states; (2) most MEAs "disallow standing for non-State or private entities;"[83] (3) enforcement authority under most MEAs does not extend to secretariats; (4) infrequent and inconsistent use of treaty enforcement provisions; (5) little guidance on liability is provided by international accords; (6) overlapping jurisdiction among treaties creates uncertainty and dispute over which regime should be applied.[84]

The Convention has only been in force for eight years; the Tribunal for a mere six. Eight cases had already been brought before the Tribunal by 2000. As Judge Higgins noted, "from 1922 to 1960 the International

---

[77] *Id.* at 914.

[78] *Id.* at 915.

[79] *See* Rudiger Wolfrum, *Intervention in the Proceedings before ICJ and ITLOS, in* LAW AND PRACTICE, *supra* note 32, at 163-64. This intervention policy is modeled after the 1907 Convention for the Pacific Settlement of International Disputes. *See id.*

[80] *See id.*

[81] *See id.* at note 13.

[82] Peggy Rodgers Kalas, *supra* note 9, at 222 (2001).

[83] The Kyoto Protocol is touted as the first MEA that will allow NGO and private entities to play a significant role in the implementation and success of the Protocol. *See* Peggy Rodgers Kalas & Alexia Herwig, *Dispute Resolution Under the Kyoto Protocol*, 27 ECOLOGY L.W. 53 (2000).

[84] *See* Kalas, *supra* note 9, at 222-24.

Court of Justice at The Hague stood alone as the forum for the resolution of international disputes."[85] Today, however, that is no longer the case. Clarification of the Convention will continue as the Convention is called upon to enforce increasing numbers of international maritime disputes. It is likely that the "International Tribunal for the Law of the Sea will itself in the future contribute to the development of the law with respect to maritime disasters."[86] It must be remembered that the movement of international treaties away from state-centeredness is also a recent development, with an increasing focus on the role to be played by NGOs, individuals, corporations, and international organizations.[87]

IV. THE INTERNATIONAL CRIMINAL COURT

The adoption of the Rome Statute establishing the International Criminal Court ("ICC") was the culmination of a long-term quest for an international criminal court, first memorialized in the Convention on the Prevention and Punishment of the Crime of Genocide in 1948. This convention provided that the crime of genocide may be tried "by such international penal tribunal as may have jurisdiction with respect to those Contracting Parties which shall have accepted its jurisdiction."[88] The Rome Statute went beyond the international penal tribunal envisioned by the Genocide Convention to create a court with "jurisdiction over the most serious crimes of concern to the international community."[89] Specifically, the Rome Statute gives the Court jurisdiction over crimes against humanity, war crimes, the crime of genocide, and the crime of aggression.[90] In defining these crimes, however, the Court is intended to address human rights abuses. The Rome Statute is not on its face conducive to complaints predicated on environmental claims. Nevertheless, the convergence in the treatment of international environmental and human rights issues discussed in Chapter 1 is establishing a clear connection between human rights and the human environment. In the light of this growing trend, the ICC does have potential as a forum for vindicating environmental crimes.

---

[85] 50 ICLQ 121 (2001).
[86] See Robinson, *supra* note 72, at 383.
[87] See Sands, *supra* note 70, at 142. There are a number of regional seas agreements and institutions, which should also be considered in seeking private access and enforcement.
[88] Convention on the Prevention and Punishment of the Crime of Genocide, 78 U.N.T.S. 277, *reprinted in* 45 AM. J. INT'L L. 7 (1951) (Supp.).
[89] See Rome Statute of the International Criminal Court, U.N. Diplomatic Conference of Plenipotentiaries on the Establishment of an International Criminal Court, preamble, U.N. Doc. A/CONF.183/9 (1998) ("Rome Statute").
[90] See *id.*

234 • *Defending the Environment*

The Rome Statute is currently structured to address three core crimes: crimes against humanity, war crimes, and genocide.[91] Acts of genocide, crimes against humanity, and war crimes may be carried out through environmental means. States, individuals, organizations, and other non-state actors that cause or permit harm to the natural environment on a massive scale could, potentially, be held criminally responsible.

Under the Rome Statute, genocide is defined as:

> Any of the following acts committed with intent to destroy, in whole or part, a national, ethnic, racial or religious group, as such: (a) Killing members of the group; (b) Causing serious mental or bodily harm to members of the group; (c) Deliberately inflicting on the group conditions of life calculated to bring about its physical destruction in whole or in part; (d) Imposing measures intended to prevent births within the group; (e) Forcibly transferring children of the group to another group.[92]

Under the Rome Statute's definition of genocide, acts that cause severe environmental degradation and in turn kill members of a distinct national, ethnic, racial or religious group, cause serious mental or bodily harm to members of the group, or inflict conditions of life that brings about the group's physical destruction would constitute genocide. The major difficulty in applying the Statute's genocide definition to environmental degradation, as in all genocide cases, lies in proving specific intent to destroy the targeted group.

Certainly, there may exist demonstrable purpose or "intent to destroy," for example, when an actor sets out to destroy a group by "polluting water sources, poisoning crop fields, or destroying a subsistence habitat."[93] The Rome Statute's required showing of specific intent may fail to encompass actors who would kill or harm distinct groups through environmental degradation merely with knowledge of their acts' consequences. It has been suggested that such situations are further precluded by the express right to development in the Rio Declaration,[94] which establishes a basis of sustainable development predicated on "acceptable" levels of environmental

---

[91] *See generally* Rome Statute, *supra* note 89. Crimes of aggression await further definition before they will be justiciable. *Id.* art 5(2).

[92] *See* Rome Statute, *supra* note 89, at art. 6

[93] Peter Sharp, *Prospects for Environmental Liability in the International Criminal Court*, 18 VA. ENVT'L L.J. 217, 235 (1999).

[94] Adoption of Agreements on Environment and Declaration: The Rio Declaration on Environment and Development, U.N. Doc. A/CONF.151/26/Rev.1 at 3 (1992), *reprinted in* 31 I.L.M. 876 (1992) (adopted by the U.N. Conference on Environment and Development (UNECD) at Rio de Janeiro, June 16, 1992) ("Rio Declaration").

degradation.[95] If a petition attempts to hold a state, individual, or organization criminally responsible for acts of genocide based on knowledge of the consequences of environmental degradation, the defendant might raise a defense that the actions were justified by the country's greater interest in sustainable development,[96] with the resultant harm to the group being incidental rather than deliberate. Such a "development defense," however, might be counterbalanced by the rights of indigenous peoples to own, develop, and control the environment of traditionally owned, otherwise occupied, or used lands.[97]

Under the Rome Statute, crimes against humanity are defined as:

> [A]ny of the following acts when committed as part of a widespread or systematic attack directed against any civilian population, with knowledge of the attack: (a) Murder; (b) Extermination; (c) Enslavement; (d) Deportation or forcible transfer of population; (e) Imprisonment or other severe deprivation of physical liberty in violation of fundamental rules of international law; (f) Torture; (g) Rape, sexual slavery, enforced prostitution, forced pregnancy, enforced sterilization, or any other form of sexual violence of comparable gravity; (h) Persecution against any identifiable group or collectivity . . . ; (i) Enforced disappearance of persons; (j) The crime of apartheid; (k) Other inhumane acts of similar character intentionally causing great suffering, or serious injury to body or to mental or physical health.[98]

The Rome Statute defines "extermination" as "the intentional infliction of conditions of life, *inter alia,* the deprivation of access to food and medicine, calculated to bring about the destruction of part of a population."[99] "Deportation or forcible transfer of population" is defined as "forced displacement of the persons concerned by expulsion or other coercive acts from the area in which they are lawfully present, without grounds permitted under international law."[100]

To establish a crime against humanity, three distinct elements must be met. First, the act must be "widespread or systematic."[101] Second, the

---

[95] See id.
[96] See Sharp, *supra* note 93, at 234.
[97] See Draft Declaration on the Rights of Indigenous Peoples as Agreed Upon by the Members of the Working Group on Indigenous Peoples at Its Eleventh Session, U.N. Doc. E/CN.4/Sub.2/1993/29; *reprinted in* 3 WESTON III.V.3.
[98] Rome Statute, *supra* note 89, at art. 7.
[99] *Id.* at art. 7(2)(b).
[100] *Id.* at art. 7(2)(d).
[101] Rome Statute, *supra* note 89, at art. 8; *see also* M. CHERIF BASSIOUNI, CRIMES AGAINST HUMANITY IN INTERNATIONAL CRIMINAL LAW 39 (1992).

act must be an "attack directed against any civilian population" which means "a course of conduct involving the multiple commission of acts referred to in paragraph 1 against any civilian population, pursuant to or in furtherance of a state or organizational policy to commit such attack."[102] Finally, the actions must fall within the proscribed actions of paragraph 1 of Article 7 and the actor must have "knowledge of the attack."[103] Compared to the Rome Statute's definition of genocide, crimes against humanity could potentially apply to a much broader range of environmental destruction.

If the foreseeable result of state, individual, or organizational action is to cause severe environmental degradation that destroys or harms civilians, a policy to continue such conduct may be deemed a policy to carry out that action—or "attack," as defined by the Statute.[104] Arguably, when actions are taken with full knowledge of their direct foreseeable results and policy perpetuates those actions, the actions' consequences become, in essence, the result of the policy. Although states, individuals, and organizations may not have a specific purpose to harm civilian populations, an environmentally conscious interpretation of the Rome Statute's language justifies holding actors criminally responsible for the likely and foreseeable consequences of their environmentally harmful conduct.

The primary difficulty in advocating an environmentally protective interpretation to crimes against humanity and genocide lies within the more general issue of how the Rome Statute's core crimes should be interpreted and how the Elements of Crimes have not been drafted to address instances of environmental degradation that affect civilian populations in the context of these crimes. Employing an expansive interpretation of the Court's jurisdiction and Elements of Crimes, the knowing destruction of an indigenous population's food source that causes mass exodus might qualify as a "forced displacement of the persons concerned by expulsion or other coercive acts from the area in which they are lawfully present,"[105] and thus qualify as a "deportation or forcible transfer of population."[106] Operating as a catch-all provision, the prohibition of acts "intentionally causing great suffering, or serious injury to body or mental or physical health,"[107] could be construed to include nearly every imaginable form of knowingly caused environmental degradation that harms civilian populations. Helpful in this regard is the *Finalized Draft Text of the Elements of Crimes*,[108] which provides that

---

[102] *Id.*
[103] Rome Statute, *supra* note 89, at art. 7.
[104] *See id.*
[105] *Id.* at 8.
[106] *Id.*
[107] *Id.* at 7.
[108] Report of the Preparatory Commission for the International Criminal Court, *Finalized Draft Text of the Elements of Crimes* (Nov. 2, 2000), *available at* http://www.un.org/law/icc; *see also* Rome Statute, art. 30.

when the mental element is not stated, intent *or* knowledge will suffice.[109] The potential for using the crimes against humanity provision of the Rome Statute to hold responsible parties accountable for massive and widespread environmental degradation would be much more promising if the elements of the crimes did not have to be strictly construed.[110]

Article 8 of the Rome Statute states that "the Court shall have jurisdiction in respect to war crimes."[111] Accordingly, the Statute divides war crimes into two general categories. Article 8 Sections 2(a) and (b) deal with international armed conflicts, while Sections 2(c), 2(d), and 2(f) deal with "armed conflict not of an international character."[112] The Court's jurisdiction over international armed conflict is much broader than it is over internal warfare.[113]

Significantly, one fully defined war crime, Article 8(2)(b)(iv), explicitly addresses environmental damage, by defining as a war crime "intentionally launching an attack in the knowledge that such attack will cause . . . widespread, long-term and severe damage to the natural environment which would be clearly excessive in relation to the concrete and direct overall military advantage anticipated."[114] The language, which requires knowledge that damage will be clearly excessive in relation to an anticipated advantage, is a balancing test. Heightened protection would be available if the environmental provision of the war crimes definition could be extended and applied to genocide and crimes against humanity. The Rome Statute specifically provides that the definitions of crimes are to be strictly construed and that the crimes cannot be extended by analogy,[115] so Article 8(2)(b)(iv) may have little relevance to the prosecution of genocide or crimes against humanity. Two obligations specified in the conventional law of war, the Additional Protocol I[116] to the Geneva Convention and the ENMOD Convention,[117] may shed some light on the environmental damage which will be actionable.

---

[109] *Id.*, General Introduction, ¶ 2.
[110] Rome Statute, art. 22(2).
[111] Rome Statute, *supra* note 89, at art. 8.
[112] *Id.*
[113] *Compare* Rome Statute, *supra* note 89, at art. 8(2)(b) (defining war crimes for international armed conflicts) with Rome Statute, *supra* note 89, at art. 8(2)(c)(e) (defining war crimes for armed conflict not of an international character).
[114] *Id.* art. 8(2)(b)(iv). The Finalized Draft Text of the Elements of the Crimes essentially repeats this language, with the clarification that the perpetrator must know the attack would cause such damage and be clearly excessive in relation to the military advantage anticipated.
[115] *See* Rome Statute, *supra* note 89, art. 22(2).
[116] Protocol Relating to the Protection of Victims of International Armed Conflict of 1977, 125 U.N.T.S. 3, *reprinted in* D. Schindler & J. Toman eds. The Laws of Armed Conflict (3d ed. 1988).
[117] Convention on the Prohibition of Military or Any Other Hostile Use of Environmental Modification Techniques, opened for signature May 18, 1977, *reprinted in* D. Schindler & J. Toman eds. *supra* note 116 ("ENMOD Convention").

238 • Defending the Environment

Articles 35(3) and 55(1) of Additional Protocol I prohibit actions "which are intended, or may be expected to cause widespread, long-term and severe damage to the natural environment."[118] Article 55(1) focuses on the protection of the individual,[119] while Article 33(3), like the Rome Statue, focuses its protections on the environment itself.[120] Just as the Rome Statute's "clearly excessive"[121] war-crimes provision language weakens the provision's deterrent effect, Articles 35(3) and 55(1) are weakened by the fact that they do not apply to damage caused by "conventional warfare."[122] Conventional warfare is not defined, but it does not include nuclear warfare or "means specifically designed to damage the environment."[123] Thus, while Articles 35(3) and 55(1) overcome the Rome Statute's "clearly excessive" language and allow for the assignment of responsibility to wartime acts intentionally directed toward the environment regardless of their military justification, the articles do not address the more common, and sometimes more serious, incidental environmental effects of conventional warfare.[124] Unfortunately, the Rome Statue does not solve the problem of incidental wartime environmental degradation either, as Article 8(2)(b)(iv) includes a "knowledge" requirement that essentially exculpates actors from responsibility for environmentally degrading conduct if the conduct's environmentally degrading effects were neither known nor foreseeable.[125]

Comparatively, Article I of the ENMOD Convention provides that "[e]ach State Party to this Convention undertakes not to engage in military or any other hostile use of environmental modification techniques having widespread, long-lasting or severe effects as the means of destruction, damage or injury to any other State Party."[126] While the Rome Statute prohibits

---

[118] Article 35(3) states: "[I]t is prohibited to employ methods or means of warfare which are intended, or may be expected, to cause widespread, long-term and severe damage to the natural environment." *Id.* at 645. Article 55(1) provides:
Care shall be taken in warfare to protect the natural environment against widespread, long-term and severe damage. This protection includes prohibition of the use or methods or means of warfare that are intended or may be expected to cause such damage to the natural environment and thereby to prejudice the health or survival of the population.
[119] *See id.* at 653.
[120] *See* ENMOD Convention, *supra* note 117.
[121] *See id.*
[122] *See* Luan Low & David Hodgkinson, *Compensation for Wartime Environmental Damage: Challenges to International Law After the Gulf War*, 35 VA. J. INT'L L. 405, 426 (1995) (citations omitted).
[123] *Id.* at 428.
[124] *See* Protocol Relating to the Protection of Victims of International Armed Conflict of 1977, 125 U.N.T.S. 3, *reprinted in* D. SCHINDLER & J. TOMAN EDS. *supra* note 116.
[125] *See* Rome Statute, *supra* note 89, at art. 8(2)(b)(iv).
[126] *See* ENMOD Convention, *supra* note 117.

wartime acts that will have known environmental degrading consequences, the Convention only prohibits "environmental modification techniques," which change the environment through the deliberate manipulation of natural processes.[127] The interpretation of "environmental modification technique," as taken by the Second Review Conference of the parties to the Convention, was that an "environmental modification technique" includes any technique that has as its direct object modification of the environment.[128] Thus, like the Rome Statute, the Convention falls short of addressing incidental, rather than purely purposeful or intentional wartime environmental degradation. In fact, the Convention is an ineffective tool to address the shortfalls of the Rome Statute's Article 8(2)(b)(iv) because it actually contains a higher standard of intent than the article, as the Convention only applies to wartime action that is purposefully directed toward the environment rather than intentional wartime acts under the Rome Statute that have foreseeable deleterious environmental effects.[129]

Procedurally, as with the ICJ, non-state actors may not bring claims directly before the Court, as only state parties or the prosecutor may do so. There is nothing, however, which precludes non-state actors from advancing a proposed claim to any state, or more likely, before the prosecutor. Indeed, Article 15 of the Rome Statute expressly authorizes the prosecutor to seek information from "intergovernmental or nongovernmental organizations, or other reliable sources that he or she deems appropriate, and [the prosecutor] may receive written or oral testimony at the seat of the Court."

Article 44(4) also provides for the ICC to

> employ the expertise of gratis personnel offered by States parties, intergovernmental organizations or NGOs to assist with the work of any of the organs of the Court. The Prosecutor may accept any such offer on behalf of the Office of the Prosecutor. Such gratis personnel shall be employed in accordance with guidelines to be established by the Assembly of States Parties.[130]

The guidelines have not yet been established. Whereas Rules 93 and 95 authorize NGOs to participate at meetings of the Assembly of States Parties, these three rules combined provide a promising opportunity for NGOs to expand their involvement in the ICC.

---

[127] Article II states "the term 'environmental modification techniques' refers to any technique for changing—through the deliberate manipulation of natural processes—the dynamics, composition or structure of the Earth, including its biota, lithosphere, hydrosphere and atmosphere, or of outer space." ENMOD Convention, *supra* note 117 art. II.
[128] *See* Low & Hodgkinson, *supra* note 122, at 432.
[129] *See* Rome Statute, *supra* note 89, at art. 8(2)(b)(iv).
[130] Rome Statute, *supra* note 89, at art. 44(4).

240 • *Defending the Environment*

The Rules of Procedure do allow for *amicus curiae* submissions by NGOs. Rule 103(1) allows for a Chamber of the Court at any stage of the proceedings to request that a State, organization, or person submit orally or in writing any observation on any issue that the Chamber deems appropriate. In contrast to the ICJ, it is clear that NGOs may play a fundamental role in both commencement of prosecutions under Article 15, the information-gathering functions of the ICC under Article 54(3), drafting of complementary legislation, and in support of the Victims and Witnesses Unit.

The main purpose of the NGO Coalition for an ICC (CICC) is to support the ICC through a variety of civil society organizations. Its activities have been recognized in a resolution at the Assembly of States Parties.[131] The resolution specifically notes Rules 93 and 95 for the future participation of NGOs in the meetings of the ASP and its subsidiary bodies.

5.1 Union Carbide in Bhopal

Increasingly, deliberate or criminally negligent environmental violations have been the basis for domestic criminal prosecutions. Perhaps the most notorious such case is the continuing litigation over the 1984 Bhopal disaster. In 2005, the Chief Judicial Magistrate of Bhopal District Court of India ordered U.S.-based Dow Chemical Corporation to show cause why its subsidiary, Union Carbide, should not appear to face criminal charges relating to the 1984 explosion at a pesticide plant.[132] As a result of the explosion, which released methyl isocyanate and other deadly gases,[133] approximately 22,000 people have died and another 120,000 are suffering serious long-term health effects.[134] Thousands of tons of toxic waste continue to contaminate the groundwater.[135]

---

[131] Resolution ICC-ASP/27Res. 8 (4th mtg. of the ASP).

[132] *See* Earthrights International, Press Release: Indian Judge Orders Dow to Explain Shielding of Subsidiary in Bhopal Criminal Case (Jan. 11, 2005), *available at* http://www.eathrights.org/news/bhopalorder1/06.05shtml (last visited Feb. 28, 2005); *see also* Unofficial Transcript of Chief Judicial Magistrate, Bhopal's Order of January 6, 2005, *available at* http://www.eathrights.org/bhopal/bhopalorder1.6.05.shmtl (last visited Feb. 28, 2005).

[133] *Id.*

[134] *See* The Short Story, at http://www.studentsforbhopal.org/what_happened.htm (last visited on Feb. 28, 2005).

[135] *Id.*

V. REGIONAL TRIBUNALS OF GENERAL JURISDICTION

A. European Union Court of Justice

The Court of Justice interprets and applies the voluminous law of the European Union ("EU"). Since its creation in 1952, the Court has handled thousands of cases addressing the ever broadening scope of law created by the EU's institutions. In 1989 a Court of First Instance was established to handle primarily cases brought by private individuals.[136]

The Council of the European Union is the legislative body of the European Union. Increasingly, its directives—binding on all members of the EU and enforceable against conflicting domestic legislation—have encompassed environmental regulation ranging from hazardous waste disposal to consumer information.

Pursuant to Article 225 of the EC Treaty, any natural or legal person can bring a proceeding before the Court of First Instance as outlined in Articles 230, 232, 235, 236 and 238 of the Treaty.[137] Of these provisions, the most generally applicable to environmental claims are Articles 230 and 232. Article 230 authorizes "any natural or legal person" to challenge EU decisions "addressed to that person" or regulations or decisions addressed to another which are of "direct and individual concern" to the complainant.[138] The complaining party may request annulment of the legal acts successfully challenged.[139] The Court of First Instance has yet to find that a general directive to member states might be subject to private party challenge, but it has also not yet ruled out that possibility.

In *Stitching Greenpeace Council v. Commission*,[140] the European Court of Justice provided some guidance on associational standing, although finding that Greenpeace did not have standing to challenge the European Commission's financing of two fossil-fueled power stations on the Canary Islands. Greenpeace asserted that the common value of environmental quality justified private party standing. The Court reaffirmed traditional case law that an association has standing: (1) when Community law expressly grants procedural rights; (2) when the association actually represents persons who have individualized standing; or (3) when the association's own interests as an association are directly affected. It is important to note as well that EC law may be enforced in the national courts of member states, as Greenpeace did in Spain in the *Stitching* case. Similarly, under Article 232 such persons may lodge a complaint against the European Parliament,

---

[136] *Available at* http://europa.eu.int/institutions/court/index_en.htm.
[137] Treaty that Established the European Union, *available at* http://europa.eu.int/eur-lex/en/treaties/dat/EC_Consol.pdf.
[138] *Id.* art. 230.
[139] *See generally* A. Arnull, *Private Applicants and the Action for Annulment under Article 173 of the EC Treaty*, 32 COMM. MKT. L. REV. 7 (1995).
[140] Case C-321/95P [1998] ECR I-1651.

242 · Defending the Environment

the Council, or the European Commission for failure to act when obligated to do so but only upon a showing that the duty was owed to the individual party.[141] Appeal of legal issues only is available to the Court of Justice.

The rules of procedure for the Court of First Instance and the Court of Justice[142] provide little explicit guidance as to whether and how non-state parties aside from EU institutions themselves may otherwise participate in court proceedings. The rules of both courts do outline the requirements for witnesses and experts.[143] The rules of the Court of First Instance allow for intervention under Article 115[144] pursuant to Article 37 of the EC Statute, which allows for intervention "by any person establishing an interest in the result of the case ... save in cases between Member States, between institutions of the Community or between member States and institutions of the Community."[145] In devising the "measures of inquiry" for a proceeding, there is nothing in the rules to preclude the Court from authorizing the filing of amicus briefs by non-state, non-EU parties.

It also deserves mention that individuals or entities (institutions or businesses) resident in the EU can apply to the European Ombudsman to protest "maladministration" of EU law by EU institutions.[146]

Although commencement of direct proceedings under Article 230, intervention, and presumably filing of amicus briefs are all options available to nongovernmental organizations, the demanding approach the ECJ and CFI have taken on standing has made it difficult for environmental NGOs to succeed. The EC is, however, a signatory to the Aarhus Convention on Access to Information, Public Participation in Decision-making and Access to Justice in Environmental Matters. Prior to ratification, the EU must bring its laws into conformity with the Convention, and specifically Article 9(2), which requires that standing requirements be formulated in keeping with the objective of wide access to justice. This provision promises to be the basis of renewed efforts by civil society to revise the EC treaty to ensure that environmental NGOs have standing before its courts.

Finally, on a separate note, as of July 1, 2004, EU member states must comply with the Strategic Environmental Assessment (SEA), which requires that the environmental impacts of many public plans and programs be evaluated in open planning procedures. There is an opportunity for public comment on the resulting environmental report as well as on the draft plan or program, and both the report and public comments must be taken into

---

[141] *Lord Bethel v. Commission,* Case 246/81, [1982] ECR 2277.
[142] *Available at* http://curia.eu.int/en/instit/txtdocfr/txtsenvigueur/txt5.pdf.
[143] *Id.; see also* Articles 25 and 26 of the Protocol on the Statute of the Court of Justice, http://europa.eu.int/abc/obj/treaties/ent/entr8b.htm.
[144] *Available at* http://curia.eu.int/en/instit/txtdocfr/txtsenvigueur/txt7.pdf.
[145] *Available at* http://europa.eu.int/abc/obj/treaties/en/entr8b.htm.
[146] *Id., available at* http://curia.eu.int/en/instit/txtdocfr/txtsenvigueur/txt5.pdf.

account in the final decision-making.[147] Additionally, the European Commission in 2004 pursued infringement actions against several countries, including Greece, Luxembourg, Spain, Austria, and Germany for noncompliance with EU environmental law.[148]

B. African Union Court of Justice

On May 26, 2001, the Constitutive Act of the African Union went into force, substantially reorganizing the Organization for African Unity. The Act in Article 18 called for the creation of the Court of Justice for the African Union, in a protocol to be subsequently drafted.[149] Although it is far too early to know what role the Court might play in international environmental disputes, two aspects of the Court suggest how it might be utilized in the future. The African Union was modeled on the European Union (although modified to reflect the African experience), and the European Union has played a major role in the development of regional and international environmental law. Secondly, the reconstitution of the OAU into the African Union was in large part designed to move the organization from a state-centric approach to an organizational framework more receptive to civil participation by NGOs, civil societies, labor unions and business organizations. If the formation of the Court reflects these considerations, it may come to play a pivotal role in the development of international environmental law, particularly with respect to issues most critical to developing countries.

VI. INTERNATIONAL ARBITRAL BODIES

Apart from the more specific arbitral and quasi-arbitral processes discussed in other chapters, two arbitral bodies of more general jurisdiction may provide additional fora in which to present an environmental harm.

A. Permanent Court of Arbitration

Established at The Hague by inter-governmental agreement in 1899 and later given permanent observer status at the United Nations, the Permanent Court of Arbitration ("PCA") administers dispute settlement through conciliation, mediation, good offices, commissions of inquiry, and

---

[147] See European Commission, *New Directive to Improve Public Participation in Environmental Impact Assessments* (July 20, 2004), *available at* http://europa.eu.int/rapid/pressReleasesAction.do?reference=IP/04/975&format=HTML&aged=1&language=EN&guiLanguage=en.
[148] *Id.*
[149] *See* http://www.au2002.gov.za/about/index.html.
[150] *See* http://www.undp.org/missions/netherlands/c-arbitration.htm.

arbitration.[150] General PCA dispute settlement is based on the United Nations Commission on International Trade Law ("UNCITRAL") Arbitration Rules or Conciliation Rules;[151] however, on June 19, 2001, the PCA Administrative Council adopted by consensus a special set of optional arbitral rules similar to the UNCITRAL rules that are specific to environmental disputes and especially designed for such environmental disputes between a state and non-state actor.[152]

The PCA has voluntary jurisdiction over disputes not only between two states or between international organizations and states but also a non-state actor and a state.[153] However, the PCA does not have compulsory jurisdiction over a dispute between two non-state actors—*i.e.*, victims and the alleged corporate actor—leaving those matters to domestic courts instead. In addition, disputes before the PCA have little transparency.

The PCA has permanent observer status with the United Nations. It has used that status to participate in international conferences devoted to environmental dispute resolution and to offer its counsel on contract and treaty language concerning such matters.[154]

5.2 Sella Field

On June 10, 2003, Ireland sought closure of Britain's Sellafield plutonium reprocessing plant before the PCA. Ireland alleged that Great Britain, in the processing of spent plutonium and uranium into usable mixed oxide fuel, had polluted the Irish Sea in violation of the UN Convention on the Law of the Sea and failed to conduct an adequate environmental assessment of the plant.[155] Ireland, in its amended claim, asserted that radioactive waste discharged from the Sellafield site posed a serious risk of harm to the Irish Sea marine environment.[156] Ireland similarly maintained that there were risks from transporting the radioactive waste through the Irish Sea to and from the Sellafield site, as well as risks from storing the waste at the site.[157]

On June 24, 2003, the PCA suspended proceedings on jurisdiction and the merits[158] after the United Kingdom raised questions of jurisdiction and

(continued)

---

[151] UNCITRAL Arbitration Rules, G.A. Res. 31/98, U.N. Commission on International Trade Law, 31st Sess., Supp. No. 17 at ch. V, sect. C, U.N. Doc. A/31/17 (1976). *See* http://www.uncitral.org.

[152] *See* Optional Rules for Arbitration of Disputes Relating to Natural Resources and/or the Environment, http://www.pca-cpa.org/ENGLISH/EDR/ENRrules.htm.

[153] *See* http://pca-cpa.org/ENGLISH/BD/1stateeng.htm.

[154] *See* http://pca-cpa.org/ENGLISH/EDR.

[155] 34 Envt. Rptr. 1399 (June 20, 2003).

[156] *Ireland v. The United Kingdom*, Permanent Court of Arbitration, Order 3, ¶ 11 (Perm. Ct. Arb. 2003), *available at* http://www.pca-cpa.org/PDF/MOX%20Order%20no3.pdf.

[157] *Id.*

[158] Order 3, ¶ 3 (Perm. Ct. Arb. 2003), *available at* http://www.pca-cpa.org/PDF/MOX%20Order%20no3.pdf.

5.2 Sella Field *(continued)*

admissibility with respect to the Convention and other international agreements cited by Ireland.[159] Additionally, the United Kingdom objected to the parties' position under European Community law, including, *inter alia*, that some matters before the PCA were actually subject to the European Court of Justice's exclusive jurisdiction.[160] After the PCA suspended proceedings, Ireland requested provisional measures pursuant to article 290 of the Convention "to preserve Ireland's rights under UNCLOS and to prevent harm to the marine environment."[161] The provisional measures Ireland sought called on the United Kingdom to ensure there were no discharges[162] from the Sellafield site into the Irish Sea, inform Ireland of any future proposals for additional processing at the Sellafield site,[163] inform the Irish Government of any vessel carrying radioactive waste to or from the Sellafield site, and inform the Irish Government monthly of any specific radionuclide discharges in liquid and aerial waste form arising from the Sellafield site.[164] The PCA refused to prescribe the provisional measures, finding Ireland failed to establish that any harm that might be caused by discharges from the Sellafield site would meet the threshold requirement of being "serious."[165]

On November 14, 2003, the PCA ordered that proceedings would remain suspended until the European Court of Justice has given judgment on a related case concerning European Community law issues, or until the PCA otherwise determines.[166]

B. International Court of Environmental Arbitration and Conciliation

In addition to the PCA, a private arbitral body was created in November 1994 called the International Court of Environmental Arbitration and Conciliation ("ICEAC").[167] It has permanent seats in Mexico and Spain, con-

---

[159] Order 3, ¶ 16 (Perm. Ct. Arb. 2003), *available at* http://www.pca-cpa.org/PDF/MOX%20Order%20no3.pdf.

[160] Order 3, ¶ 20 (Perm. Ct. Arb. 2003), *available at* http://www.pca-cpa.org/PDF/MOX%20Order%20no3.pdf.

[161] Order 3, ¶¶ 31-34 (*citing* Convention on the Law of the Sea, Dec. 10, 1982, art. 290, 21 I.L.M. 1261).

[162] Order 3, ¶ A (Perm. Ct. Arb. 2003), *available at* http://www.pca-cpa.org/PDF/MOX%20Order%20no3.pdf.

[163] Order 3, ¶ B (Perm. Ct. Arb. 2003), *available at* http://www.pca-cpa.org/PDF/MOX%20Order%20no3.pdf.

[164] Order 3, ¶ B (Perm. Ct. Arb. 2003), *available at* http://www.pca-cpa.org/PDF/MOX%20Order%20no3.pdf.

[165] Order 3, ¶ 10 (Perm. Ct. Arb. 2003), *available at* http://www.pca-cpa.org/PDF/MOX%20Order%20no3.pdf.

[166] Order 4, ¶ 6 (Perm. Ct. Arb. 2003), *available at* http://www.pca-cpa.org/PDF/MOX%20Order%20no3.pdf.

[167] *See* http://iceac.sarenet.es.

sists of 28 volunteer judges and lawyers, and aims to settle, through voluntary conciliation, disputes submitted by states and non-states, including NGOs.[168] Moreover, it gives consultative opinions "on legal questions of international concern relating to the environment at the request of any natural or legal person, whether public or private, national or international."[169]

5.3 Mendivil

The first request for an ICEAC advisory opinion was submitted by petitioner Domingo Gutierrez Mendivil on August 17, 1998.[170] Mendivil sought the court's opinion as to whether waste and dangerous substances deposited by Alco Pacifico de Mexico, S.A. de C.V. in the El Florido Ranch in Tijuana between 1987 and 1991, and transferred to the CYTRAR waste deposit in the Mexican town of Hermosillo, Sonora must be returned to the United States.[171] The waste was transferred from the United States to El Florido by U.S.-based company Alco Pacific, Inc.,[172] where it was dumped at the CYTAR deposit in Hermosillo, an area bordering the United States.[173] The court found that CYTRAR's location, six kilometers from the nearest township, breached several Mexican environmental regulations, which establish standards for geohydrological and surface hydrology conditions.[174]

Despite concluding that there was a dearth of international regulation to govern the matter, and that the Basel Convention[175] could not be applied retroactively, the court found that the United States and Mexico could be obliged to return the waste to the United States, as the country of origin, as part of a specialized yet general obligation to repair the damage caused to the natural and human environment in Hermosillo.[176] The court found that this general obligation could be based upon the doctrine of objective liability for causing environmental damage even in the absence of a breach by Mexico or the United States of an international responsibility or a violation of international law.[177] Under this kind of objective liability, which is a kind of strict liability, possible causes of exoneration are precluded from being considered.[178]

---

[168] See http://iceac.sarenet.es/Ingles/Stat.html.
[169] See http://iceac.sarenet.es/Ingles/Stat.html#Cap4, at art. 12.
[170] Consultative Opinion in the Senora Case, International Court of Environmental Arbitration and Conciliation, 3 (Apr. 7, 1999), *available at* http://iceac.sarenet.es/Ingles/cases/caso_sonora.html.
[171] *Id.* at 1.
[172] *Id.* at 2.
[173] *Id.* at 4.
[174] *Id.* at 3.
[175] Mar. 22, 1989, 28 I.L.M. 649.
[176] ICEAC, *supra* note 150.1, at 5.
[177] *Id.*
[178] *Id.* at 6.

5.3 Mendivil *(continued)*

The court also found that Mexico and the United States had breached the cooperation provision relating to environmental matters set forth in Principle 24 of the 1972 Stockholm Statement.[179] Specifically, the court found that both states failed in their respective duties to exchange information relevant to protecting the environment, take actions to further research, obtain technical and financial aid, and establish environmental appraisal programs with respect to the border zone between the states.[180] Additionally, the court said both states violated their responsibility to ensure that activities carried out within their jurisdiction or under their control do not damage the environment of the other states or areas located outside the limits of their national jurisdiction.[181]

In an additional finding, the court recognized that Alco Pacific, Inc. could face liability for environmental damage in the border zone caused by CYRTRAR under the Comprehensive Environmental Response, Compensation and Liability Act of 1980 (CERCLA).[182] CERCLA establishes that a party that generates dangerous substances can be held liable for potential damage affecting the United States as well as its consumers.[183] The court found that the United States could be required to repair the contaminated area and subsequently exercise its right of recovery against Alco Pacific, Inc. under the provisions of the Hazardous Substances Response Fund, otherwise known as the American Superfund.[184]

Concluding its opinion, the court found that the Hermosillo authorities may request the Mexican government to remove the CYRTRAR deposit and properly treat the waste that was dumped there.[185] In addition to holding that the United States would have to fund the cleanup through its Superfund, the court said Mexico and the United States may appoint the ICEAC as a mediator during the cleanup. Furthermore, the court said the Hermosillo authorities could bring forth formal claims before the U.S. courts if their requests were not heeded.[186] Thus, while the ICEAC advisory opinion was not a binding statement, it presented actionable information about states' potential liability for environmental damage.

---

[179] *Declaration of the United Nations Conference on the Human Environment*, U.N. Conference on the Human Environment, 21st mtg., Chapter 11 (1972), *available at* http://www.unep.org/Documents.multilingual/Default.asp?DocumentID=97&ArticleID=1503&l=en.

[180] ICEAC, *supra* note 167, at 7.

[181] U.N. Conference on the Human Environment, *supra* note 179 at Principle 21, *available at* http://www.unep.org/Documents.multilingual/Default.asp?DocumentID=97&ArticleID=1503&l=en.

[182] 42 U.S.C. §§ 103, 9607(a) (1980).

[183] *Id.*

[184] *Id.*

[185] ICEAC, *supra* note 167, at 13.

[186] *Id.*

VII. CONCLUSION

Although international courts and tribunals of general jurisdiction have broader subject matter jurisdiction to consider environmental problems whether or not they are linked to a human rights violation or to a finance or trade issue, these courts and tribunals unfortunately have a narrower jurisdiction over parties than the human rights, finance, and investment fora discussed in earlier chapters in this book. Consequently, this limitation hinders the ability of non-state actors to make submissions and appear at the outset before these fora. This dilemma has fostered the promotion in academic and even some government circles of the creation of an international environmental court of general jurisdiction open to state and non-state actors alike. Given the lack of financial and human resources available for existing international courts and tribunals, the creation of a new supranational forum focused on one area of world problems (albeit a fundamental and highly important area) seems unrealistic at this time. The momentum for its creation perhaps will forge a compromise between diplomats and international lawyers to expand the scope of jurisdiction for the existing international courts of general jurisdiction discussed in this chapter. One vitally important element that could tip the scales in favor of such change is the continued pursuit by non-state actors of access to the fora discussed in this chapter to resolve environmental problems. As limited as the access is, the more NGOs and others knock on these courts' doors, the greater the likelihood that eventually they will answer.[187]

---

[187] As noted in the introduction, this book does not separately address UN Specialized Agencies and UN Related Agencies. Some of the Strategies in this chapter may be appropriate for use with these agencies. For more information on these entities, please consult http://www.un.org/aboutun/chart.html.

CHAPTER 6

ENFORCING ENVIRONMENTAL LAW THROUGH DOMESTIC LAW MECHANISMS

I. INTRODUCTION

There are advantages and disadvantages to pursuing a domestic strategy instead of an international one. The advantage is that domestic fora, at least in the United States, can provide binding and enforceable relief, whether injunctive, declaratory, or compensatory, unlike most international fora. The disadvantage is that many domestic fora may lack jurisdiction over a matter occuring abroad or a matter that violates international rather than domestic laws or norms. When these barriers preclude domestic judicial remedies, other non-litigation domestic strategies may be available.

6.1 India Supreme Court's Monitoring Committee on Hazardous Waste

India's Supreme Court has established a Monitoring Committee on Hazardous Wastes.[1] While noncompliance will generally result in a factory's closing,[2] in one instance a factory that was polluting the groundwater had to supply untainted water to villages.[3] The Committee has begun to enforce rights under the Basel Convention on the Control of Transboundary Movements of Hazardous Wastes and their Disposal by returning wrongly imported hazardous waste, and working with pollution control boards.[4] Many factories were closed until proper waste disposal procedures were implemented, and until the boards allowed them to reopen.[5] Companies were charged fines if they did not follow the required procedures when handling waste. In just three Indian states, 100 million rupees (U.S. $2.2 billion) has already been spent in treating hazardous waste.[6] Local Area Environment Committees made up of Pollution Control Board officials, industry representatives, and NGOs monitor and ensure implementation.[7]

---

[1] See ENS-Newswire, *India's Supreme Court Panel Cracks Down on Hazardous Waste* (Nov. 19, 2004), *available at* http://www.ens-newswire.com/ens/nov2004/2004-11-19-01.asp (last visited Feb. 21, 2005).
[2] *Id.*
[3] *Id.*
[4] *Id.*
[5] *Id.*
[6] *Id.*
[7] *Id.*

This chapter begins with these domestic non-litigation strategies. Where such strategies are not sufficient, the chapter then turns to litigation strategies focusing first on the Alien Tort Claims Act and its coverage of non-state defendants. Alternatively, the provisions of U.S. domestic environmental laws can in some cases be applied extraterritorially to provide equal or even greater protection than international law for environmental resources. Another method for domestic prevention of the weakening of environmental regulation is to file court actions to compel disclosure of requested information or to challenge the disclosed governmental action. General obstacles to domestic litigation are outlined, and domestic non-litigation strategies are once again reviewed as an alternative when the obstacles are insurmountable.

For the most part, the strategies presented in this chapter are limited to only those domestic strategies that relate to international strategies presented earlier in this book. The litigation strategies concerning the Alien Tort Claims Act and the Federal Tort Claims Act and the non-litigation strategy for holding corporations accountable relate to the strategies to enforce environmental human rights, as presented in Chapter 1. The non-litigation strategy concerning Executive Order 12114 and the litigation strategy concerning extraterritorial application of the National Environmental Policy Act both relate to strategies to enforce the environmental review standards of international finance and trade fora, as presented in Chapter 2. The non-litigation and litigation strategies concerning advisory committee participation and concerning transparency relate to the intersection of international trade and investment rules and environmental protection, as presented in Chapter 3. The litigation strategy concerning extraterritorial application of environment laws besides NEPA relate to the strategies for enforcing the environmental protection standards set forth in the multilateral environmental agreements as presented in Chapter 4. Finally, all of the strategies in this chapter relate more generally to the claims one can raise in the fora discussed in Chapter 5.

II. NON-LITIGATION STRATEGIES

A. Corporate Citizenship

Citizen Works, in cooperation with Public Citizen, supports the efforts of Bob Hinkley, a former securities lawyer and Skadden corporate partner, to amend corporate law with a short phrase called the Code of Corporate Citizenship.[8] The Code would restrict the pursuit of profit to situations in which it would not come "at the expense of the environment, human rights,

---

[8] For an interview with Hinkley, see http://www.citizenworks.org/issues/latest_news/hinkley.php.

the public safety, the welfare of the communities in which the corporation operates or the dignity of its employees."[9] This amendment to state corporate statutes would subject companies and directors who violate the provision to suits by individual members of the public or NGOs for damages (*i.e.*, if a corporation damaged the environment, affected individuals or environmental NGOs could sue).

Some states (Maine, Massachusetts, New Hampshire, Vermont, Minnesota, California) have already started to form groups to advocate for the Code in the legislature and make the Code a campaign issue for hopeful candidates. Individuals can become involved by communicating with state officials and legislators to have corporate law in their state include the Code. Individuals can also contact Citizen Works at 202-265-6164 or info@citizenworks.org for more information on involvement in this campaign.

B. Participating on Advisory Committees

In the United States, several trade acts since 1974 have established advisory committees that help the president, the United States Trade Representative, and relevant cabinet secretaries (*e.g.*, Agriculture, Defense, Environment, Labor) shape international trade and investment policy and rules. The committees fall into three tiers: the President's Advisory Committee for Trade Policy and Negotiations ("ACTPN"); 6 policy advisory committees; and 26 technical, sectional, and functional advisory committees. Details about the composition, scope, and membership procedures of these committees can be found at http://www.ustr.gov/outreach/advise.shtml.

The following committees either currently include an environmentalist or a court has allowed such participation.

- Advisory Committee for Trade Policy and Negotiations ("ACTPN"). *See* http://www.ustr.gov/outreach/actpnroster.htm (currently includes Frederick Krupp, Environmental Defense).
- Trade and Environment Policy Advisory Committee ("TEPAC"), one of the six policy advisory committees chaired by the U.S. Trade Representative ("USTR") and the Environmental Protection Agency. *See* http://www.ustr.gov/outreach/tepacroster.htm. (Currently includes:
  Brent Blackwelder, Friends of the Earth
  Daniel Esty, Yale Forestry School and Environmental Studies
  Patricia Forkan, The Humane Society of the United States
  Jonathan Lash, World Resources Institute

---

[9] *Id.*

252 • *Defending the Environment*

John Mizroch, World Environmental Center
Frederick O'Regan, International Fund for Animal Welfare
Durwood Zaelke, Center for International Environmental Law
Lyuba Zarsky, The Nautilus Institute for Security and Sustainable Development.)

- Industry Sector Advisory Committee for Lumber & Wood, one of the 26 technical, sectional, and functional advisory committees. See http://www.ita.doc.gov/td/icp/Finalist10.html (environmental representative permitted per court order in *Northwest Ecosystems Alliance v. USTR*, Civ. No. C99-1165R (W.D. Wa. 1999) but not yet appointed).
- Industry Sector Advisory Committee for Paper and Paper Products, one of the 26 technical, sectional, and functional advisory committees. See http://www.ita.doc.gov/td/icp/Finalist12.html. (Currently includes Doug Norlen, Policy Director, Pacific Environment Resources Center per court order in *Northwest Ecosystems Alliance v. USTR*, Civ. No. C99-1165R (W.D. Wa. 1999).)
- Industry Sector Advisory Committee for Chemical and Allied Products, one of the 26 technical, sectional, and functional advisory committees. See http://www.ita.doc.gov/td/icp/Finalist3.html. (Environmental representative permitted per court order in *Washington Toxics Coalition, et al. v. Office of the United States Trade Representative*, Civ. No. C00-0730R (W.D. Wa. 2001) but not yet appointed.)

C. Demanding Transparency from Domestic Governments on Matters Adversely Affecting the Environment Abroad

Another means for combating the weakening of regulations to protect the environment and public health and safety is to obtain information about domestic matters affecting the environment abroad. Such information can be obtained by submitting written requests to government agents or by participating on government advisory committees, and then filing court actions when the government fails to cooperate. The information can then be used to submit public comments to the appropriate administrative agencies about the government's current or future program or activities set forth in the information obtained, or to launch a legislative campaign to change the outcome.

It strengthens the strategy to coordinate efforts with NGOs in other countries also affected by or concerned about the particular matter in question in order to request information and design a response. For the Latin American region, contact the Inter-American Association for Environmental Defense (AIDA) in Oakland, California at acederstav@aida-americas.org. For other countries, contact the Environmental Law Alliance Worldwide (E-LAW) in Eugene, Oregon at elawus@elaw.org.

To obtain information from an agency of the U.S. government, submit a written request to that agency in accordance with the rules that agency has promulgated pursuant to the Freedom of Information Act ("FOIA").[10] General information about making requests is available from the American Civil Liberties Union ("ACLU") at http://www.aclu.org/library/foia.html. Moreover, once it has been determined to which agency to make the request, the Internet site for that agency should have a section devoted to FOIA requests that specifies how to draft the request and to whom to send it. To make sure that the agency responds to the request as quickly as possible and to best preserve the ability to file a court action should the agency either fail to respond or deny your request, it is wise to consult a public interest legal organization such as the ACLU to help draft the request. Because attorneys who file court actions under FOIA and prevail are entitled to receive court-awarded fees, there may also be attorneys outside public interest legal organizations willing to assist.

This strategy is particularly useful when multilateral trade and investment affects the environment. For example, when 34 governments in the Americas decided to negotiate a Free Trade Agreement of the Americas that promises to include investment dispute processes potentially detrimental to environmental, health, and safety regulations, the Center for International Environmental Law ("CIEL"), a NGO based in Washington, D.C., became concerned that the general public was not allowed to participate in the process in part because it did not know the status of the negotiations. CIEL submitted a FOIA request to the Office of the U.S. Trade Representative, the appropriate agency in this case, asking for the United States' negotiating positions and related records.

D. Calling for U.S. Federal Agency Compliance with Executive Order 12114

Another non-litigation strategy is to lobby U.S. administrative agencies that take actions abroad impacting the environment to comply with Executive Order 12114.[11] This Executive Order requires federal agencies to undertake environmental review for any actions, findings, or conclusion that may have an impact abroad. Although a judicial challenge cannot be brought against the federal agency for failing to comply with the Executive Order, because the text of the order bars such actions, the federal agency can be pressured to comply with the requirement given the possibility of media attention if the agency does not.

---

10   5 U.S.C. § 552, as amended (FOIA), http://www.frwebgate1.access.gpo.gov/cgi-bin/waisgate.cgi?WAISdocID=38026532081+22+0+0&WAISaction=retrieve.

11   44 Fed. Reg. 1957 (Jan. 4, 1978), *at* http://ceq.eh.doe.gov/nepa/regs/eos/eo12114.pdf.

E. Lobbying Congress to Impose Environmental Standards on Appropriations

Another domestic strategy that civil society can pursue is lobbying for the inclusion of environmental review requirements for particular foreign operation appropriations. Both the U.S. Senate and the U.S. House of Representatives have Foreign Operations Subcommittees to their Committee on Appropriations. These subcommittees handle appropriations for nearly all non-military U.S. government activity abroad. Given the ubiquitous nature of U.S. activity abroad undertaken each year, the environmental impact of the United States on the globe is tremendous. Therefore, if Congress were to condition such appropriations on environmental review, then the amount of environmental harms attributable to direct U.S. foreign government activity would be significantly reduced. In turn, the United States could emerge as a world environmental leader, achieving such results through an effective alternative to treaty regimes.

A recent example of such a lobbying effort is one undertaken by several different Latin American advocacy groups in Washington, D.C.—led by the Amazon Alliance and counseled by Earthjustice—to condition the appropriation of money for herbicide spraying in Colombia on environmental and public health review. Their hard work resulted in the addition of the following language in the 2002 budget:

> Provided further, That funds appropriated by this Act that are used for the procurement of chemicals for aerial coca fumigation programs may be made available for such programs only if the Secretary of State, after consultation with the Administration of the Environmental Protection Agency, the Secretary of the Department of Agriculture, and, if appropriate, the Director of the Centers for Disease Control and Prevention, determines and reports to the Committees on Appropriations that: (1) aerial coca fumigation is being carried out in accordance with regulatory controls required by the Environmental Protection Agency as labeled for use in the United States, and after consultation with the Colombian Government to ensure that the fumigation is in accordance with Colombian laws; (2) the chemicals used in the aerial fumigation of coca, in the manner in which they are being applied, do not pose unreasonable risks or adverse effects to humans or the environment; and (3) procedures are available to evaluate claims of local citizens that their health was harmed or their licit agriculture crops were damaged by such aerial coca fumigation, and to provide fair compensation for meritorious claims; and such funds may not be made available for such purposes after six months from the date of enactment of this Act unless alternative development programs have been developed, in consultation with communities and local authorities in the departments in which such aerial coca fumigation is planned,

and in the department in which such aerial coca fumigation has been conducted such programs are being implemented.[12] Such a strategy involves several steps, in no particular order.

1. Target the members of the two Foreign Operations subcommittees by meeting with their staff and providing factually and legally accurate material about your issue. Draft for them the exact language you seek and then defend it.[13]
2. Call for hearings on the issue while the draft language is being debated and after it has been implemented by the appropriate administrative agency.
3. To the degree your proposed language calls upon multiple administrative agencies to take action, you can refer any subsequent problems with inter-agency cooperation on the matter to the U.S. House Governmental Relations Committee or the U.S. Senate Government Affairs Committee and ask for an investigative hearing.
4. Challenge in court any failure to comply with the new language.

F. Pelly Amendment

The Pelly Amendment to the Fishermen's Protection Act of 1967, 22 U.S.C. § 1978 (the "Pelly Amendment") enables civil society to petition the U.S. Secretaries of Commerce and Interior to certify foreign governments that engage in activities harmful to endangered or threatened species. Such certification can result in the imposition of trade sanctions against that foreign government by the U.S. President and/or the monitoring and investigating of the foreign government's practices by the Secretary of Commerce or Interior, depending upon which certified the foreign government. Both trade sanction imposition and periodic monitoring and investigation are designed to pressure the foreign government to cease its harmful actions.

The Pelly Amendment provides that "[w]hen the Secretary of Commerce or the Secretary of the Interior finds that nationals of a foreign country, directly or indirectly, are engaging in trade or taking which diminishes the effectiveness of any international program for endangered or threatened species, the Secretary making such finding shall certify such fact to the President." 22 U.S.C. § 1978(a)(2). Certification can then lead to imposition of trade sanctions and/or monitoring and investigations.

---

[12] P.L. 107-115 at 115 Stat. 2130-2131 (2002), http://frwebgate.access.gpo.gov/cgi-bin/getdoc.cgi?dbname=107_cong_public_laws&docid=f:publ115.107. That same language was retained in the FY 2003 budget as well and continues to evolve and strengthen. See P.L. 108-7 at 117 Stat. 173, http://frwebgate.access.gpo.gov/cgi-bin/getdoc.cgi?dbname=108_cong_public_laws&docid=f:publ007.108.

[13] A list of the Senate subcommittee members can be found at http://appropriations.senate.gov/. A list of the House subcommittee members can be found at http://appropriations.house.gov/.

"Upon receipt of certification, the President may direct the Secretary of the Treasury to prohibit the bringing or the importation into the United States of any products from the offending country for any duration as the President determines appropriate and to the extent that such prohibition is sanctioned by the World Trade Organization (as defined in section 2(8) of the Uruguay Round Agreements Act [19 USCS § 3501(8)] or the multilateral trade agreement (as defined in section 2(4) of that Act [19 USCS § 3501(4)]." 22 U.S.C. § 1978(a)(4). "Within sixty days following certification by the Secretary of Commerce or the Secretary of the Interior, the President shall notify the Congress of any action taken by him pursuant to such certification." 22 U.S.C. § 1978(b). Although certification has occurred on many occasions, trade sanction imposition has yet to happen.[14]

Alternatively, certification requires the Secretary of Commerce or the Secretary of the Interior, as appropriate, to "(A) periodically monitor the activities of foreign nationals that may affect the international programs. . . . ; (B) promptly investigate any activity by foreign nationals that, in the opinion of the Secretary, may be cause for certification. . . ; and (C) promptly conclude; and reach a decision with respect to; any investigation recommended under subparagraph (B)."

To pursue the Pelly Amendment strategy, identify a foreign government engaging in activity that harms an endangered or threatened species. Then, determine whether such action diminishes the effectiveness of an international program or treaty involving the United States. The simple test is whether the endangered or threatened species is listed on or generally referred to in a treaty to which the United States is a party, even if the foreign government engaging in the harmful activity is not.

If both requirements are met, then one should draft a letter petition that details the harm occurring, the foreign government responsible, and the international program involved, and that requests certification. One should submit the petition to the Secretary of Commerce or the Secretary of Interior. For any marine or anadromous species, as generally discussed in 50 C.F.R. Parts 223 and 224, submit the petition to the Secretary of Commerce. Addressed are:

The Honorable Donald Evans
US Secretary of Commerce
1401 Constitution Avenue, N.W.
Washington, D.C. 20230

---

[14] For an account of Pelly Amendment case studies, *see* Steve Charnovitz, *Recent Developments: Environmental Trade Sanctions and the GATT: An Analysis of the Pelly Amendment on Foreign Environmental Practices*, 9 AM. U. J. INT'L. & POL'Y 751, 763-772 (Spring 1994). On a few occasions, the President has come close to imposing sanctions, instead reaching an agreement with the certified nation to cease the acts harming the endangered or threatened species.

William T. Hogarth, Ph.D.
Assistant Administration for Fisheries
National Marine Fisheries Service
NOAA Fisheries
1315 East West Highway, SSMC3
Silver Spring, MD 20910

Similarly, for any other endangered or threatened species, as generally discussed in 50 C.F.R. Parts 1-199, submit to the Secretary of the Interior. Addresses for each are:

The Honorable Gale Norton
US Secretary of the Interior
1849 C Street, NW
Washington, D.C. 20240

Steven A. William
Director, U.S. Fish & Wildlife Service
1849 C Street, NW
Washington, D.C. 20240

Consult the list of experts in the Appendix to review your petition before submitting it.

III. LITIGATION STRATEGIES

6.2 Indonesian Illegal Logging Law

There is a new law in Indonesia making illegal logging a capital offense.[15] The law is pending in the House of Representatives, but a temporary law is now in effect.[16] Illegal logging has been linked to human rights abuses, environmental degradation, and civil wars, and is costly for the state. Largely a result of illegal logging, 2.6 million hectares of natural forest are lost annually and companies in the timber-processing industry have closed due to decreases in supply.[17] The government has prosecuted some illegal loggers, but is overwhelmed by the number. In fact, police are investigating more illegal logging cases each year. Minister of Forestry M. Prakosa blames the police, the port authority, and the navy for the crime's scale.[18] The ministry has gradually lowered logging quotas, and requires domestic timber and pulp-and-paper companies to address issues relating to biodiversity and the livelihoods of indigenous communities.[19]

---

[15] See Bill Guerin, *Illegal loggers: Shoot them, Jakarta Says*, ASIAN TIMES (July 7, 2004), *available at* http://www.atimes.com/atimes/Southeast_Asia/FG07Ae03.html (last visited Feb. 28, 2005).
[16] *Id.*
[17] *Id.*
[18] *Id.*
[19] *Id.*

A. The Alien Tort Claims Act

The Alien Tort Claims Act of 1789 ("ATCA") provides U.S. district courts with "original jurisdiction of any civil action by an alien for a tort only, committed in violation of the law of nations or a treaty of the United States."[20] While the ATCA was rarely invoked for a long stretch of our history, there have been a number of definitive cases in the past 30 years.

In *Hilao v. Estate of Marcos*, families whose members had been subjected to torture, summary executions, and disappearances brought an action against the former President of the Philippines for damages. The U.S. Appeals Court for the Ninth Circuit held, in part, that a "suit as an alien for the tort of wrongful death, committed by military intelligence officials through torture *prohibited by the law of nations*, is within the jurisdictional grant of [the ATCA] § 1350."[21] Relying on the landmark case of *Filartiga v. Pena-Irala*, the court found the ATCA "creates a universal cause of action for violations of specific, universal and obligatory international human rights which 'confer [] fundamental rights upon all people vis-à-vis their own governments'"[22] Plaintiffs must demonstrate the tortious act involved either violation of a universally recognized principle of international law or tortious conduct in violation of a treaty of the United States.[23]

In *Kadic v. Karadzic*,[24] the U.S. Court of Appeals for the Second Circuit found that individual, non-state actors may be held liable for acts widely recognized as being in violation of international law. In this case, groups of Bosnian refugees sought damages against the self-proclaimed leader of the Bosnian-Serb Republic (then unrecognized by the United States) for acts of genocide, rape, torture, and summary execution, among

---

[20] 28 U.S.C. § 1350. In the landmark case of *Filartiga v. Pena-Irala*, 630 F.2d 876 (2d Cir. 1980), two Paraguayan citizens brought a wrongful death suit in federal district court against the Inspector General of Police in Asuncion, Paraguay, who lived in the United States. Filartiga's son had been tortured to death allegedly in retaliation for Filartiga's criticism of the Paraguayan government. On appeal, the Second Circuit reversed the district court's finding of lack of subject matter jurisdiction and held that deliberate torture perpetrated under color of official authority violates customary international law. The court recognized that torture perpetrated by public officers is renounced by virtually all nations, and clearly violates the law of nations within the meaning of the ATCA.

[21] *Hilao v. Estate of Marcos*, 25 F.3d 1467, at 1473, quoting previous related case *Estate I*, 978 F.2d at 499 (emphasis added).

[22] *Id.* at 1475, quoting *Filartiga v. Pena-Irala*, 630 F.2d 876, at 885–87.

[23] *See* Virginia A. Melvin, *Case Comment: Tel-Oren v. Libyan Arab Republic: Redefining the Alien Tort Claims Act*, 70 MINN. L. REV. 211 (Oct. 1985).

[24] 70 F.3d 232 (2d Cir. 1995).

other violations. The refugees sued under the ATCA and the Torture Victim Prevention Act ("TVPA"). The district court and the Second Circuit concluded that since the Bosnian-Serb Republic was not a recognized state, and therefore Karadzic was not a state actor, the TVPA did not confer subject matter jurisdiction because of its explicit reference to "actual or apparent authority, or color of law." The argument can still be made, however, that "*apparent*" authority, and "*color* of law" within the definition of torture encompass non-state actors with some form of official authority or control short of formal state authority. The Second Circuit did acknowledge that the trial court might on remand find that Karadzic was a *de facto* state actor despite the failure of the international community to recognize the Bosnian-Serb Republic. The appeals court was left to determine whether non-state actors could commit other torts "in violation of the law of nations," and found that there are certain acts for which non-state actors may be held liable under modern international law, namely genocide and war crimes.[25]

After the holding in *Karadzic* applying the ATCA to non-state actors, numerous alien victims of environmental degradation have filed environmental human rights claims against non-state actors, particularly multinational corporations, and have referred to the ATCA as the basis for the court's jurisdiction.[26] Initially, the courts seemed inclined in suits against private individuals to hold that the ATCA can apply to non-state actors, but in cases of human rights claims not involving environmental human rights claims.[27] In subsequent cases filed against multinational corporations pursuant to the ATCA and specifically involving environmental human rights claims, the courts have applied a four-part judicial test common to domestic civil rights litigation that considers whether the non-state actor acted like a state in connection with the environmental human rights claim alleged.[28]

---

[25] *See generally* Judith Hippler Bello & Theodore R. Posner, *Alien Tort Claims Act—Genocide—War Crimes—Violations Of International Law By Nonstate Actors*, 90 AM. J. INT'L L. 658 (1996).

[26] *See Doe v. Unocal*, 248 F.3d 915 (9th Cir. 2001); *see also Wiwa v. Royal Dutch Petroleum Co.*, 226 F.3d 88 (2d Cir. 2000); *Bowoto v. Chevron*, No. C99-2506 (N.D. Cal. filed May 27, 1999).

[27] *See In re Estate of Ferdinand E. Marcos Human Rights Litig.*, 978 F.2d 493, 499 (9th Cir. 1992); *see also Tel-Oren v. Libyan Arab Republic*, 726 F.2d 774 (D.C. Cir. 1984).

[28] *See Doe v. Unocal*, 110 F. Supp. 2d 1294, 1304 (C.D. Cal. 2000) (holding that ATCA did not apply to Unocal, a multinational petroleum corporation, because Unocal did not satisfy the test).

6.3 Malaysia—Chemor

An out-of-court settlement protected the right to health[29] when Chemor residents sued the owner of a rubber factory that was releasing noxious fumes.[30] The factory had to relocate its operations to a new site before March 30, 2005, or entirely stop operating.[31] The factory has also agreed to reduce its emissions, treat its anaerobic ponds and effluent processors,[32] and allow the Department of the Environment to test their emissions.[33]

In *Doe v. Unocal Corporation*,[34] several Burmese villagers sued under the ATCA, alleging that the corporation had aided and abetted the military government of Myanmar in using the plaintiffs as forced laborers and that members of the military had killed, tortured, and raped villagers. These human rights violations were designed to discourage opposition to a pipeline project in the Tenasserim region. Myanmar had granted Total S.A., a French oil company, a license to explore coastal gas deposits. The project involved building the Yadana Gas Pipeline Project from the coast through the Tenasserim region to Thailand. Unocal acquired 28 percent of the project from Total.

The court cited the Second Circuit's decision in *Kadic v. Karadzic*,[35] for the proposition that ATCA liability may attach to non-state actors. The ATCA, according to the court, not only confers jurisdiction, but also creates a cause of action against non-state actors in some circumstances. As to Unocal's liability for knowingly aiding the violations, the court adopted the reasoning of the International Criminal Tribunal for the former Yugoslavia in *The Prosecutor v. Furundzija*,[36] that the *actus reus* of aiding and abetting in international criminal law requires practical assistance, encouragement, or moral support that substantially affects the criminal behavior. The court concluded that there were genuine issues of fact as to whether Unocal as a non-state actor satisfied the *actus reus* and *mens rea* required under the ATCA for aiding and abetting the state's alleged commission of forced labor, murder, and rape. The court found insufficient evidence, however, to support the torture claims against dismissal. The Ninth Circuit Court of Appeals granted a rehearing *en banc*, vacating the panel decision.[37]

---

[29] See Chan Li Leen, *Residents Discontinue Legal Action*, THE STAR (May 11, 2004), available at http://www.elaw.org/news/partners/text.asp?id=2422 (last visited Mar. 2, 2005).
[30] *Id.*
[31] *Id.*
[32] *Id.*
[33] *Id.*
[34] 2002 U.S. App. Lexis 19263 (9th Cir. Sept. 18, 2002).
[35] 70 F.3d 232, 240 (2d Cir. 1995).
[36] International Tribunal for Yugoslavia, Case No. IT-95-17/1-T (Dec. 10, 1998), available at http://www.un.org/icty/furundzija/trialcz/judgement/fur_tj 981210e.pdf.
[37] 2003 U.S. App. Lexis 2716 (9th Cir. Feb. 14, 2003).

Following the Ninth Circuit Court of Appeals decision to vacate and rehear *en banc Doe v. Unocal Corporation* in February, 2003, Unocal encountered major setbacks in what it hoped would be a dismissal of the case against them. The first major setback was the U.S. Supreme Court decision in *Sosa v. Alvarez-Machain* to uphold the Alien Tort Claims Act.[38] The second major setback came in September 2004, when Unocal's appeal for dismissal was rejected, thus urging the case into the beginning stages of a jury trial.[39] Rather than stand trial, Unocal decided to settle out of court in December 2004.[40] The actual terms of the settlement remained undisclosed, but in a joint statement both parties said that the settlement would compensate the villagers and provide money to develop community programs "to improve living conditions, health care, and education, and protect their rights in the pipeline region."[41]

Although neither side would comment on the size of the settlement, Unocal filed suit against its insurance companies for personal injuries coverage in the settlement of the case. The insurance companies, who insure Unocal for up to $60 million, denied the claim, but Unocal sued both its primary and secondary insurers, leading analysts to speculate that the settlement was quite large.[42] Attorneys' fees alone are estimated at $15 million.[43]

Business groups and the Bush administration have heavily criticized the Alien Tort Claims Act. Attorney General John Ashcroft filed a brief to the Ninth Circuit Court of Appeals in the *Unocal* case broadly stating that United States courts should not allow alien claims under ATCA.[44] The Bush administration further indicated that allowing alien claims under the ATCA would complicate foreign policy administration.[45]

---

[38] ASIA TIMES, "Foreign Crimes Come Home to the US" (Dec. 16, 2004), *available at* http://www.atimes.com/atimes/Southeast_Asia/FL16Ae01.html (last visited May 23, 2005). *See also* discussion *infra* and *Rasul v. Bush*, 124 S. Ct. 2686 (2004) (holding federal district courts able to exercise jurisdiction over claims filed by aliens under the Alien Tort Statute).

[39] ASIA TIMES, "Foreign Crimes Come Home to the U.S." (Dec. 16, 2004), *available at* http://www.atimes.com/atimes/Southeast_Asia/FL16Ae01.html (last visited May 23, 2005).

[40] Robert Benson, Professor of Law at Loyola Law School who specializes in international human rights law, speculated that Unocal "wanted to avoid a trial where humble villagers get on the stand and talk about rape and murder." Mark Lifsher, "Unocal Settles Human Rights Lawsuit over Alleged Abuses at Myanmar Pipeline," L.A. TIMES, Mar. 22, 2005, at C1.

[41] *Report of Earthjustice: Human Rights and the Environment*, U.N. Commission on Human Rights, 61st Sess. (2005) at 54, *available at* http://www.earthjustice.org/news/display.html?ID=983.

[42] Daphne Eviatar, "A Big Win for Human Rights," THE NATION (May 9, 2005), *available at* http://www.thenation.com/doc.mhtml?i=20050509&s=eviatar.

[43] *Id.*

[44] *Id.*

[45] Mark Lifsher, "Unocal Settles Human Rights Lawsuit over Alleged Abuses at Myanmar Pipeline," L.A. TIMES, Mar. 22, 2005, at C1.

Human rights organizations hope that the settlement in *Unocal* will have an influential impact on the way other big businesses conduct their affairs abroad. With several cases pending in the courts against major U.S. companies, the impact of *Unocal* may be seen in the near future.[46] One difference in the *Unocal* case, however, was the amount of documentation indicating that the Unocal Corporation knew about the human rights abuses that occurred during the building of the pipeline.[47]

The announcement of the settlement came just two weeks before Unocal's announcement of a merger with Chevron Texaco, a much larger company facing its own problems in court. There was some speculation that the settlement was part of the merger agreement.[48] The courts officially dismissed the case when both parties filed a joint motion to dismiss.[49]

Unocal follows upon the procedural success of another group of alien litigants challenging the environmental/human rights practices of corporate entities. In *Wiwa v. Royal Dutch Shell Petroleum Co.*,[50] four Nigerians, including three United States residents, sued Royal Dutch Petroleum of the Netherlands and Shell Transport and Trading Company of the United Kingdom.[51] Allegedly Shell Nigeria recruited the Nigerian police and military to attack villages and suppress opposition to its oil development activities in the Ogoni region.[52] In addition, the complaint states that Shell encouraged Nigerian government officials to imprison, torture, and kill plaintiffs and their families, and forcibly took land without adequate compensation while causing pollution of the air and water.[53] Shell allegedly gave the Nigerian military money, weapons, vehicles, ammunition, and other logistical support in the village raids.[54] On February 22, 2002, the district court rejected almost all of the grounds for dismissal, allowing the case to move to discovery.[55] The human rights violations from environmental harm

---

[46] See, e.g., *Bowoto v. Chevron Texaco Corp.*, 312 F. Supp. 2d 1229, 2004 U.S. Dist. LEXIS 4603 (N.D. Cal. 2004); *Estate of Rodriguez v. Drummond Co.*, 256 F. Supp. 2d 1250, 2003 U.S. Dist. LEXIS 6657 (N.D. Ala. 2003); *Aldana v. Fresh Del Monte Produce, Inc.*, 305 F. Supp. 2d 1285, 2003 U.S. Dist. LEXIS 24343 (S.D. Fla. 2003). In all three district court cases, plaintiffs' claims under the ATCA were dismissed without prejudice.

[47] Daphne Eviatar, "A Big Win for Human Rights," THE NATION (May 9, 2005), *available at* http://www.thenation.com/doc.mhtml?i=20050509&s=eviatar.

[48] "Without a settlement, Unocal would have doubled Chevron Texaco's potential liability for human rights violations and compounded its public embarrassment." Daphne Eviatar, "A Big Win for Human Rights," THE NATION (May 9, 2005), *available at* http://www.thenation.com/doc.mhtml?i=20050509&s=eviatar.

[49] *Doe v. Unocal Corp.*, 403 F.3d 708, 2005 U.S. App. LEXIS 6070 (9th Cir. 2005).
[50] No. 96 Civ. 8386, 2002 U.S. Dist. LEXIS 3293 (S.D. N.Y. Feb. 22, 2002).
[51] *Id.* at *3.
[52] *Id.* at *5.
[53] *Id.* at *4, *41.
[54] *Id.* at *42.
[55] *Id.* at *101.

include crimes against humanity against Doe and Owens Wiwa, torture of Doe, cruel, inhuman, and degrading treatment of Doe and Wiwa, violation of the right to peaceful assembly and association for Doe and Wiwa, as well as the rights to life, liberty, and security of person for Doe.[56]

In denying the motion to dismiss, the court found sufficient the allegations that Royal Dutch/Shell were in collusion with the state of Nigeria, and that the acts of Shell Nigeria were sufficiently attributable to its parent company Royal Dutch/Shell for claims under the Torture Victim Protection Act and ATCA to be brought against the parent company and Brian Anderson, the Nigerian chairman for Royal Dutch/Shell and managing director of Shell Nigeria. The court also rejected the act of state doctrine as warranting dismissal, noting that the public interest outweighed any threat of embarrassment to the Nigerian government.

The ATCA cases in United States federal court are relevant and instructive in several respects. First, the ATCA complaints are establishing a new form of linkage between environmental harm and human rights—the violation of human rights to oppress opposition to environmental degradation.[57] Secondly, the law developing the liability of non-state actors conversely sheds light on when nation-state responsibility may be predicated on the acts of non-state actors, either individuals or private corporations.[58] Finally, litigation of these international torts of environmental oppression may lay a foundation of expanded use of supranational fora within the United Nations system (*e.g.*, the Committee Against Torture) and outside (*e.g.*, the International Criminal Court and domestic courts for crimes against humanity).[59] This last factor has become increasingly important in light of two decisional setbacks to ATCA litigation in which circuit courts have placed more stringent requirements on pleadings when plaintiffs attempt to use human rights arguments to challenge environmental pollution.

In *Beanal v. Freeport-McMoran*,[60] the U.S. Court of Appeals for the Fifth Circuit affirmed a district court judge's dismissal of Beanal's claims under the ATCA and TVPA for environmental pollution and human rights violations, holding that *Beanal*'s pleadings failed to state a claim under Federal Rules of Civil Procedure 12(b)(6). In 1996, Beanal, the leader of the

---

[56] *Id.*
[57] *See Bano v. Union Carbide*, 273 F.3d 120 (2d Cir. 2001); *Sarei v. Rio Tinto* PLC, 221 F. Supp. 2d 1116 (C.D. Cal. 2002).
[58] *See, e.g.*, William Aceves, *Affirming the Law of Nations in U.S. Courts: The Karadzic Litigation and the Yugoslav Conflict*, 14 BERKELEY J. INT'L L. 137 (1996); Peggy Rodgers Kalas, *International Environmental Dispute Resolution and the Need for Access by Non-State Entities*, 12 COLO. J. INT'L ENVTL. L. & POL'Y 191 (2001).
[59] *Doe v. Unocal*, Nos. 00-56603, 00-57197, Nos. 00-56628, 00-57195.
[60] 197 F.3d 161 (5th Cir. 1999).

Amungme Tribal Council in Irian Jaya, Indonesia, filed suit against Freeport for alleged violations of international law in connection with Freeport's operation of an open-pit copper, silver and gold mine in Irian Jaya. Specifically, Beanal claimed that Freeport "caused harm and injury to the Amungme's environment and habitat" and "that Freeport's private security force acted in concert with the Republic to violate international human rights."[61] The Fifth Circuit addressed each of these issues separately. Beginning with the human rights claim, the court upheld the trial judge's dismissal by noting that Beanal's claims failed to provide adequate notice under Federal Rules of Civil Procedure 8(a). "Beanal's claims are devoid of names, dates, locations, times or any facts that would put Freeport on notice as to what conduct supports the nature of his claims."[62]

More generally, in upholding the dismissal of Beanal's environmental claims, the court found that Beanal failed to show that Freeport's mining activities violated "any universally accepted environmental standards or norms."[63] Specifically, the court stated that international treaties and agreements on which Beanal relied, including the Rio Declaration,[64] "merely refer to a general sense of environmental responsibility and state abstract rights and liberties devoid of articulable or discernible standards and regulations to identify practices that constitute international environmental abuses or torts."[65] In addition, the court expressed reluctance to impose U.S. environmental policy on other nations, especially when the alleged harms occur entirely within a state's borders without impacting neighboring countries.[66]

In September, 2003, the U.S. Court of Appeals for the Second Circuit upheld a district court judge's dismissal on similar grounds. In *Flores v. Southern Peru Copper Corporation*,[67] ("SPCC") a group of Peruvian plaintiffs brought personal injury claims under the ATCA against SPCC, a U.S. company, alleging that pollution from SPCC's copper mining, refining, and smelting operations caused plaintiffs' or their decedents' lung disease, violating the plaintiffs' "right to life" and "right to health."[68] Relying in part on the Fifth Circuit's decision in *Beanal v. Freeport-McMoran*, the Second Circuit upheld dismissal of plaintiffs' claims for failure to state a cause of action on which relief could be granted.[69] In so doing, the *Flores* court

---

[61] *Id.* at 163.
[62] *Id.* at 165.
[63] *Id.* at 166.
[64] Rio Declaration on Environment and Development, June 13, 1992, U.N. Doc. A/CONF. 15 1/5 rev. 1 (1992).
[65] *Beanal*, 197 F.3d 161, 167.
[66] *Id.* at 167.
[67] *Flores v. Southern Peru Copper Corporation*, 343 F.3d 140 (2d Cir. 2003).
[68] 343 F.3d at 143.
[69] FED. R. CIV. P. 12(b)(6).

provided an in-depth examination of the types of claims it concluded are and are not actionable under international law pursuant to the ATCA.

The court stated that for any ATCA claim to succeed, it must allege a violation of customary international law. As defined by the Second Circuit, customary international law consists only of those clear and unambiguous rules that states universally abide by out of a sense of legal obligation, and mutual concern.[70] Although based on several international agreements, including the Universal Declaration of Human Rights[71] and the Rio Declaration on Environment and Development,[72] the court found that the plaintiffs' "right to life" and "right to health" to be "vague and amorphous," far from establishing a "clear and unambiguous" rule of customary international law sufficient to provide a basis for a claim under the ATCA.[73] The court quoted *Beanal v. Freeport-McMoran*, noting that international agreements such as these "state abstract rights and liberties devoid of articulable or discernible standards and regulations."[74]

As for the plaintiffs' specific environmental claims, the court found, as in *Beanal*, no rule of customary international law prohibiting international pollution.[75] In response to the plaintiffs' reliance on treaties to demonstrate international agreement, the court held that "a treaty will only constitute *sufficient proof* of a norm of customary international law if an overwhelming majority of States have ratified the treaty, *and* consistently act in accordance with its principles."[76] Without providing an example of such a treaty, the court concluded that none of the treaties relied on by the plaintiffs met this standard because they were either not ratified by the United States or Peru or both, and thus not binding; or worse, they failed to provide clear and unambiguous regulations and standards for international pollution.[77] The court then dismissed the possibility that any non-binding international agreement could serve as a source of customary international law, including: non-binding United Nations General Assembly resolutions,[78] other multinational declarations, including the Rio Declaration,[79] or decisions of multinational tribunals.[80]

---

[70] *Flores*, 343 F.3d at 154-57.
[71] Universal Declaration of Human Rights, art. 25, G.A. Res. 217(III), U.N. GAOR, 3d Sess., U.N. Doc. A/810, at 71 (1948).
[72] *Rio Declaration on Environment and Development*, June 13, 1992, U.N. Doc. A/CONF. 15 1/5 rev. 1 (1992).
[73] *Flores*, 343 F.3d at 160.
[74] *Id.*, quoting *Beanal*, 197 F.3d at 167.
[75] *Flores*, 343 F.3d at 161-162.
[76] 343 F.3d at 162-163.
[77] 343 F.3d at 160-170.
[78] 343 F.3d at 168.
[79] 343 F.3d at 169-70.
[80] 343 F.3d at 170.

266 • Defending the Environment

In the wake of *Beanal v. Freeport-McMoran* and *Flores v. Southern Peru Copper Corporation*, enforcing environmental law under the ATCA, at least in these two circuits, has become much more difficult. In particular, it is clear that plaintiffs must allege violations of specific "articulable or discernible standards and regulations [that] identify practices that constitute international environmental abuses or torts."[81] Moreover, as both cases demonstrate, these courts are extremely hesitant to impose U.S. environmental standards on other nations via the ATCA, especially when the alleged pollution is purely intranational. Even if a plaintiff succeeds in avoiding dismissal on Federal Rules of Civil Procedure 12(b)(6) grounds, there is no guarantee that the claim would not be dismissed for *forum non conveniens*.[82]

In sum, then, despite the notable successes that some plaintiffs have enjoyed in enforcing environmental regulations by linking environmental degradation to other human rights recognizably protected under the ATCA, even against non-state actors, it appears that enforcing a human right to a safe and healthy environment, if not completely closed, has been severely restricted at least in these circuits. Whether this trend will continue remains to be seen, but for claims involving pollution entirely within a nation's borders by non-state actors, litigants must overcome these detrimental precedents.

To paraphrase Mark Twain, the anticipated death of the ATCA before the U.S. Supreme Court in *Sosa v. Alvarez-Machain*[83] was greatly exaggerated. The Supreme Court refused to limit the reach of the ATCA to the very limited category of international law claims understood in 1789, as urged by the U.S. Solicitor General. The Court concluded that no development in the two centuries since its passage had categorically precluded federal courts from recognizing a claim under the law of nations as part of U.S. common law. Although requiring that enforceable norms of custom under the ATCA be norms accepted by the civilized world and defined with the specificity of the recognized 1789 norms, this limitation need not be interpreted as any more demanding than that previously formulated by the lower courts or, in fact, required for recognition generally of a norm as custom under international law (although environmental advocates should pay close attention to the possible procedural limitations which the opinion suggests in footnotes might play a more important role in limiting ATCA actions in the future). The decision, despite much cautionary language and dismissal of Sosa's particular claim, confirms the availability of the ATCA for victims of serious violations of international law that may include plaintiffs who tie environmental degradation to well established human rights abuses.[84]

---

[81] *Beanal*, 197 F.3d 161, 167.
[82] *Flores*, 343 F.3d at 172.
[83] 542 U.S. 692 (2004).
[84] See Human Rights First, *Press Release: Supreme Court Denies Claim of Alvarez-Machain, but Upholds Important Human Rights Law* (June 29, 2004), *available at* http://www.humanrightsfirst.org/media/2004_alerts/0629.htm (last visited Feb. 27, 2005).

Turning to a related matter, the Preliminary Draft Convention on Jurisdiction and Foreign Judgments in Civil and Commercial Matters seeks to harmonize jurisdictional rules and to limit the places where proceedings can be instituted to a few appropriate fora, so as to avoid a multiplicity of proceedings as well as irreconcilable judgments. The Preliminary Draft Convention also seeks to simplify and expedite the recognition and enforcement of judgments.[85] If ratified, it might increase the likelihood of enforcing environmental law under the ATCA and other domestic laws.

Article 18 of the Preliminary Draft Convention limits contracting states' grounds for jurisdiction, but Variants One and Two provide exceptions to the limits.[86] The exceptions granted by Variant One extend to conduct that constitutes genocide; a crime against humanity or a war crime, as defined in the Statute of the International Criminal Court;[87] a grave violation of a natural person's non-derogable fundamental rights established under international law;[88] or a serious crime against a natural person under international law. Variant Two's exception applies to a serious crime under international law, provided that the contracting state has established its criminal jurisdiction over that crime in accordance with an international treaty to which it is a party and that the claim is for civil compensatory damages for death or serious bodily injury.[89]

The Preliminary Draft Convention, if ratified, would provide enhanced enforceability among contracting states under the Alien Tort Claims Act for environmental law violations that rise to the level of genocide, crimes against humanity, war crimes, serious crimes against persons under international law, or grave violations against natural person of non-derogable fundamental rights established under environmental law.

B. Extraterritorial Application of United States Environmental Laws to U.S. Government Activity Abroad

The global presence of the U. S. government and U.S. corporations causes a certain amount of environmental degradation in the world, attributable in part to particular U.S. government decisions and/or actions. Whereas much of this book has discussed strategies to challenge such harms before international courts and tribunals, an arguably more effective forum in which to hold the United States accountable and enjoin it from continuing environmental degradation is domestic federal court. The

---

[85] *Available at* http://www.wipo.int/sct/en/documents/session_3/doc/sct3_3.doc.
[86] Preliminary Draft Convention on Jurisdiction and Foreign Judgments in Civil and Commercial Matters, Oct. 30, 1999, art. 18, para. 3, *available at* http.www.wipo.int/sct/en/documents/session_3/doc/sct_3.doc.
[87] *Id.*
[88] *Id.*
[89] *Id.*

United States is immune from suit in federal court unless it waives its sovereign immunity. Nevertheless, some domestic litigation avenues discussed in this section may prove fruitful.

As reviewing the litigation avenues suggested by this subsection will reveal, a number of obstacles exist to using these avenues because the law remains unclear as to whether U.S. courts have jurisdiction over allegations that U.S. activity abroad is resulting in adverse environmental harms abroad. Currently, the grounds for such extraterritorial remedies are extremely limited. Nevertheless, civil society needs to continue to bring these suits if a broadening of availability and effectiveness is ever to occur. U.S. courts often do provide greater relief than any comparable international fora, so the challenge of widening the domestic courts' jurisdiction with respect to these claims is a battle worth fighting. Of course, change in established jurisprudence is likely to take decades, much like every other radical change in jurisprudence in the history of U.S. courts. The faster the cases can be filed, the faster the clock begins ticking.

1. Common Law Tort Actions Against a Domestic Government

Apart from an Alien Tort Claims Act court action discussed above, a common law tort action might be another way to hold the U.S. government accountable for environmental degradation abroad. In the case of the United States, the U.S. government's waiver of sovereign immunity with respect to tort suits is limited to the terms of the Federal Tort Claims Act, 28 U.S.C. Sections 1346(b) and 2671-2680. This results in less room for challenging government actions and decision-making than tortious acts of individual government employees. Consult an expert in the List of Practitioner Experts for further assistance with this strategy.[90]

2. Administrative Procedures Act

The federal Administrative Procedures Act ("APA"),[91] allows civil society to compel federal government agencies to take action unlawfully withheld or unreasonably delayed, and allows civil society to challenge federal government final agency actions, findings and conclusions that, among other things, are "[1] arbitrary, capricious, an abuse of discretion, or otherwise not in accordance with law; [2] contrary to constitutional right, power, privilege, or immunity; [3] in excess of statutory jurisdiction, authority, or limitations, or short of statutory right; [or 4] without observance of

---

[90] *See supra.*
[91] 5 U.S.C. §§ 701 *et seq.* ("APA").

procedure required by law."[92] Thus, when a federal government decision has potentially adverse environmental affects abroad, the APA provides a means for holding the government accountable.

6.4 Costa Rica—Shark Finning

In 2004, the Supreme Court of Costa Rica ruled that the Customs Office violated the right to a healthy and balanced environment by allowing shark fins to be unloaded at private docks without inspectors present, and by taking too long to address a complaint that officials take more precautions so as to prevent the practice.[93] The court called for an end to shark finning—a practice whereby the fins are sliced off and the body is discarded in the ocean—stating that customs officials "should take all necessary measures to prevent shark finning and sanction . . . all those persons who commit this act."[94]

The good news about undertaking a strategy of domestic litigation using the APA is that the APA provides a broader waiver of sovereign immunity for government decision making than the Federal Tort Claims Act.[95] However, the bad news about this strategy is that for any U.S. actions, findings, and conclusions taken abroad, the law remains unclear whether the underlying federal environmental laws that are the basis for the APA claim can be applied extraterritorially. Whereas federal courts fully support use of the APA as a means for challenging such government decision making when damage occurs within the United States, the law is less certain with respect to actions abroad. However, it seems that the APA can sometimes justify challenges against U.S. government decisions taken with respect to a matter abroad. In *Rosner v. United States*,[96] for example, the court allowed the APA to provide a basis for two of the plaintiffs' three claims against the U.S. military for its seizure of and failure to return property of Hungarian Jews originally stolen by the pro-Nazi Hungarian government and sent to Germany.

Another issue in APA cases is that the action, finding or conclusion challenged must be considered "final." In *Sabella v. United States*[97] the plaintiffs sought injunctive relief preventing enforcement of an International Dolphin Conservation Act ("IDCA") provision banning the use of purse

---

[92] *Id.* § 706.
[93] *See* Steve Barry, *High Court Rules on Shark-Finning Issue*, TICO TIMES (Aug. 11, 2004), *on file with Earthjustice*.
[94] *Id.*
[95] *See* III.B.1, *supra*.
[96] 231 F. Supp. 2d 1202, 1211–12 (S.D. Fla. 2002).
[97] *Sabella v. U.S.*, 863 F. Supp. 1 (D.D.C.1994).

seine nets on vessels operated by persons subject to U.S. jurisdiction.[98] Plaintiffs claimed jurisdiction under the APA on the grounds that a letter from the National Oceanic and Atmospheric Administration's General Counsel stating the probability of the IDCA's application to the vessel in question was a final agency action. The court determined that the letter was not final agency action.[99]

In the environmental realm, the APA has been used to hold the U.S. government accountable for adverse environmental impacts abroad in two general ways. Both strategies should be undertaken *only* with the assistance of legal counsel. Consult the List of Practitioner Experts for such assistance.

a. Claims of a Violation of the National Environmental Policy Act

The first use of the APA to challenge environmental harms abroad that result from the U.S. government's actions is to claim that the U.S. government failed to comply with the National Environmental Policy Act ("NEPA")[100] in its undertaking of environmental review of a particular federal action. Unlike the other major federal environmental laws, NEPA lacks a citizen enforcement provision so that NEPA challenges are brought using the APA rather than citizen enforcement provisions discussed below. For such NEPA challenges, the struggle is not whether the APA can be used to maintain the case but, rather, whether Congress ever intended the environmental review provisions of NEPA to apply extraterritorially.

Generally speaking, the Foley/Aramco doctrine[101] creates a presumption against extraterritorial application of U.S. law. In determining whether Congress intended a statute to apply extraterritorially, U.S. courts look to the language of the statute, its legislative history, and the overall statutory scheme.

Apart from evidence of Congressional intent in favor of extraterritorial application, the courts often will overcome the presumption in the case of the extraterritorial application of environmental laws, including NEPA, if evidence exists that the action taken abroad will adversely impact: (1) the United States;[102] (2) a global commons;[103] or (3) another sovereign

---

[98] *See id.* at 2.
[99] *See id.* at 3.
[100] 42 U.S.C. §§ 4321–4345.
[101] *Foley Bros., Inc. v. Filardo*, 336 U.S. 281 (1949); *see also EEOC v. Arabian American Oil Co.*, 499 U.S. 244 (1991).
[102] *See, e.g., Sierra Club v. Adams*, 578 F.2d 389 (D.C. Cir. 1978); *see also* http://www.earthjustice.org/news/documents/5-03/borderdecision.pdf and http://www.earthjustice.org/news/display.html?ID=594.
[103] *See, e.g., Environmental Defense v. Massey*, 986 F.2d 528 (D.C. Cir. 1993), discussed *infra*.

country that has not provided its consent to the action occurring within its jurisdiction.

Environmental Defense Fund v. Massey,[104] was an important case in which the court was persuaded to overcome the presumption against extraterritorial application.[105] *Massey* involved the application of NEPA to federal activities in Antarctica. On one level, *Massey* may be interpreted as concluding that the presumption against extraterritorial application does not apply when the federal agency activities occur outside of sovereign territory in an area of the global commons. Alternatively, it may be read more broadly as concluding that, because NEPA applies to federal agency decision making, if the decision-making processes for the agency action occur within the United States, extraterritorial application is not even at issue. This headquarters theory of *Massey*, however, may have been somewhat negatively affected by a subsequent decision of the U.S. District Court for the District of Columbia.[106]

Also helpful is the U.S. Court of Appeals for the Eighth Circuit decision in *Defenders of Wildlife v. Massey*[107] in which the court held that the consultation requirements of the Endangered Species Act did apply to federal projects in foreign countries. Although reversed by the United States Supreme Court for the plaintiffs' lack of standing, the Supreme Court did not specifically address the extraterritoriality issue.[108]

b. Claims that an Agency Action, Finding or Conclusion Made Pursuant to Any Other U.S. Federal Environmental Law *Except NEPA* Was Arbitrary, Capricious and/or an Abuse of Agency Discretion

This approach involves a core APA challenge against agency decisions that adversely impact the environment abroad. The same jurisprudence about the presumption against extraterritorial application of the federal environment law in question—Clean Air Act, Endangered Species Act, National Historic Preservation Act,—would apply. Again, consult the List of Practitioner Experts for further assistance with this approach.

---

[104] 986 F.2d 528 (D.C. Cir. 1993).
[105] *Id.*
[106] See *NEPA Coalition of Japan v. Aspin*, 837 F. Supp. 466 (D.D.C. 1993). With respect to NEPA actions specifically, reference should also be made to Executive Order 12114 (Jan. 1979) setting forth its own requirements for environmental impact analysis of federal agency actions with extraterritorial environmental impacts. The Order itself states that it creates no enforceable cause of action.
[107] 911 F.2d 117 (8th Cir. 1990).
[108] *Lujan v. Defenders of Wildlife*, 504 U.S. 555 (1992).

One clever use of this strategy, undertaken by Earthjustice on behalf of several non-state actors, is the use of equivalency provision in the National Historical Preservation Act, 16 U.S.C. §§ 470 et seq. ("NHPA") to protect endangered species.[109] Generally speaking, pursuant to the NHPA, the U.S. Secretary of the Interior maintains a National Register of Historic Places. Section 402 of the NHPA, 16 U.S.C. § 470a-2, pertains to international federal activities affecting historic properties and provides that:

> Prior to the approval of any Federal undertaking outside the United States which may directly and adversely affect a property which is on the World Heritage List or on the applicable country's equivalent of the National Register, the head of a Federal agency having direct or indirect jurisdiction over such undertaking shall take into account the effect of the undertaking on such property for purposes of avoiding or mitigating any adverse effects.

Consequently, where the World Heritage List or an "applicable country's equivalent of the National Register" includes a natural place or species, one could apply the Administrative Procedure Act to this provision and challenge any U.S. agency acting abroad in a manner that fails to avoid or mitigate adverse effects of such property.

6.5 Dugong

In March 2005, the United States District Court for the Northern District of California decided that the National Historic Preservation Act (NHPA) could be applied to a Department of Defense airbase building project in Okinawa, Japan. The project threatens the last remaining habitat of the dugong, a marine mammal protected as a cultural monument in Japan.[110] The dugong were listed as a "National Monument" under Japan's Cultural Properties Protection Law. Therefore, under the equivalency standard of the NHPA, plaintiffs argued that the dugong were protected under the NHPA.[111] The dugong are considered a significant part of native Okinawan culture and tradition. In Japanese mythology, the dugong were revered as a creature similar to a mermaid or siren that brought helpful warnings of impending tsunamis.[112] The proposed airbase threatens the coral reefs along Okinawa's northeast coast where the dugong graze.[113] Under the NHPA, the Department

---

[109] See http://www.earthjustice.org/urgent/display.html?ID=154.
[110] Dugong v. Rumsfeld, 2005 U.S. Dist. LEXIS 3123 (N.D. Ca. 2005).
[111] Id.
[112] The Dugongs vs. The Department of Defense, Earthjustice Backgrounder (Apr. 26, 2005), available at http://www.earthjustice.org/backgrounder/print.html?ID=103 (last visited Jun. 25, 2005).
[113] Id.

6.5 Dugong (continued)

of Defense would have to ensure protection on the dugong habitat and avoid death or serious injury to the dugong.[114]

The Department of Defense argued that the Japanese register protecting the dugong did not meet the NHPA's requirement of equivalency and filed for summary judgment. The court disagreed, finding that the registers need only correspond or have identical effects.[115] The court dismissed the Department of Defense's motion for summary judgment and as a result the Department of Defense must conduct a public assessment of the impact of the airbase construction on the dugong habitat.[116] The key question in the assessment is whether building the proposed airbase would adversely affect the dugong habitat. The Department of Defense will have to consult with Japanese environmentalists and cultural officials in a completely public process before any further construction on the airbase. The discovery phase should determine whether the proposed building site actually provides an active habitat for the dugong.[117]

6.6 Australian Bluefin Tuna Fishing Challenge

Following an announcement in December 2004 by Australian Environment Minister Ian Campbell that fishing bluefin tuna complies with the definition of an approved trade under the Environment Protection and Biodiversity Conservation Act of 1999 (EPBC Act) of Australia, the Human Society International (HIS) began petitioning for review of the declaration of the Administrative Appeals Tribunal. The HIS contended that in order for a trade to be approved under the EPBC Act, the minister must be able to show that the trade will not endanger the survival or conservation status of the species involved. Before Campbell's declaration, the Department of Environment and Heritage (DEH) issued an assessment of the bluefin tuna spawning stock, indicating it had become "severely depleted." The assessment, however, also indicated that reduction of fishing by Australia alone would not be enough because other nations in the region, including Japan, Korea, and Taiwan, would simply add Australia's allocation to their own stocks. The Tribunal, which can overturn the minister's declaration, met with both parties on May 25, 2005 for a preliminary conference. The Tribunal is likely to hear the case before the end of the year.[118]

---

[114] *Complaint, Dugong v. Rumsfeld*, Civil Action No, C-03-4350 (MHP), *available at* http://www.earthjustice.org/news/documents/11-03/03_11_24_AMENDED_DUGONG_COMPLAINT.pdf (last visited Jun. 8, 2005).

[115] Dugong, *supra* at note 112, at 22.

[116] Press Release, Judge Rules US Defense Department Must Consider Fate of Okinawan Dugong (Mar. 2, 2005), *available at* http://www.earthjustice.org/news/display.html?ID=964 (last visited Jun. 20, 2005).

[117] Stephen Getlein, Natural Resources Manager for the Marine Corps Base Camp Butler in Okinawa, claims that dugong have not been sighted for years in the proposed building site area. Dugong, *supra* at note 112, at 61.

[118] *Australia's Decision to Continue Fishing of Tuna Challenged by Environmental Group*, 28 INT'L ENV'T REP. (BNA) No. 11, at 386 (June 1, 2005).

3. Citizen Suit Provisions

The other mechanism apart from the APA by which the United States has waived its sovereign immunity with respect to environmental litigation are the various citizen suits provisions in each of the major federal environmental laws aside from NEPA (*i.e.*, Comprehensive Environmental Response, Compensation and Liability Act, Resource Conservation and Recovery Act, Clean Water Act, Clean Air Act, and Endangered Species Act, etc.).[119] Among other things, these provisions allow citizens and citizen groups like NGOs to bring suit against the United States for violating the particular environmental law, or to bring suit against the specific agency responsible for implementing and enforcing the particular environmental law for failing to comply with a mandatory duty under that particular environmental law. However, because such an action once again rests on whether the environmental law allegedly violated was intended by Congress to apply extraterritorially, the court will likely undertake the same assessment as was done in *Massey*.

A similar mechanism exists in Scandinavia. On October 5, 1976, the landmark citizen-suit protections of the Convention on the Protection of the Environment between Denmark, Finland, Norway, and Sweden[120] entered into force. The Nordic Convention allows for private enforcement within national courts by any person in one of the contracting states—Denmark, Finland, Norway, and Sweden—who is or may be affected by a nuisance caused by environmentally harmful activities in another contracting state.[121] Affected persons in a contracting state have the right to question the permissibility of the harmful activities occurring in another contracting state before the latter state's appropriate Court of Administrative Authority.[122] In addition to questioning the harmful activities' permissibility, affected persons may also raise questions on measures to prevent damage and may appeal the Court of Administrative Authority's decision to the same extent and on the same terms as a legal entity of the state where the harmful activities are occurring.[123]

---

[119] *See, e.g.*, Section 505 of the Clean Water Act, 33 U.S.C. § 1365.
[120] Feb. 19, 1974, 1092 U.N.T.S. 279 [hereinafter Nordic Convention].
[121] Nordic Convention, *supra* note 120, art. III, 1092 U.N.T.S. at 592.
[122] *Id.*
[123] *Id.*

6.7 Teck Cominco

Relying on the citizen suit provision of the Comprehensive Environmental Response, Compensation, and Liability Act (CERCLA), a suit was brought against Teck Cominco, the owners of a lead and zinc smelter ten miles north of the U.S.-Canadian border. The smelter deposited smelting by-product into some of Washington's bodies of water.[124] The court was asked to enforce the fines and penalties imposed on Teck Cominco by the U.S. Environmental Protection Agency. Teck Cominco claimed that it is not subject to CERCLA and that the U.S. district court had no jurisdiction. The district court for the Eastern District of Washington denied the motion to dismiss, stating that the U.S. presumption against extraterritoriality "does not apply where conduct in a foreign country produces adverse effects within the United States."[125] The court also found that: "[b]ecause the fundamental purpose of CERCLA is to ensure the integrity of the domestic environment, we expect that Congress intended to proscribe conduct associated with the degradation of the environment, regardless of the location of the agents."[126]

6.8 Ballast Water

On March 31, 2005 the United States District Court for the Northern District of California struck down an EPA regulation exempting ship ballast water from discharge permits in U.S. ports.[127] The court held that the EPA acted outside its authority in creating the exemptions and the EPA was ordered to repeal the regulations codified in 40 C.F.R. § 122.3 (a). The ruling further requires that all ship owners and operators follow the National Pollutant Discharge Elimination System or accept penalties under the Clean Water Act.[128]

Several environmental groups filed the lawsuit in 2003. Discharge of ballast water can introduce foreign aquatic species into U.S. waters, which in turn can destroy native aquatic species and habitats. Plaintiffs introduced evidence reporting the annual discharge of ballast water at over 21 billion

(continued)

---

[124] See Nicholas K. Gernaios, *Teck Cominco Seeks Dismissal of Suit over Pollution in Lake Roosevelt* (Aug. 27, 2004), *available at* http://seattlepi.nwsource.com/local/ 188145_roosevelt27.html (last visited Feb. 27, 2005).

[125] *Id.* at *17.

[126] *Pakootas v. Tech Cominco Metals, Ltd.*, 2004 U.S. Dist. LEXIS 23041 at *51 (EDNY 2004).

[127] *Northwest Environmental Advocates v. EPA*, N.D. Cal., No. 03-05760 SI, (Mar. 31, 2005).

[128] *U.S. Court Orders EPA to Regulate Ballast Water from Ships in U.S. Ports*, 28 INT'L ENV'T REP. (BNA) No. 7, at 215 (April 6, 2005).

276 • Defending the Environment

> **6.8 Ballast Water** *(continued)*
>
> gallons per year. In forming its decision, the court relied on the language of the Clean Water Act, which prohibits the "discharge of any pollutant except as authorized by an NPDES permit."[129] The court further indicated that for the purposes of the Clean Water Act, a ship could be considered a source of pollution and biological materials could be considered pollutants.[130]

C. Court Action to Demand Transparency on Domestic Actions Affecting the Environment Abroad

One of the non-litigation strategies outlined above suggested requesting documents from government agencies in an effort to increase transparency. Because of the cutting-edge nature of the documents that civil society is likely to request, many government agencies will rely upon exceptions under the Freedom of Information Act to withhold documents.

Should the government not provide requested trade and investment information, non-state actors should contemplate filing a court action *with the assistance of legal counsel*. The U.S. Freedom of Information Act provides the party requesting information from the government with a right of action against the government agency that either fails to respond within the required amount of time or that withholds information.[131] The government has several defenses and exceptions available to it in such actions which, at times, may be open to interpretation by the court.

In December 2002, the U.S. District Court for the District of Columbia rendered its opinion in *Center for International Environmental Law, et al. v. Office of the United States Trade Representative*.[132] CIEL, along with two other non-profit groups, filed suit under the FOIA against the Office of the U.S. Trade Representative and Robert B. Zoellick, in his official capacity, for wrongfully withholding information relating to the U.S.-Chile Free Trade Agreement negotiations. The court refused to dismiss Zoellick over the defendant's claim that the FOIA precludes suits against individuals acting in their official capacities.

The court declared that the FOIA requires public disclosure of agency records unless the requested records fall within one or more of nine carefully structured statutory exemptions.[133] The agency bears the burden of demonstrating that either the document is unidentifiable, has been pro-

---

[129] *Id.*
[130] *Id.*
[131] *See* 5 U.S.C. § 552(a)(4).
[132] Civil Action No. 01-2350 (PLF).
[133] *Id.*

duced as per the request, or is exempted by the FOIA. In *CIEL v. USTR*, the USTR withheld documents produced by or shared with Chile during the FTA negotiations under Exemption 5, which excludes "inter-agency or intra-agency memorandums or letters which would not be available by law to a party other than an agency in litigation with the agency."[134] The court rejected the USTR's characterization of Chile as a mutually benefitted partner or outside consultant whose communications are protected as inter-agency, and ordered the documents withheld under this exemption released.

USTR also withheld documents under Exemption 1, which protects records that are "(A) specifically authorized under criteria established by an Executive order to be kept secret in the interest of national defense or foreign policy and (B) are in fact properly classified pursuant to such Executive order."[135] The court gave "substantial weight" to affidavits given by the USTR in determining that the documents fit the requirements of Exemption 1 after finding the affidavits were reasonably specific in detail. Documents withheld under Exemption 1 were found properly withheld.

Finally, CIEL claimed USTR waived the right to withhold certain documents by publicly releasing similar information. The court found CIEL failed to demonstrate with sufficient specificity the nature of the information released to the public and withheld, and so dismissed that particular claim.

CIEL's partial success in enjoining USTR's withholding is enhanced by at least two more effective results:

- press coverage;[136] and
- a specific example for future campaigns about the lack of transparency in globalization decision-making processes by the U.S. government.

D. Court Action to Assure Environmental Representation on Federal Advisory Committee Act

Section 5(b)(2) of the Federal Advisory Committee Act ("FACA"),[137] requires that the membership on trade advisory committees be "fairly balanced in terms of the points of view represented and the functions to be performed." Consequently, whenever the scope of the above trade advisory committees includes programs or activities that could directly or indirectly

---

[134] 5 U.S.C. § 522(b)(5).
[135] 5 U.S.C. § 522(b)(1).
[136] *See* Nora Boustany, *Diplomatic Dispatches: U.N.'s Opportunity to Make Peace in Congo*, THE WASH. POST, Mar. 9, 2001, at A21; Doug Palmer, *U.S. Green Group Sues USTR for Trade Talk Papers*, REUTERS NEWS SERVICE, Mar. 7, 2001, *available at* http://www.globalexchange.org/campaign/ftaa/news2001/reuterso30701.html; Campion Walsh, *Green Groups Sue for Disclosure on US-Chile Trade Talks*, WALL ST. J. Nov. 9, 2001.
[137] 5 U.S.C. App. 1.

impact the environment, non-state actors can and should request that environmentalists be included on these committees pursuant to this fair balance requirement.

The Administrative Procedure Act[138] provides a non-state actor told by the government that he or she cannot participate on an advisory committee with a private right of action to counter the government's decision on grounds that it is arbitrary and capricious or otherwise did not accord with the law which, in this case, would be the "fair balance" requirement.

To date, two federal court actions have been filed concerning the appointment of environmentalists to trade advisory committees.[139] In the *Northwest Ecosystems Alliance* case, environmentalists took issue with the USTR's decision not to allow them to sit on either the Industry Sector Advisory Committee for Lumber and Wood or the Industry Sector Advisory Committee for Paper and Paper Products. In *Washington Toxic Coalition, et al.*, members of the advisory committee took issue with the USTR's decision to allow environmentalists to sit on the Industry Sector Advisory Committee for Chemicals and Allied Products. In both cases, the environmentalists have prevailed and current membership on the committees is required to include them.

E. General Litigation Obstacles

Although domestic courts are particularly suited to enforce international environmental law because of their authority over the assets of the most common polluters, corporations and individuals, significant obstacles stand in the way of enforcement. These obstacles are addressed only briefly, because ultimately the difficulties they pose are very fact-specific.

In *British Columbia v. Canadian Forest Products Ltd.*, Canada's Supreme Court allowed provincial governments to bring suits against companies causing environmental damage by stating, "it is open to the Crown in a proper case to take action as *parens patriae*, for compensation and injunctive relief on account of public nuisance or negligence causing environmental damage to public lands."[140] Because the Crown brought its claim as a "landowner of a tract of forest" rather than as a trustee of a public good, and likewise failed to present evidence quantifying environmental damage, the Court restored the decision of the trial court, which had "rejected

---

[138] 5 U.S.C. §§ 701 *et seq.*

[139] *Northwest Ecosystems Alliance v. USTR*, Civ. No. C99-1165R (W.D. Wa. 1999); *Washington Toxics Coalition, et al. v. Office of the United States Trade Representative*, Civ. No. C00-0730R (W.D. Wa. 2001).

[140] *British Columbia v. Canadian Forest Products Ltd.*, 2 S.C.R. 74 (2004), *available at* http://www.lexum.umontreal.ca/csc-scc/en/pub/2004/vol2/html/2004scr2_0074.html (last visited Mar. 2, 2005).

the Crown's claim for financial compensation for 'environmental loss' on the facts of this case."[141] Unfortunately, however, these limitations—some jurisdictional, others discretionary—often provide all the reason a judge needs to avoid deciding a controversial, highly politicized case.

Sovereign immunity ensures that a state will not be subjected to the courts of another co-equal state. This doctrine is not as broadly protective as it once was.[142] Foreign states or officials are generally not protected for commercial acts or torts.[143] Subject to certain exceptions contained in the language of the Act, the Foreign Sovereign Immunities Act ("FSIA") immunizes foreign states from the jurisdiction of United States courts. FSIA defines "foreign state" as an "agent or instrumentality" of a foreign sovereign. Questions arise, however, as to whether an individual official qualifies as an "agent or instrumentality." In *Trajano v. Marcos*,[144] the court found that the FSIA may exclude individual officials from the immunity. Although this finding is consistent with *Filartiga v. Pena-Irala*, the court in *Trajano* modified it by claiming it would extend immunity to an individual acting within his official capacity and not exceeding the scope of his authority.[145] In *Hilao v. Estate of Marcos*, the court found that Marcos' acts of torture were not within his official mandate, nor were they governmental or public acts, and therefore could not be considered acts of a state for the purposes of sovereign immunity.[146] As one commentator has suggested, "It is not a stretch to assert that domestic courts are just as capable of holding foreign sovereigns to international law as the sovereign's own courts."[147]

The APA is useful in overcoming immunity in that it provides an immunity waiver, allowing suits against the United States.[148] Plaintiffs in *Rosner v. United States* invoked this waiver to apply property laws to U.S. military actions in Austria at the close of World War II.[149] Plaintiffs' property was originally confiscated in Hungary by the Nazis and shipped to Germany on what is known as the "Gold Train."[150] American soldiers intercepted the train in Austria and held it there for several months before determin-

---

[141] *Id.*
[142] Mary Ellen O'Connell, *Symposium; Enforcement and the Success of International Environmental Law*, 3 IND. J. GLOBAL LEGAL STUD. 47 (1995).
[143] *See* The Foreign Service Immunity Act of 1976, 28 U.S.C. §§ 1330, 1602-11.
[144] 978 F.2d 493 (9th Cir. 1992).
[145] *See* Michelle M. Meloni, *Regional Report: The Alien Tort Claims Act: A Mechanism for Alien Plaintiffs to Hold Their Foreign Nations Liable for Tortious Conduct*, 5 DETROIT C.L.J. INT'L L. & PRAC., 349 (1996).
[146] *Hilao*, at 1469-73.
[147] O'Connell, *supra* note 76, at 60.
[148] *See* 5 U.S.C. § 702.
[149] *Rosner v. United States*, 231 F. Supp. 2d 1202, 1211 (2002).
[150] *See id.* at 1204-1205.

ing that ownership could not be restored; the property was subsequently sold, distributed, and/or requisitioned.[151] The court ruled that if plaintiffs can prove that the military action was not during a time of war and thus not protected under the APA's military-authority exception, plaintiffs were entitled to a full accounting and return of their property.[152]

Standing poses another obstacle to domestic enforcement. The United States Supreme Court addresses standing under the U.S. Constitution's Article III requirement that the Court may only decide a "case or controversy."[153] The Court has determined that, for citizens bringing environmental suits, the constitution requires: (1) an injury in fact (actual or imminent), (2) a causal connection between the injury and the alleged conduct, and (3) that the Court's decision could offer relief or redress.[154] "Injury in fact" has been defined by the Court to include recreational or aesthetic damage along with traditional economic or physical damage, although "[i]t requires that the party seeking review be himself among the injured."[155]

A court must also examine the standing of parties in relation to the environmental law at issue.[156] While "most [domestic] environmental laws include broad statutes granting jurisdictional standing to sue within their citizen suit provisions,"[157] often courts find persons are not injured by a violation of *international* law.[158] Many courts find that in order for an international law to be the basis of a cause of action, the cause must be clearly implied,[159] or even explicit, as seen in *Beanal* and *Flores*.[160]

Forum non conveniens allows courts to dismiss suits for being inconvenient to that forum. Many courts find suits "inconvenient" because they

---

[151] See *id.* at 1205.

[152] See *id.* at 1212, 1218.

[153] See *Lujan v. Defenders of Wildlife*, 504 U.S. 555 (1992). In *Lujan*, an environmental group challenged a statute that failed to include certain extraterritorial applications of the Endangered Species Act, discussed in II1., *supra*.

[154] 504 U.S. 555, at 560–61.

[155] See *Sierra Club v. Morton*, 405 U.S. 727, at 734–35 (1972).

[156] Michael I. Jeffery, *Intervenor Funding as the Key to Effective Citizen Participation in Environmental Decision-Making: Putting the People Back into the Picture*, 19 ARIZ. J. INT'L & COMP. L. 643, (2002).

[157] *Id.* at 654.

[158] O'Connell, *supra* note, at 81. See also Johanna Rinceanu, *Enforcement Mechanisms in International Environmental Law: Quo Vadunt? Homo Sanus In Natura Sana*, 15 J. ENVTL. L. & LITIG. 147 (2000).

[159] *Id.* O'Connell also gives the example of *Committee of U.S. Citizen Living in Nicaragua v. Reagan*, 859 F.2d 929 (D.C. Cir. 1988) (holding the group had no cause of action to enforce judgments of the ICJ with which Reagan failed to comply by ordering military interference in Nicaragua).

[160] *Beanal v. Freeport-McMoran, Inc.*, 197 F.3d 161 (5th Cir. 1999); *Flores v. Southern Peru Copper Corporation*, 343 F.3d 140 (2d Cir. 2003).

include application of international law, which is often not the law usually applied by the court.[161] Furthermore, many courts refuse to decide cases involving what they deem to be "political questions" or matters touching on foreign affairs.[162] In *Hilao*, however, the court refused to dismiss the case on *forum non conveniens* grounds because the Marcos family held assets in the U.S.[163]

In *Aguinda v. Texaco, Inc.*,[164] the Second Circuit dismissed a class action suit brought by citizens of Ecuador and Peru claiming the oil company damaged the environment and caused personal injuries by polluting the rainforests and rivers. The court in *Aguinda* dismissed partly on grounds of *forum non conveniens*, finding Texaco had adequately demonstrated "(1) that there exists an adequate alternative forum, and (2) that the ordinarily strong presumption favoring the plaintiff's chosen forum is overcome by a balance of the relevant factors of private and public interest weighing heavily in favor of the alternative forum."[165] *Aguinda* stands as an example of the uphill battle many environmental plaintiffs face when filing a suit in a domestic court concerning injuries inflicted abroad by domestic companies.

A decision out of the Northern District of California, however, provides some useful arguments against dismissal on *forum non conveniens* grounds, positing that such claims against domestic companies are particularly suitable for resolution by its own domestic courts, despite the extraterritorial nature of the injury. In May 1999, several Nigerian citizens brought suit against the Chevron Corporation of California claiming that human rights abuses resulted from the response by Chevron and the Nigerian military to an effort of local residents to protect the environment and human health. The plaintiffs allege that Chevron provided helicopter, boat, and personnel support and paid the Nigerian military to violently attack the peaceful occupation of an offshore oil rig by local residents in May 1998. The attack killed two protestors and injured hundreds of others. The protestors were demanding that Chevron meet with community leaders to discuss the destruction of the delta environment caused by oil exploitation activities. The plaintiffs are seeking damages and injunctive relief under the Alien Tort Claims Act[166] and under California state law.

On June 16, 2000, Judge Charles Legge of the U.S. District Court for the Northern District of California denied Chevron's *forum non conve-*

---

[161] O'Connell, *supra* note 75, at 69.
[162] *Id.*
[163] *Id.* at 63.
[164] 142 F. Supp. 2d 534 (2001).
[165] *Id.* at 538 (2001).
[166] 28 U.S.C. § 1350.

niens motion and ordered discovery to proceed.[167] Using the reasons for his decision in two earlier bench rulings on April 7, 2000, and May 12, 2000, Judge Legge found that "there are at least two categories of allegations here that do fall within the norms of international law, and that is the torture and summary execution and the prolonged arbitrary detention."[168] He emphasized California has an interest in "regulating the conduct of corporations that are headquartered here, even if the conduct of the corporations . . . is overseas."[169] On June 16, 2000, Judge Legge filed a written order denying Chevron's motion to dismiss, and also granted the plaintiffs' request to file a newly amended complaint. The case is now in discovery.

Plaintiffs invoke the APA in many of these cases to establish their right to review of "final agency action" for which there is no other adequate remedy.[170] The right to this review allows a plaintiff to challenge activities occurring abroad when those activities are the result of final agency action; however, it is difficult to determine that an action is final, and cases are often dismissed for lack of ripeness. For instance, in *Sabella v. United States*,[171] plaintiffs sought injunctive relief preventing enforcement of an International Dolphin Conservation Act ("IDCA") provision banning the use of purse seine nets on vessels operated by persons subject to U.S. jurisdiction.[172] Plaintiffs claimed jurisdiction under the APA on the grounds that a letter from the National Oceanic and Atmospheric Administration's General Counsel stating the probability of the IDCA's application to the vessel in question was a final agency action.[173] The court determined that the letter was not a "final" action,[174] yet the extraterritorial application of the IDCA would likely have come under the court's jurisdiction otherwise.

Should final agency action be established, there are numerous other obstacles to extraterritorial application of environmental laws. Most often, foreign policy considerations will prevent a court from granting relief in an APA case. For instance, the court in *Hirt v. Richardson*[175] determined

---

[167] *Bowoto v. Chevron*, No. C-99-2506 (N.D. Cal. June 16, 2000) (order denying defendant's motion to dismiss; granting in part and denying in part plaintiffs' motion to amend; and denying defendant's countermotion for sanctions).

[168] Transcript of Proceedings at 9:12-15, *Bowoto v. Chevron*, No. C-99-2506 (N.D. Cal. May 12, 2000).

[169] Transcript of Proceedings at 12:17-19, *Bowoto v. Chevron*, No. C-99-2506 (N.D. Cal. Apr. 7, 2000).

[170] 5 U.S.C. § 704.
[171] 863 F. Supp. 1 (1994).
[172] *See id.* at 2.
[173] *See id.* at 3.
[174] *See id.* at 5.
[175] 127 F. Supp. 2d 833 (1999).

that while "the facts in this case warrant extraterritorial application of NEPA,"[176] the delicate nature of foreign relations between the United States and Russia precluded such relief.[177] While extraterritorial application of environmental law is often unsuccessful, the APA has been the basis for review and extraterritorial application of various American property and constitutional laws for both its review provision and waiver of U.S. sovereign immunity.

Under the APA, if plaintiffs establish any final agency action, the court may then strike down such actions that are found to be "an abuse of discretion" or "in excess of statutory jurisdiction, authority, or limitations."[178] In *Haitian Centers Council, INC. v. Sale*,[179] plaintiffs claimed deprivation of due process and invoked the APA to review the Attorney General's screening and detainment of HIV-positive Haitians on Guantanamo Bay Naval Base in Cuba. The court reasoned that plaintiffs, "as persons 'adversely effected or aggrieved by agency action' . . . have a cause of action under the APA."[180] The court found the Attorney General's actions pursuant to the Immigration and Nationality Act an abuse of discretion under the APA and held unlawful her decision not to parole the Haitian detainees.[181] The court further affirmed the right to apply the Constitution extraterritorially in Guantanamo Bay.[182]

IV. NEWLY INDEPENDENT STATES

After the fall of the Soviet Union, the newly independent states ("NIS") and areas of Eastern Europe realized many challenges faced the enforcement of environmental laws in those regions. Newly formed environmental groups, referred to as public interest environmental law organizations ("PIELOs"), have approach the problems in a two-fold manner, through legislation and litigation.

When creating their new constitutions, many of the NIS countries included general rights to access to information, public participation in decision-making, and access to justice.[183] Many NIS countries have legislation specifically dealing with access to environmental information, but governments are less than forthcoming with information and often claim

---

[176] *Id.* at 844.
[177] *See id.* at 849.
[178] 5 U.S.C. § 706(2)(A).
[179] 823 F. Supp. 1028 (1993).
[180] *Id.* at 1046, *quoting* 5 U.S.C. § 702.
[181] *See id.* at 1049–50.
[182] *See id.* at 1040–42.
[183] Svitlana Kravchenko, *New Laws on Public Participation in the Newly Independent States*, in Donald Zillman, Alastair R. Lucas and George (Rock) Pring, eds., HUMAN RIGHTS IN NATIONAL RESOURCES DEVELOPMENT (Oxford University Press, 2002).

the information constitutes state secrets. Some NIS countries have tried to combat this problem by creating laws about the dispersal of environmental information or obligations of state authorities to provide information.[184]

Lawmaking on public participation is another gray area in NIS countries. One of the most powerful ways to encourage public participation is through environmental impact assessments ("EIAs"), which are necessary to gain licensing in any commercial enterprise.[185] In NIS countries, however, EIAs are the responsibility of the developer and the government later reviews the information before final approval is given. The same problem exist with EIAs as with access to information—no dissemination of information to the public and no checks on the government.

Public interest lawyers in Eastern European countries have also tried legislative techniques such as participating in law-drafting, but many activities in Eastern Europe are focused on educating those people already in the legal system. Activities include: clinical programs for judges, prosecutors, and organizations; conferences and networking for environmental public interest lawyers; publications and libraries; and building an international framework for support.[186]

Although access of justice has become more available in NIS countries, citizens and NGOs cannot sue the government in criminal courts, only in civil courts, arbitration or special economic courts. Many organizations in Eastern Europe and NIS countries are modeled after United States environmental NGOs and the key purpose of these organizations is to bring lawsuits against the government or corporations on behalf of citizens or environmental organizations.[187] Most lawsuits have focused on five areas of environmental law: (1) cases involving environmental impact assessments (EIAs); (2) cases involving access to information; (3) cases involving the right to a safe or healthy environment; (4) cases involving compensation for damages;[188] (5) cases defending violations of environmental human rights.[189] Although the PIELOs have been successful in the court system, there are many challenges to successful litigation, including Strategic Lawsuits against Public Participation ("SLAPPs"), which usually involve gov-

---

[183] Svitlana Kravchenko, *New Laws on Public Participation in the Newly Independent States,* in Donald Zillman, Alastair R. Lucas and George (Rock) Pring, eds., HUMAN RIGHTS IN NATIONAL RESOURCES DEVELOPMENT (Oxford University Press, 2002).

[184] *Id.* at 477–478.

[185] *Id.* at 487.

[186] Svitlana Kravchenko, *Citizen Enforcement of Environmental Law in Eastern Euorpe,* 10 WIDENER L. REV. 475, 492–498 (2004).

[187] *Id.* at 477.

[188] Under a civil law system, damages are usually called "moral damages" and are similar to what, under common law, would be considered damages for pain and suffering. *Id.* at 486.

[189] *Id.* at 479.

ernment lawsuits against environmental whistleblowers, intimidation techniques by governments or corporations, and lack of financial support.[190] In most Eastern European and NIS countries, the party who loses the lawsuit must pay all court costs, therefore it can be very expensive to bring high-profile environmental lawsuits, especially if the outcome is uncertain. PIELOs also gain most of their funding from foreign donors as many domestic donors are unreliable or their money comes from questionable means.[191]

One of the most powerful remedies available, however, is injunctive relief and one of the most effective litigation techniques in this area of the world is to ask the courts for a prohibition against actions that are harmful to the environment and health or an order to stop all activities currently taking place that may be harmful to the environment or health. Even injunctive relief can be difficult for the plaintiff monetarily due to a court obligation forcing the plaintiff to reimburse the defendant for monies lost during the injunctive period.[192]

V. CONCLUSION

This final chapter brings the environmental advocate back full circle to the first chapter, suggesting how litigation and non-litigation strategies should incorporate international and domestic remedies. As noted in Chapter 1, a valid environmental human rights claim before the UN or regional systems requires a specific act or omission by a nation-state, that results in or contributes to environmental degradation. Examples include, but once again are hardly limited to, the granting of permits to emit air pollutants and discharge hazardous waste, the allowance of or failure to prevent ecosystem destruction, especially from development and extraction projects that often result in air, water, soil and/or ecosystem destruction, the forbiddance of, or affirmative efforts to, combat protests against environmental degradation, and the provision of military or other support to safeguard an activity giving rise to environmental harm. Such environmental claims linked to human rights have the advantage of a number of international fora for human rights which may be utilized, but the drawbacks of being limited to violations by nation-states and limited enforceability. One alternative is the possibility of a complaint in United States federal court pursuant to the Alien Tort Claims Act to hold non-state actors accountable. Domestic remedies generally provide more of an opportunity for binding injunctive, declaratory, and compensatory relief than most international fora. The drawbacks to domestic remedies are the often significant barriers to domestic jurisdiction over international environmental claims. When

---

[190] *Id.* at 487–502.
[191] *Id.* at 499–501.
[192] Kravchenko, "New Laws," *supra* note 121.1, at 494.

these barriers preclude domestic judicial remedies, other non-litigation strategies may be available for domestic initiatives, and the usefulness of intranational fora should be reassessed.

On June 10, 2005, Spain announced that it would create a special court for prosecuting environmental crimes and appoint a special prosecutor to bring such cases. The legislation would allow Spain's Director of Public Prosecutions to appoint a special public prosecutor for environmental cases, similar to those Spain already has for terrorism, corruption, and domestic violence. The environmental prosecutor will also cooperate with the national police Special Protection Service and other law enforcement officials as needed. The legislation is expected to go into effect in 2006.[193]

6.9 Canada—Use of Land Claimed by Aboriginal Peoples

Canada's Supreme Court is protecting the rights of indigenous people by requiring that provincial governments must consult with them about the use of their traditional territory even if no title has been recognized.[194] In one case, the Court held that the Haida Nation was not adequately consulted before issuing a timber license.[195] In another, the Court held that there should have been a consultation before the reopening of a mining road was approved.[196] The Court stated: "The duty to consult and accommodate is part of a process of fair dealing and reconciliation that begins with the assertion of sovereignty and continues beyond formal claims resolution. The foundation of the duty in the Crown's honour and the goal of reconciliation suggest that the duty arises when the Crown has knowledge, real or constructive, of the potential existence of the Aboriginal right or title and contemplates conduct that might adversely affect it."[197] The Court's ruling does not apply to private companies,[198] and only consultation is necessary.[199]

---

[193] Brett Allan King, *Spanish Legislation Would Designate Specialized Environmental Prosecutor*, 28 INT'L ENVT'L RPTR. (BNA) 402-03 (June 15, 2005).

[194] *See* Canada's Supreme Court sides with First Nations (Nov. 19, 2004), *available at* http://www.indianz.com/News/2004/005438.asp (last visited Feb. 28, 2005).

[195] *Id.*

[196] *Id.*

[197] *Haida Nation v. British Columbia (Minister of Forests)*, 2004 SCC 73 (Nov. 18, 2004), *available at* http://www.lexum.umontreal.ca/csc-scc/en/rec/html/2004scc073.wpd.html (last visited Feb. 28, 2005).

[198] *See* Canada's Supreme Court sides with First Nations, *supra*, n. 1.

[199] *Id.*

Domestic strategies may yet be the most valuable and viable alternative to international ones for holding accountable a non-state actor acting under the auspices of or in collusion with a state. The recent decision in *Beanal* and *Flores* and the rehearing in *Unocal* suggest, however, that a human right to an adequate environment will not be cognizable under the ATCA unless other, more universally and unequivocally recognized human rights are violated by the challenged actions whether those of a nation-state or nonstate actor. In most cases, this impediment can be addressed by careful reformulation of a complaint to encompass any recognized human rights violations—such as torture, forced labor, and various forms of abuse directed to identifiable, protected groups—which so often accompany such abusive environmental projects and actions.

> Traditionally international lawyers tend to regard domestic decisions as the middle-brow replication of international law, akin to the provincial production of a famous play, with its cast of awkward amateurs and bungled bits of stage business. But instead of thinking of the local production as second-rate, we might think of it as embedding the play in that time and place, and forging a bond with other productions in other times and places. Beyond this, each and every local production might be seen to change the meaning of the play.[200]

As the quote above indicates, international lawyers may view domestic mechanisms as more limited than they are, and domestic lawyers may be uncomfortable or unfamiliar with international fora and international law itself for environmental protection. This is in itself an obstacle to be overcome. Integrated, coordinated, and repetitive utilization of domestic and international fora and laws is the most effective way to compel recognition of international environmental law at all levels of authority.

---

[200] Karen Knop, *Here and There: International Law in Domestic Courts*, 32 N.Y.U. J. INT'L L. & POL. 501 (2000). The focus of this chapter is on domestic remedies in United States courts. A number of environmental treaties allow individuals to bring claims of treaty violations in national courts although such individual access is more unusual in other areas of international law. A few such treaties are the Nordic Convention, the Convention on Third Party Liability in the Field of Nuclear Energy, the Vienna Convention on Civil Liability for Nuclear Damage, and the International Convention on Civil Liability for Oil Pollution Damage.

CONCLUSION

The overriding message of this book is that there are mechanisms and strategies for effective enforcement of international environmental law by civil society. It is no longer correct to conclude that enforcement is the province of nation-states, with civil society as merely the third-party, incidental beneficiary of whatever measures states choose to take or the victim of their inaction. Individuals, community groups, NGOs, and international organizations, among others, have a pivotal role in monitoring and enforcement of the established and emerging norms, which is not dependent on state support or initiation. Recognition of the vitality and significance of this function of civil society is not only crucial but essential when it is a state or group of states that are the perpetrators of environmental degradation.

This book has set forth the most widely available and useful of these strategies and mechanisms, but due regard should also be given to national or localized fora and remedies that may also exist. Also generalities about which methods may be most effective are generalities, and the effectiveness of any particular strategy will be largely fact-dependent upon the environmental problem to be addressed. Finally, it must be stressed once again that it is important to proceed on all available fronts, with an integrated strategy that makes full use of international and domestic opportunities. Equally important, one should consult appropriate individuals in the List of Practitioner Experts on the appendix in this book when undertaking these strategies.

By way of example, the following analysis suggests some of the ways in which the strategies outlined in this book might be utilized to protect a specific habitat or species.

1. Applicable strategies from *Chapter 1: Exercising Environmental and Public Health Human Rights*.

Although linkage of environmental claims to human rights violations often provides the most prolific assortment of fora and remedies, environmental human rights strategies for protection of a non-human species and its habitat are limited. Three plausible strategies may exist. First, because protection of the species and its habitat likely falls within the scope of the scientific work of UNESCO, make a written submission to UNESCO calling on the organization to take ameliorative steps on its own or in conjunction with a government harming the species or habitat. Second, if the preservation of the species is essential to human health in any way, the matter can be brought to the attention of the UN Rapporteur on Health. Third, if any of the countries that are home to the species and its habitat thwart or punish any protesters who are in favor of protecting the species and its habitat, a petition with the UN Human Rights Committee pursuant to the International Covenant on Civil and Political Rights or the regional human rights commission for the region in which the violating country exists may be filed.

2. Applicable strategies from *Chapter 2: Advocating for International Finance and Trade Institutions to Adhere to Environmental and Public Health Standards*.

If the species or habitat is adversely affected in any way by any development project for which funding has been or will be provided by the World Bank or a regional development bank, the issue may be brought to the dispute resolution panel or ombudsmen process for the given lending institution. It is advisable to think broadly about all of the potential direct and indirect adverse affects from any given development project so that project undergoes environmental review.

If the species or habitat is harmed by the failure of the United States, Canada, and/or Mexico to enforce or implement a domestic environmental law, or by the failure of Canada or Chile to enforce or implement a domestic environmental law, there is also the option of a petition before the North American Commission on Environmental Cooperation or a petition before the Canada-Chile Commission on Environmental Cooperation, respectively.

3. Applicable strategies from *Chapter 3: Preventing New International Trade and Investment Dispute Resolution Mechanisms from Undermining Current Environmental and Public Health Regulations*.

If any trade or investment dispute is ever filed in which a government or investor challenges as a trade or investment violation any measure designed to safeguard the species or its habitat (or a measure that indirectly benefits such a species or habitat), then a request should be sent to the dispute resolution institution to appear as *amicus curiae*, including with that request a written submission.

If any trade or investment measure appears to pose a threat to a species or its habitat, advocate for a domestic government, not necessarily one's own, to file a claim before the appropriate dispute resolution body to prevent such threat from occurring.

If any new trade or investment treaties are emerging that establish provisions or operations that could harm the species or its habitat, then demand an environmental review of that trade or investment treaty and notify the government's review body of this concern. Challenge the environmental review body in court if the environmental review fails to adequately assert and address the threat to the species or its habitat.

4. Applicable strategies from *Chapter 4: Encouraging Secretariats of Multilateral Environmental and Public Health Agreements to Enforce Current International Environmental Standards.*

Compile a list of MEAs relevant to the protection of the species and its habitat. First, consult the table attached to Chapter 4 to determine if any of the listed treaties pertain to the species and its habitat. The Convention on Biological Diversity will likely apply to almost any species and its habitat. The Convention on International Trade in Endangered Species will apply if the species is threatened by trade of the species or its parts. The Convention on Migratory Species will apply if the species migrates. The Food and Agriculture Organization Constitution will apply if fisheries are involved. The United Nations Law of the Sea Convention will apply for any marine species.

Second, consult the internet for additional regional treaties and species-specific treaties not included on the table. For example, in the Americas, the Convention on Nature Protection and Wildlife Preservation in the Western Hemisphere may apply. Similarly, the International Convention for the Regulation of Whaling would apply for endangered or threatened whales.

After compiling a list of relevant treaties, use any or all of the following strategies. Send a letter petition to the secretariats of those treaties calling on the secretariats to take steps on their own or in conjunction with the violating nation-state parties to safeguard the species and its habitat. Lobby domestic governments to raise the issue with the secretariat. Ask domestic governments to commence an action before the MEA's dispute resolution process against those nation-state parties that are harming or failing to protect the species and its habitat in violation of the MEA. Become an observer to the next Conference of the Parties for the MEA and bring to the attention of attendees the threats against the species and its habitat.

5. Applicable strategies from *Chapter 5: Enforcing International Environmental Law in Tribunals of General Jurisdiction.*

Many international tribunals, including the International Court of Justice (ICJ), the Permanent Court on Arbitration, the International Criminal Court, the European Court of Justice, and the African Court of Justice can hear environmental disputes. However, their jurisdiction over parties is often limited only to nation-states. With the right strategy, non-state actors can succeed in having at least one of these bodies hear environmental claims.

While the International Court of Justice ("ICJ") may only hear cases brought by states, it can also render advisory opinions at the request of the organs and specialized agencies of the United Nations. With successful lobbying to either a national government or a U.N. body with standing

292 • Defending the Environment

to bring a claim, a NGO with sufficient resources may be able to have issues raised before the ICJ.

In the case of marine pollution, the Law of the Sea Treaty Regime ("LOS") not only creates a cause of action against governments that fail to protect the marine environment, it provides a forum for the airing of disputes—the International Tribunal for the Law of the Sea. Individuals, NGOs, corporations and international organizations may participate in LOS proceedings as parties or intervenors. In addition, it may also be possible to bring suit against offenders in domestic courts.

The International Criminal Court has jurisdiction currently over crimes against humanity, war crimes, and crimes of genocide. Because such crimes may be carried out through environmental means, states, individuals, organizations and other non-state actors that cause or permit harm to the natural environment on a massive scale could, potentially, be held criminally responsible for the effects of environmental degradation. However, since only state parties, the Security Council and the Prosecutor may bring claims before the court, non-state actors should advance proposed claims to them with the most receptive prospect for such advocacy most likely being the Prosecutor.

In addition to the courts mentioned above, the Permanent Court of Arbitration and the International Court of Environmental Arbitration and Conciliation have developed special rules to settle environmental disputes through voluntary conciliation.

6. Applicable strategies from *Chapter 6: Enforcing International Environmental Law Through Domestic Law Mechanisms*

Within the United States, interested parties have a wide range of options for influencing environmental actions by both governmental and private actors. Non-litigation strategies often entail public information campaigns, such as calling for U.S. federal agencies to comply with Executive Order 12114. In addition, submitting written requests to government agencies for information on activities impacting the environment or participating on advisory committees can mandate transparency for governmental activity. To prevent private actors from taking actions that harm the environment, interested parties should advocate for the Code of Corporate Citizenship to be adopted as part of their state's Corporation statute, creating a right of action against companies and directors for actions that negatively impact the environment, human rights, the public safety, the welfare of the communities in which the corporation operates or the dignity of its employees.

The Alien Tort Claims Act ("ATCA") provides U.S. district courts with original jurisdiction of civil actions by aliens for tortious violations of international custom and treaties of the United States. Significantly, some ATCA plaintiffs have successfully linked environmental harm and human rights violations. As seen in *Beanal* and *Flores*, however, some Circuit courts are imposing more stringent requirements for recognizing international law violations in such cases. Continued, aggressive litigation of these claims has never been important for developing this area of law.

Despite the U.S. federal courts' hesitancy to impose U.S. environmental law extraterritorially, federal court can offer an effective forum in which to hold the U.S. government accountable for environmental harms it causes outside the U.S. Although the U.S. is immune from suit in federal court unless it waives its sovereign immunity, under a "headquarters theory" of the Federal Tort Claims Act, the U.S. government is not immune from suits for acts and decisions occurring in the U.S. that have effects abroad. Thus, if decisions made in the U.S. have effects abroad, the acts (decisions) occurred in U.S. territory.

Under the Administrative Procedures Act ("APA"), plaintiffs can challenge federal government final agency actions, or force federal government agencies to take action unlawfully withheld or unreasonably delayed. However, the law remains unclear whether the underlying federal environmental laws that are the basis for the APA claim can be applied extraterritorially. The exception to this rule involves claims that the U.S. government failed to comply with the National Environmental Policy Act when the action taken abroad will adversely impact the United States, a global commons, or another sovereign country that has not provided its consent to the action occurring within its jurisdiction. As with Federal Tort Claims Act suits, if a decision having an adverse impact abroad was actually made at the agency's headquarters in the U.S., a "headquarters theory" can make the challenged action domestic, thereby avoiding the extraterritorial liability question altogether.

Most major federal environmental laws also include provisions specifically allowing citizens to bring suit against the U.S. for violating the particular environmental law, or to bring suit against the specific agency responsible for implementing and enforcing the particular environmental law for failing to perform a nondiscretionary duty.

The U.S. Freedom of Information Act ("FOIA") provides non-state actors requesting information from the government with a cause of action against the government agency that either fails to respond within the designated response time or withholds information. The agency bears the burden of demonstrating that either the document is unidentifiable, has been produced as per the request, or is exempted by the FOIA.

Whenever the scope of trade advisory committees could directly or indirectly impact the environment, non-state actors can and should request that environmental advocates be included on these committees pursuant to the "fair balance" requirement. A non-state actor told by the government that he or she cannot participate on an advisory committee has a private right of action through the Administrative Procedures Act to counter the government's decision on the grounds that it is arbitrary and capricious or did not accord with the "fair balance" requirement.

The continued dedication and commitment of civil society to environmental improvement is at a critical juncture at both the international and domestic levels. At the international level, NGOs have achieved a level of recognition that allows them to move from "behind the scenes" lobbying to formally recognized functions in a number of international fora. International and regional organizations, such as the European Union, have demonstrated a willingness to pursue environmental priorities with recalcitrant states, and the various regional human rights treaties in Africa, the Americas and Europe have codified a healthy environment as a human right. At the same time, however, a revitalization of national security as a state concern has become for other states a convenient excuse for relaxation or outright rejection of environmental protections, and diversion of national monies to military security rather than environmental security.

The detrimental impact on environmental protection of the current destabilization of international relations and its "trickle-down impact" on domestic protection is explicitly illustrated in the briefs of the United States Department of Justice in the *Unocal* case before the Ninth Circuit Court of Appeals *en banc*,[1] and even more recently as this book was going to press, in the United States' supporting petition for certiorari to the United States Supreme Court in *Alvarez-Machain v. Sosa and United States of America*.[2] In both briefs, the United States asserts that the Alien Tort Claims Act does not create a private cause of action in federal court, particularly with respect to unratified or non-self-executing treaties and General Assembly resolutions, essentially adopting the separate, concurring opinion of Judge Robert Bork in *Tel-Oren v. Libyan Arab Republic*. The United States necessarily acknowledges that its advocated limitation on the ATCA would render it "superfluous" (in other words, meaningless) given the statutory provision for federal question jurisdiction in 28 U.S.C. section 1331.[3] In the *Alvarez-Machain* brief, the United States actively seeks review by the Supreme Court to adopt the Bork view of the ATCA, despite agreement in all Circuit Court opinions addressing the issue that the ATCA creates a private cause of action, because "... the importance of the questions concerning the ATS [ATCA], and the fact that the case law discussed above substantially fleshes out the competing positions on the scope of the ATS that have been adopted by the lower courts, counsel against waiting for a more concrete

---

[1] See pages 246–247 *supra*.

[2] *Alvarez-Machain v. United States and Sosa*, 331 F.3d 604 (9th Cir. June 3, 2003). The brief for the United States in support of the petition for certiorari is *available at* http://www.usdoj.gov/asg/briefs/2003/Oresponses/2003-0339.resp.html (hereinafter cited as "Alvarez-Machain Government Brief").

[3] Brief for the United States of America as Amicus Curiae in *Doe v. Unocal*, summarized in "Department of Justice Position in *Unocal* Case," 97 A.J.I.L. 703–706 (hereinafter cited as "Government Brief in Unocal").

circuit conflict to materialize...."[4] In *Unocal*, the government's brief on appeal to the Ninth Circuit makes the following argument, later repeated with slightly different workding in the *Alvarez-Machain* brief:

> ... [T]he types of claims that are being asserted today under the ATS are fraught with policy implications. They often involve our courts in deciding suits between foreigners regarding events that occurred with the borders of other nations, and in the exercise of foreign governmental authority. The ATS has been wrongly interpreted to permit suits requiring the courts to pass factual, moral, and legal judgment on these foreign acts. And, under this Court's approach, ATS actions are not limited to rogues and outlaws. As mentioned above, such claims can easily be asserted against this Nation's friends, including our allies in our fight against terrorism. A plaintiff merely needs to accuse a defendant of, for example, arbitrary detention to support such a claim. Indeed, that approach has already permitted an alien to sue foreign nationals who assisted the United States in its conduct of international law enforcement efforts. *See Alvarez-Machain, 266 F.3d at 1051* [footnote omitted]. As noted above, this Court's approach to the ATS therefore bears serious implications for our current war against terrorism, and permits ATS claims to be asserted against our allies in that war. Notably, such claims have already been brought against the United States itself in connection with its efforts to combat terrorism. [citing *Al Odah v. United States*, 321 F. 3d 1134(D.C.Cir. 2003)].[5]

Thus the war against terrorism has become a covert war against judicial review of even the most fundamental human rights and civil liberties claims. As the government sought to eviscerate the ATCA in *Unocal*, even for such widely recognized human rights violations as slavery and torture, 30,000 impoverished Ecuadoreans took on the petroleum giant Texaco in an Ecuadorean court for exploiting their lax domestic laws. It was the first time that a multinational oil company had been subjected to Ecuadorean jurisdiction for 20 years of drilling which the plaintiffs claim poisoned their soil and water, causing cancer and other illnesses. The case had been sent to Ecuador by the United States Second Circuit Court of Appeals, which

---

[4] Alvarez-Machain Government Brief, *supra* note 2, at 6.
[5] Government Brief as Amicus Curiae on appeal to the Ninth Circuit in *Unocal*, at 21-22.
The D.C. Circuit Court of Appeals dismissed the ATCA claims of the Guantanamo Bay detainees in *Al Odah* because they were detained outside the sovereign territory of the U.S., precluding habeas corpus jurisdiction. It did not reach any issue as to the scope of the ATCA. 321 F.3d 1134 (D.C. Cir. 2003), *petition for cert. pending*, Nos. 03-334 & 03-343 (filed Sept. 2, 2003).

ruled it should be heard where the damage occurred. A legal adviser for the oil company said in opening arguments that the case would scare away other multinational corporations considering investing in Ecuador.

For the people who had seen their land and water destroyed, and their families dying, and for civil society, this statement is more in the nature of a promise than a threat for dedicated advocacy of a safe and healthy environment.

APPENDIX

LIST OF PRACTITIONER EXPERTS

Most of the strategies in this book have been used only a few times if at all. Therefore, your submissions are likely to be precedent setting, and your interaction with the international institution involved may determine definitively how that international institution treats in the future submissions from other individuals and groups. To assure that your efforts do not hinder others, it is essential that you either seek assistance from the appropriate individual(s) or organization(s) listed in this appendix or at least notify them of your undertaking. These practitioner experts are extremely knowledge about how to apply the strategies in this book and likely are aware of others who may be using them. Should you have difficulty reaching these people, please contact the authors of this book who can help facilitate a connection.

CHAPTER 1: EXERCISING ENVIRONMENTAL HEALTH HUMAN RIGHTS IN THE UNITED NATIONS AND REGIONAL SYSTEMS

1. United Nations System

    Marcos Orellana
    Center for International Environmental Law (CIEL)
    1367 Conn. Ave., NW Suite #300
    Washington, D.C. 20036
    USA
    (202) 785-8700
    morellana@ciel.org
    www.ciel.org

Constance de la Vega
Law Professor
University of San Francisco Law School
2130 Fulton Street
San Francisco, CA 94117
USA
(415) 422-6752
delavega@usfca.edu

Yves Lador
Independent Consultant
CH-1219 Chatelaine
Geneva
Switzerland
41 79 705 06 17
y.lador@bluewin.ch

Alice Palmer
Director
Foundation for International Environmental Law and Development (FIELD)
52-53 Russell Square
London WC1B 4HP
United Kingdom
44 (0) 20 7637-7950
apalmer@field.org.uk
www.field.org.uk

Marcello Mollo
Associate Attorney, International Program
Earthjustice
426 Seventeenth Street, 7th Floor
Oakland, CA 94612
USA
(510) 625-6700
mmollo@earthjustice.org
www.earthjustice.org/regional/international

International Human Rights Law Group
1200 18th Street NW, Suite 602
Washington D.C. 20036
USA
(202) 822-4600
HumanRights@hrlawgroup.org
www.hrlawgroup.org

2. Inter-American System

Marcos Orellana
Center for International Environmental Law (CIEL)
1367 Conn. Ave., NW Suite #300
Washington, D.C. 20036
USA
(202) 785-8700
morellana@ciel.org
www.ciel.org

Jorge Daniel Taillant
Executive Director
Center for Human Rights and Environment (CEDHA)
General Paz, 186, 10A
Córdoba 5000
Argentina
(54) 351 425 6278
daniel@cedha.org.ar
www.cedha.org.ar

Martin Wagner
Director, International Program
Earthjustice
426 Seventeenth Street, 7th Floor
Oakland, CA 94612
USA
(510) 625-6700
mwagner@earthjustice.org
www.earthjustice.org/regional/international

Center for Justice and International Law (CEJIL)
1630 Connecticut Ave., NW
Suite 555
Washington D.C. 20009-1053
USA
(202) 319-3000
washington@cejil.org
www.cejil.org

3. European System

Environmental Law Service
Kostnicka 1324
390 01 Tabor

Czech Republic
42 (0) 381 256 662
tabor@eps.cz
www.i-eps.cz

Yves Lador
Independent Consultant
CH-1219 Chatelaine
Geneva
Switzerland
41 79 705 06 17
y.lador@bluewin.ch

Alice Palmer
Director
Foundation for International Environmental Law and Development (FIELD)
52-53 Russell Square
London WC1B 4HP
United Kingdom
44 (0)20 7637-7950
apalmer@field.org.uk
www.field.org.uk

4. **African System**

Lawyers' Environmental Action Team (LEAT)
Mazingira House, Mazingira Street
Mikocheni Area
P. O. Box 12605
Dar es Salaam
Tanzania
leat@twiga.com
www.leat.or.tz

Irene Makumbi
Senior Researcher
Uganda Wildlife Society
P.O. Box 7422
Kampala
Uganda
uws@imul.com

Kenneth Kakuru
Greenwatch
P.O. Box 6256
Kampala
Uganda
256.41.344613
greenwatch@infocom.co.ug

Legal Resource Centre
South Africa
www.lrc.org.za

CHAPTER 2: ADVOCATING FOR INTERNATIONAL FINANCE AND TRADE INSTITUTIONS TO ADHERE TO ENVIRONMENTAL AND PUBLIC HEALTH STANDARDS

1. **World Bank Inspection Panel**

   Monti Aguirre
   Latin America Campaigner
   International Rivers Network
   1847 Berkeley Way
   Berkeley, CA 94703
   USA
   (510) 848-1155
   info@irn.org
   www.irn.org

   Dana Clark
   President
   International Accountability Project
   Berkeley, CA 94709
   USA
   danaclark7@mindspring.com

   David Hunter
   Anne Perrault
   Center for International Environmental Law (CIEL)
   1367 Conn. Ave., NW Suite #300
   Washington, D.C. 20036
   USA
   (202) 785-8700
   dhunter@ciel.org
   aperrault@ciel.org
   www.ciel.org

Claudia Saladin
World Wildlife Federation
1250 24th Street, NW
Washington, D.C. 20037
USA
(202) 293-4800
Claudia.Saladin@WWFUS.ORG
www.wwf.org

2. **IFC Compliance Advisor Ombudsman**

Graham Saul
Bank Information Center
Washington, D.C.
USA
info@bicusa.org
www.bicusa.org

3. **Asian Development Bank**

Satoru Matsumoto and Kenji Fukuda
Mekong Watch Japan
2F Makuko Bldg.
1-20-6 Hugashi Ueno
Taito-ku
Tokyo 110-0015
Japan
info@mekongwatch.org
www.mekongwatch.org

Mishka Zaman and Alvin Carlos
Bank Information Center
Washington, D.C.
USA
info@bicusa.org
www.bicusa.org

4. **European Bank for Reconstruction and Development**

Heike Mainhardt-Gibbs
Bank Information Center
Washington, D.C.
USA
info@bicusa.org
www.bicusa.org

Tomasz Terklecki
Petr Hlobil,
CEE Bankwatch Network
Jicinska 8
130 00 Praha 3
The Czech Republic
main@bankwatch.org
www.bankwatch.org

5. **African Development Bank**

Nikki Reisch
Bank Information Center
Washington, D.C. 20005
USA
info@bicusa.org
www.bicusa.org

6. **North American Commission on Environmental Cooperation**

Jake Caldwell
Director of Policy for Resources for Global Growth
Center for American Progress
1333 H Street, NW
10th Floor
Washington, D.C. 20005
(202) 682-1611
progress@americanprogress.org
www.americanprogress.org

Gustavo Alanís Ortega
Centro Mexicano de Derecho Ambiental (CEMDA)
Atlixco # 138
Col. Condesa 06140
Mexico D.F.
(568) 6-33-23
general@cemda.org.mx
www.cemda.org.mx

David Hunter
Anne Perrault
Center for International Environmental Law (CIEL)
1367 Conn.Ave., NW Suite #300
Washington, D.C. 20036
USA

(202) 785 8700
dhunter@ciel.org
aperrault@ciel.org
www.ciel.org

Martin Wagner
Director, International Program
Earthjustice
426 Seventeenth Street, 7th Floor
Oakland, CA 94612
USA
(510) 625-6700
mwagner@earthjustice.org
www.earthjustice.org/regional/international

7. **Canada-Chile Commission on Environmental Cooperation**

Fernando Dougnac
Fiscalia del Medio Ambiente (FIMA)
Guardia Vieja 408
Providencia
Santiago, Chile
56-2-421-7563
fima@fima.cl
www.fima.cl

Marcos Orellana
Center for International Environmental Law
1367 Conn. Ave., NW Suite #300
Washington, D.C. 20036
USA
(202) 785 8700
morellana@ciel.org
www.ciel.org

CHAPTER 3: PREVENTING NEW INTERNATIONAL TRADE AND INVESTMENT DISPUTE RESOLUTION MECHANISMS FROM UNDERMINING CURRENT ENVIRONMENTAL AND PUBLIC HEALTH REGULATIONS

1. **World Trade Organization**

Jake Caldwell
Director of Policy for Resources for Global Growth
Center for American Progress
1333 H Street, NW

10th Floor
Washington, D.C. 20005
(202) 682-1611
progress@americanprogress.org
www.americanprogress.org

Martin Wagner
Director, International Program
Earthjustice
426 Seventeenth Street
Oakland, CA 94612
USA
(510) 550-6700
mwagner@eajus.org
www.earthjustice.org/regional/international

Nathalie Bernasconi
Center for International Environmental Law (CIEL)
1367 Connecticut Avenue, NW
Suite 300
Washington, D.C. 20036
USA
(202) 785-8700
nbernasconi@ciel.org
www.ciel.org

2. **NAFTA Chapter 11**

Howard Mann
Special Counsel
International Institute for Sustainable Development
250 Albert St., Suite 1360
Ottawa, Ontario K1P 6M1
Canada
(613) 238-2296
(613) 729-0621
howard@howardmann.ca
info@iisd.ca
www.iisd.org

Daniel Magraw
Nathalie Bernasconi
Center for International Environmental Law (CIEL)
1367 Connecticut Avenue, NW Suite #300
Washington, D.C. 20036
USA

(202) 785-8700
dmagraw@ciel.org
nbernasconi@ciel.org
www.ciel.org

Martin Wagner
Director, International Program
Earthjustice
426 Seventeenth Street
Oakland, CA 94612
USA
(510) 550-6700
mwagner@eajus.org
www.earthjustice.org/regional/international

3. Bilateral Investment Treaties (BITs)

Marcos Orellana
Center for International Environmental Law
1367 Conn. Ave., NW Suite #300
Washington, D.C. 20036
USA
(202) 785-8700
morellana@ciel.org
www.ciel.org

Martin Wagner
Director, International Program
Earthjustice
426 Seventeenth Street
Oakland, CA 94612
USA
(510) 550-6700
mwagner@eajus.org
www.earthjustice.org/regional/international

David Waskow
Friends of the Earth
1717 Massachusetts Avenue, NW
Suite 600
Washington, D.C. 20036
(877) 843-8687
foe@foe.org
www.foe.org

CHAPTER 4: ENCOURAGING SECRETARIATS OF MULTILATERAL ENVIRONMENTAL AND PUBLIC HEALTH AGREEMENTS TO ENFORCE CURRENT INTERNATIONAL ENVIRONMENTAL STANDARDS

Donald Goldberg
Glenn Wiser
Center for International Environmental Law (CIEL)
1367 Connecticut Avenue, NW Suite #300
Washington, D.C. 20036
USA
(202) 785-8700
dgoldberg@ciel.org
gwiser@ciel.org
www.ciel.org

Martin Wagner
Director, International Program
Earthjustice
426 Seventeenth Street
Oakland, CA 94612
(510) 550-6700
USA
mwagner@eajus.org
www.earthjustice.org/regional/trade

Inter-American Association for Environmental
    Defense (AIDA)
c/o Earthjustice
426 Seventeenth Street, 6th Floor
Oakland, California 94612
(510) 550-6700
acederstav@aida-americas.org
www.aida-americas.org

Rolando Castro
Cedarena
Apdo. 134
2050 San Pedro
Costa Rica
(506) 253-7080
cedarena@racsa.cu.cr
www.cedarena.org

CHAPTER 5: ENFORCING INTERNATIONAL ENVIRONMENTAL LAW IN TRIBUNALS OF GENERAL JURISDICTION

Lawyers' Committee on Nuclear Policy
211 East 43rd Street
New York, NY 10017
(212) 818-1861
lcnp@lcnp.org
www.lcnp.org

Daniel Magraw
Marcos Orellana
Center for International Environmental Law (CIEL)
1367 Conn. Ave., NW Suite #300
Washington, D.C. 20036
USA
(202) 785-8700
dmagraw@ciel.org
morellana@ciel.org
www.ciel.org

Alice Palmer
Director
Foundation for International Environmental Law and
   Development (FIELD)
52-53 Russell Square
London WC1B 4HP
United Kingdom
44 (0)20 7637 7950
apalmer@field.org.uk
www.field.org.uk

Durwood Zaelke
Director
International Network for Environmental
   Compliance & Enforcement
2141 Wisconsin Ave. NW
Suite D2
Washington, D.C. 20007
(202) 338-1300
dzaelke@inece.org
www.inece.org

CHAPTER 6: ENFORCING INTERNATIONAL ENVIRONMENTAL LAW THROUGH DOMESTIC LAW MECHANISMS

1. Transparency and Public Participation

Patti Goldman
Earthjustice
203 Hoge Building
705 Second Avenue
Seattle, WA 98104-1711
(206) 343-7340
eajuswa@earthjustice.org

Lori Wallach
Director, Global Trade Watch
Public Citizen
215 Pennsylvania Avenue, SE
Washington, D.C. 20003
(202) 546-4996
gtwinfo@citizen.org
www.citizen.org/trade

David Waskow
Friends of the Earth
1025 Vermont Ave., NW, Suite 300
Washington, D.C. 20005
(877) 843-8687
foe@foe.org
www.foe.org

2. Extraterritorial Application of U.S. Environmental Laws

Marcello Mollo
Associate Attorney, International Program
Earthjustice
426 Seventeenth Street
Oakland, CA 94612
USA
(510) 550-6700
mmollo@eajus.org
www.earthjustice.org/regional/international

3. Alien Tort Claims Act and Related Issues

Terry Collingsworth
Executive Director
International Labor Rights Fund
733 15th St., NW #920
Washington, D.C. 20005
(202) 347-4100
laborrights@lrf.org
www.laborrights.org

Günther Handl
Professor of Law
Tulane Law School
Weinmann Hall
6327 Fretet St.
New Orleans, LA 70118-6231
(504) 865-5939
ghandl@law.tulane.edu

Rick Herz
Litigation Coordinator
Earth Rights International
1612 K St. NW
Suite 401
Washington, D.C. 20006
(202) 466-5188
infousa@earthrights.org
www.earthrights.org

Martin Wagner
Director, International Program
Earthjustice
426 Seventeenth Street
Oakland, CA 94612
USA
(510) 550-6700
mwagner@eajus.org
www.earthjustice.org/regional/international

4. Coordinating Domestic Strategies in Multiple Countries

Anna Cederstav
Executive Director
Inter-American Association for Environmental
   Defense (AIDA)
c/o Earthjustice
426 Seventeenth Street, 6th Floor
Oakland, California 94612
acederstav@aida-americas.org
www.aida-americas.org

Bern Johnson
Executive Director
Environmental Law Alliance Worldwide (E-LAW)
1877 Garden Avenue
Eugene, OR 97403
(541) 687-8454
elawus@elaw.org
www.elaw.org

Durwood Zaelke
Director
International Network for Environmental
   Compliance & Enforcement
2141 Wisconsin Ave. NW
Suite D2
Washington, D.C. 20007
(202) 338-1300
dzaelke@inece.org
www.inece.org

Authors

Linda Malone
Marshall-Wythe Foundation Professor of Law
College of William & Mary School of Law
Williamsburg, VA 23187
lamalo@wm.edu
(757) 221-3800

Scott Pasternack
Environmental Division
New York City Law Department
spastern@law.nyc.gov
(212) 788-0303

BIBLIOGRAPHY

CHAPTER 1

BOOKS

A SYSTEMATIC GUIDE TO THE CASE-LAW OF THE EUROPEAN COURT OF HUMAN RIGHTS (Peter Kempees ed., 1999).
AFRICA AND EUROPE: RELATIONS OF TWO CONTINENTS IN TRANSITION (Stefan Brune et al. eds., 1994).
AN EU CHARTER OF FUNDAMENTAL RIGHTS: TEXT AND COMMENTARIES (Kim Feus ed., 2000).
ANKUMAH, EVELYN A., THE AFRICAN COMMISSION ON HUMAN AND PEOPLE'S RIGHTS: PRACTICES AND PROCEDURES (1996).
BANTON, MICHAEL P., INTERNATIONAL ACTION AGAINST RACIAL DISCRIMINATION (1996).
BEDDARD, RALPH, HUMAN RIGHTS AND EUROPE: A STUDY OF THE MACHINERY OF HUMAN RIGHTS PROTECTION OF THE COUNCIL OF EUROPE (2d. ed. 1980).
BEYOND CONFRONTATION: INTERNATIONAL LAW FOR THE POST-COLD WAR ERA (Lori Fisler Damrosch et al. eds., 1995).
BEYOND WESTPHALIA?: STATE SOVEREIGNTY AND INTERNATIONAL INTERVENTION (Gene M. Lyons & Michael Mastanduno eds., 1995).
BROADENING THE FRONTIERS OF HUMAN RIGHTS: ESSAYS IN HONOUR OF ASBJORN EIDE (Donna Gomien ed., 1993).
CASTBERG, FREDE, THE EUROPEAN CONVENTION ON HUMAN RIGHTS (Torkel Opsahl & Thomas Ouchterlony eds., Gytte Borch trans., 1974).
CHASZAR, EDWARD, THE INTERNATIONAL PROBLEM OF NATIONAL MINORITIES (1999).
CHINA JOINS THE WORLD: PROGRESS AND PROSPECTS (Elizabeth Economy & Michel Oksenberg eds., 1999).
Clapham, Andrew, *Human Rights, in* THE PREVENTION OF HUMANITARIAN EMERGENCIES 232 (E. Wayne Nazfiger & Raimo Vayrynen eds., 2002).
CLARK, ROGER STEVENSON, A UNITED NATIONS HIGH COMMISSIONER FOR HUMAN RIGHTS (1972).
Clark, Roger S., *How International Human Rights Law Affects Domestic Law, in* HUMAN RIGHTS: NEW PERSPECTIVES, NEW REALITIES 185 (Adamantia Polis & Peter Schwab eds., 2000).
CLEMENTS, L.J., EUROPEAN HUMAN RIGHTS: TAKING A CASE UNDER THE CONVENTION (2d ed. 1999).

COMMISSION TO STUDY THE ORGANIZATION OF PEACE, THE UNITED NATIONS AND HUMAN RIGHTS: EIGHTEENTH REPORT OF THE COMMISSION (1968).
COMMON GROUND OR MUTUAL EXCLUSION?: WOMEN'S MOVEMENTS AND INTERNATIONAL RELATIONS (Marianne Braig & Sonja Wolte eds., 2002).
CONCLUDING OBSERVATIONS OF THE UN COMMITTEE ON THE RIGHTS OF THE CHILD: THIRD TO SEVENTEENTH SESSION, 1993-1998 (Leif Holmstrom ed., 2000).
COUNCIL OF EUROPE, CASE LAW ON THE EUROPEAN SOCIAL CHARTER (1978).
COUNCIL OF EUROPE, EXPLANATORY REPORTS ON THE SECOND TO FIFTH PROTOCOLS TO THE EUROPEAN CONVENTION FOR THE PROTECTION OF HUMAN RIGHTS AND FUNDAMENTAL FREEDOMS (1971).
CRIMINAL JUSTICE IN EUROPE: A COMPARATIVE STUDY (Phil Fennell ed., 1995).
DAVIDSON, J. SCOTT, THE INTER-AMERICAN HUMAN RIGHTS SYSTEM (1997).
DAVIDSON, SCOTT, THE INTER-AMERICAN COURT OF HUMAN RIGHTS (1992).
DAVIS, SHELTON H., LAND RIGHTS AND INDIGENOUS PEOPLES: THE ROLE OF THE INTER-AMERICAN COMMISSION ON HUMAN RIGHTS (1988).
Davis, Michael C., *Human Rights, Political Values, and Development in East Asia, in* HUMAN RIGHTS: NEW PERSPECTIVES, NEW REALITIES 139 (Adamantia Polis & Peter Schwab eds., 2000).
Dejeant-Pons, M., *The Right to Environment in Regional Human Rights Systems, in* HUMAN RIGHTS IN THE TWENTY-FIRST CENTURY 595 (P. Mahoney & K. Mahoney eds. 1993).
DEJEANT-PONS MÁ & M. PALLEMAERTS, DROITS DE L'HOMME ET ENVIRONNEMENT (2002).
DeMars, William E., *Transnational Non-Governmental Organizations: The Edge of Innocence, in* THE PREVENTION OF HUMANITARIAN EMERGENCIES 193 (E. Wayne Nazfiger & Raimo Vayrynen eds., 2002).
DOCUMENTS OF THE AFRICAN COMMISSION ON HUMAN AND PEOPLE'S RIGHTS (Malcolm D. Evans & Rachel Murray eds., 2001).
Donini, Antonio, *The Geopolitics of Mercy: Humanitarianism in the Age of Globalization, in* THE PREVENTION OF HUMANITARIAN EMERGENCIES 253 (E. Wayne Nazfiger & Raimo Vayrynen eds., 2002).
Donnelly, Jack, *Ethics and International Human Rights, in* ETHICS AND INTERNATIONAL AFFAIRS: EXTENT AND LIMITS 128 (Jean-Marc Coicaud & Daniel Warner eds., 2001).
Donnelly, Jack, *Progress in Human Rights, in* PROGRESS IN POSTWAR INTERNATIONAL RELATIONS 312 (Emanuel Adler & Beverly Crawford eds., 1991).
EARTH RIGHTS: LINKING THE QUEST FOR HUMAN RIGHTS AND ENVIRONMENTAL PROTECTION (Jed Greer & Tyler Giannini eds., 1999).
ECOLOGICAL INTEGRITY: INTEGRATING ENVIRONMENT, CONSERVATION, AND HEALTH (David Pimentel et al. eds., 2000).
ECOLOGISTS AND ETHICAL JUDGMENTS (N.S. Cooper & R. C. J. Carling eds., 1995).

Elliot, Lorraine, *Environmental Security, in* ASIA'S EMERGING REGIONAL ORDER: RECONCILING TRADITIONAL AND HUMAN SECURITY 157 (William T.Tow et al. eds., 2000).
ENVIRONMENT, HUMAN RIGHTS, AND INTERNATIONAL TRADE (Francesco Francioni ed., 2001).
ENVIRONMENTAL CHANGE AND INTERNATIONAL LAW: NEW CHALLENGES AND DIMENSIONS (Edith Brown Weiss ed., 1992).
ENVIRONMENTAL HUMAN RIGHTS: POWER, ETHICS, AND LAW (Jan Hancock ed., 2003).
ENVIRONMENTAL RIGHTS: LAW, LITIGATION & ACCESS TO JUSTICE (Sven Deimann & Bernard Dyssli eds., 1995).
EUROPEAN CONVENTION ON HUMAN RIGHTS, TEXTS AND DOCUMENTS (Herbert Miehsler & Herbet Petzold eds., 1982).
FREEDOM OF ASSOCIATION: A USER'S GUIDE: STANDARDS, PRINCIPLES AND PROCEDURES OF THE INTENTIONAL LABOUR ORGANIZATION (David Tajgman & Karen Curtis eds., 2000).
FROM CAPE TO CONGO: SOUTHERN AFRICA'S EVOLVING SECURITY CHALLENGES (Mwesiga Baregu & Christopher Landsberg eds., 2003).
FUNDAMENTAL RIGHTS IN EUROPE: THE EUROPEAN CONVENTION ON HUMAN RIGHTS AND ITS MEMBER STATES, 1950-2000 (Robert Blackburn & Jorg Polakiewicz eds., 2001).
FUNDAMENTALS OF RISK ANALYSIS AND RISK MANAGEMENT (Vlasta Molak ed., 1997).
GOMIEN, DONNA, LAW AND PRACTICE OF THE EUROPEAN CONVENTION ON HUMAN RIGHTS AND THE EUROPEAN SOCIAL CHARTER (1996).
Goodin, Robert E., *International Ethics and the Environmental Crisis, in* ETHICS AND INTERNATIONAL AFFAIRS: A READER 257 (Joel H. Rosenthal ed., 1995).
Haas, Peter M., *Making Progress in International Environmental Protection, in* PROGRESS IN POSTWAR INTERNATIONAL RELATIONS 273 (Emanuel Adler & Beverly Crawford ed., 1991).
HAJNAL, PETER I., GUIDE TO UNESCO (1983).
Handl, G., *Human Rights and Protection of the Environment: A Mildly 'Revisionist' View, in* HUMAN RIGHTS AND ENVIRONMENTAL PROTECTION (A.A. Cancado Trindade ed., 1992).
HARRIS, D.J., THE EUROPEAN SOCIAL CHARTER (2001).
Harris, Stuart, *Environmental Challenges, in* AUSTRALIAN FOREIGN POLICY: INTO THE NEW MILLENNIUM 113 (F.A. Mediansky ed., 1997).
HERMAN, WALTER, ET AL., UNESCO: PURPOSE, PROGRESS, PROSPECTS (1968).
HUMAN RIGHTS AND DEVELOPMENT IN AFRICA (Claude E. Welch & Ronald I. Meltzer eds., 1984).
HUMAN RIGHTS AND DISABLED PERSONS: ESSAYS AND RELEVANT HUMAN RIGHTS INSTRUMENTS (Theresia Degener & Yolan Koster-Dreese eds., 1995).
HUMAN RIGHTS APPROACHES TO ENVIRONMENTAL PROTECTION (Alan E. Boyle & Michael R. Anderson eds., 1996).

INDIGENOUS PEOPLES AND THE FUTURE OF AMAZONIA: AN ECOLOGICAL ANTHROPOLOGY OF AN ENDANGERED WORLD (Leslie E. Sponsel ed., 1995).
INTERNATIONAL COURTS AND TRIBUNALS: SELECTED DOCUMENTS AND MATERIALS (W. van der Wolf & S. de Haardt eds., 2d ed. 2001).
INTERNATIONAL LABOUR ORGANIZATION, INTERNATIONAL LABOUR CONVENTIONS AND RECOMMENDATIONS (1996).
ISLAM AND ECOLOGY: A BESTOWED TRUST (Richard Foltz et al. eds., 2003).
JANIS, MARK W., EUROPEAN HUMAN RIGHTS LAW: TEXT AND MATERIALS (1995).
JAPANESE FOREIGN POLICY TODAY: A READER (Takashi Inoguchi & Purnendra Jain eds., 2000).
Johnston, Barbara Rose, *Human Environmental Rights, in* HUMAN RIGHTS: NEW PERSPECTIVES, NEW REALITIES 95 (Adamantia Polis & Peter Schwab eds., 2000).
JUDICIAL CONTROL: COMPARATIVE ESSAYS ON JUDICIAL REVIEW (Rob Bakkar et al. eds., 1995).
JUDICIAL DISCRETION IN EUROPEAN PERSPECTIVE (Ola Wiklund ed., 2003).
JUSTICE AND NATURAL RESOURCES: CONCEPTS, STRATEGIES, AND APPLICATIONS (Kathryn M. Mutz et al. eds., 2002).
Juviler, Peter, *Political Community and Human Rights in Postcommunist Russia, in* HUMAN RIGHTS: NEW PERSPECTIVES, NEW REALITIES 115 (Adamantia Polis & Peter Schwab eds., 2000).
Kibreab, Gaim, *Protecting Environmental Resources and Preventing Land Degradation, in* THE PREVENTION OF HUMANITARIAN EMERGENCIES 115 (E. Wayne Nazfiger & Raimo Vayrynen eds., 2002).
Kiss, A.-Ch., *An introductory note on a human right to environment, in* ENVIRONMENTAL CHANGE AND INTERNATIONAL LAW 551 (E. Brown Weiss ed., 1992).
KISS, ALEXANDRE, & DINAH SHELTON, INTERNATIONAL ENVIRONMENTAL LAW (3d ed. 2004).
KISS, ALEXANDRE, & DINAH SHELTON, MANUEL OF ENVIRONMENTAL LAW (2d ed. 1997).
Kumpula, Anne, *Environmental Law, in* AN INTRODUCTION TO FINNISH LAW 499 (Juha Poyhonen ed., 2d ed. 2002).
LAMBERT-ABDELGAWAD, ELISABETH, THE EXECUTION OF JUDGMENTS OF THE EUROPEAN COURT OF HUMAN RIGHTS (2002).
LAW ABOVE NATIONS: SUPRANATIONAL COURTS AND THE LEGALIZATION OF POLITICS (Mary L. Volcansek ed., 1997).
LEACH, PHILLIP, TAKING A CASE TO THE EUROPEAN COURT OF HUMAN RIGHTS (2001).
LEBLANC, LAWRENCE J., THE OAS AND THE PROMOTION AND PROTECTION OF HUMAN RIGHTS (1977).
LINDHOLT, LONE, QUESTIONING THE UNIVERSALITY OF HUMAN RIGHTS: THE AFRICAN CHARTER ON HUMAN AND PEOPLE'S RIGHTS IN BOTSWANA, MALAWI, AND MOZAMBIQUE (1997).

LOUCAIDÉS, LOUPES G., ESSAYS IN THE DEVELOPING LAW OF HUMAN RIGHTS (1995).
LUBIN, CAROL RIEGELMAN, SOCIAL JUSTICE FOR WOMEN: THE INTERNATIONAL LABOR ORGANIZATION AND WOMEN (1990).
MACKAY, FERGUS, A GUIDE TO INDIGENOUS PEOPLES' RIGHTS IN THE INTER-AMERICAN HUMAN RIGHTS SYSTEM (2002).
MCGOLDRICK, DOMINIC, THE HUMAN RIGHTS COMMITTEE: ITS ROLE IN THE DEVELOPMENT OF THE INTERNATIONAL COVENANT ON CIVIL AND POLITICAL RIGHTS (1991).
MERRILLS, J. G., HUMAN RIGHTS IN EUROPE: A STUDY OF THE EUROPEAN CONVENTION ON HUMAN RIGHTS (4th ed. 2001).
MERRILLS, J. G., THE DEVELOPMENT OF INTERNATIONAL LAW BY THE EUROPEAN COURT OF HUMAN RIGHTS (2d ed. 1993).
MULTILATERALISM AND U.S. FOREIGN POLICY: AMBIVALENT ENGAGEMENT (Stewart Patrick & Shepard Forman eds., 2002).
MURRAY, RACHEL, THE AFRICAN COMMISSION ON HUMAN AND PEOPLE'S RIGHTS AND INTERNATIONAL LAW (2000).
NGOS, THE UN, AND GLOBAL GOVERNANCE (Thomas G. Weiss & Leon Gordenker eds., 1996).
NUGENT, NEILL, GOVERNMENT AND POLITICS OF THE EUROPEAN UNION (5th ed. 2003).
OELSCHLAGER, MAX, *What is Environmental Ethics?*, in ETHICAL ISSUES FOR A NEW MILLENNIUM 102 (John Howie ed., 2002).
OURS BY RIGHT: WOMEN'S RIGHTS AS HUMAN RIGHTS (Joanna Kerr ed., 1993).
OVEY, CLARE & ROBIN, WHITE, JACOBS AND WHITE: THE EUROPEAN CONVENTION ON HUMAN RIGHTS (3d ed. 2002) (1996).
PANFORD, KWAMINA, AFRICAN LABOR RELATIONS AND WORKER'S RIGHTS: ASSESSING THE ROLE OF THE INTERNATIONAL LABOR ORGANIZATION (1994).
PASQUALUCCI, JO M., THE PRACTICE AND PROCEDURE OF THE INTER-AMERICAN COURT OF HUMAN RIGHTS (2003).
PETZOLD, ERBERT, THE EUROPEAN CONVENTION ON HUMAN RIGHTS: CASES AND MATERIALS: A READER FOR STUDENTS OF THE INTERNATIONAL LAW OF HUMAN RIGHTS (1981).
PONTICELLI, CHARLOTTE M., U.S.-UNESCO RELATIONS (1989).
POSEY, D., TRADITIONAL RESOURCE RIGHTS: INTERNATIONAL INSTRUMENTS FOR PROTECTION AND COMPENSATION FOR INDIGENOUS PEOPLES AND LCOAL COMMUNITIES (1996).
PRESTON, WILLIAM, HOPE AND FOLLY: THE UNITED STATES AND UNESCO, 1945-1985 (1989).
RACING TO REGIONALIZE: DEMOCRACY, CAPITALISM, AND REGIONAL POLITICAL ECONOMY (Kenneth P. Thomas & Mary Ann Tetreault eds., 1999).
RAMCHARAN, BERTRAND, THE UNITED NATIONS HIGH COMMISSIONER FOR HUMAN RIGHTS: THE CHALLENGES OF INTERNATIONAL PROTECTION (2002).

REDGWELL, CATHERINE, *Life, the Universe and Everything: A Critique of Anthropocentric Rights*, HUMAN RIGHTS APPROACHES ENVIRONMENTAL PROTECTION 71 (Alan E. Boyle & M. Anderson eds., 1996).
REID, KAREN, A PRACTITIONER'S GUIDE TO THE EUROPEAN CONVENTION ON HUMAN RIGHTS (1998).
ROBERTSON, A. H., HUMAN RIGHTS IN EUROPE: BEING AN ACCOUNT OF THE EUROPEAN CONVENTION FOR THE PROTECTION OF HUMAN RIGHTS AND FUNDAMENTAL FREEDOMS SIGNED IN ROME ON 4 NOVEMBER 1950, OF THE PROTOCOLS THERETO AND OF THE MACHINERY CREATED THEREBY, THE EUROPEAN COMMISSION OF HUMAN RIGHTS AND THE EUROPEAN COURT OF HUMAN RIGHTS (2d ed. 1977).
SATHYAMURTHY, T. V., THE POLITICS OF INTERNATIONAL COOPERATION: CONTRASTING CONCEPTIONS OF U.N.E.S.C.O. (1964).
SCHEININ, MARTIN, *Constitutional Law and Human Rights*, in AN INTRODUCTION TO FINNISH LAW 31 (Juha Poyhonen ed., 2d ed. 2002).
SCHREIBER, ANNA P., THE INTER-AMERICAN COMMISSION ON HUMAN RIGHTS (1970).
SCHWAB PETER S., & ADAMANTIA POLLIS, *Globalization Impact on Human Rights*, in HUMAN RIGHTS: NEW PERSPECTIVES, NEW REALITIES 209 (2000).
SCHWLEB, EGON, HUMAN RIGHTS AND THE INTERNATIONAL COMMUNITY: THE ROOTS AND GROWTH OF THE UNIVERSAL DECLARATION OF HUMAN RIGHTS, 1948-1963 (1964).
SHELTON, DINAH, *Environmental Rights*, in PEOPLES RIGHTS (Philip Alston ed., 2001).
SMIL, VACLAV, *Development and Destruction: The Dimensions of China's Environmental Challenge*, in CHINA BEYOND THE HEADLINES 195 (Timothy B. Weston & Lionel M. Jensen eds., 2000).
SPAULDING, SETH & LIN, LIN, HISTORICAL DICTIONARY OF THE UNITED NATIONS EDUCATIONAL, SCIENTIFIC AND CULTURAL ORGANIZATION (UNESCO) (1997).
STRUGGLES FOR SOCIAL RIGHTS IN LATIN AMERICA (Susan Eckstein & Timothy P. Wickham-Crowley eds., 2003).
STUMBING TOWARD SUSTAINABILITY (John C. Dernbach ed., 2002).
THE AFRICAN CHARTER ON HUMAN AND PEOPLE'S RIGHTS: THE SYSTEM IN PRACTICE, 1986-2000 (Malcolm D. Evans & Rachel Murray eds., 2002).
THE CHANGING WORLD (Patricia Fara et al. eds., 1996).
THE EUROPEAN CONVENTION FOR THE PROTECTION OF HUMAN RIGHTS: INTERNATIONAL PROTECTION VERSUS RESTRICTIONS (Mireille Delmas-Marty ed., Christine Chodkiewicz trans. et ed., 1992).
THE EXECUTION OF STRASBOURG AND GENEVA HUMAN RIGHTS DECISIONS IN THE NATIONAL LEGAL ORDER (T. Barkhuysen et al. eds., 1999).
THE INTER-AMERICAN SYSTEM OF HUMAN RIGHTS (David J. Harris & Stephen Livingstone eds., 1998).
TRIPP, BRENDA M.H., UNESCO IN PERSPECTIVE (1954).
UNITED NATIONS COMMISSION OF THE STATUS OF WOMEN, THE STATUS OF THE

UNMARRIED MOTHER: LAW AND PRACTICE: REPORT OF THE SECRETARY-GENERAL (1971).
UNITED NATIONS: COMMITTEE ON THE ELIMINATION OF DISCRIMINATION AGAINST WOMEN, THE WORK OF CEDAW: REPORTS OF THE COMMITTEE ON THE ELIMINATION OF DISCRIMINATION AGAINST WOMEN (CEDAW) (1989).
UNITED NATIONS SECRETARY-GENERAL, PARTICIPATION OF WOMEN IN COMMUNITY DEVELOPMENT: REPORT OF THE SECRETARY-GENERAL (1972).
UMOZURIKE, U.O., THE AFRICAN CHARTER ON HUMAN AND PEOPLE'S RIGHTS (1997).
U.S. POLICY AND THE FUTURE OF THE UNITED NATIONS (Roger A. Coate ed., 1994).
VAN DIJK, P., ET AL., THEORY AND PRACTICE OF THE EUROPEAN CONVENTION ON HUMAN RIGHTS (3d ed. 1998).
WOMEN'S RIGHTS: A GLOBAL VIEW (Lynn Walter ed., 2001).
YOUNG, KIRSTEN A., THE LAW AND PROCESS OF THE U.N. HUMAN RIGHTS COMMITTEE (2002).
YOUNG, KIRSTEN A., THE LAW AND PROCESS OF THE U.N. HUMAN RIGHTS LINKING HUMAN RIGHTS AND THE ENVIRONMENT (Romina Picolottie & Jorge Daniel Taillant eds., 2003).
YOUNG, ORAN R., *Environmental Ethics in International Society, in* ETHICS AND INTERNATIONAL AFFAIRS: EXTENT AND LIMITS 161 (Jean-Marc Coicaud & Daniel Warner eds., 2001).
ZOELLE, DIANA GRACE, GLOBALIZING CONCERN FOR WOMEN'S HUMAN RIGHTS: THE FAILURE OF THE AMERICAN MODEL (2000).
ZWART, TOM, THE ADMISSIBILITY OF HUMAN RIGHTS PETITIONS: THE CASE LAW OF THE EUROPEAN COMMISSION OF HUMAN RIGHTS AND THE HUMAN RIGHTS COMMITTEE (1994).

ARTICLES

Acevedo, Mariana T. Note: *The Intersection of Human Rights and Environmental Protection in the European Court of Human Rights*, 8 N.Y.U. ENVTL. L.J. 437 (2000).

Agbakwa, Shedrack C., *Reclaiming Humanity: Economic, Social, and Cultural Rights as the Cornerstone of African Human Rights*, 5 YALE H.R. & DEV. L.J. 177 (2002).

Akinseye-George, Yemi, *Conflict Resolution in Africa: New Trends in African Human Rights Law: Prospects of an African Court of Human Rights*, U. MIAMI INT'L & COMP. L. REV. 159 (2001).

Ala'I, Padideh, *Global Trade Issue in the New Millennium: A Human Rights Critique of the WTO: Some Preliminary Observations*, 33 GEO. WASH. INT'L L. REV. 537 (2001).

Alfredson, G., & A., Ovsiouk, *Human Rights and the Environment*, 60 NORDIC J. INT'L L. 19 (1991).

Alvarez, Jose E., *Trade and the Environment: Implications for Global Governance: How Not to Link: Institutional Conundrums of an Expanded Trade Regime*, 7 WID. L. SYMP. J. 1 (2001).

Anaya, S. James, *Indigenous Rights Norms in Contemporary International Lawi*, 8 ARIZ. J. INT'L & COMP. L. 1 (1991).

Anaya, S. James, & Claudio Grossman, *The Case of Awas Tingni v. Nicaragua: A New Step in the International Law of Indigenous Peoples*, 19 ARIZ. J. INT'L & COMP. LAW 1 (2002).

Anaya, S. James, & Robert A. Williams, Jr., *The Protection of Indigenous Peoples' Rights over Lands and Natural Resources Under the Inter-American Human Rights System*, 14 HARV. HUM. RTS. J. 33 (2001).

Berman, Paul Schiff, *The Globalization of Jurisdiction*, 151 U. PA. L. REV. 311 (2002).

Bhala, Raj, *Clarifying the Trade-Labor Link*, 37 COLUM. J. TRANSNAT'L L. 11 (1998).

Black-Branch, Jonathan L., *Observing and Enforcing Human Rights Under the Council of Europe: The Creation of a Permanent European Court of Human Rights*, 3 BUFF. JOUR. INT'L L. 1 (1996).

Bodansky, Daniel, *The Legitimacy of International Governance: A Coming Challenge for International Environmental Law?*, 93 A.J.I.L. 596 (1996).

Bol, Jennifer, *Using International Law to Fight Child Labor: A Case Study of Guatemala and the Inter-American System*, 13 AM. U. INT'L L. REV. 1135 (1998).

Bridgeman, Natalie L., *Human Rights Litigation Under the ATCA as a Proxy for Environmental Claims*, 6 YALE H.R. & DEV. L.J. 1 (2003).

Bruch, Carl, et al., *Constitutional Environmental Law: Giving Force to Fundamental Principles in Africa*, 26 COLUM. J. ENVTL L. 131 (2001).

Carozza, Paolo G., *Propter Honoris Respectum: Uses and Misuses of Comparative Law in International Human Rights: Some Reflections on the Jurisprudence of the European Court of Human Rights*, 73 NOTRE DAME L. REV. 1217 (1998).

Cooper, Jessica B. Note: *Environmental Refugees: Meeting the Requirements of the Refugee Definition*, 6 N.Y.U. ENVTL. L.J. 480 (1998).

Cosgrove, Michael F., Note: *Protecting the Protectors: Preventing the Decline of the Inter-American System for the Protection of Human Rights*, 32 CASE W. RES. J. INT'L L. 39 (2000).

Cullett, P., *Definition of an Environmental Right in a Human Rights Context*, 13 NETH. Q. HUM. RTS. 25 (1995).

D'Amato, Anthony, & Sudhir K. Chopra, *Whales: Their Emerging Right to Life*, 85 AJIL 21 (1991).

Defeis, Elizabeth F., *Human Rights and the European Union: Who Decides? Possible Conflicts Between the European Court of Justice and the European Court of Human Rights*, 19 DICK. J. INT'L L. 301 (2001).

Desgagne, Richard, *Integrating Environmental Values into the European Convention on Human Rights*, 89 A.J.I. L. 263 (1995).
Dias, Clarence J., *Human Rights, Environment and Development in South Asia: The Importance of International Human Rights Law*, 6 ILSA INT'L & COMP L. 415 (2000).
Dommen, Caroline, *Claiming Environmental Rights: Some possibilities Offered by the Untied Nations' Human Rights Mechanisms*, 11 GEO. INT'L ENVTL. L. REV. 1 (1998).
Donoff, Jeffery L., *From Green to Global: Toward the Transformation of International Environmental Law*, 19 HARV. ENVTL. L. REV. 241 (1995).
Eaton, J. P., *The Nigerian Tragedy, Environmental Regulation of Transnational Corporations and the Human Right to a Healthy Environment*, 15 B.U.I.L.J. 261 (1997).
Ehrmann, Markus, *Procedures of Compliance Control in International Environmental Treaties*, 13 COLO. J. INT'L ENVTL. L. & POL'Y 377 (2002).
Eshbach, Roseann, *A Global Approach to the Protection of the Environment: Balancing State Sovereignty and Global Interests*, 4 TEMP. INT'L & COMP. L.J. 271, 271 (1990).
Furtado, Charles F., Jr., *Guess Who's Coming to Dinner? Protection for National Minorities in Eastern and Central Europe Under the Council of Europe*, 34 COLUM. HUMAN RIGHTS L. REV. 333 (2003).
Gamble, John King, et al., *Human Rights Treaties: A Suggested Typology, An Historical Perspective*, 7 BUFF. HUM. RTS. L. REV. 33 (2001).
Gammie, Beth, *Human Rights Implications of the Export of Banned Pesticides*, 25 SETON HALL L. REV. 558 (1994).
Gavouneli, Maria, *Access to Environmental Information: Delimitation of a Right*, 13 TUL. ENVTL. L.J. 303 (2000).
Gordon, Joy, *The Concept of Human Rights: The History and Meaning of its Politicization*, 23 BROOKLYN J. INT'L L. 689 (1998).
Hagler, Megan, *News from the Inter-American System*, 10 HUM. RTS. BR. 28 (2002).
Hagler, Megan, & Francisco Rivera, *Bamaca Velasquez v. Guatemala: An Expansion of the Inter-American System's Jurisprudence on Reparations*, 9 HUM. RTS. BR. 2 (2002).
Harrington, Joanna, *Punting Terrorists, Assassins and Other Undesirables: Canada, the Human Rights Committee and Requests for Interim Measures of Protection*, 48 McGILL L.J. 55 (2003).
Hitchcock, R., *International Human Rights, the Environment, and Indigenous Peoples*, 1 COLO. J. I. L.P. 1 (1994).
Jellema, Calvin P., *The Redheaded Stepchild of Community Competition Law: The Third Party and Its Rights to be Heard in Competition Proceedings*, 20 B.U. INT'L L.J. 211 (2002).
Kalas, Peggy Rodger, *International Environmental Dispute Resolution and the Need for Access by Non-State Entities*, 12 COLO. J. INT'L ENVTL. L. & POL'Y 191 (2001).

Kane, M. J., *Promoting Political Rights to Protect the Envrionment*, 18 YALE J. INT'L L. 389.

King-Hopkins, Kimberly D. Comment: *Inter-American Commission on Human Rights: Is Its Bark Worse Than Its Bite in Resolving Human Rights Disputes?*, 35 TULSA L.J. 421 (2001).

Kiss, A.-Ch., *Le Droit a law Conservation de l'environnement*, 1 REV. UNIVERSELLE DES DROITS DE L'HOMME 445 (1990).

Kiss, A.-Ch., *Peut-on définir le droit de l'homme à l'environnement?*, 1976 REV. JURIDIQUE DE L'ENVIRONNEMENT 15.

Kruger, Hans Christian, *Symposium on Continuing Progress in Institutionalizing Legal Education—21st Century Global Challenges: Promoting and Protecting Human Rights in Europe: Reflection Concerning Accession of the European Communities to the European Convention on Human Rights*, 21 PENN ST. INT'L L. REV. 89 (2002).

Lee, John, *The Underlying Legal Theory to Support a Well-Defined Human Right to a Healthy Environment as a Principle of Customary International Law*, 25 COLUM. J. ENVTL. L. 283 (2000).

Leuprecht, Pete, *Introduction to the Symposium: Innovations in the European System of Human Rights Protection: Is Enlargement Compatible with Reinforcement?*, 8 TRANSNAT'L L. CONTEMP. PROBS. 313 (1998).

Lindholt, Lone, *Regional Human Rights Systems: Questioning the Universality of Human Rights: The African Charter on Human and Peoples' Rights in Botswana, Malawi and Mozambique*, 24 YALE J. INT'L L. 359, (1999).

Malone, Linda A., & Scott Pasternack, *Exercising Environmental Human Rights and Remedies in the United Nations System*, 27 WM. & MARY ENVTL. L. & POL'Y REV. 365 (2002).

McClymonds, J.T., *The Human Right to a Healthy Environment: An International Legal Perspective*, 37 N.Y. L. S. L. REV. 583 (1992).

Montalvo, Andres E., *Reservations to the American Convention on Human Rights: A New Approach*, 16 AM. U. INT'L L. REV. 269 (2001).

Mowery, Lauren A., Note, *Earth Rights, Human Rights: Can International Environmental Human Rights Affect Corporate Accountability?*, 13 FORDHAM ENVTL. LAW J. 343 (2002).

Mugwanya, George William, *Realizing Universal Human Rights Norms Through Regional Human Rights Mechanisms: Reinvigorating the African System*, 10 IND. INT'L & COMP. L. REV. 35 (1999).

Mullen de Bolivar, Maura, *A Comparison of Protecting the Environmental Interests of Latin American Indigenous Communities from Transnational Corporations under International Human Rights and Environmental Law*, 8 J. TRANSNAT'L L. & POL'Y 105 (1998).

Nash, James A., *The Case for Biotic Rights*, 18 YALE J. INT'L L. 235 (1993).

Nowrot, Karsten, *The Rule of Law in the Era of Globalization: Legal*

Consequences of Globalization: The Status of Non-Governmental Organizations under International Law, 6 IND. J. GLOBAL LEG. STUD. 579 (1999).

Oloka-Onyango, J., *Reinforcing Marginalized Rights in an Age of Globalization: International Mechanisms, Non-State Actors, and the Struggle for Peoples' Rights in Africa*, 18 AM. U. INT'L L. REV. 851 (2003).

Osofsky, Hari M., *Environmental Human Rights under the Alien Tort Statute: Redress for Indigenous Victims of Multinational Corporations*, 20 SUFFOLK TRANSNAT'L L. REV. 335 (1997).

Park, Ann I., *Human Rights and Basic Needs: Using International Human Rights Norms to Inform Constitutional Interpretation*, 34 UCLA L. REV. 1195 (1987).

Pasqualucci, Jo M., *Advisory Practice of the Inter-American Court of Human Rights: Contributing to the Evolution of International Human Rights Law*, 38 STAN. J INT'L L. 241 (2002).

Pasqualucci, Jo M., *Preliminary Objections Before the Inter-American Court of Human Rights: Legitimate Issues and Illegitimate Tactics*, 40 VA. J. INT'L L. 1 (1999).

Popovic, Neil A. F., *In Pursuit of Environmental human Rights: Commentary on the Draft Declaration of Principles on Human Rights and the Environment*, 27 COLUM. HUMAN RIGHTS L. REV. 487 (1996).

Popovic, Neil A. F., *Pursuing Environmental Justice with International Human Rights and State Constitutions*, 15 STAN. ENVTL. L.J. 338 (1996).

Popovic, Neil A. F., *The Right to Participate in Decisions That Affect the Environment*, 10 PACE ENVTL. L. REV. 683 (1993).

Quinn, Gerard, *The European Union and the Council of Europe on the Issue of Human Rights: Twins Separated at Birth*, 46 MCGILL L.J. 849 (2001).

Reed, RoseMary, *Rising Seas and Disappearing Islands: Can Island Inhabitants Seek Redress under the Alien Tort Claims Act?*, 11 PAC. RIM L. & POL'Y 399 (2002).

Rescia, Victor Rodriguez, & Marc David Seitles, *The Development of the Inter-American Human Rights System: A Historical Perspective and a Modern-Day Critique*, 16 N.Y.L. SCH. J. HUM. RTS. 593 (2000).

Rincenau, Johanna, *Enforcement Mechanisms in International Environmental Law: Quo Vadunt?*, 15 J. ENVTL. L. & LITIG. 147 (2000).

Rivera, Michael, *Bi-Polar and Polycentric Approaches to Human Rights and the Environment*, 28 COLUM. J. ENVTL. L. 371 (2003).

Rodriguez-Rivera, Luis E., *Is the Human Right to Environment Recognized Under International Law? It Depends on the Source*, 12 COLO. J. INT'L ENVTL. L. & POL'Y 1 (2001).

Rosencranz, Armin, & Richard, Campbell, *Foreign Environmental and Human Rights Suits Against U.S. Corporations in U.S. Courts*, 18 STAN. ENVTL. L.J. 145 (1999).

Sands, Philippe, *The "Greening" of International Law: Emerging Principles and Rules*, 1 IND. J. GLOBAL LEG. STUD. 293 (1994).

Schorn, Timothy J., *Drinkable Water and Breathable Air: A Livable Environmental as a Human Rights*, 4 GREAT PLAINS NAT. RESOURCES J. 121 (2000).

Shaughnessy, Meaghan, *Human Rights and the Environment: The United Nations Global Compact and the Continuing Debate about the Effectiveness of Corporate Voluntary Codes of Conduct*, 2000 COLO. J. INT'L ENVTL. L. & POL'Y 159 (2000).

Shelton, Dinah, *Fair Play, Fair Pay: Protecting the Traditional Knowledge and Resources of Indigenous Peoples*, 1993 YBIEL (1994).

Shelton, Dinah, *Human Rights and the Hierarchy of International Law Sources and Norms: Hierarchy of Norms and Human Rights: Of Trumps and Winners*, 65 SASK. L. REV. 299 (2002).

Shelton, Dinah, *Human Rights, Environmental Rights, and the Right to Environment*, 28 STAN J. INT'L L. 103 (1991).

Shelton, Dinah, *The Boundaries of Human Rights Jurisdiction in Europe*, 13 DUKE J. COMP. & INT'L L. 95 (2003).

Shelton, Dinah, *What Happened in Rio to Human Rights?*, 4 Y. B. INT'L ENVT'L L. 75 (1994).

Shutkin, W., *International Human Rights Law and the Earth: The Protection of Indigenous Peoples and the Environment*, 31 VA. J. INT'L L. 479 (1991).

Slater, Pam, *Environmental Law in Third World Countries: Can it be Enforced by Other Countries?*, 5 ILSA J INT'L & COMP L 519 (1999).

Smith, David, *Human Rights and the Environment: Clean Air and a Clean Environment as Fundamental Human Rights*, 1999 COLO. J. INT'L ENVTL. L. Y. B. 149 (1999).

Spyke, Nancy Perkins, *The Promotion and Preservation of Culture as Part of Environmental Policy*, 20 WM. & MARY ENVTL. L. & POL'Y REV. (1996).

Stever, Tara C., *Protecting Human Rights in the European Union: An Argument for Treaty Reform*, 20 FORDHAM INT'L L.J. 919 (1997).

Sullivan, Danile S., *Effective International Dispute Settlement Mechanisms and the Necessary Condition of Liberal Democracy*, 81 GEO. L.J. 2369 (1993).

Swepston, L., *A New Step in the International Law on Indigenous and Tribal Peoples: ILO Convention 169 of 1989*, OKLA. CITY U. L. REV. 677 (1990).

Taylor, Prudence E., *From Environmental to Ecological Human Rights: A New Dynamic in International Law?*, 10 GEO. INT'L ENVTL. L. REV. 309 (1998).

Thorme, M., *Establishing Environment as a Human Right*, 19 DEN. J. INT'L L. & POL'Y 302 (1991).

Tinker, Catherine, *Is a United Nations Convention the Most Appropriate Means to Pursue the Goal of Biological Diversity?: Responsibility*

for Biological Diversity Conservation Under International Law, 28 VAND. J.TRANSNAT'L L. 777 (1995).
Trindade, Antonio Augusto Cancado, *Current State and Perspectives of the Inter-American System of Human Rights Protection at the Dawn of the New Century*, 8 TUL. J. INT'L & COMP. L. 5 (2000).
Udombana, Nsongurua J., *So Far, So Fair: The Local Remedies Rule in the Jurisprudence of the African Commission on Human and Peoples' Rights*, 97 A.J.I.L. 1 (2003).
Udombana, Nsongurua J., *Toward the African Court on Human and Peoples' Rights: Better Late Than Never*, 3 YALE H.R. & DEV. L.J. 45 (2000).
Uhlmann, Eva M. Kornicker, *State Community Interests, Jus Cogens and Protection of the Global Environment: Developing Criteria for Peremptory Norms*, 11 GEO. INT'L ENVTL. L. REV. 101 (1998).
Van Dyke, Brennan, *Proposal to Introduce the Right to a Healthy Environment into the European Convention Regime*, 13 VA. ENVTL. L.J. 323 (1994).
Weber, S., *Environmental Information and the European Convention on Human Rights*, 12 HUM. RTS. L.J. 177 (1991).
Weisburd, A. M., *Implications of International Relations Theory for International Law of Human Rights*, 38 COLUM. J. TRANSNAT'L L. (1999).
Weisburd, A. Mark, *International Courts and American Courts*, 21 MICH. J. INT'L L. 877 (2000).
Werssbrodt, David, & Isabel, Horteiter, *The Principle of Non-Refoulement: Article 3 of the Convention Against Torture and Other Cruel, Inhuman or Degrading Treatment or Punishment in Comparison with the Non-Refoulement Provisions of Other International Human Rights Treaties*, 5 BUFF. HUM. RTS. L. REV. 1 (1999).
Wiggins, A., *Indian Rights and the Environment*, 18 YALE J. INT'L L. 345 (1993).
Wilson, Richard J., and Jan Perlin, *The Inter-American Human Rights System: Activities During 1999 through October 2000*, 16 AM. U. INT'L L. REV. 315 (2001).
Yoshida, O., *Soft Enforcement of Treaties: The Montreal Protocol's Non-compliance Procedure and the Functions of Internal International Institutions*, 10 COLO. J. INT'L ENVTL. L. & POL'Y 95 (1999).

CHAPTER 2

BOOKS

ALFREDSSON, GUNMUNDUR, & ROLF RING, THE INSPECTION PANEL OF THE WORLD BANK: A DIFFERENT COMPLAINTS PROCEDURE (Gunmundur Alfredsson & Rolf Ring eds., 2000).

BRAINARD, JOHN C., THE DIRECTORY OF NATIONAL ENVIRONMENTAL ORGANIZATIONS (John C. Brainard ed.,. 5th ed. 1996).
CLARK, DANA, DEMANDING ACCOUNTABILITY: CIVIL SOCIETY CLAIMS AND THE WORLD BANK INSPECTION PANEL (Dana Clark et al. eds., 2003).
MENKVELD, PAUL A., ORIGIN AND ROLE OF THE EUROPEAN BANK FOR RECONSTRUCTION AND DEVELOPMENT (Paul A. Menkveld ed., 1991).
NANDA, VED P., INTERNATIONAL ENVIRONMENTAL LAW FOR THE 21ST CENTURY (Ved P. Nanda & George R. Pring eds., 2003).
SANDS, PHILLIPPE, GREENING INTERNATIONAL LAW (Phillippe Sands ed., 1993).
SANDS, PHILLIPPE, PRINCIPLES OF INTERNATIONAL ENVIRONMENTAL LAW (Phillippe Sands ed., 2d ed. 2003).
STEINBERG, RICHARD H., THE GREENING OF TRADE LAW: INTERNATIONAL TRADE ORGANIZATIONS AND ENVIRONMENTAL ISSUES (Richard H. Steinberg ed., 2002).
SHIHATA, IBRAHIM F. I., THE WORLD BANK INSPECTION PANEL IN PRACTICE (2d ed. 2000).
SHIHATA, IBRAHIM F. I., THE WORLD BANK INSPECTION PANEL (Ibrahim F. I. Shihata ed., 1994).
SIERRA CLUB, WORLD DIRECTORY OF ENVIRONMENTAL ORGANIZATIONS (5th ed. 1996).
SULLIVAN, THOMAS F. P., DIRECTORY OF ENVIRONMENTAL INFORMATION SOURCES (Thomas F. P. Sullivan ed., 1995).

ARTICLES

Bialos Jeffery P., & Deborah E. Siegel, *Dispute Resolution Under the NAFTA: The Newer and Improved Model*, 27 INT'L LAW. 603 (1993).
Bruch, Carl. E., & Roman Czebiniak, *Globalizing Environmental Governance: Making the Leap From Regional Initiatives on Transparency, Participation, and Accountability in Environmental Matters*, 32 ENVTL. L. REP. 10428 (2002).
Carmody, Chi, *Beyond the Proposals: Public Participation in International Economic Law*, 15 AM. U. INT'L L. REV. 1321 (2000).
Housman, Robert, *Integrating Labor and Environmental Concerns into the North American Free Trade Agreement: A Look Back and a Look Ahead*, 8 AM. U. J. INT'L L. & POL'Y 719 (1993).
Housman, Robert, *The North American Free Trade Agreement's Lessons for Reconciling Trade and the Environment*, 30 STAN. J. INT'L L. 379 (1994).
Housman, Robert, *The Treatment of Labor and Environmental Issues in Future Western Hemisphere Trade Liberalization Efforts*, 10 CONN. J. INT'L L. 301 (1995).
Housman, Robert, & Durwood J. Zaelke, *Making Trade and Environmental Policies Mutually Reinforcing: Forging Competitive Sustainability*, 23 EVNTL. L. 545 (1993).

Hunter, David, *Using the World Bank Inspection Panel to Defend the Interests of Project-Affected People*, 4 CHI. J. INT'L L. 201 (2003).

Kalas, Peggy Rodgers, *International Environmental Dispute Resolution and the Need for Access by Non-State Entities*, 12 COLO. J. INT'L ENVTL. L. & POL'Y 191 (2001).

Leighton, Michelle, & Elena Castaneda, *Civil Society Concerns in the Context of Economic Globalization*, 15 TRANSNAT'L LAW. 105 (2002).

Patton, Kevin W. Note: *Dispute Resolution Under the North American Commission on Environmental Cooperation*, 5 DUKE J. COMP. INT'L L. 87 (1994).

Peel, Jacqueline, *Giving the Public a Voice in the Protection of the Global Environment: Avenues for Participation by NGOs in Dispute Resolution at the European Court of Justice and World Trade Organization*, 12 COLO. J. INT'L ENVTL. L. & POL'Y 47 (2001).

Spracker, Stanley M., et al., *Environmental Protection and International Trade: NAFTA as a Means of Eliminating Contamination as a Competitive Advantage*, 5 GEO. INT'L ENVTL. L. REV. 669 (1993).

Stewart, Richard B., *The NAFTA: Trade, Competition, Environmental Protection*, 27 INT'L LAW. 751 (1993).

CHAPTER 3

BOOKS

AELIE, DURWOOD, ET AL., TRADE AND THE ENVIRONMENT: LAW, ECONOMICS, AND POLICY (1993).

ANDERSON, KYM, THE GREENING OF WORLD TRADE ISSUES (1992).

AUDLEY, JOHN J., GREEN POLITICS AND GLOBAL TRADE: NAFTA AND THE FUTURE OF ENVIRONMENTAL POLITICS (1997).

CAMERON, JAMES, TRADE AND THE ENVIRONMENT: THE SEARCH FOR BALANCE (1994).

COPELAND, BRIAN RICHARD, TRADE AND THE ENVIRONMENT: THEORY AND EVIDENCE (2003).

ESTY, DANIEL C., GREENING THE GATT: TRADE, ENVIRONMENT, AND THE FUTURE (1994).

FRANCIONI, FRANCESCO, ENVIRONMENT, HUMAN RIGHTS AND INTERNATIONAL TRADE (2001).

FREDRIKSSON, PER, TRADE, GLOBAL POLICY, AND THE ENVIRONMENT (1999).

FRENCH, HILARY F., COSTLY TRADEOFFS: RECONCILING TRADE AND THE ENVIRONMENT (1993).

INTERNATIONAL INSTITUTE FOR SUSTAINABLE DEVELOPMENT, ENVIRONMENT AND TRADE: A HANDBOOK (2000).

JHA, VEENA, RECONCILING TRADE AND THE ENVIRONMENT: LESSONS FROM CASE STUDIES IN DEVELOPING COUNTRIES (1999).

KISS, ALEXANDRE CHARLES, & DINAH SHELTON, MANUAL OF EUROPEAN ENVIRONMENTAL LAW (1997).

LEE, JAMES R., EXPLORING THE GAPS: VITAL LINKS BETWEEN TRADE, ENVIRONMENT, AND CULTURE (2000).
LOFDAHL, COREY L., ENVIRONMENTAL IMPACTS OF GLOBALIZATION AND TRADE: A SYSTEMS STUDY (2002).
LOW, PATRICK, INTERNATIONAL TRADE AND THE ENVIRONMENT (1992).
RAO, P. K., ENVIRONMENTAL TRADE DISPUTES AND THE WTO (2001).
SAMPSON, GARY P., TRADE, ENVIRONMENT, AND THE WTO: THE POST-SEATTLE AGENDA (2000).
SCHULZE, GÜNTHER G., INTERNATIONAL ENVIRONMENTAL ECONOMICS: A SURVEY OF THE ISSUES (2001).
STEINBERG, RICHARD H., THE GREENING OF TRADE LAW: INTERNATIONAL TRADE ORGANIZATIONS AND ENVIRONMENTAL ISSUES (2002).
TUSSIE, DIANA, THE ENVIRONMENT AND INTERNATIONAL TRADE NEGOTIATIONS: DEVELOPING COUNTRY STAKES (1999).
UIMONEN, PETER, ENVIRONMENTAL ISSUES IN THE NEW WORLD TRADING SYSTEM (1997).
UNITED STATES. OFFICE OF THE U.S. TRADE REPRESENTATIVE, THE GATT URUGUAY ROUND AGREEMENTS: REPORT ON ENVIRONMENTAL ISSUES (1994).
XU, XINPENG, INTERNATIONAL TRADE AND ENVIRONMENTAL REGULATION: A DYNAMIC PERSPECTIVE (1999).
ZAELKE, DURWOOD, TRADE AND THE ENVIRONMENT: LAW, ECONOMICS, AND POLICY (1993).

ARTICLES

Anderson, Terry L., & J. Bishop Grewell, *It Isn't Easy Being Green: Environmental Policy Implications for Foreign Policy, International Law, and Sovereignty*, 2 CHI. J. INT'L L. 427 (2001).

Bernabe-Riefkohl, Alberto, *"To Dream the Impossible Dream": Globalization and Harmonization of Environmental Laws*, 20 N.C. J. INT'L L. & COM. REG. 205 (1995).

Block, Greg, *Trade and Environment in the Western Hemisphere: Expanding the North American Agreement on Environmental Cooperation in the Americas*, 33 ENVT'L L. 501 (2003).

Brunner, Annick Emmenegger, *Conflicts Between International Trade and Multilateral Environmental Agreements*, 4 ANN. SURV. INT'L & COMP. L. 74 (1997).

Bugeda, Beatriz, *Is NAFTA Up to its Green Expectations? Effective Law Enforcement Under the North American Agreement on Environmental Cooperation*, 32 U. RICH. L. REV. 1591 (1999).

Carlson, Scott N., *The Montreal Protocol's Environmental Subsidies and GATT: A Needed Reconciliation*, 29 TEX. INT'L L.J. 211 (1994).

Charnovitz, Steve, *Trade and the Environment: The Environment vs. Trade Rules: Defogging the Debate*, 23 ENVTL. L. 475 (1992).

Dixon, Craig A. A. Note: *Environmental Survey of WTO Dispute Panel Resolution Panel Decisions Since 1995:"Trade at All Costs?,"* 24 WM. & MARY ENVTL. L. & POL'Y REV. 89 (2000).

Elmilady, Suzanne, *A Step in the Right Direction: How to Make the Free Trade Agreement of the Americas a Cohesive Agreement That Will Better Serve Integration of Free Trade in the Western Hemisphere*, 11 CURRENTS INT'L TRADE L.J. 70 (2002).

Feketekuty, Geza, *The Link Between Trade and Environmental Policy*, 2 MINN. J. GLOBAL TRADE 171 (1993).

Gaines, Sanford E., *Rethinking Environmental Protection, Competitiveness, and International Trade*, 1997 U. CHI. LEGAL F. 231 (1997).

Goldman, Patti A., *Resolving the Trade and Environmental Debate: In Search of a Neutral Form with Neutral Principles*, 49 WASH. & LEE L. REV. 1279 (1993).

Horwitz, Thomas M. Note: *International Environmental Protection After the GATT Tuna Decision: a Proposal for a United States Reply*, 25 CASE W. RES. J. INT'L L. 55 (1993).

Kometani, Kazumochi, *Trade and Environment: How Should WTO Panels Review Environmental Regulations Under GATT Articles III and XX?*, 16 NW. J. INT'L L. & BUS. 441 (1996).

Lind, Samuel N., *ECO-Labels and International Trade Law: Avoiding Trade Violations While Regulating the Environment*, 8 INT'L LEGAL PERSP. 113 (1996).

Martin, Lana, *World Trade Organization and Environmental Protection: Reconciling the Conflict*, 9 CURRENTS INT'L TRADE L.J. 69 (2000).

Miller, Stefan R., *NAFTA: A Model for Reconciling the Conflict Between Free Trade and International Environmental Protection*, 56 U. PITT. L. REV. 483 (1994).

Mugwanya, George William, *Global Free Trade Vis-a-Vis Environmental Regulation and Sustainable Development: Reinvigorating Efforts Towards a More Integrated Approach*, 14 J. ENVTL. L. & LITIG. 401 (1999).

O'Connell, Mary Ellen, *Using Trade to Enforce International Environmental Law: Implications for United States Law*, 1 IND. J. GLOBAL LEG. STUD. 273 (1994).

Pitschas, Christian, *GATT/WTO Rules for Border Tax Adjustment and the Proposed European Directive Introducing a Tax on Carbon Dioxide Emissions and Energy*, 24 GA. J. INT'L & COMP. L. 479 (1995).

Roht-Arriaza, Naomi, *Precaution, Participation, and the "Greening" of International Trade Law*, 7 J. ENVTL. L. & LITIG. 57 (1992).

Runge, C. Ford, *Trade Protectionism and Environmental Regulations: The New Nontariff Barriers*, 11 NW. J. INT'L L. & BUS. 47 (1990).

Schoenbaum, Thomas J., *Trade and Environment: Free International Trade and Protection of the Environment: Irreconcilable Conflict?*, 86 A.J.I.L. 700 (1992).

Schultz, Jennifer, *The Demise of "Green" Protectionism: The WTO Decision on the US Gasoline Rule*, 25 DENV. J. INT'L L. & POL'Y 1 (1996).
Soloway, Julie A., *Environmental Trade Barriers Under NAFTA: The MMT Fuel Additives Controversy*, 8 MINN. J. GLOBAL TRADE 55 (1999).
Strauss, Andrew L., *From GATT-zilla to the Green Giant: Winning the Environmental Battle for the Soul of the World Trade Organization*, 19 U. PA. J. INT'L ECON. L. 769 (1998).
Tollefson, Chris, *Games Without Frontiers: Investor Claims and Citizen Submissions Under the NAFTA Regime*, 27 YALE J. INT'L L. 141 (2002).
Villegas, Pedro, *Nature Beyond The Nation State Symposium: The Environmental Challenge of the Common Market in South America: REMA Under MERCOSUR*, 29 GOLDEN GATE U.L. REV. 445 (1999).
Wagner, J. Martin, *International Investment, Expropriation and Environmental Protection*, 29 GOLDEN GATE U. L. REV. 465 (1999).
Wagner, J. Martin, *The WTO's Interpretation of the SPS Agreement Has Undermined the Right of Governments to Establish Appropriate Levels of Protection Against Risk*, 31 LAW & POL'Y INT'L BUS. 855 (2000).
Wiener, Jonathan Baert, *On the Political Economy of Global Environmental Regulation*, 87 GEO. L.J. 749 (1999).
Winter, Ryan L., Note and Comment: *Reconciling the GATT and WTO with Multilateral Environmental Agreements: Can We Have Our Cake and Eat It Too?*, 11 COLO. J. INT'L ENVTL. L. & POL'Y 223 (2000).
Wirth, David A., *International Trade Agreements: Vehicles for Regulatory Reform?*, 1997 U. CHI. LEGAL F. 331 (1997).

CHAPTER 4

BOOKS

HULL, E. W. SEABROOK & ALBERT W. KEERS, INTRODUCTION TO A CONVENTION ON THE INTERNATION ENVIRONMENTAL PROTECTION AGENCY (1971).
HURRELL, ANDREW, & BENEDICT KINGSBURY EDS., THE INTERNATIONAL POLITICS OF THE ENVIRONMENT (1992).
SAND, PETER H., THE EFFECTIVENESS OF INTERNATIONAL ENVIRONMENTAL AGREEMENTS: A SURVEY OF EXISTING LEGAL INSTRUMENTS (1992).
SANDS, PHILIPPE, PRINCIPLES OF INTERNATIONAL ENVIRONMENTAL LAW: FRAMEWORK, STANDARDS, AND IMPLEMENTATION (1995).

ARTICLES

Anderson, Steven M., *Reforming International Institutions to Improve Global Environmental Relations, Agreements, and Treat Enforcement*, 18 HASTINGS INT'L & COMP. L. REV. 771 (1995).
Ardia, David S., *Does the Emperor Have no Clothes? Enforcement of International Laws Protecting the Marine Environment*, 19 MICH. J. INT'L L. 497 (1998).

Bacon, Brad L., *Enforcement Mechanisms in International Wildlife Agreements and the United States: Wading Through the* Murk, 12 GEO. INT'L ENVTL. L. REV. 331(1999).
Brown Weiss, Edith, *Understanding Compliance with International Environmental Agreements: The Baker's Dozen Myths*, 32 U. RICH. L. REV. 1555 (1999).
Brown Weiss, Edith, *International Environmental Law: Contemporary Issues and the Emergence of a New World Order*, 81 GEO. L.J. 675 (1993).
Churchill, Robin R., & Geir Ulfstein, *Autonomous Institutional Agreements in Multilateral Environmental Agreements: A Little-Noticed Phenomenon in International Law*, 94 A.J.I.L. 623 (2000).
DiMatteo, Larry A., Kiren Dosanjh, Paul L. Frantz, Peter Bowal, Clyde Stoltenberg, *The Doha Declaration and Beyond: Giving a Voice to Non-Trade Concerns Within the WTO Trade Regime*, 36 VAND. J. TRANSNAT'L L. 95 (2003).
Drumbl, Mark A., *Poverty, Wealth, and Obligation in International Environmental Law*, 76 TUL. L. REV. 843 (2002).
Dunoff, Jeffrey L., *Institutional Misfits: The GATT, the ICJ and Trade-Environment Disputes*, 15 MICH. J. INT'L L. 1043 (1994).
Hanafi, Alex G., *Joint Implementation: Legal and Institutional Issues for an Effective International Program to Combat Climate Change*, 22 HARV. ENVTL. L. REV. 441 (1998).
Handl, Gunther, *Environmental Security and Global Change: The Challenge to International Law*, 1 Y.B. INT'L ENVTL. L. 3 (1990).
Hicks, Bethany L., *Treaty Congestion in International Environmental Law: The Need for Greater International Coordination*, 32 U. RICH. L. REV. 1643 (1999).
Hierlmeier, Jodie, *UNEP: Retrospect and Prospect—Options for Reforming the Global Environmental Governance Regime*, 14 GEO. INT'L ENVTL. L. REV. 767 (2002).
Kelly, Michael J., *Overcoming Obstacles to the Effective Implementation of International Environmental Agreements*, 9 GEO. INT'L ENVTL. L. REV. 447 (1997).
Murray, Paula C., *The International Environmental Management Standard, ISO 14000: A Non-Tariff Barrier or a Step to an Emerging Global Environmental Policy?*, 18 U. PA. J. INT'L ECON. L. 577 (1997).
Ramlogan, Rajendra, *The Environment and International Law: Rethinking the Traditional* Approach, 3 RES COMMUNES: VERMONT'S J. ENV'T 4 (2001).
Raustiala, Kal, *The "Participatory Revolution" in International Environmental Law*, 21 HARV. ENVTL. L. REV. 537 (1997).
Shaffer, Gregory C., *The World Trase Organization Under Challenge: Democracy and the Law and Politics of the WTO's Treatment of Trade and Environment Matters*, 25 HARV. ENVTL. L. REV. 1 (2001).

Trachtman, Joel P., & Philip M. Moremen, *Costs and Benefits of Private Participation in WTO Dispute Settlement: Whose Right is it Anyway?*, 44 HARV. INT'L L.J. 221 (2003).

CHAPTER 5

Books

ACCOUNTABILITY FOR ATROCITIES: NATIONAL AND INTERNATIONAL RESPONSES (Jane Stromseth ed., 2003).
ALTER, KAREN J., ESTABLISHING THE SUPREMACY OF EUROPEAN LAW: THE MAKING OF AN INTERNATIONAL RULE OF LAW IN EUROPE (2001).
BARRETT, SCOTT, ENVIRONMENT AND STATECRAFT: THE STRATEGY OF ENVIRONMENTAL TREATY-MAKING (2003).
BASSIOUNI, M. CHERIF, CRIMES AGAINST HUMANITY IN INTERNATIONAL CRIMINAL LAW (1992).
BASSIOUNI, M. CHERIF, INTRODUCTION TO INTERNATIONAL CRIMINAL LAW (2003).
BEACH, DEREK, BETWEEN LAW AND POLITICS: THE RELATIONSHIP BETWEEN THE EUROPEAN COURT OF JUSTICE AND EU MEMBER STATES (2001).
BIRNIE, PATRICIA W., & ALAN E. BOYLE, INTERNATIONAL LAW AND THE ENVIRONMENT (2d ed., 2002).
BIRNIE, PATRICIA W., & ALAN E. BOYLE, BASIC DOCUMENTS ON INTERNATIONAL LAW AND THE ENVIRONMENT (1995).
BODIE, THOMAS J., POLITICS AND THE EMERGENCE OF AN ACTIVIST INTERNATIONAL COURT OF JUSTICE (1995).
BOWETT, D.W., THE INTERNATIONAL COURT OF JUSTICE: PROCESS, PRACTICE AND PROCEDURE (1997).
BROOMHALL, BRUCE, INTERNATIONAL JUSTICE AND THE INTERNATIONAL CRIMINAL COURT: BETWEEN STATE CONSENT AND THE RULE OF LAW (2003).
BROWN WEISS, EDITH, INTERNATIONAL ENVIRONMENTAL LAW AND POLICY (1998).
BROWN, EDWARD D., THE INTERNATIONAL LAW OF THE SEA (1994).
BROWN, LIONEL N., & TOM KENNEDY, THE COURT OF JUSTICE OF THE EUROPEAN COMMUNITIES (2000).
BUILDING ON THE KYOTO PROTOCOL: OPTIONS FOR PROTECTING THE CLIMATE (Kevin A. Baumert et al. eds., 2002).
BURROUGHS, JOHN, THE (IL)LEGALITY OF THREAT OR USE OF NUCLEAR WEAPONS: A GUIDE TO THE HISTORIC OPINION OF THE INTERNATIONAL COURT OF JUSTICE (1998).
Caminos, Hugo, *The Establishment of Specialized Courts, in* CURRENT MARINE ENVIRONMENTAL ISSUES AND THE INTERNATIONAL TRIBUNAL FOR THE LAW OF THE SEA 35 (Myron H. Nordquist & John Norton Moore eds., 2001).
CENTER FOR OCEANS LAW AND POLICY, UNIVERSITY OF VIRGINIA, THE STOCKHOLM DECLARATION AND THE LAW OF THE MARINE ENVIRONMENT (Myron H. Nordquist et al. eds., 2003).

Bibliography • *333*

CHITTY, GRITAKUMAR E., *A Brief History of the Post Conference Development of the Tribunal as an International Judicial Body, in* CURRENT MARINE ENVIRONMENTAL ISSUES AND THE INTERNATIONAL TRIBUNAL FOR THE LAW OF THE SEA 43 (Myron H. Nordquist & John Norton Moore eds. 2001).
CULLET, PHILIPPE, DIFFERENTIAL TREATMENT IN INTERNATIONAL ENVIRONMENTAL LAW (2003).
DE BÚRCA, GRÁINNE, & J. H. H. WEILER, THE EUROPEAN COURT OF JUSTICE (2001).
DiMENTO, JOSEPH F., THE GLOBAL ENVIRONMENT AND INTERNATIONAL LAW (2003).
ELSEA, JENNIFER, INTERNATIONAL CRIMINAL COURT: OVERVIEW AND SELECTED LEGAL ISSUES (2003).
ENVIRONMENTAL PROTECTION AND INTERNATIONAL LAW (Winfried Lang et al. eds., 1991).
GENOCIDE: CONCEPTUAL AND HISTORICAL DIMENSIONS (George J. Andreopoulos ed., 1994).
GLOBAL ENVIRONMENTAL POLICIES: INSTITUTIONS AND PROCEDURES (Ho-Won Jeong, ed., 2001).
GRUBB, MICHAEL, ET AL., THE KYOTO PROTOCOL: A GUIDE AND ASSESSMENT (1999).
HALVORSSEN, ANITA M., EQUALITY AMONG UNEQUALS IN INTERNATIONAL ENVIRONMENTAL LAW: DIFFERENTIAL TREATMENT FOR DEVELOPING COUNTRIES (1999).
HANGIN, XUE, TRANSBOUNDARY DAMAGE IN INTERNATIONAL LAW (2003).
HEY, ELLEN, REFLECTIONS ON AN INTERNATIONAL ENVIRONMENTAL COURT (2000).
INCREASING THE EFFECTIVENESS OF THE INTERNATIONAL COURT OF JUSTICE: PROCEEDINGS OF THE ICJ/UNITAR COLLOQUIUM TO CELEBRATE THE 50TH ANNIVERSARY OF THE COURT (Connie Peck & Roy S. Lee eds., 1997).
INTERNATIONAL COURTS AND TRIBUNALS: SELECTED DOCUMENTS AND MATERIALS (W. van der Wolf & S. de Haardt eds., 2d ed., 2001).
INTERNATIONAL ENVIRONMENTAL LAW ANTHOLOGY (Anthony D'Amato & Kristen Engel eds., 1996).
INTERNATIONAL CRIMES, PEACE, AND HUMAN RIGHTS: THE ROLE OF THE INTERNATIONAL CRIMINAL COURT (Dinah Shelton ed., 2000).
INTERNATIONAL ENVIRONMENTAL LAW REPORTS (Cairo A. R. Robb et al. eds., 1999).
INTERNATIONALIZATION OF THE ECONOMY AND ENVIRONMENTAL POLICY OPTIONS (Paul J. J. Welfens ed., 2001).
JONASSOHN, KURT, & KARIN SOLVEIG BJÖRNSON, GENOCIDE AND GROSS HUMAN RIGHTS VIOLATIONS IN COMPARATIVE PERSPECTIVE (1998).
JONES, JOHN R. W. D., INTERNATIONAL CRIMINAL PRACTIVE (3d ed. 2003).
JUSTICE FOR CRIMES AGAINST HUMANITY (Mark Lattimer & Philippe Sands eds., 2003).
KIBEL, PAUL S., THE EARTH ON TRIAL: ENVIRONMENTAL LAW ON THE INTERNATIONAL STAGE (1999).

KISS, ALEXANDRE CHARLES, & DINAH SHELTON, INTERNATIONAL ENVIRONMENTAL LAW (3rd ed. 2003).
KNOOPS, GEERT-JAN ALEXANDAER, AN INTRODUCTION TO THE LAW OF INTERNATIONAL TRIBUNALS: A COMPARATIVE STUDY (2003).
KUOKKANEN, TUOMAS, INTERNATIONAL LAW AND THE ENVIRONMENT: VARIATIONS ON A THEME (2002).
KWIATKOWSKA, BARBARA, DECISIONS OF THE WORLD COURT RELEVANT TO THE UN CONVENTION ON LAW OF THE SEA (2002).
LASOK, K. P. E., THE EUROPEAN COURT OF JUSTICE: PRACTICE AND PROCEDURE (2d ed. 1994).
LAW OF THE SEA: THE COMMON HERITAGE AND EMERGING CHALLENGES (Harry N. Scheiber ed., 2000).
LAW OF THE SEA (Hugo Caminos ed., 2001).
LEE, ROY S., THE INTERNATIONAL CRIMINAL COURT: ELEMENTS OF CRIMES AND RULES OF PROCEDURE AND EVIDENCE (2001).
LEVERING, RALPH B., & MIRIAM LEVERING, CITIZEN ACTION FOR GLOBAL CHANGE: THE NEPTUNE GROUP AND LAW OF THE SEA (1999).
MCWHINNEY, EDWARD, JUDICIAL SETTLEMENT OF INTERNATIONAL DISPUTES: JURISDICTION, JUSTICIABILITY, AND JUDICIAL LAW-MAKING ON THE CONTEMPORARY INTERNATIONAL COURT (1991).
MEYER, HOWARD N., THE WORLD COURT IN ACTION: JUDGING AMONG THE NATIONS (2002).
MOLITOR, MICHAEL R., INTERNATIONAL ENVIRONMENTAL LAW: PRIMARY MATERIALS (1991).
MORRIS, VIRGINIA, AND MICHAEL SHARF, AN INSIDER'S GUIDE TO THE INTERNATIONAL CRIMINAL TRIBUNAL FOR THE FORMER YUGOSLAVIA (1995).
NANDA, VED P., & GEORGE PRING, INTERNATIONAL ENVIRONMENTAL LAW FOR THE 21ST CENTURY (2003).
NANDA, VED P., INTERNATIONAL ENVIRONMENTAL LAW AND POLICY (1995).
OBERTHÜR, SEBASTIAN, & HERMANN OTT, THE KYOTO PROTOCOL: INTERNATIONAL CLIMATE POLICY FOR THE 21ST CENTURY (1999).
POLAR POLITICS: CREATING INTERNATIONAL ENVIRONMENTAL REGIMES (Oran R. Young & Gail Osherenko eds., 1993).
RAO, P. K., INTERNATIONAL ENVIRONMENTAL LAW AND ECONOMICS (2002).
RAO, P. K., ENVIRONMENTAL TRADE DISPUTES AND THE WTO (2002).
RAO, P. CHANDRASEKHARA, *International Tribunal for the Law of the Sea: An Overview, in* THE INTERNATIONAL TRIBUNAL FOR THE LAW OF THE SEA: LAW AND PRACTICE 1 (P. Chandrasekhara Rao & Rahmatullah Khan eds., 2001).
REMEDIES IN INTERNATIONAL LAW: THE INSTITUTIONAL DILEMMA (Malcolm D. Evans ed., 1998).
ROBINSON, DAVIS R., *Recourse Against Flag States for Breaches of Their International Obligations Under the 1982 Law of the Sea Convention, in* CURRENT MARINE ENVIRONMENTAL ISSUES AND THE INTERNATIONAL

TRIBUNAL FOR THE LAW OF THE SEA 374 (Myron H. Nordquist & John Norton Moore eds., 2001).

ROMANO, CESARE, THE PEACEFUL SETTLEMENT OF INTERNATIONAL ENVIRONMENTAL DISPUTES: A PRAGMATIC APPROACH (2000).

ROSENNE, SHABTAI, THE LAW AND PRACTICE OF THE INTERNATIONAL COURT (2d ed. rev. 1985).

ROSENNE, SHABTAI, THE WORLD COURT—WHAT IT IS AND HOW IT WORKS (5th ed. rev. 1995).

ROSENNE, SHABTAI, *The Case-Law of ITLOS (1997-2001):An Overview, in* CURRENT MARINE ENVIRONMENTAL ISSUES AND THE INTERNATIONAL TRIBUNAL FOR THE LAW OF THE SEA 127 (Myron H. Nordquist & John Norton Moore eds., 2001).

SADAT, LEILA NADYA, THE INTERNATIONAL CRIMINAL COURT AND THE TRANSFORMATION OF INTERNATIONAL LAW: JUSTICE FOR THE NEW MILLENNIUM (2002).

SAND, PETER H., TRANSNATIONAL ENVIRONMENTAL LAW: LESSONS IN GLOBAL CHANGE (1999).

SANDS, PHILIPPE, *ITLOS:An International Lawyer's Perspective, in* CURRENT MARINE ENVIRONMENTAL ISSUES AND THE INTERNATIONAL TRIBUNAL FOR THE LAW OF THE SEA 142 (Myron H. Nordquist & John Norton Moore eds., 2001).

SANDS, PHILIPPE, PRINCIPLES OF INTERNATIONAL ENVIRONMENTAL LAW (2003).

SCHABAS, WILLIAM, AN INTRODUCTION TO THE INTERNATIONAL CRIMINAL COURT (2001).

SCHNEIDER, JAN, WORLD PUBLIC ORDER OF THE ENVIRONMENT: TOWARDS AN INTERNATIONAL ECOLOGICAL LAW AND ORGANIZATION (1979).

SOHN, LOUIS B., & KRISTEN GUSTAFSON, THE LAW OF THE SEA: IN A NUTSHELL 210 (1984).

SPRINGER, ALLEN L., THE INTERNATIONAL LAW OF POLLUTION: PROTECTING THE GLOBAL ENVIRONMENT IN A WORLD OF SOVEREIGN STATES (1983).

SZAFARZ, RENATA, THE COMPULSORY JURISDICTION OF THE INTERNATIONAL COURT OF JUSTICE (1993).

T.M.C. ASSER INSTITUUT, INTERNATIONAL ENVIRONMENTAL LAW (1997).

THE EFFECTIVENESS OF INTERNATIONAL ENVIRONMENTAL AGREEMENTS: A SURVEY OF EXISTING LEGAL INSTRUMENTS (Peter H. Sand ed., 1992).

THE GLOBAL ENVIRONMENT: INSTITUTIONS, LAW, AND POLICY (Norman J. Vig & Regina S. Axelrod eds., 1999).

THE IMPLEMENTATION AND EFFECTIVENESS OF INTERNATIONAL ENVIRONMENTAL COMMITMENTS: THEORY AND PRACTICE (David Victor et al. eds., 1998).

THE INTERNATIONAL COURT OF JUSTICE: ITS FUTURE ROLE AFTER FIFTY YEARS (A.S. Muller et al. eds., 1997).

THE INTERNATIONAL POLITICS OF THE ENVIRONMENT: ACTORS, INTERESTS AND INSTITUTIONS (Andrew Hurrell & Benedict Kingsbury eds., 1992).

THE OCEANS AND ENVIRONMENTAL SECURITY: SHARED U.S. AND RUSSIAN PERSPECTIVES (James M. Broadus & Raphael V. Varanov eds., 1994).
THE ROME STATUTE FOR AND INTERNATIONAL CRIMINAL COURT: A COMMENTARY (Antonio Cassese et al. eds., 2002).
THE WIDENING CIRCLE OF GENOCIDE (Israel W. Charny ed., 1994).
THE WORLD COURT REFERENCE GUIDE: JUDGMENTS, ADVISORY OPINIONS AND ORDERS OF THE PERMANENT COURT OF INTERNATIONAL JUSTICE AND THE INTERNATIONAL COURT OF JUSTICE (1922-2000) (Bimal N. Patel ed., 2002).
UNITED NATIONS CONVENTION ON THE LAW OF THE SEA, 1982: A COMMENTARY (Myron H. Nordquist ed., 2000).
WEITZ, ERIC D., A CENTURY OF GENOCIDE: UTOPIAS OF RACE AND NATION (2003).
WOLFRUM, RUDIGER, *Intervention in the Proceedings before ICJ and ITLOS*, in THE INTERNATIONAL TRIBUNAL FOR THE LAW OF THE SEA: LAW AND PRACTICE 161 (P. Chandrasekhara Rao & Rahmatullah Khan eds., 2001).
YOUNG, STEVEN S., INTERNATIONAL LAW OF ENVIRONMENTAL PROTECTION (1995).

ARTICLES

Arnull, A., *Private Applicants and the Action for Annulment Under Article 173 of the EC Treaty*, 32 COMM. MKT. L. REV. 7 (1995).
Bodansky, Daniel, et al., *Invoking State Responsibility in the Twenty-First Century*, 96 AM. J. INT'L L. 798 (2002).
Botchway, Francis N., *The Context of Trans-Boundary Energy Resource Exploitation: the Environment, the State, and the Methods*, 14 COLO. J. INT'L ENVTL. L. & POL'Y 191 (2003).
Chanbonpin, Kim David, *Holding the United States Accountable for Environmental Damages Caused by the U.S. Military in the Philippines, a Plan for the Future*, 4 ASIAN-PAC. L. & POL'Y J. 10 (2003).
Danner, Allison Marston, *Enhancing the Legitimacy and Accountability of Prosecutorial Discretion at the International Criminal Court*, 97 AM. J. INT'L L. 510 (2003).
Delbruck, Jost, *A More Effective International Law of New "World Law"?—Some Aspects of the Development of International Law in a Changing International System*, 68 IND. L.J. 705 (1993).
Dewes, Kate, & Robert Green, *The World Court Project: How a Citizen Network Can Influence the United Nations*, 7 PACIFICA REV. 22 (NO. 2, 1995).
DiMento, Joseph, *International Environmental Law: A Global Assessment*, 33 ENVTL. L. REP. 10387 (2003).
Dunoff, Jeffrey L., *Institutional Misfits: the Gatt, the ICJ & Trade-Environment Disputes*, 15 MICH. J. INT'L L. 1043 (1999).

Girouard, Robert J., Note, *Water Export Restrictions: A Case Study of WTO Dispute Settlement Strategies and Outcomes*, 15 GEO. INT'L ENVTL. L. REV. 247 (2003).

Kalas, Peggy Rodgers, *International Environmental Dispute Resolution and the Need for Access by Non-state Entities*, 12 COLO. J. INT'L ENVTL. L. & POL'Y 191 (2001).

Kalas, Peggy Rodgers, & Alexia Herwig, *Dispute Resolution Under the Kyoto Protocol*, 27 ECOLOGY L.W. 53 (2000).

Low, Luan, & David Hodgkinson, *Compensation for Wartime Environmental Damage: Challenges to International Law After the Gulf War*, 35 VA. J. INT'L L. 405 (1995).

McCallion, Kenneth F., & H. Rajan Sharma, *Environmental Justice Without Borders: The Need for an International Court of the Environment to Protect Fundamental Rights*, 32 GEO. WASH. J. INT'L. L. & ECON. 351 (2000).

Murphy, Sean D., *Does the World Need a New Environmental Court?*, 32 GEO. WASH. J. INT'L. L. & ECON. 333 (2000).

Oxman, Bernard H., *The Third United Nations Conference on the Law of the Sea: Tenth Session*, 76 AM. J. INT'L L. 1 (1982).

Reed, Lucy, *Great Expectations: Where Does the Proliferation of International Dispute Resolution Tribunals Leave International Law?*, 96 AM. SOC'Y INT'L L. PROC. 219 (2002).

Rinceanu, Johanna, *Enforcement Mechanisms in International Environmental Law: Quo Vadunt? Homo Sanus in Natura Sana*, 15 J. ENVTL. L. & LITIG. 147 (2000).

Rollé, Mary Elliott Note: *Unraveling Accountability: Contesting Legal and Procedural Barriers in International Toxic Tort Cases*, 15 GEO. INT'L ENVTL. L. REV. 135 (2003).

Sharp, Peter, *Prospects for Environmental Liability in the International Criminal Court*, 18 VA. ENVT'L L.J. 217 (1999).

Udombana, Nsongurua J., *An African Human Rights Court and an African Union Court: A Needful Duality or a Needless Duplication?*, 28 BROOK. J. INT'L L. 811 (2003).

Udombana, Nsongurua J., *Articulating the Right to Democratic Governance in Africa*, 24 MICH. J. INT'L L. 1209 (2003).

Uhlmann, Eva M. Kornicker, *State Community Interests, Jus Cogens and Protection of the Global Environment: Developing Criteria for Peremptory Norms*, 11 GEO. INT'L. ENVTL. L. REV. 101 (1998).

Wu, Charles Qiong, *A Unified Forum? The New Arbitration Rules for Environmental Disputes Under the Permanent Court of Arbitration*, 3 CHI. J. INT'L L. 263 (2002).

Zaelke, Durwood, *Making Law Work: Environmental Compliance and Sustainable Developments*, CAMERON MAG. LONDON (2005).

CHAPTER 6
BOOKS

A GUIDE TO FEDERAL AGENCY ADJUDICATION (Michael Asimow ed., 2003).

BAXI, UPENDRA, INCONVENIENT FORUM AND CONVENIENT CATASTROPHE: THE BHOPAL CASE (1986).

CAMPIGLIO, LUIGI, THE ENVIRONMENT AFTER RIO: INTERNATIONAL LAW AND ECONOMICS (1994).

COHEN, BENEDICT S., & DIRK D. HAIRE, *Environmental Citizen Suits: Standing and the Proper Scope of Relief,* in CITIZEN SUITS AND QUI TAM ACTIONS: PRIVATE ENFORCEMENT OF PUBLIC POLICY 21 (James T. Blanch ed., 1996).

DEFENDERS OF WILDLIFE, THE PUBLIC IN ACTION: USING STATE CITIZEN SUIT STATUTES TO PROTECT BIODIVERSITY (1996).

INTERNATIONAL ENVIRONMENTAL SOFT LAW: COLLECTION OF RELEVANT INSTRUMENTS (W. E. Burhenne & Marlene Jahnke eds., 1993).

LEVY, DAVID, INTERNATIONAL LITIGATION: DEFENDING AND SUING FOREIGN PARTIES IN U.S. FEDERAL COURTS (2003).

MACDONALD, JAMES B., & JOHN E. CONWAY, ENVIRONMENTAL LITIGATION (1972 and supplements).

MILLER, JEFFREY G., CITIZEN SUITS: PRIVATE ENFORCEMENT OF FEDERAL POLLUTION CONTROL LAWS (1987).

SHELTON, DINAH, COMMITMENT AND COMPLIANCE: THE ROLE OF NON-BINDING NORMS IN THE INTERNATIONAL LEGAL SYSTEM (2000).

STEPHENS, BETH, INTERNATIONAL HUMAN RIGHTS LITIGATION IN U.S. COURTS (1996).

THE ALIEN TORT CLAIMS ACT: AN ANALYTICAL ANTHOLOGY (Ralph G. Steinhardt & Anthony A. D'Amato eds., 1999).

VISCUSI, W. KIP, REGULATION THROUGH LITIGATION (2002).

WILLETT, LINDA A., ET AL., THE ALIEN TORT STATUTE AND ITS IMPLICATIONS FOR MULTINATIONAL CORPORATIONS (2003).

ARTICLES

Bazyler, Michael J., & Amber L. Fitzgerald, *Trading with the Enemy: Holocaust Restitution, the United States Government, and American Industry*, 28 BROOK. J. INT'L L. 683 (2003).

Blumberg, Phillip I., *Asserting Human Rights Against Multinational Corporations under United States Law: Conceptual and Procedural Problems*, 50 AM. J. COMP. L. 493 (2002).

Burghelea, Gabriela, *The Extraterritorial Application of Antitrust Law and the National Environmental Policy Act: a Comparative Study*, 8 GEO. INT'L ENVTL. L. REV. 351 (1996).

Cameron, Beatrice A., *Global Aspiration, Local Adjudication: a Context for the Extraterritorial Application of Environmental Law*, 11 WIS. INT'L L.J. 381 (1993).
Carroll, Wayne J., *International Application of the National Environmental Policy Act*, 4 ISLA J. INT'L & COMP. L. 1 (1997).
Clagget, Brooke, *Forum Non Conveniens in International Environmental Tort Suits: Closing the Doors of U.S. Courts to Foreign Plaintiffs*, 9 TUL. ENVTL. L.J. 513 (1996).
Digan, Thomas E., *NEPA and the Presumption Against Extraterritorial Application: the Foreign Policy Exclusion*, 11 J. CONTEMP. HEALTH L. & POL'Y 165 (1994).
Donaldson, Russell G., *Construction and Application of Alien Tort Statute (28 U.S.C.A. sec. 1350), Providing for Federal Jurisdiction over Alien's Action for Tort Committed in Violation of Law of Nations or Treaty of United States*, 116 A.L.R. FED. 387 (1993).
Dupuy, Pierre-Marie, *Soft Law and the International Law of the Environment*, 12 MICH. J. INT'L L. 420 (1991).
Free, Brian C., *Awaiting Doe v. Exxon Mobil Corp.: Advocating the Cautious Use of Executive Opinions in Alien Tort Claims Act Litigation*, 12 PAC. RIM L. & POL'Y 467 (2003).
Garmon, Tina, *Domesticating International Corporate Responsibility: Holding Private Military Firms Accountable Under the Alien Tort Claims Act*, 11 TUL. J. INT'L & COMP. L. 325 (2003).
Hing Wen, Abigail, *Suing the Sovereign's Servant: The Implications of Privatization for the Scope of Foreign Sovereign Immunities*, 103 COLUM. L. REV. 1538 (2003).
Holwick, Scott, *Transnational Corporate Behavior and Its Disparate and Unjust Effects on the Indigenous Cultures and the Environment of Developing Nations: Jota v. Texaco, a Case Study*, 11 COLO. J. INT'L ENVTL. L. & POL'Y 183 (2000).
Krolikowski, Susanne B. Case Note: *A Sovereign in a Sovereignless Land? The Extraterritorial Application of United States Law*, 19 N.C. J. INT'L L. & COM. REG. 333 (1994).
Lu, Justin, *Jurisdiction over Non-State Activity under the Alien Tort Claims Act*, 35 COLOM. J. TRANSNAT'L L. 531 (1997).
Lutz, Ellen L., Essay, *The Marcos Human Rights Litigation: Can Justice Be Achieved in U.S. Courts for Abuses That Occurred Abroad?*, 14 B.C. THIRD WORLD L.J. 43 (1994).
Mayer, Tomea C., *The Federal Tort Claims Act: a Sword or Shield for Recovery from the Government for Negligent Hazardous Waste Disposal?* 39 WASH. U. J. URB. & CONTEMP. L. 173 (1991).
McHarg, W. Herbert, *The Federal Advisory Committee Act: Keeping Interjurisdictional Ecosystem Management Groups Open and Legal*, 15 J. ENERGY NAT. RESOURCES & ENVTL. L. 437 (1995).

Ni, Kuei-Jung, *Contemporary Prospects for the Application of Principle 12 of the Rio Declaration*, 14 GEO. INT'L ENVTL. L. REV. 1 (2001).

Rankin, Jennifer K., *U.S. Laws in the Rainforest: Can a U.S. Court Find Liability for Extraterritorial Pollution Caused by a U.S Corporation? An Analysis of Aguinda V. Texaco, Inc.*, 18 B.C. INT'L & COMP. L. REV. 221 (1995).

Resseter, Robert, *The Role of Collaborative Groups in Federal Land and Resource Management: a Legal Analysis*, 23 J. LAND RESOURCES & ENVTL. L. 67 (2003).

Riechel, Silvia M., *Governmental Hypocrisy and the Extraterritorial Application of NEPA*, 26 CASE W. RES. J. INT'L L. 115 (1994).

Rumrell, Richard G., *Use of Circumstantial Evidence to Prove an Environmental Case Against the Federal Government under the Federal Tort Claims Act*, 7 COOLEY L. REV. 389 (1990).

Shepard, Julia C., *The Lacey Act: Extraterritorial Application Based on an Antitrust Paradigm*, 29 SAN DIEGO L. REV. 67 (1992).

Shermer, Steven D., *The Efficiency of Private Participation in Regulating and Enforcing the Federal Pollution Control Laws: a Model of Citizen Involvement*, 14 J. ENVTL. L. & LITIG. 461 (1999).

Siegle, Jennifer M., *Suing U.S. Corporations in Domestic Courts for Environmental Wrongs Committed Abroad Through the Extraterritorial Application of Federal Statutes*, 2 U. MIAMI BUS. L. REV. 393 (2002).

Stilo, Terri, *Failure to Warn of a Known Environmental Danger: Limits on United States Liability under the Federal Tort Claims Act (FTCA)*, 6 PACE ENVTL. L. REV. 589 (1989).

Thompson, Barton H., Jr., *The Continuing Innovation of Citizen Enforcement*, 2000 U. ILL. L. REV. 185.

Unger, Russell, *Brandishing the Precautionary Principle Through the Alien Tort Claims Act*, 9 N.Y.U. ENVTL. L.J. 638 (2001).

Wells, Bill Charles, *The Grin Without the Cat: Claims for Damages from Toxic Exposure Without Present Injury*, 18 WM. & MARY L. REV. 285 (1994).

White, Molly M., *Home Field Advantage: the Exploitation of Federal Forum Non Conveniens by United States Corporations and Its Effects on International Environmental Litigation*, 26 LOY. L.A. L. REV. 491 (1993).

Wu, Jean, *Pursuing International Environmental Tort Claims under the ATCA: Beanal V. Freeport-McMoran*, 28 ECOLOGY L.Q. 487 (2001).

Zaelke, Durwood, *Making Law Work: Environmental Compliance and Sustainable Developments*, CAMERON MAG. LONDON (2005).

INDEX

Aarhus Compliance Commission, 191-193, 192n
Aarhus Convention, 97, 99, 191-194, 212-214, 242
Aboriginal people, 20-21, 63, 186
ACHPR. *See* African Commission on Human and Peoples' Rights
ACHR, 96, 99, 100-102, 104
ACLU, 253
ACTPN, 251-252
Additional Protocol to the American Convention, 48-50, 52n, 237
Administrative Procedures Act
  advisory committees and, 278
  bluefin tuna and, 272-273
  National Environmental Policy Act and, 270-271
  overview of, 268-270, 293
  right to review and, 282
Adverse Effects from Toxics Resolution, 78, 79, 80, 89, 92
Advisory Committee for Trade Policy and Negotiation, 251-252
Advisory committees, 251-252, 277-278
African Charter on Human and Peoples' Rights, 45-48, 79, 117-118
African Commission on Human and Peoples' Rights
  private rights of action and, 128-129
  protocol to, 45-48, 117-118
  specific human rights and, 90, 98-102, 104, 116-117
African Convention on Conservation of Nature and Natural Resources, 78
African Court on Human and Peoples' Rights, 117-118
African Development Bank Group, 157-159
African Development Fund, 157
African Protocol, 45-48, 117-118
African Union, 73, 243
Aguinda v. Texaco, Inc., 281
AIDA, 252, 307, 310
Alco Pacific, Inc., 246-247
Alien Tort Claims Act of 1749
  dispute resolution and, 14n
  enforcement and, 285
  federal district courts and, 261n
  Guantanamo Bay and, 295n
  human rights claims and, 10n
  jurisdiction and, 267, 292-293
  specific lawsuits and, 11n, 258-266, 259n
Alternatives for the Americas, 187
Alvarez-Machain, Sosa v., 266, 294-295, 294n
Amaggi, 141-142
American Civil Liberties Union, 253
American Convention on Human Rights
  Additional Protocol to, 48-50, 52n, 237
  countries ratifying, 48n-49n

341

American Convention on Human
  Rights (*continued*)
  Inter-American Commission on
    Human Rights and, 51-53,
    118-119
  jurisdiction and, 58-61
  petitions to, 50n, 51n, 53n
  right to food and, 93
American Declaration of the Rights
  and Duties of Man, 48-50,
  52-53, 56-57, 90
Amicus curiae
  Africa and, 46n, 181
  America and, 63
  Canada-Chile Free Trade
    Agreement and, 179-180
  criteria for, 124-129
  defined, 6
  Europe and, 67, 180
  International Criminal Court and,
    240
  Llaka Honat and, 20-21, 63
  NAFTA and, 174-179
  Office of the High Commission
    for Human Rights and, 71-72
  other submissions of, 182-183
  preparation and filing of,
    183-184
  species protection and, 290
  World Trade Organization and,
    172-174
Amoco Transport Company,
  231-232
Apartheid, 235
APEC, 182
*Apirana Mahuila et al. v. New
  Zealand*, 104
Appropriations, 254-255
Arab Republic, Tel-Oren v., 294
Argentina, 20-21, 63
Armed conflicts, 237
Asian Coalition for Housing Rights,
  96, 99, 100-102, 104
Asian Development Bank

accountability and, 147
Chasma Right Bank Irrigation
  Project and, 154-155
compliance review and, 152-
  153
consultation phase of, 148
contact information for, 302
filing requests with, 149-152
remedial actions of, 154
Asian Pacific Economic
  Community, 182
*Aspin, NEPA Coalition of Japan
  v.*, 271n
Association, freedom of, 12, 100,
  110, 111, 116-123
Astilleros Espanoles, S.H., 232
ATCA. *See* Alien Tort Claims Act
ATCPN, 251-252
ATS, 294

Ballast water, 275-276
Bank for Reconstruction and
  Development, 132, 155-156,
  302-303
Bank Information Center, 302,
  303
Basel Convention on the Control
  of Transboundary Movements
  of Hazardous Waste and Their
  Disposal, 208, 249
Beanal v. Freeport-McMoran,
  263-264, 280
Bechtel Corporation, 182
Beef importation ban, 184
*Belgium, Democratic Republic of
  Congo v.*, 223n
Belize Barrier Reef, 203-204
Belize Institute of Environmental
  Law and Policy, 203
Belize-Maya, 56-57
BELPO, 203
Berezovka, 142-143
Bergama, 68
Bhopal, 241

Bilateral investment treaties, 182, 184n
Biodiversity, 205, 273. *See also* Convention on Biological Diversity
BITs, 182, 182n
Bladet Tromsø et Stensaas v. Norway, 101
Bluefin tuna, 230, 273
Board of Experts of African Development Bank Group, 157-159
Boise Cascade, 166
Bolivia, 182
Bowota v. Chevron Corporation, 262n, 282n
Brazil, 90, 141-142
Briefs, *amicus curiae. See Amicus curiae*
Bulgaria, 201

Camouco case, 230
Canada, 89-90, 103-104, 286
Canada-Chile Agreement on Environmental Cooperation, 163-164, 165-166, 290, 304
Canada-Chile Free Trade Agreement, 163-166, 179-180
Canadian Fisheries Act, 162
Canadian Forest Products Ltd., British Columbia v., 278-279
CAO, 138
Cartagena Protocol on Biosafety, 205
Cascada-Chile project, 165-166
CBD, 97, 99, 190n, 205, 291
CCAEC, 163-164, 165-166, 290, 304
CCFTA, 163-166, 179-180
Cedarena, 307
CEDAW convention. *See* Convention on the Elimination of All forms of Discrimination against Women

CEDHA, 20-21, 20n, 63, 63n, 299
CEE Bankwatch Network, 303
CEJIL, 299
CEM, 223
CEMDA, 303
Center for American Progress, 303, 304-305
Center for Economic and Social Rights, 47-48, 77
Center for Human Rights and Environment, 20-21, 20n, 63, 63n, 299
Center for International Environmental Law
 contact information for, 299-305, 307, 308
 defined, 20n, 63n
 freedom of information and, 276-277
 Free Trade Agreement of the Americas and, 253
 Llaka Honat and, 20-21, 63
 San Mateo de Huanchor and, 55-56
 World Bank Inspection Panel and, 133
Center for International Environmental Law, et al. v. Office of the United States Trade Representative, 276
Center for Justice and International Law, 299
Center for the Settlement of Investment Disputes, 174-175, 183
Centers for Disease Control, 254-255
Central Forestry Board, 23-24
Centro Mexicano de Derecho Ambiental, 303
CEQ, 185-186
CERCLA, 247, 274, 275
CERD, 26-28, 26n, 109, 124

CESCR. *See* Committee on Economic, Social, and Cultural Rights
Chaisiri Reefer case, 230
Chamber for Environmental Matters, 223
Charter-based human rights, 15
Charter of Fundamental Rights of the European Union, 64, 69, 79, 122, 157
Chasma Right Bank Irrigation Project, 154-155
Chassagnou and Others v. France, 101
Chemicals. *See* Hazardous chemicals
Chemor, 260
Chevron Corporation, 266n, 281-282, 282n
Children, 109. *See also* Committee on the Rights of the Child; Convention on the Rights of the Child
Chile, 163-166, 179-180, 276-277, 290, 304
Chorote people, 20-21, 63
CHR. *See* Inter-American Commission on Human Rights
Chulupo people, 20-21, 63
CIEL. *See* Center for International Environmental Law
CIEL v. USTR, 277
Citizen Works, 250-251
Clean Air Act, 274
Clean Water Act, 162, 274, 276
Climate change, 204, 206
Coal Fired Power Plants, 162
Coca fumigation programs, 254-255
Cochabamba, 182
Code of Corporate Citizenship, 250-251, 292
COMESA, 181
Commission of Inquiry, 45

Commission on Human Rights. *See* Inter-American Commission on Human Rights
Commission on the Promotion and Protection of Human Rights. *See* Sub-Commission on the Promotion and Protection of Human Rights
Commission on the Status of Women, 32-34, 36, 119
Committee Against Torture, 263
Committee for the Elimination of Discrimination Against Women, 28-31, 125
Committee for the Elimination of Racial Discrimination, 26-28, 26n, 109, 124
Committee of Experts, 69
Committee of Ministers, 69, 74-75
Committee of U.S. Citizens Living in Nicaragua v. Reagan, 280n
Committee on Appropriations, 254-255
Committee on Conventions and Recommendations, 40-41
Committee on Economic, Social, and Cultural Rights
  human rights claims and, 24-26
  jurisdiction of, 108
  private rights of action and, 124
  specific human rights and, 81, 86-87, 90, 95
  website for, 24n
Committee on Petitions of the European Parliament, 75, 122-123, 129, 156-157
Committee on the Rights of the Child, 31-32, 96, 125
Common Market for Eastern and Southern Africa, 181
Compliance Advisor Ombudsman of the International Finance Corporation, 138

Compliance Commission, 191-193, 192n
Comprehensive Environmental Response, Compensation and Liability Act of 1980, 247, 274, 275
Concluding Observations on Romania, 103-104
Conference of the Parties, 197-198
Conference participation, 197-198
Confurco case, 230
Consultative status, 17, 198, 199-201, 202
Contentious jurisdiction, 58-60
Convention for the Prevention of Pollution from Ships, 218
Convention on Biological Diversity, 97, 99, 190n, 205, 291
Convention on International Trade of Endangered Species, 206, 291
Convention on Migratory Species, 171n, 207, 291
Convention on Nature Protection and Wildlife Preservation in the Western Hemisphere, 291
Convention on Prohibition of Military or Any Other Hostile Use of Environmental Modification Techniques, 237, 238-239, 239n
Convention on the Conservation of Migratory Species and Wild Animals, 171n, 207, 291
Convention on the Elimination of All forms of Discrimination against Women
  implementation of, 30-31
  specific human rights and, 82, 93, 96, 103, 109
  state reservations and, 29-30, 29n-30n, 33n

Convention on the Elimination of Racial Discrimination, 103, 109
Convention on the Law of the Sea
  Amoco Transport Company and, 231-232
  critiques of, 232-233
  enforcement and, 291
  formation of, 225-226
  International Tribunal for, 229-231, 292
  overview of, 211
  pollution and, 231n, 292
  Sellafield and, 244-245
  structure of, 227-229
  submission eligibility, 230-231
  swordfish and, 230n
Convention on the Prevention and Punishment of the Crime of Genocide, 233
Convention on the Protection of the Environment, 274
Convention on the Rights of the Child
  overview of, 31-32
  specific human rights and, 82, 90-93, 96, 100-104, 109
Convention on Third Party Liability in the Field of Nuclear Energy, 287n
COP, 197-198
Coral bleaching, 204
Corporations, transnational, 80, 85-86
Costa Rica, 182, 269
Council of Europe, 64n, 69, 74-75
Council on Environmental Quality, 185-186
Court of Administrative Authority, 274
Court of First Instance, 180, 242
Court of Justice, 180, 241-243
Court of Justice of the Andean Community, 180

Covenant and Protocol, 18
CRC Convention. *See* Convention on the Rights of the Child
Crimes against humanity, 70, 234–237, 292
Critiques, 5, 124–129, 232–233
Croatia, 200
Culture, 104, 108, 116–123
Customary international law, 69–71
CYTRAR waste deposit, 246–247

Damages, moral, 284n
Danube River delta, 193–194
Defenders of Wildlife, Lujan v., 280n
Defenders of Wildlife v. Massey, 271
Degradation of environment, 9–14, 236–239, 238n, 239n, 259
Democratic Republic of Congo v. Belgium, 223n
Department of Defense, 273
Department of Environment and Heritage, 272–273
Deportation, 235
Desertification, 208
Detention, 70
Discrimination. *See* Gender discrimination; Racial discrimination
Dispute resolution. *See also* Amicus curiae
Convention on the Conservation of Migratory Species and Wild Animals and, 171n
Convention on the Law of the Sea and, 229–231
domestic governments and, 14n, 184–185
human rights claims and, 68–69
International Court of Justice and, 171n, 190n, 221–225
international financial organizations and, 131–132
international vs. domestic regulations, 167–169
intervention and, 170–172
investment treaties and, 182, 182n
public participation and, 185–187
Dispute Resolution Panels, 173
Dispute Settlement Body, 173
Dispute Settlement Understanding of the World Trade Organization, 171n
Doe v. Unocal Corporation, 263n, 260–262, 265n, 294–296, 298n
Dolphins, 269–270, 282
Domestic courts, 14n, 287n
Domestic enforcement mechanisms. *See also* Alien Tort Claims Act
Administrative Procedures Act, 268–274
advisory committees and, 251–252
appropriations and, 254–255
citizen suits, 274–276
corporate citizenship, 250–251
Federal Advisory Committee Act, 277–278
newly independent states and, 283–285
obstacles to, 278–283
Pelly Amendment and, 255–257
pros and cons of, 249–250
transparency as, 252–253, 276–277
Domestic governments, 184–185, 287n, 290–291
Dow Corporation, 240
DRC, 96, 102
Drought effects, 208
DSB, 173
Dugong, 272–273, 273n

Index • 347

Dutch Shell Petroleum Co., Wiwa v., 11n, 262-263

EAC, 181
Earthjustice, 272, 298, 299, 304-310
Earth Rights International, 310
East African Community Court of Justice, 181
ECHR, 64-66, 92, 96, 100-102
Economic and Social Council
 consultative status to, 17, 198
 private rights of action and, 128
 resolution of, 110, 114-115
 website for, 33n
Economic and Social Council Resolution, 110, 114-115
Economic Community of Western African States, 181
ECOSOC, 114, 114-115
ECOWAS, 181
Ecuador, 61-62, 89, 98-99, 183
Ecuador, Hourani v., 98-99
EHP v. Canada, 89-90
EIAs, 98, 193, 200, 214-215, 284
E-LAW, 252, 311
Elements of Crimes, 236-237, 237n
E.M. Eurogold Madencilik, 68
Emissions, 260
EnCana, 183
Endangered species, 206, 274, 280n, 291. *See also* Pelly Amendment
Endangered Species Act, 271, 274, 280n
ENMOD convention, 237, 238-239, 239n
Enslavement, 70, 235
Environmental Defense Fund v. Massey, 271
Environmental degradation, 9-14, 236-239, 238n, 239n, 259

Environmental Impact Assessments, 98, 193, 200, 214-215, 284
Environmental Law Alliance Worldwide, 252, 311
Environmental modification techniques, 237, 238-239, 239n
Environmental Protection Agency, 251, 254-255, 275
Environmental Protection and Biodiversity Conservation Act, 272-273
Environmental warfare. *See* War crimes
EPBC Act, 272-273
Equal protection, 103-104, 107, 116-123
Erica disaster scenario, 231
ESC, 64, 90, 123, 129
Estate of Marcos, Hilao v., 258, 281
EU Court of Justice, 180, 241-243
Eurogold Madencilik, 68
European Bank for Reconstruction and Development, 155-156, 302-303
European Commission, 64-66, 68
European Convention for the Protection of Human Rights and Fundamental Freedoms, 64-66, 92, 96, 100-102
European Council, 64n, 69, 74-75
European Court of Human Rights, 66-68, 66n, 74-75, 120-121
European Law Service, 299-300
European Parliament
 Charter of Fundamental Rights of the European Union and, 64, 69, 79, 122, 157
 Committee on Petitions of, 75, 122-123, 129, 156-157
European Social Charter, 64, 90, 123, 129

European Union
  Aarhus Convention and, 242
  Charter of Fundamental Rights
    of, 64, 69, 79, 122, 157
  Court of Justice of, 180, 241-243
  globalization and, 167-169
  transparency and, 212-214
European Union Court of Justice,
  180, 241-243
Executive Order 12114, 253, 292
Expression, freedom of, 100, 108,
  116-123
Extermination, 235

FACA, 277-278
Factoran, Oposa v., 200
Family, 107
FAO, 116-123, 201, 209-210, 291
Federal Advisory Committee Act,
  277-278
Federal Tort Claims Act, 268, 293
FIELD, 298, 300, 308
Filartiga v. Pena-Irala, 258, 258n,
  279
FIMA, 304
Finnish Wilderness Act, 23-24
Fiscalia del Medio Ambiente, 304
Fisheries. *See also* Law of the Sea
    Treaty Regime
  Administrative Procedures Act
    and, 269-270, 272-273
  bluefin tuna and, 230, 272-273
  dugong and, 272-273, 273n
  Montreal Technoparc and, 162
  Pelly Amendment and, 255-257,
    256n
  swordfish and, 230n
  treaties concerning, 209-210,
    226n
  whaling and, 291
*Flores v. Southern Peru Copper
    Corporation*, 264-265, 280
FOIA, 253, 276, 293
Foley/Aramco doctrine, 270

Food
  human rights laws for, 93-96
  jurisdiction and, 108
  United Nations Food and
    Agriculture Organization and,
    116-123, 201, 209-210, 291
Food and Agriculture Organization,
  116-123, 201, 209-210, 291
Foreign Relations Law of the
  United States, 70
Foreign Sovereign Immunities Act,
  279
Forestry
  advisory committees and, 252
  *British Columbia v. Canadian
    Forest Products Ltd.* and,
    278-279
  Haida Nation and, 286
  logging and, 257
  reindeer and, 23-24
  treaties concerning, 209-210
Foro Ecológico del Peru, 203
Forum non conveniens, 280-
  282
Foundation for International
  Environmental Law and
  Development, 298, 300, 308
France, 101, 231-232
Freedom of association, 12, 100,
  110, 107, 116-123
Freedom of expression, 100, 108,
  116-123
Freedom of information, 11, 98-99,
  107, 116-123. *See also*
  Freedom of Information Act
Freedom of Information Act, 253,
  276, 293
Freeport-McMoran, Beanal v.,
  263-264, 280
Free Trade Agreement of the
  Americas, 169, 187, 253
Free trade agreements. *See also*
  NAFTA
  of the Americas, 169, 187, 253

Canada-Chile, 163–166, 179–180
General Agreement on Tariffs and Trade, 168, 171n, 173n
U.S.-Chile, 276–277
Free Trade Area of the Americas, 187
Free Trade Commission, 175
Friends of the Earth, 306, 309
FSIA, 279
FTAA, 187
FTC, 175
Fumigations, 254–255
Furundzija, Prosecutor v., 260

Gabcikovo-Nagymaros Project, 222n–223n
GATT 1907, 168, 171n, 173n
Gender discrimination, 28–31, 103, 109, 115, 125. *See also* Convention on the Elimination of All forms of Discrimination against Women
General Agreement on Tariffs and Trade, 168, 171n, 173n
Geneva Convention, 237
Genocide, 70, 233–236, 258–259, 292
Germany, 66
Global Exchange, 187
Globalization, 167–172, 185–187
Global Trade Watch, 187, 309
Gold Train, 279–280
Governmental Social Committee, 69
Grand Prince case, 230
Greece, 65, 96
Greenhouse gases, 206
Greenpeace, 241
Greenwatch, 301
Gross human rights violations, 36–40
Groundwater, 178–179
Guantanamo Bay, 295n

Guerra and Others v. Italy, 92
Guidelines on Compliance with and Enforcement of Multilateral Environmental Agreements, 199

Haida Nation, 286
Haiti, 283
Harken Energy Corp, 182
Hatton and Others v. U.K., 92
Hazardous chemicals. *See also* Pollution
 appropriations and, 254–255
 Basel Convention on, 208, 249
 International Court of Environmental Arbitration and Conciliation and, 246–247
 metals as, 55–56
 pesticides, 98, 216–217
 resolution on adverse effects from, 78, 79, 80, 89, 92
 treaties concerning, 98, 208, 216–217
 Washington Toxic Coalition, et al. and, 278
Hazardous Substances Response Fund, 247
HCHR, 71–72, 71n
Health
 jurisdiction and, 108, 116–123
 laws pertaining to, 90–92
 United Nations Rapporteur on, 290
 World Health Organization and, 82–83, 224–225
Hemispheric Social Alliance, 187
Herbicides, 254
Heritage protection, 203–204, 215–216
High Commission for Human Rights, 71–72, 71n
Hilao v. Estate of Marcos, 258, 281
Himalayas, 204
Hinkley, Bob, 250–251

Hirt v. Richardson, 282–283
HIS, 273
Hourani v. Ecuador, 89, 98–99
Housing, 96, 99, 100–102, 104, 108
HRC. See Human Rights
   Committee
Huascaran National Park, 203
Humane treatment, 102, 116–123
Humanity, crimes against, 70,
   234–237, 292
Human Rights Committee
   amicus curiae and, 20–21
   ICCPR article 40(1) and, 22–24
   indigenous peoples and, 105
   inter-state complaints and, 21–22
   jurisdiction of, 107
   optional protocols and, 10n, 18–20
   private rights of action and, 124
   species protection and, 290
   website for, 18n
Human Society International, 273

IACHR. See Inter-American
   Commission on Human Rights
IACt.HR. See Inter-American Court
   of Human Rights
IALANA, 224–225, 308
IBRD, 132
ICC. See International Criminal
   Court
ICCPR, 100, 101, 102, 104
ICCPR article 40(1), 22–24, 98, 99
ICEAC, 245–247, 246–247, 292
ICSID, 174–175, 183
IDA, 132
IDCA, 269–270, 282
IISD, 178–179, 305
ILO, 41–45
ILO 165. See Indigenous and Tribal
   Peoples Convention of 1989
Immigration and Nationality Act, 283

Imprisonment, 235
India, 201, 249
Indigenous and Tribal Peoples
   Convention of 1989
   countries ratifying, 41n
   human rights and, 41–45, 78, 96
   industrial associations and, 42n
   International Labor Organization
      and, 116
Indigenous peoples, 105–110, 110, 116–123, 125
Individual petitions, 18, 18n
Indonesia, 257
Industrial associations, 42n
Industry Sector Advisory
   Committees, 252, 278
Information, freedom of, 11, 98–99, 107, 116–123. See also
   Freedom of Information Act
Inhumane treatment, 116–123
Injunctive relief, 285
Intent, Rome Statute and, 234–235
Inter-American Association for
   Environmental Defense, 252, 307, 310
Inter-American Commission on
   Human Rights
   Belize-Maya and, 56–57
   overview of, 32–34, 50, 290
   petition prerequisites and, 53–54
   private rights of action and, 127, 128, 129
   procedure of, 55
   Sarayacu community and, 61–62
   scope of authority of, 51–53
   specific human rights and, 118–119
   website for, 32n
Inter-American Court of Human
   Rights
   advisory jurisdiction and, 60–62
   contentious jurisdiction and, 58–60
   enforcement and, 74

overview of, 57-58
private rights of action and, 129
specific human rights and, 118-119
website for, 57n
Inter-American Development Bank, 143-147, 154
Inter-American system, 74
International Accountability Project, 301
International Association of Lawyers Against Nuclear Arms, 224-225, 308
International Bank for Reconstruction and Development, 132
International Center for the Settlement of Investment Disputes, 174-175, 183
International Convention for the Prevention of Pollution from Ships, 218
International Convention for the Regulation of Whaling, 291
International Convention on Civil and Political Rights, 93
International Convention on Civil Liability for Oil Pollution Damage, 218, 291n
International Convention on Oil Pollution Preparedness, Response and Cooperation, 218
International Convention on the Elimination of All Forms of Racial Discrimination, 24-26
International Court of Arbitration and Conciliation, 245-247, 292
International Court of Justice
advisory opinions of, 222
Article 38(1) of, 7
claims submission to, 291-292
Committee for the Elimination of Racial Discrimination and, 28
Convention on the Law of the Sea and, 232-233
Dispute resolution and, 171n, 190n
impediments to use of, 223-224
International Physicians for the Prevention of Nuclear War and, 224-225
MEA disputes and, 189-190
NGOs and, 223n
International Covenant on Civil and Political Rights, 107
International Covenant on Economic, Social, and Cultural Rights
overview of, 24-26
specific human rights and, 82, 93, 96, 104, 108
International Criminal Court
Alien Tort Claims Act and, 263, 267
crimes against humanity and, 235-237
establishment of, 233-234
genocide and, 234-235
jurisdiction of, 292
NGO participation in, 239-240
war crimes and, 237-239
International Development Association, 132
International Dolphin Conservation Act, 269-270, 282
International Finance Corporation
Brazil and, 141-142
complaint submission to, 138-140
contact information for, 302
Kazakhstan and, 142-143
overview of, 137-138
results of complaints to, 140-141
World Bank Inspection Panel and, 141-143

International Human Rights Law Group, 298
International Institute for Sustainable Development, 178-179, 305
International Labor Convention, 78
International Labor Organization, 41-45
International Labor Rights Fund, 309
International Maritime Organization, 218-219
International Peace Bureau, 224-225
International Physicians for the Prevention of Nuclear War, 224-225
International Rights Convention on the Elimination of all Forms of Racial Discrimination, 109
International Rivers Network, 301
International Status of South-West Africa, 223n
International Tribunal for the Law of the Sea, 229-231, 292. *See also* Convention on the Law of the Sea
Inter-state complaints, 20-22, 63-64
Intervention, 170-172, 232
IPB, 224-225
IPPNW, 224-225
Italy, Guerra and Others v., 92

Japan, 275n, 272-273, 273n
Johannesburg Summit Plan of Implementation, 97
Jurisdiction, 16, 58-60, 60-62, 237. *See also* Tribunals of general jurisdiction
Jurisdiction and Foreign Judgements in Civil and Commercial Matters, 267

Kadic v. Karadzic, 258-259, 260
Karachaganak Oil and Gas Condensate Field, 142-143
Karadzic, Kadic v., 258-259, 260
Kazakstan, 142-143
Kichwa peoples, 61-62
Kidnapping, 70
Kitok v. Sweden, 104
KOGCF, 142-143
Korea, 200
Kyoto conference, 232n
Kyoto Protocol to the UNFCCC, 206

Law of the Sea Treaty Regime. *See* Convention on the Law of the Sea
Lawyers' Committee on Nuclear Policy, 224-225, 308
Lawyers' Environmental Action Team, 300
Left Bank Outfall Drain, 136-137
Legality of the Threat or Use of Nuclear Weapons, 222n
Legal Resource Centre, 301
Letter petitions, 5
Liability, 218, 247, 274, 275, 287n
Liberty, 101, 107, 116-123
Libyan Arab Republic, 294
Life, 89, 107, 116-123
Llaka Honat, 20-21, 63
Loans, 132-133
Lobbying, 63-64, 196-197, 254-255, 294
Logging, 23-24, 257. *See also* Forestry
Lopez Ostra v. Spain, 92
LOS Convention. *See* Convention on the Law of the Sea
Lubicon Lake Band v. Canada, 103, 104
Lujan v. Defenders of Wildlife, 280n
Lukoil Overseas Project, 142-143
Luxembourg, 65

Macedonia, 200
Madencilik, 68
Malaysia-Chemor, 260
Marcos, Trajano v., 279
Marcos (Estate of), Hilao v., 258, 281
Maritime safety, 218
MARPOL, 218
Massey, Defenders of Wildlife v., 271
Massey, Environmental Defense Fund v., 271
Mathieu, Gregory, 75
Mayagna (Sumo) Awas Tingni Community Case, 96
Maya lands, 56–57
MEAs. *See* Multilateral environmental agreements
Mendivil, 246–247
Mercosur, 182
Mercury, 106
Methanex Corporation, 174, 175, 178–179
Methyl isocyanate, 240
Methyl tertiary-butyl ether, 178–179
Middle East, 9n
MIGA, 138–141
Migratory species, 171n, 207, 291
Military, 238–239, 239n. *See also* War crimes
Mining, 264
Mobilized existing human rights, 11–14
Model Rules of Procedure, 177
Mongolia, 201
Montreal Protocol on Substances that Deplete the Ozone Layer, 205
Montreal Technoparc, 162
Moral damages, 284n
Mount Everest, 204
MOX Plant case, 230
MTBE, 178–179

Multilateral environmental agreements
 critiques of, 232–233
 enforcement and, 189–191
 Kyoto conference as, 236n
 lobbying state parties and, 196–197
 non-party submissions and, 191–194
 petitioning secretariats and, 194–195
 public participation and, 197–202
 species protection and, 291
 states and, 195–196
Multilateral Investment Guarantee Agency, 138–141
Murder, 70, 235, 258–259, 260–261
M/V Saiga case, 229–230

NAAEC, 159–162
NAFTA, 163–169, 174–179, 305–306
NAFTA Chapter 11, 174–177
NAFTA Chapter 20, 177
NAFTA environmental side agreement, 159–162
Nagymaros Project, 222n–223n
National Drainage Program Project, 136–137
National Environmental Policy Act, 270–271, 293
National Historical Preservation Act, 272
National Pollutant Discharge Elimination System, 275
NDP, 136–137
NEPA Coalition of Japan v. Aspin, 271n
New Zealand, 104
NGOs. *See also* Center for International Environmental Law
 citizen suits and, 274–276
 Convention on the Law of the Sea and, 230–231, 292

NGOs (*continued*)
International Court of Justice and, 227n, 224
International Criminal Court and, 239–240
lobbying by, 294
newly independent states and, 284
UN consultative status and, 17
Nicaragua, 280n
Niger Delta Development Commission, 47–48
Nigeria, 12n, 47–48, 77, 262–263, 281–282
Non-governmental Organizations. *See* NGOs
Non-party submissions, 191–194
Nordic Convention, 274, 287n
Normandy Madencilik, 68
North American Agreement on Environmental Cooperation, 159–162
North American Commission on Environmental Cooperation, 159–162, 171n, 190n, 290
North American Free Trade Agreement (NAFTA). *See* NAFTA
Northwest Ecosystems Alliance case, 278
Norway, 101
Nuclear weapons, 226n, 224–225, 308

OAS, 49–50, 49n, 74, 202
Occidental Petroleum, 183
Oceania, 9n
Oceans. *See also* Convention on the Law of the Sea
ballast water and, 275–276
dugong and, 272–273, 273n
regional protection of, 233n
Seabed Disputes Chamber and, 229, 230
species protection and, 291
treaties concerning, 211
ODB-OP, 143–147, 154
OECD, 169
OECS, 182
Office of the High Commission for Human Rights, 71–72, 71n
Office of the United States Trade Representative, 185–186, 276–277
Ogoniland, Nigeria, 12n, 47–48, 262–263
Oil pollution, 183, 218, 228, 231–232, 287n
In re:Oil Spill by Amoco Cadiz off the Coast of France, 231–232
Okinawa, 272–273, 273n
Operational policies, 133
Oposa v. Factoran, 200
OPRC, 218
Optional Protocol to the International Covenant on Civil and Political Rights, 10n, 18–20
Oral statements, 5
Organization of African Unity, 73, 243
Organization of American States, 49–50, 49n, 74, 202
Organization of Eastern Caribbean States, 182
Organization of Economic Cooperation and Development, 169
Ovacik, 68
Ozone Layer, 205

Pakistan, 136–137, 154–155
Panels, dispute resolution, 173
Parliament. *See* European Parliament
Participation. *See* Public participation
PCA, 243–245, 292

Peace and Security Council of the African Union, 73
Pelly Amendment to the Fishermen's Protection Act of 1927, 255-257, 256n
Pena-Irala, Filartiga v., 258, 258n, 279
Permanent Court of Arbitration, 243-245, 292
Permanent Forum on Indigenous Issues, 114, 125
Permanent Sovereignty over Natural Resources, 105
Persistent organic pollutants, 217
Peru, 55-56, 264-265
Pesticides, 98, 216-217, 240
Petition Committee of the European Parliament, 64
Petitioning secretariats, 194-195
Petitions
  American Convention on Human Rights and, 51n, 53n
  Belize Barrier Reef and, 203-204
  defined, 4
  European Commission and, 64-66
  individual, 18, 18n
  to MEA secretariat, 194-195
  submissions and, 124-129
Petitions Committee, 75, 122-123, 129, 156-157
Pialopoulos and Others v. Greece, 96
Plan of Implementation, 97, 201
Plutonium, 244-245
Pollution. *See also* Hazardous chemicals
  Aguinda v. Texaco, Inc. and, 281
  Alien Tort Claims Act and, 263-264
  ballast water as, 276
  Convention on the Law of the Sea and, 227-229, 227n, 292
  conventions on, 218, 287n
  International Court of Environmental Arbitration and Conciliation and, 246-247
  plutonium as, 244-245
  toxic metals and, 55-56
  treaties concerning, 214, 218
POPs, 217
Power plants, 162
Presidents Advisory Committee for Trade Policy and Negotiations, 251-252
Prevention of Discrimination and Rights of Minorities, 110
Principles Relating to the Human Rights Conduct of Companies, 79
Privacy, 92-93, 107, 116-123
Profit, 250-251
Promotion and Protection of Human Rights. *See* Sub-Commission on the Promotion and Protection of Human Rights
Property, 96, 108, 116-123
Prosecutor v. Furundzija, 260
Prostitution (forced), 235
Protection, 103-104, 107, 116-123
Protocol of San Salvador, 48-50, 52n, 237
Protocol on Pollutant Release and Transfer Registers, 192n, 214
Protocol on Strategic Environmental Assessment, 191-193, 214-215
Protocol to the African Charter on Human and Peoples' Rights, 45-48, 117-118
PRTR, 99
PSC, 73
Public Citizen's Global Trade Watch, 187, 250-251, 309
Public interest environmental law organizations, 283-285

Public participation
  Environmental Impact
    Assessments and, 284
  Environmental Protection Agency
    and, 251
  Federal Advisory Committee Act
    and, 277-278
  human rights laws and, 98-99
  jurisdiction and, 108, 116-123
  Multilateral environmental agreements and, 197-202
  right to, 11
  Strategic Environmental
    Assessments and, 242-243
  trade agreements and, 185-187

Racial discrimination, 24-28, 26n, 103, 109, 124
Ramsar Convention on Wetlands of International Importance, 136, 207
Rape, 235, 258-259
Rapporteurs. *See* Special Rapporteurs
Reagan, Committee of U.S. Citizens Living in Nicaragua v., 280n
Reindeer, 23-24
Relief, 4
Relief, injunctive, 285
Remedial actions, 154, 154-155
Report on the Situation of Human Rights in Ecuador, 89
Reservations and Declarations Made Upon Signature, 29n-30n, 33n
Residence, 93, 108, 116-123
Resolution. *See* Dispute resolution
Restatement, 70
Richardson, Hirt v., 282-283
Rights of the Child. *See* Committee on the Rights of the Child; Convention on the Rights of the Child

Right to Adequate Food, 95
Right to Freedom of Opinion and Expression, 100
Right to the Highest Attainable Standard of Health, 90
Right to water, 88-89
Rio Declaration on Environment and Development, 97, 98, 234-235, 264, 265
Romania, 103-104
Rome Statute, 233-237
Rosner v. United States, 269-270, 279-280
Rotterdam Convention, 98, 216-217
Royal Dutch Petroleum, 11n, 262-263

Sabella v. United States, 269-270, 282
Sagarmatha National Park, 204
Saiga case, 229-230
Sale, Haitian Centers Council, Inc. v., 283
Sanctions, trade, 168-169, 255
Sanitary Protection Zone, 142-143
San Mateo de Huanchor, 55-56
San Salvador, Protocol of, 48-50, 52n, 237
Sarayacu, 61-62
Scandinavia, 274
SEA. *See* Strategic Environmental Assessments
Seabed Disputes Chamber, 229, 230
Seas. *See* Oceans
Security Council, 72, 190n
Sellafield, 244-245
Shell Petroleum Development Corporation, 11n, 47-48, 262-263
Shell Transport and Trading Company, 262-263
Sherpas, 204

Shipping, 228–229, 275–276
Shrimp importation, 168, 173n
SLAPPs, 284–285
Slavery, 70, 235
Smelters, 275
Social and Economic Rights Action Center, 47–48, 77
Sosa v. Alvarez-Machain, 266, 294–295, 294n
Southern Bluefin Tuna case, 230
Sovereign immunity, 279
Spain, 65, 92, 286
Special Rapporteurs
 claims and, 32–34, 290
 hazardous chemicals and, 80
 jurisdiction of, 111–114
 private rights of action available with, 125–127
 specific human rights and, 93–94, 100, 102, 105
Standard Oil Company, 231–232
State actions, 10, 222, 223, 232
Statements, 5, 124–129
State parties, 232
Statute of the Council of Europe, 64n
Statutes of Limitations, 149
Sterilization (forced), 235
Stitching Greenpeace Council v. Commission, 241
St. Lawrence River, 162
Stockholm Convention on Persistent Organic Pollutants, 217
Stockholm Declaration on the Human Environment, 77
Stockholm Statement, 247
Stop the FTAA Coalition, 187
Strategic Environmental Assessments, 99, 191–193, 214–215, 242–243
Strategic Lawsuits Against Public Participation, 284–285
Sub-Commission on the Promotion and Protection of Human Rights
 human rights claims and, 34–35
 indigenous peoples and, 110
 private rights of action and, 128
 reports of, 81, 92, 94–95, 104
 right to humane treatment and, 102
 right to water and, 87–88
 Special Rapporteurs and, 111
 website for, 34n
Superfund, 247
Sustainable development
 International Institute for, 178–179, 305
 right to, 78, 84
 Rio Declaration and, 234–235
 United Nations Division for, 201
Sustenance, 96, 108
Sweden, Kitok v., 104
Swordfish, 230, 230n

Tapiete people, 20–21, 63
Taskin, 68
Teck Cominco, 275
Tel-Oren v. Libyan Arab Republic, 294
TEPAC, 251
Texaco, Inc., Aguinda v., 281
Third Restatement of the Foreign Relations Law of the United States, 70
Toba people, 20–21, 63
Tort Claims Acts, 268, 288. *See also* Alien Tort Claims Act
Torture, 70, 258–259, 262n, 263
Torture Victim Prevention Act, 258–259, 263
Total S.A., 260–261
Toxic chemicals. *See* Hazardous chemicals
Toxic metal pollution, 55–56
Trade agreements. *See* Free Trade Agreements

Trade and Environmental Policy Advisory Committee, 251
Trade sanctions, 168–169, 255
Trajano v. Marcos, 279
Transboundary impact assessments, 98, 193, 208, 211, 214–215
Transnational Corporations, 80, 85–86
Transparency, 170, 186–187, 212–214, 252–253, 276–277
Treaties. *See also Individual treaties*
  species protection and, 291
  summary tables of, 77–110, 205–219
  wetlands conservation and, 136, 207
Tribunals of general jurisdiction. *See also* International Court of Justice
  African Union Court of Justice, 243
  European Union Court of Justice, 180, 241–243
  International Court of Arbitration and Conciliation, 245–247
  International Criminal Court, 233–240
  Law of the Sea Treaty Regime, 225–233, 292
  Permanent Court of Arbitration, 243–245
Tulane Law School, 310
Tuna, 230, 272–273
Turkey, 68
Turtles, 168, 173n

UDHR. *See* Universal Declaration of Human Rights
Uganda Wildlife Society, 300
U.K., Hatton and Others v., 92
Ukraine, 193–194
UNCITRAL. *See* United Nations Commission on International Trade Law
UNCLOS. *See* Convention on the Law of the Sea; Law of the Sea Treaty Regime
UNEP, 199–201, 224n
UNESCO. *See* United Nations Educational, Scientific, and Cultural Organization
UNFCCC, 99
Union Carbide, 240
United Nations Commission on International Trade Law Arbitration Rules, 174, 243–244
United Nations Convention on the Law of the Sea. *See* Convention on the Law of the Sea
United Nations Convention to Combat Desertification, 99, 208
United Nations Division for Sustainable Development, 201
United Nations Educational, Scientific, and Cultural Organization, 40–41, 40n, 119, 201, 289–290
United Nations Environmental Program, 199–201, 224n
United Nations Food and Agriculture Organization, 116–123, 201, 209–210, 291
United Nations Framework Convention on Climate Change, 97, 206
United Nations Rapporteurs. *See* Special Rapporteurs
United Nations Related Organizations, 3
United Nations Security Council, 72, 190n
United Nations Specialized Agencies, 3

United Nations System, 3, 71-73, 297-298
United States, Rosner v., 269-270, 279-280
United States, Sabella v., 269-270, 282
United States- Chile Free Trade Agreement, 276-277
United States of America, Methanex Corporation v., 174, 175, 178-179
United States Trade Representative, 185-186, 276-277
Universal Declaration of Human Rights
customary human rights law and, 71-72
public participation and, 98, 99
specific human rights and, 82, 93, 96-97, 100-102, 104
Unocal Corporation, Doe v., 259n, 260-262, 261n, 294-296, 294n
USTR, 185-186, 276-277
USTR, CIEL v., 277

Vessel integrity, 228-229
Vienna Convention for Protection of the Ozone Layer, 205
Vienna Convention on Civil Liability for Nuclear Damage, 287n
Vienna Convention on the Law of Treaties, 232
Vote, 12, 101, 108, 116-123
Vrete, 65

War crimes, 233-237, 237-239, 238n, 239n, 292
Washington Toxic Coalition, et al., 278

Water, 82-89, 108, 162, 178-179, 274-276
Wetlands conservation, 136, 207
Wichi people, 20-21, 63
Wildlife, 171n, 207, 291, 300, 302. *See also* Endangered species
Wiwa v. Royal Dutch Shell Petroleum Co., 11n, 262-263
Women. *See* Gender discrimination
Working Procedures of Appellate Review, 173
World Bank Inspection Panel
contact information for, 301-302
document availability of, 135-136
International Finance Corporation and, 141-143
overview of, 132-133
Pakistan and, 136-137
request submission to, 133-134, 134-135
World Court Project, 224-225
World Health Organization, 82-83, 224-225
World Heritage Committee, 203-204
World Heritage Convention, 215-216
World Heritage List, 272
World Trade Organization, 167-169, 171n, 172-174, 173n, 304-305
World Wildlife Federation, 302
Written statements, 5, 124-129

Yadana Gas Pipeline Project, 260-261
Yanomami v. Brazil, 90

Zaire, 90
Zoellick, Robert B., 276